The Great Western
Migration to the
Gold Fields of California,
1849–1850

The Great Western Migration to the Gold Fields of California, 1849–1850

Robert J. Willoughby

McFarland & Company, Inc., Publishers
Jefferson, North Carolina, and London

The present work is a reprint of the softcover edition of The Great Western Migration to the Gold Fields of California, 1849–1850, first published in 2003 by McFarland.

Library of Congress Cataloguing-in-Publication Data

Willoughby, Robert J.
　　The great western migration to the gold fields of California, 1849–1850 / by Robert J. Willoughby.
　　　　p.　　cm.
　　Includes bibliographical references and index.

　　ISBN 978-0-7864-7394-6
　　softcover : acid free paper ∞

　　1. Frontier and pioneer life — West (U.S.)　2. Overland journeys to the Pacific.　3. Pioneers — West (U.S.) — History — 19th century.　4. Immigrants — West (U.S.) — History — 19th century.　5. Pioneers — West (U.S.) — Diaries.　6. Immigrants — West (U.S.) — Diaries.　7. West (U.S.) — Description and travel.　8. West (U.S.) — History — 1848–1860.　9. West (U.S.) — History, Local.　I. Title.
　　F593.W476　2012
　　979'.02 — dc21　　　　　　　　　　　　　　　　　　2002152483

British Library cataloguing data are available

© 2003 Robert J. Willoughby. All rights reserved

No part of this book may be reproduced or transmitted in any form or by any means, electronic or mechanical, including photocopying or recording, or by any information storage and retrieval system, without permission in writing from the publisher.

On the cover: Wagon Train at Independence Rock (courtesy Denver Public Library)

Manufactured in the United States of America

McFarland & Company, Inc., Publishers
　Box 611, Jefferson, North Carolina 28640
　www.mcfarlandpub.com

For my children,
Rob, Sean, Kevin, Eric, and Amy,
who from their births have blessed and inspired me,
amazed and challenged me,
and always left me smiling.

"and knowledge is pleasant to your soul"
— Proverbs 2:10

Acknowledgments

The following organizations, libraries, and collections have graciously granted permission to reproduce excerpts from diaries held in their collections. The assistance of all of these fine institutions is deeply appreciated and their cooperation highly commended. *The Yale University Collection of Western Americana*, held in the *Beinecke Rare Book and Manuscript Library*, New Haven, Connecticut, for the diaries of: Caleb Booth, John Birney Hill, Sarah Davis, Margaret Frink, and William Frush; The *Illinois State Historical Library*, Springfield, Illinois, for the letters of John Nevin King, and the diary of Franklin Starr; The *Department of Special Collections of the Stanford University Libraries* for the journal of Lucena Parsons; The *Western Historical Manuscript Collection*, Columbia, Missouri, for the diaries of James A. Pritchard and Henry Wellenkamp; The *California State Library*, Sacramento, for the diaries of Mica Littleton and Amos Piatt Josselyn; The *Society of California Pioneers* for the diary of Israel Hale; The *Iowa State Historical Society* for the journal of William Edmundson; The *Bancroft Library*, University of California–Berkeley, for the diary of Niles Searls, the *Henry Huntington Library*, San Marino, California, for the diary and drawings of J. Goldsborough Bruff, and the *Nevada Historical Society* for the Diary of Samuel Jamison.

A special word of thanks to Mrs. Rodema Gnuschke and the staff of the inter-library loan department at Missouri Western State College for her assistance in filling my numerous requests for research materials. My appreciation and thanks to Ms. Lindsey O'Donnell and Ms. Kelly Hobson, student aids who provided valuable diary transcriptions for this book. Love and appreciation go to my brother Vince Willoughby for preparing the graphics for the maps in this book. And last, but most importantly, I thank my wife Christine for her constant encouragement of my work, and the love she gives to one so unworthy as I am.

Table of Contents

Acknowledgments	vii
Preface	1
Introduction	3

PART I
FROM THE BANKS OF THE
MISSOURI TO FORT LARAMIE 9

Getting Ready to Go	9
Leaving from Independence	15
Leaving from Weston/Fort Leavenworth	27
Leaving from St. Joseph	30
Along the Blue River Road to the Platte	36
Other Roads to the Platte	41
Falling in Along the Platte	45
Leaving from Kanesville/Council Bluffs	48
Fort Kearney	54
Fort Kearney to the Platte Fork	58
The Fork of the Platte	70
Crossing the South Fork of the Platte to Ash Hollow	74
Ash Hollow	78
Sioux Country Along the North Platte	80
Landmarks of the Western Plains	84
Scotts Bluff	90
On to Fort Laramie	94
Around Fort Laramie	98

Part II
From Fort Laramie to Fort Hall and Salt Lake City   107

Into the Black Hills	107
Around Deer Creek	115
Ferry on the Upper Platte	119
North Platte Ferry to the Sweetwater	123
The Sweetwater, Independence Rock and the Devil's Gate	129
Along the Sweetwater	135
Ice Spring	138
South Pass and Pacific Springs	140
Pacific Springs to the Road Fork on Big Sandy	144
Sublette/Greenwood Cut-off	149
Big Sandy to Fort Bridger	153
At the Green River	157
Toward the Bear River Road	161
Around Thomas's Fork	169
Soda Springs and Steamboat Springs	174
Junction with Hudspeth Cut-off	177
On to Fort Hall	180
Fort Hall	182
Fort Bridger to Salt Lake City	186

Part III
From Fort Hall and Salt Lake to the Sierra Nevada   193

Salt Lake to the City of Rocks	193
Fort Hall to the City of Rocks	198
Raft River Road	201
Merger of Fort Hall and Salt Lake Roads at the City of Rocks	204
Goose Creek to the Upper Humboldt River	206
Starting the Humboldt Run	213
Carlin Canyon	217
Dust, Deprivation, Depredation	219
Junction with the Lassen/Myers Cut-off	230

Table of Contents

The Lassen Route from the Humboldt to Goose Lake	233
On to the Sink	245
At the Big Meadow	248
The Humboldt Sink	250
The Truckee Route to the Crest of the Sierras	253
The Carson Route Across the Desert	258
Along the Carson River	261
The Elephant — Up the Eastern Wall of the Sierras	265
Promised Land — Into the Sacramento Valley	271
Epilogue	274
Notes	275
Index	287

Preface

I believe diaries, and other personal writings and recollections, in the form of letters, papers, or journals, provide the core of the best kind of written history. Whom or what a person observed first hand, at any given time or place, and then recounted makes a most authentic record. In this work, the diaries of those who actually went to California in 1849 and 1850 are opened up and laid side by side for the reader. Tens of thousands went and the number of diaries, or fragments thereof, that survive must be in the hundreds. As this is not a multi-volume set it is in no way inclusive of them all. I selected about twenty, which I felt represented the spectrum of writers. There are both men and women diarists, who went out to "see the elephant" in both years. The writings range from the highly literate style of a young, well educated attorney, to the simplistic ramblings of a barely literate young wife and mother accompanying her husband, who wrote with no working concept of English grammar.

But within the broad literary range, I found them all useful and marvelous. Some diarist wrote in an almost technical style, recounting every mile traveled and every bend rounded and little of hardship. Others seemed to have found solace from the difficult trail life in recounting their personal feelings, putting their fears and apprehensions down on paper. Still other diaries are full of observations of the people around them, and the interpersonal relationships that developed, elaborating on the good and evil in so many men rushing to find their El Dorado. Wonderful descriptions of the wilderness trail, from the last outposts of civilization on the banks of the Missouri River, to the great granite wall of the Sierra Nevada, abound in nearly all of them.

I have tried to minimize my narration of the diary passages, and offer some historical perspective or explanation where I felt it might be needed. Otherwise, the diarists speak for themselves. All of the diaries have been excerpted or edited for this work. Complete diaries can be found in various other sources. In some cases, to make the diary entry more readable, I have taken the liberty of inserting some grammatical marks and notations regarding spelling. My comments or explanations are enclosed in square brackets, [] thusly. Explanations by the diarists themselves are marked with ordinary parentheses. In nearly every case I have left the original spelling and punctuation as it originally appeared. In the case of the diary entries by Sarah Davis, I have left everything as near to the original as possible to illustrate the true form of her own writings.

As the road progresses ever westward, I hope the narration and accompanying maps will keep the reader on course, just as the guidebooks the emigrants depended on, and the dust clouds of those ahead of them, kept the gold seekers on the right road, going to see the elephant.

Introduction

> The fall of 1848 found me travelling through the western part of the State of Missouri in quest of a location suitable for a future home and for the practice of my profession. I was beginning to make preparations for my return home to New York [my native state] when I received intelligence from a friend, that he was soon to leave New York for California, via Independence, and at the same time urgently requesting me to accompany him in the anticipated journey. As I had already more than half decided upon "Seeing the Elephant," which is but another name for going to California, I was not long in deciding that the present opportunity was quite as favorable as any I could expect for visiting the gold region.[1]
>
> Niles Searls, May 8, 1849

The trek west, from the banks of the Missouri River to the Pacific Coast, made by some quarter of a million Americans during the decades of the 1840s and 1850s, stands as one of the great human adventure stories of all time. During those two decades a number of emigrants both preceded and followed the great migration. They were settlers interested in putting down more permanent roots, in farming and business. With the discovery of gold in California at Sutter's Mill in 1848, the migration of 1849–1850 took on an urgency and a scope that would never be matched again.

The phrase "to see the elephant," a slang or euphemism in that day, implied the immensity, or unusual nature of an undertaking or journey, and came to stand for the entire western migration experience, particularly its dangers and hardships. There are many intriguing questions associated with this marvelous endeavor. Obviously, why they went, and what they hoped to find when they got there, are important. The motivation in its simplest form, of course, was the treasure hunt, which has throughout human history held immense appeal to men and women of all ages and social extraction. When the news of the discovery reached the east coast of the United States it spread like wildfire, fanned by a press that was hungry for new headlines to equal those generated by the recent war with Mexico. The *New York Herald* of December 11, 1849, succinctly summed up the situation when it reported, "The Gold mania rages with intense vigor, and is carrying off its victims hourly and daily.... Ships, freighted with all the necessary articles of life, are being got in readiness.... Vessels are about to sail from all Atlantic ports, and our young men — including mechanics, doctors, lawyers, and we may add, clergymen — are taking leave of old associations, and embarking for the land of wealth, where the only capital required for making a fortune is a spade, a sieve, or tin colender, and a small stock of patience and industry."

To me, the matter of how they got there presents the greatest interest and the most intriguing point of inquiry. It is true that they could go by sea, as the newspaper excerpt of that day indicates, but to do so entailed a grueling trip around the southern tip of South America. Even on the fastest ship at that time, it still took over 100 days, and was dangerous and costly. The great majority chose to go overland. I recently flew from Kansas City to San Francisco, mirroring the route taken one hundred and fifty years earlier from Independence to Sacramento, on a flight of four hours, by commercial jet. As I looked down on the fields, mountains, plateaus and deserts, rivers and canyons from seven miles up, the monumental question of how anyone could make such a trip on foot or even by a horse drawn wagon, with not a single modern amenity, over a distance of 2,000 miles and a period of four months, took on staggering proportions.

After thinking about it for a long while, from the perspective of the modern jet traveler, and that of a student of history, I had to wonder, just how did they pull it off? Thus began my research. This account of the migration is based almost exclusively on the diaries, letters, and recollections of those who made the trip to California in 1849 and 1850. I do not intend this as an anthology of every diary written between those years, but rely on a selected few, those which I found to be representative and which contained the greatest elements of interest. My aim in this work is to capture some of the best examples of human nature and the indomitable character of anyone who, in those days, would make a very long and dangerous trek in search of their personal El Dorado. Though the "rush" proved to be a male dominated historical event, women did make the trip and I have included them in my selection of diarists. Their insights offer a view that is often a less rigid account of miles traveled or road conditions, but one of an increased sensitivity to everyone and everything around them. For most that rushed west, "seeing the elephant" became a journey they would in the end, because very few ever got rich in the gold fields, simply "chalk up to nothing but the experience."

Those searchers, whom you shall meet and get to know in some intimacy from their writings in this book, though driven by similar motivations,

Introduction

offer a variety of backgrounds, viewpoints, and styles. They are, in alphabetical order:

Caleb Booth, a young man, not yet 25 years old, who left to go see the elephant in 1850, from Farmington, Iowa.

Joseph Goldsborough Bruff, often referred to as Captain Bruff, a man of 45 years, cultured, articulate and disciplined from an upper-class eastern family (District of Columbia), he studied at West Point, and, despite the soldier's demeanor he carried throughout his life, never, as far as records show, served in the army. His captaincy was more likely earned from his experience on the deck of a ship or working in naval yards. Caught up in the fever, he made hand written copies of John C. Frémont's reports from his trip to California and urged among his friends the formation of the Washington City Mining Company. He went out in 1849.

Sarah Davis, a young woman of Quaker extraction, recently married and a new mother, was 24 years old at the time of her trip in 1850. She traveled out with her husband, Zeno, after having spent the winter of 1849 in St. Joseph. They might have gone the year before but she was with child and did not give birth to her baby girl until August of 1849. It was not until well into their journey that the family made the decision between the farmlands of Oregon and the prospects of California. They veered off to the latter. Her writing is from a grammatical standpoint only marginally literate, yet because it is from a woman and offers her views and insights it provides an important contrast to the male accounts of this historical event, which are much more numerous.

William Edmundson was from Oskaloosa, Iowa. He traveled to California with his brother David in 1850.

Margaret A. Frink, born Margaret Alsip, in 1818 in Maryland, married Ledyard Frink and accompanied him to California from their home in Martinsville, Indiana in 1850. Like that of Sarah Davis, her diary presents a woman's view of the hardships of trail life.

William Frush went out in 1850 with his brother John, leaving from Newark, Missouri.

Israel F. Hale traveled out in 1849 with his brother Titus.

Sallie Hester, 14 years old, from Bloomington, Indiana, traveled to California in 1849 with her entire immediate family; her father, mother, two brothers, and one sister. One of the briefest diaries kept, it nonetheless adds another woman's insights into the hardships.

Samuel M. Jamison was from Indiana, Pennsylvania. A young man, probably in his early 20s at the time of his trip (he died in 1909 nearly 60 years after the event), he went out with a group of friends in 1850.

Amos Piatt Josselyn was from Zanesville, Ohio. Married and leaving his wife at home, the 21 year old Josselyn went out in 1849 with a group of friends from his hometown, taking a steamer from Cincinnati down the Ohio, through St. Louis, and up the Missouri to Independence.

John Nevin King, a young man of some religious conviction, who had served in the army during the Mexican War on the Rio Grande, recounted parts of his 1850 journey in letters to his father, mother, and brothers.

Micajah Littleton went out in 1850, keeping a detailed diary that recorded nearly every grave marker on the road from Independence to the Sierra Nevada.

Lucena Parsons, born in 1821, was 28 years old and married when she left Janesville, Wisconsin, and went to California in 1850.

James A. Pritchard, titled Captain, from Petersburgh, Kentucky, kept a finely detailed diary of his trip to California in 1849, leading a group of men from his hometown.

Niles Searls, 24 years old, a young lawyer from New York, got caught up in the fever in 1849 while searching out a place to practice law in Missouri and went west with a group of friends, paying $200 to an express company for transport. His diary is probably the most literary of any; an obviously well educated man, he blends his powers of observation, philosophy, and descriptive powers into a marvelous narrative.

Franklin Starr left from Alton, Illinois, in 1849 in company with three friends.

Henry Wellenkamp, from Washington, Missouri, kept one of the briefest diaries, but when he had something to comment on offered a succinct quality that proved that sometimes fewer words are best. He went to see the elephant in 1850.

The demographic profile of migration paints an interesting picture. True, most of those rushing to the gold fields were young men, from 20 to 30 years old. But there were men well into their sixties that went, as well as infant boys brought along by their fathers. Women went too, of all ages, from infants to elderly, although in much lower numbers and in nearly every case in the accompaniment of their husbands, bringing their children with them. People of every profession and occupation went: lawyers, doctors, former soldiers (some through desertion were only recently so), sailors, farmers, carpenters, and mechanics. They referred to themselves as "emigrants" and tended to form into groups or "companies," of familiar faces that came from every state and community east of the Mississippi River; from big cities like New York, Philadelphia, Washington, D.C., and Cincinnati, to literally hundreds of small towns, counties and townships. They also came from England, Wales, Scotland, Germany, Ireland, and the Cherokee lands in Oklahoma. Nearly all were white, although on rare occasion an African- or Hispanic American would be reported. Native Americans, the Indians, though not technically emigrants, made their presence felt throughout the migration, and the interaction between those going to the gold fields and those who owned the land through which they passed covered the entire gamut of human relationships, from fear and loathing to admiration.

Sometimes the emigrants bonded themselves together with formal contracts or constitutions, which set down such matters as how much each member's financial obligation would be, exactly who would be in charge, whether decisions would be dictated or democratically arrived at, how often they would stand guard duty and if they missed it, what the penalty would be. Some even included by-laws that extended beyond the trek into the gold fields, stating how the bounty from the earth would be divided up once the nuggets were harvested. Some formed actual joint stock companies. One of the emigrants wrote of encountering such a train from Ithaca, New York, which consisted of 50 members with a capital investment of $25,000.

For nearly all, it began as an exciting opportunity to get rich, a great four-month camping trip, along a 2,000-mile long wilderness trail with unimaginable scenery. Some of the diaries are very detailed, others quite sketchy. As noted earlier, the level of literacy, beyond the basic ability to write, varies greatly. Diaries written by the well educated, like Niles Searls, a lawyer, or J. Goldsborough Bruff, a West Pointer and member of the eastern upper class society, are reflective of the best grammatical standards of their time and are more verbose in their descriptions and explanations of what their composers saw and did. More rudimentary diaries, with gross grammatical and spelling errors, are no less valuable. They often convey clearly in a few words what another might have taken a paragraph to describe. Some of the diarists follow the trek from the perspective of reporting on the road, writing with the detail of a surveyor. Another kept copious notes on the weather, wind directions, elevations, precipitation, a marvelous record of western climate kept with all the accuracy of a modern meteorologist. Another diary is written as a morbid yet poignant chronicle of a trail of death and dying, while another says little of the hardship, preferring to find some silver lining in each cloud. Nearly all the diarists reach some nadir at which even the most optimistic can no longer find justification for what they have undertaken and the suffering it has led to. Still they staggered westward toward their ultimate goal.

Part I
From the Banks of the Missouri to Fort Laramie

Getting Ready to Go

Once the emigrants decided they had to go to California, the next questions they likely asked were, "where and when do I leave from?," "what do I need to take?," "how do I get there?" The needs to answer those questions and ultimately supply the emigrants with nearly everything they needed for the grand adventure led to the development of a new industry in the American West. The overland outfitting business evolved quickly at the various jumping-off sites. The term "jumping-off," which I often use here, is an apt one. These people were literally stepping off a ledge, the ledge between the last vestiges of civilization, as they knew it, into a span of 2,000 miles of wilderness with only those comforts and amenities they could carry with them, and little or no "in place" support to provide even the most basic necessities of body or soul. Other than what they read in recently printed guidebooks, and a smattering of letters and articles in the newspapers, because in 1849, very few had actually preceded them, emigrants stepping onto the Great Plains for the first time, departing on their westward trek, really were jumping-off into the unknown.

In the case of the earliest western migration, which began fairly soon after 1840, Independence, Missouri, had taken the place of preeminence. The town had established itself as the trailhead and eastern supply center of the Santa Fe trade in the Southwest during the 1820s, and as such had very little trouble making the transition to outfitting emigrants going to the Pacific Coast region, first to Oregon and then California when the rush started.

St. Joseph, Missouri, which eventually came to dominate the outfitting business, began as a bustling river town, supplying the burgeoning farm community developed in the Platte Purchase region of northwest Missouri. The mercantile community there took the transition from supplying farmers to outfitting thousands of emigrants completely in stride, and indeed the town reveled in it.

The other major jumping-off point, Council Bluffs, or Kanesville, in Iowa, opposite present day Omaha, started as a fur trading outpost on the upper Missouri River and evolved into a supply and outfitting center as migration from states north of the Ohio River brought settlers into western Iowa. The displacement of the Mormons from the banks of the Mississippi River at Nauvoo, Illinois, also provided a powerful impetus for the supply and ferry business, as their trek to Utah brought them through western Iowa. Between Independence and Council Bluffs there were a dozen other smaller towns and ferry points that also served as jumping-off points, like Weston, Missouri; Fort Leavenworth, Kansas; Savannah, Missouri; and Bellevue, Nebraska, to name a few.

Emigrants got to their jumping-off site of choice by one of two means. They traveled overland by wagon, horse, or coach from the East, depending on what they wished to bring with them. Some chose to outfit themselves at home, for convenience or for price, and therefore by the time they reached the edge of the plains they were already packed and needed only to be ferried over the river to begin. In 1849 no railroad crossed Missouri, so the other option consisted of traveling up the Missouri River by steamboat to the jumping-off points. Companies of emigrants often collected and consolidated in St. Louis, at the confluence of the Missouri and Mississippi Rivers, and the steamboat companies loaded and overloaded their boats with emigrants for the often dangerous, one-week trip upstream. Depending on one's plans, Independence, which did not sit directly on the river, had a landing, and provided the first opportunity to disembark. Agents representing that town competed with agents from Weston and St. Joseph, further up the Missouri, to entice people off the boats. Independence boasted that it was the oldest and most established supply base and offered the earliest opportunity to hit the Plains without having to ferry the Missouri. Weston and St. Joseph could rightfully boast that by staying aboard the steamers for another day of comfortable upriver travel the emigrants could save themselves a hundred miles and a week's hard overland travel.

The towns were, of course, not necessarily looking out for the best interest of the impetuous emigrants, but for the prosperity of their own merchants and outfitters. Newspapers in both Independence and St. Joseph went to war with each other, blasting the shortcomings of their opponent and singing the praises of their own town as a jumping-off site with hardly a nod toward journalistic integrity. Rumors of disease, shortages of supplies, long waits at ferries, and generally bad access roads, were reported as gospel by the rival towns and circulated not only in St. Louis but as far as the east coast. St. Joseph even turned to "celebrity" endorsements of its trailhead citing Mexican War hero Commodore Robert F. Stockton saying, "The St. Joseph road was nearer and better than the one leading from Independence." They also quoted Major "Black" Harris, a well known military scout and pathfinder, as saying the route beginning at St. Joseph was "the best and nearest by upward of one hundred miles."[1]

As the number of emigrants swelled the number of business houses grew proportionally. St. Joseph soon surpassed Independence as the primary jumping-off point for both the Oregon and California emigrants. In 1845 St. Joseph incorporated as a town and had eleven mercantile houses. By 1852 it boasted over twenty large supply establishments with gross receipts ranging from $10,000 to $50,000, much of which came directly from the outfitting business. One emigrant who observed the bustle that surrounded that city in 1850 wrote, "I could not begin to tell you how many their [are] in St. Joseph that are going to Oregon and California but thousands of them. It is a sight to see the tents and wagons on the banks of the river and through the country they are as thick as camp meeting tents 20 or 30 miles and some say 50 miles." She added, "we did not stop at Independence. Tomorrow we go to St. Jo to lay in our provisions and cross the river to Indian territory."[2] Kanesville, described in 1851 by an emigrant woman on her way west, had eight large stores, a ferry, and "houses mostly hewed log, 2 story and on main street they have sided them up and they present quite a fine appearance." Another added, "Provision in Kanesville is very reasonable; beautiful potatoes for 40&45 cents per bushell and great plenty of them."[3]

The outfitting business basically handled three general categories of necessities for the emigrant — a few specific product lines to fill everyone's needs. The first general category consisted of wagons and harness components, as the wagon made up the primary vehicle of choice for overland travel over primitive at best roads. Occasionally a buggy or a coach might attempt the trip but the choice of wheeled vehicles had definite limits. Secondly, the outfitters sold livestock to pull the wagons, literal horsepower, riding and packing animals, and sometimes animals to provide meat and milk on the hoof to the emigrants. The third general category consisted of the varied supplies to fill the wagon and sustain the travelers with the most modest creature comforts, hopefully for the full length of their journey with some left over to sustain them once they arrived.

In regard to the wagons, they were not the great Conestoga type freight wagons that dominated the migration and overland trade in the eastern part of the nation. For the Oregon and California Trails, a strengthened, wooden farm wagon was common. From an engineering standpoint these were no great marvels. The bed or box measured ten feet long, three and a half feet wide, and three feet deep. Some had built boxes with false floors for extra or out-of-sight storage space. The bottom of the box might also be coated with pitch to give it a degree of waterproofing when the wagon had to serve as an amphibious craft during fording. Exterior mounted iron brackets held large tools, and side boxes added extra storage room over wheels. Some were built with a bench seat across the front, and in a very few cases the seat actually had some type of spring or recoil mechanism, such as a heavy leather rebound strap, to damp vibration for the rider. Otherwise one might prop a regular household chair at the front of the box and ride that way.

The box rested on the axles and heavy cross members front and rear. Attached with strap iron or a U-bolt assembly, this allowed the bed to be raised by placing spacers between the axle assembly and the bottom of the box. To the "hounds," heavy angular braces, the running gear was attached. The forward axle assembly mounted with an iron swivel pin that allowed for steering. That joint and the hub pins where the wheels actually attached to the axle were heavily greased. The wagon's tongue, which extended forward between the first set of draft animals, was the primary steering mechanism. It attached to the front axle assembly, with strap iron and harness chain eyelets reinforcing it. A wooden reach or centerline beam ran under the center of the bed from the front axle to the rear axle as a stabilizer. The rear axle, like the front, had no damping device, or shock absorber, and mounted directly to the rear hound.

The entire vehicle was borne on five to six feet diameter rear wheels and four feet diameter front wheels. They had wooden spokes and an iron rim or tire was necessary. Enclosed by a top of hemp canvas, impregnated with linseed oil for waterproofing and stretched over hickory bows, the bed, if properly packed, could haul up to 3,000 lbs. with some stability. As one emigrant guide stressed, "The wagon should be new, made of thoroughly seasoned timber, and well ironed and not too heavy; with good light beds, strong bows, and a large double sheets."[4] While many emigrants, as a matter of economics, brought their own farm wagons with them as they moved from their old homes to new land in Oregon, a large number of new wagons had to be produced at or near the jumping-off points for those rushing to the gold fields who chose to come upriver by steamboat and buy their complete overland outfit on the fly.

Between 1845 and 1850, Independence boasted at least four major wagon manufacturing shops, all of which had been previously active in production for the Santa Fe trade. Each shop produced from 80 to 120 heavy wagons per year. An 1846 article in the St. Joseph *Gazette* assured emigrants, "There are a sufficient number of Black-smiths, Wagon Makers, Saddlers and other mechanics who are always prepared with plenty of stock on hand."[5] Prices for the wagons varied, but the St. Joseph *Adventure* in February 1849 listed the going rate from $70 to $100, with demand and shortages by manufacturers pushing the price up to $150 according to some emigrant accounts. Wagon parts such as wheels, chains, axles, and tongues were in short supply due to demand. Sometimes the demand was artificially created.

One character in St. Joseph, named Tom Farris, was described as a "pestiferous" petty criminal, who perpetrated countless local break-ins and specialized in various larcenies against emigrants waiting to cross on St. Joseph's ferries. He led a gang of thugs who during the night would steal wheels and harness chains from emigrants' wagons. When the morning came, the emigrants, desperate to get on the trail, scurried about to buy replacements. Sometimes they bought their very own back from Farris, after his gang had repainted them to hide the origins of the stolen property. Farris always resold his loot at exorbitant prices. He ran his operation for two years, always outwitting the town constable and the handful of night watchmen. Finally, in May 1851, and in the typical fashion of western justice, a mob of citizens took matters into their own hands. Reportedly they took "Old Tom and his first lieutenant, a handsome and finely dressed man," to the top of Prospect Hill, overlooking St. Joseph, and gave each of them 100 lashes with a rawhide whip, along with an admonition to leave town immediately. Tom Farris and his gang disappeared after that.[6]

By the middle of the 1840s, livestock breeders were producing large numbers of oxen, mules, and draft horses. Some brokers bought oxen from as far east as Ohio to meet demands for the traveling season. If time permitted, mules and horses had to be broken to the constraints of harness work, but as the rush built, often animals were broken in as the trek progressed. Individual oxen were paired in a yoke and most guides recommended at least four yokes for an average wagon with spare yoke in reserve. If mules were used, six were recommended, but four animals often sufficed. Teams of draft horses were most commonly used, but because most were regularly fed grain, to supplement grazing, the transition to grass only on the prairie led to a sometimes substantial reduction in the animals' stamina and health. Enough grain to supplement grazing was expensive and bulky to haul, and while some emigrants attempted to do so it soon ran out. Horses also often had a more brutal time in the rugged mountain country, throwing shoes and splitting hoofs, where oxen and mules demonstrated better footing characteristics, though they could be just as tender at the hoof. Mules moved faster than oxen but were also more expensive. Oxen cost $30–$45 per yoke during the heyday of the migration while mules cost on average $40–$50 each. Again, supply and demand dictated prices and during the spring rush prices could double if one was desperate enough to pay.

Once a person had the wagon and the proper team of animals to pull it, what one needed to take was generally agreed upon by all the emigrant guides, the newspapers that promoted their town and merchants, and those who had survived previous treks and wrote back to those who were to follow them. Each person started with 200 pounds of bread stuffs, either wheat flour or corn meal for baking or ready made crackers; 75–100 pounds of bacon — because it had been smoked or salted it was the one meat that would not otherwise spoil due to no refrigeration; 12 pounds each of coffee and sugar, and five pounds of salt. For each wagon holding at least a family of five add: two bushels of beans, two bushels of dried fruit, prunes, plums, or raisins, 50 pounds of rice, as well as cheese, pumpkins, onions, corn meal for making mush, and anything that an individual might have a particular taste for that would keep at least part of the way. One young woman emigrant reported that her father searched the region around Kanesville, Iowa, frantic to find pickled cucumbers for the journey.[7]

Emigrants were warned against taking furniture, other than a feather bed mattress to make the wagon bed or ground beneath them a bit easier to sleep on, and a small sheet metal cooking stove. Tents of varying sizes from dog size to large room size were in general use and considered a necessity. Often a wagon was too full initially to find a place to lie down, so the tent was pitched beside it. At least an extra waterproof sheet could be used to make a lean-to shelter against the side of the wagon at night. A large canvas floor for the tent proved a worthwhile luxury. Travelers were told to pack a good supply of clothing, including weatherproof oilskins to go over hats and coats, a good selection of tools, including an ax, saw, hammer and nails, and a grease pot to do wagon repairs, soap, and some medicine. Elizabeth Dixon Smith, who passed over the trail in 1848, wrote back to affirm the advice she had received. "No one should travle [sic] this road without medicine for they are al most sure to have the summer complaint. Each family should have a box of phisic pills and a quart of caster oil, a quart of the best rum, and a large vial of peppermint essence."[8] Nearly everything in the medicine chest worked to relieve a bowel problem or stomachache but they carried nothing for more serious maladies like the cholera, which decimated some wagon trains and whole families. Future prospectors for the California gold fields were warned against taking heavy mining machinery; a pick, shovel, and pan were plenty to pack across the continent and the first two of those items would be needed if the wagon got stuck on the way.

The alternative to providing all of one's own kit for the trip presented itself in the form of the express company. The demand for what the consumer, the emigrant with some ready cash and little else, wanted and needed, created an explosion of so called express companies that provided everything for a price. Niles Searls paid $200, which was probably typical of the charge. What the express companies promised was comfortable, spring mounted carriages for six to twelve persons, baggage wagons, teams of mules or horses, to make faster time, trained teamsters to do the driving, all the camping amenities, like stoves and tents, plenty of food, and all the pleasures of a grand sightseeing excursion. Some even offered a guaranteed departure window and arrival date, and signed up well known guides, former mountainmen and trailblazers in their declining years, to lead them through in under 100 days. What they actually delivered we shall see.

They began collecting at the jumping-off sites as early as February in 1849, and flyers circulated in the east encouraged emigrants to be in place on the edge of the Great Plains by April for the earliest possible start, once the snow had all melted, the spring thaws and the swollen streams had dropped, and most importantly, the grass, the fuel for the animals, began to come on in quantity. Some left as early as the middle of April, depending on whether or not they listened to or took the conventional advice, but the first week in May became the target window for departure. The next six weeks after that offered the best chance of getting through before the snows closed the mountain passes of the high Sierra Nevada at the other end. By 1849, no emigrant had to be told the story of the Donner Party, who didn't make it through in time and resorted to cannibalism before help reached them from the California side.

Leaving from Independence

It is appropriate that we begin the journey to see the elephant with our diarist who left from Independence as it was the first major jumping-off point, up the Missouri River, on the edge of the Great Plains. After arriving at Independence, the emigrants went through the routine of getting themselves and their companies, trains, or messes, five or six men assigned to a particular wagon or carriage, together, and then waiting for the day of departure. Anticipation built quickly, and may emigrants complained of constant delays until those first few miles were under their belts. From Independence, the road led west along the old Santa Fe Trail for a short distance and then turned northwest, across what is today east central Kansas toward the Blue River. The Blue River and the confluence of its tributary, the Little Blue, lay approximately 185 miles from Independence. Depending on the weather, sickness, inexperience, and any number of other types of delays, that initial stretch of road might take anywhere from ten days to three weeks.

Samuel M. Jamison arrived in Independence, Missouri, on April 19, 1850. Originally from Pennsylvania, he and a number of friends had shipped 20 horses and mules along with wagons and supplies to St. Louis. Those materials were shipped by steamboat up the Missouri River to Independence. They spent time repairing their wagons, buying more horses and mules, washing clothes, writing letters, and going to church. He also bought a violin.[9]

Amos Josselyn briefly recounted his first days on the trail from Independence, in late April, 1849, writing, "Arrived at Independence landing at day light and spent the day in getting up the Bluff. Camped just up the hill. Left Camp and went up to Independence and found it to be quite a business place. Rain nearly all day which prevented us from moving but being in no hurry put it off until next day. Left camp at 8 o'clock and drove 6 miles and camped three miles S.W. of Independence."[10]

Captain J. A. Pritchard's company had sent their baggage up river from St. Louis on a steamer, but drove their wagons and mules overland across the state, reaching Independence on April 22, 1849. He reported the city, "is a handsome flourishing town with a high healthy situation — three miles from the Missouri River on the south side And Surrounded by one of the most beautiful and fertile countries of any Town in the Nation. The emigrants were encamped in every direction for miles around the placewaiting the time to

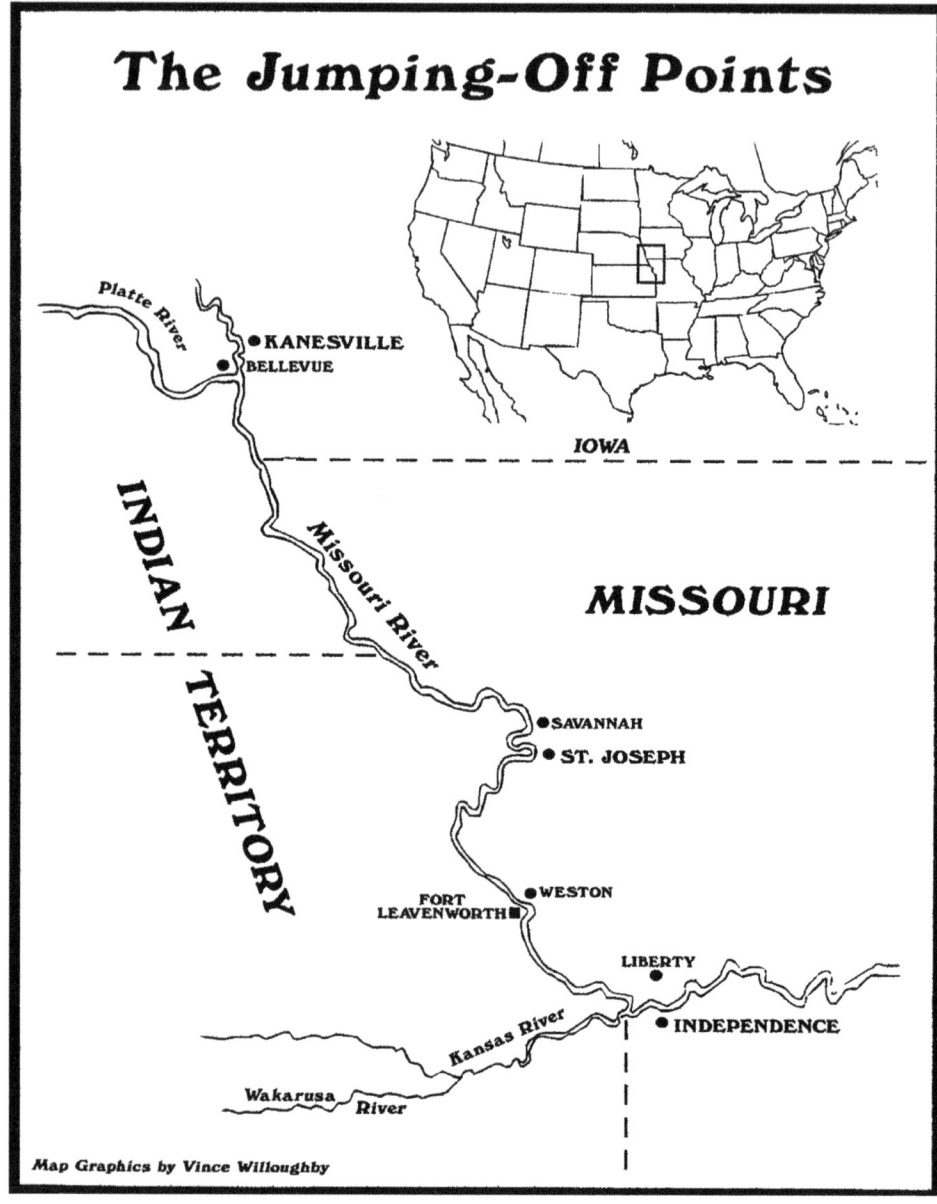

The Jumping-off Points — Missouri River Valley from Independence to Kanesville.

come for their departure. Such were the crowded conditions of the streets of Ind. By long trains of Ox teams, mules, teams of men there with stock to sale and men there to purchase stock that it was all most impossible to pass a long."[11]

Pritchard continued his entry giving a wonderful description of the excitement around Independence. "And the California fever rageing [sic] to such a fearful extent that it was carrying off its thousands pr day. Being all ready now to bid adieu to home, friends, and happy country, as it were — for we were about separating our selfs from the abodes of civilization, its peace, comforts, and its safety, for a period we knew not how long, and to some for ever, to launch a way upon the broad and extensive plaines [sic] which Straches [sic] away and away, until it fades from the sight in the dim distance, and bounded only by the blue wall of the Sky. While thus laying round in suspense the reflections of home were forcibly crowding upon our minds the happy influences that we had torn our selves from to enter up on a wild and in all probability a chimerical enterprise."[12]

Micajah Littleton, who began his trek in May, 1850, travelling with an express company, remarked about the slow start from Independence in his journal, "After having sold our outfit to Gelen & Co. we left Independence for camp 5 miles East of Independence lay there until Wednesday the 22nd when the train left for a new camping place all being dissatisfied with the management and delay we pitched 10 miles south of Independence the same day and lay there until Friday morning. Started and came on 11 miles. 2 miles west of Blue River [stream mis-identified] and pitched again and lay until Monday morning at 9 o'clock. The passengers of the train becoming very much dissatisfied on Sunday morning called a meeting and appointed a committee of 7 to draft Resolutions and present to the company of owners and requiring some action prompt and definite demanding a set time to start and that to be prompt also not to allow them to take any other passengers also that if what waggons & carriages they had were not sufficient to carry what they already had engaged, that they should have no privileges to ride in carriages as those who first engaged. There are not a more handsome piece of Road and scenery has ever been presented to my view than on this Road, not a tree or Bush to be seen except now and then a small group of timer [timber] in the lower parts of some ravine and that look as it were put there to Beautify the sight."[13]

Niles Searls, a young lawyer, and the source of the first quote in the introduction of this book, had made up his mind to go see the elephant after a friend from his home state of New York encouraged him to join on an expedition. They met in Independence and signed on with one of the many express companies, or "pioneer lines" promising a guided tour across the plains to California. His journal began in May 1849. "My friend arrived in the latter part of April, 1849, and we immediately set about making preparations for our departure. Our first intentions were to fit out a mule team to convey our provisions and baggage across the plains, but after a few lessons in the troubles of such an outfit and the perplexities of such a conveyance to the uninitiated, we gave up this idea and concluded to go out as passengers in the 'Pioneer line,' an organization for the conveyance of passengers from Independence, Mo., to San Francisco. The conveyance is by carriages capable of containing six persons each, covered, seated upon springs and drawn by mules. Accompanying these is a number of baggage wagons sufficient to contain the provisions and baggage for the company, the former of which as well as tents, cooking apparatus, etc., are furnished by Turner Allen & Co., the proprietors of the 'line.' Determined to go well prepared both for comfort and pleasure, we procured each a good horse, to be used in hunting and to ride when fatigued with the carriage. After procuring the necessary outfit in Independence, we sought a temporary retreat from the dense throng that crowded that place."[14]

Searls' eloquent and detailed journal entry from May 9, 1849, does a good job providing a description of how the express companies operated. "Our company will consist of about one hundred and twenty passengers, who are to be formed into messes of six persons each, each mess to occupy their own carriage—to be furnished with a set of camp equipage, do their own cooking and to drive their own mules when put before the carriage. This is the day appointed for our final departure, but owing to the want of several additional baggage wagons we shall only move a few miles at a time till Saturday which is now named as the day for our 'Rolling' in good earnest. Today everything has been tumult and confusion in camp.

"The business of 'hitching up,' as it is termed, commenced at nine o'clock this morning but owing to the difficulties of harnessing one hundred and fifty mules for the first time, it was not completed till late in the evening. Nearly every animal was caught with the lasso and choked down, harnessed by main strength and placed before the wagons, there to perform sundry feats that would astonish any but a juggler or one accustomed to ground and lofty tumbling. After sundry mishaps such as breaking wagon tongues, harnesses, etc., we at length got under way and proceeded two miles, where we again encamped for the night.

"Our first business after picketing our horses for the night and pitching our tent, was to seek for wherewithal to satisfy the cravings of appetite. After an hour's delay we succeeded to the number of four in procuring some coffee, bacon, pilot bread and sugar. One of our number soon levied upon a fence rail with which a fire was kindled and culinary operations were for the first time commenced. Another hour and we were seated in a circle around our humble supper eating by moonlight this, the first fruits of our own cooking. No useless table was spread. The Earth is to be our future bed, seat and table and we reclined upon her bosom. We partook of our creature comforts with a relish that in our former plentiful hours was wholly unknown."[15]

Generally speaking, the express companies, despite what they promised, did little more than provide the basic equipage, food, and mode of transportation, anyone with a little time and energy could have put together themselves. The time factor, being in a hurry to get to the gold fields, or self-doubt about one's organizational skills, or simply having the money to buy into the company's promotional literature brought many to their office doors to book passage. The proprietors could generally calculate the cost per head for emigrants, figuring a one way trip for all capital expenditures, adding a profit margin, and then hiring someone, not necessarily checking the references for leadership or management skills, to lead the emigrants out.

For those with the knowledge, or at least one of the often published plans, packing one's own equipage and food, buying or bringing from home a team of draft animals, left them with the simple task of signing on with a train and agreeing to its by-laws. As many were already part of an organized company of persons from a given community, individuals with leadership qualities, like previous military experience, were already well known within those groups. Most emigrant companies felt no compulsion to go out looking for an experienced mountaineer to lead them through, as the widely published emigrant guides would show the way. Still there seemed to have been a nearly universal want for someone to assume a clear leadership role, and many trains elected "captains" or committees to provide guidance and decision making when the situation overwhelmed or left in question the individual. Trains or companies went through a nearly constant process during those first few days of consolidation, adding groups, individuals joining or leaving, depending on their perceived needs for protection, speed of travel, or just social connection. Samuel Jamison's brief entries on April 24–25, 1850, make the point clearly. "Left Independence at 2 o'clock. Went ten miles to Col. Grants and encamped. Joined up with Green County Company and traveled 25 miles. Camped called a meeting. elected Capt. Tangaman."[16]

Just getting used to the trail and the type of travel it required, back tracking for supplies they knew they would not find again until California, or just collecting some forgotten of perceived necessity, slowed the initial pace from the jumping-off points considerably, as Amos Josselyn pointed out in his late April, 1849 entry. "drove to Mr. Rices [nine miles from Ind.] where corn was pleanty at 1.25 per bll. Drove back 1 mile to a smith shop and got our tyre cut. In camp all day working at wagons, fixing ox tongue, &c. Hitched up and drove 8 miles to Blue river [probably Bull Creek] before leaving Rice's we bought corn enough to feed our teams for 6 or 7 days thinking that the grass would be good enough for grazing by the time the corn was out."[17]

Life on the trail, the camping, the handling of the barely broken teams, and the wagon ride itself immediately demonstrated the hardness by most accounts. Those accustomed to physical labor at first managed without too much complaint, but the easterners, the townspeople, and professionals found it quite brutal. "Rose this morning from our bed upon the ground with sensations similar to those I imagine must pervade the frame of the inebriated after a week's spree,"[18] wrote Niles Searls on May 10, 1849. He continued his comments the next day writing, "Rose this morning under the influence of a severe cold contracted from exposure in camp and in sleeping on the ground." Riding in the wagons or carriages offered little comfort after a bad night's sleep. "At one moment we might all be seen rolling on at a slow pace with all the solemnity of a funeral procession; while in the next, some refractory team, enraged at their recent captivity, would plunge from the procession and, after a few gyrations by way of ascertaining if their locomotives were in moving order, dart off across the broad Prairie at top of their speed and in utter defiance of all restraint."[19]

Some companies saw the first few days on the trail as a race. While many companies or trains complained of a slow pace, others made sport of, or boasted about how many they passed in their rush to see the elephant. Jamison's early, brief diary entries, from the end of April and early May, 1850 indicated a group of young men in a hurry. "April 29 ... let wagons down into the creek with ropes. 2 miles very bad swamp. Passed one grave. Drove 22 miles, past 64 wagons, drove 30 miles more. April 30... Left camp at 5 o'clock in a hurry to pass the ox trane [sic] which passed before day light to get to the river before us. traveled 15 miles before 9 o'clock. windy and cold. May 2 ... got up at 3 o'clock to pass St. Lewis [Louis] Company."[20]

The difficulty of beginning trail life caused the normal physical hardship, due to ignorance or just poor preparation and the same led to accidents, as Amos Josselyn recorded on May 1, 1849. "Left camp at 7 o'clock and when three miles form camp one of the Newark teams got fritened [sic] at a man throwing a blanket over his shoulders and ran off: the driver in attempting to jump from the wagon fell and the four wheels of the wagon ran over him which has injured him very much, but it may not be fatal they not having any convenient way to carry him, he was put in our wagon. There being no water near we had to drive on and it took us nearly all day to drive 7 miles (the nearest watering place), having to stop every few minutes to let our wounded man get his breath."[21]

Serious accidents, broken bones, or internal injuries, presented on a surprisingly regular basis, but the routine of trail life must have banged up or strained body parts almost daily, as Samuel Jamison recounted as they raced along. "May 6... Left camp at half past 5 o'clock. Passed 2 tranes [sic] one with 27 wagons and the other 15. Passed 6 graves from the appearance they had been last years dead. We had two mules give out. When I was called on g[u]ard in passing around the encampment I tripped on the rope of a mule and skinned my shin."[22]

And then there was the weather to get use to. It appears from the accounts of nearly all the emigrants that the early spring months of April and May, in both 1849 and 1850 were quite cold. Many remarked about having to wear coats, and that plenty of wind and rain made for wet springs. "Cold and windy, so cold that every man had to put on two or three coats,"[23] wrote Amos Josselyn about conditions on May 1, 1849. Niles Searls' May 15, 1849, comments reflect how the emigrant, unaccustomed to the weather of the Great Plains, reacted to the first big thunderstorm. "We are awakened from a sound repose this morning at about two A.M. by a pelting shower of rain, which soon penetrated and ran under our canvas home till most of us were completely saturated by the swift descending flood. Books, papers, guns, coats and baggage of every kind were wet or soiled by the tremendous gale. Seldom have I witnessed a more vivid display of electricity than accompanied this storm."[24]

Sickness accompanied nearly every train, in various degrees of severity. Searls began identifying those with maladies early on in his journal, the first references being reported with some optimism about recovery. "Our Commissary, Mr. Charles Falkner, has been since yesterday morning laboring under a severe attack of Cholera. The obstacles to be surmounted in preparing so large a train for an extensive journey are more numerous and of greater magnitude than can be well imaged by an individual unacquainted with the trip. Some few are complaining, but judging from the number of Doctors in the train, if any suffer from sickness it will not be for want of medical advisers," he wrote on May 12, 1849, but a few days onto the trail. The next day he added pessimistically, "One of our teamsters, California Bob, was attacked with Cholera last night and will not probably survive the day and night."[25]

Amos Josselyn kept track of the man in his train who had been run over by the wagon. On May 4, 1849, three days after the accident he wrote, "the wounded man appearing to be able to ride, we got him into the wagon and drove to Blackjack point about 8 miles. It rained nearly all the time and the roads very bad." Then, on May 5, he added, "The wounded man appeared to stand it verry well but when we stopped he fainted away. The wounded man died at 10 o'clock this morning and it took us untill 11 o'clock to attend to the funeral ceremonies."[26]

Despite the initial hardships many emigrants kept their spirits up and had positive comments to make about their condition and their surroundings. "The roads the best I ever seen," wrote Amos Josselyn on May 1, 1849. A simplistic and positive comment imbedded in his journal, in comparison to those of other emigrants dominated by tales of misery. The more literate Niles Searls wrote lengthy philosophical prose early into his trek, despite seeing much misery within the first week. "We have launched out upon those broad plains which for months must be our home, and what is the object of our present journey? Are we led on by a kind of indefinite whim to roam over creation's broad expanse without any particular object in view; or, by the more laudable one of seeking for knowledge at her primeval source, or surveying and admiring the majestic work of Providence as displayed in their native grandeur? And what is to be the result of this expedition upon our future lives and fortunes?"[27]

The next day, Searls continued in his thoughtful mode, writing, "How beautiful are the works of nature and how has Thou, as it were in Thy playful moments decorated the wild solitude of earth with Thy most refulgent splendor! Well may the untutored savage while roaming in perfect freedom o'er these boundless wilds, exult in his native freedom and adore the Great Spirit that gave birth to his extended domain."[28]

Whether expressed in the eloquent prose of a man well educated, or in the simplistic words of the less literate, the illness and sometimes dying that accompanied the trains tempered even the most philosophically optimistic. "Two of our passengers were attacked last night with Cholera and left behind with no prospect but that of death to put an end to their sufferings," wrote Searls on May 17, 1849. "One of them, I learned was from Toronto, Canada; the other, from Connecticut." Searls' express company moved on, and he reported, "Those who had been left in the morning with the sick came in at a late hour, after having performed the last solemn duty towards them required here on earth. They died a little before five this evening and both within a period of five minutes, and were buried in one grave on the ground where we had encamped the preceding night."[29]

Emigrants saw the results of illness not only in their own trains but also in others that they passed. "A wagon containing a woman and a young man have just passed in front of camp and are returning to the States," recorded Searls on May 18, 1849. "They were bound for the modern 'Ophir' and had reached a point fifteen miles beyond the Kansas when her husband died and she, solitary and bereaved, was making her way back." But in that case death presented an opportunity, as Searls added, "by this means we are enabled to send back letters to our friends." When a close travelling companion became ill, as in the case of Niles Searls' friend named Sinclair, hoping with cautious optimism remained the only solace. "[He] has been growing worse during the day, having had several spells of vomiting. A physician was called this evening who administered some medicine and pronounced his case to be Cholera, but thinks him in a fair way to recover."[30]

Spring thunderstorms on the Great Plains, and particularly in that part today commonly referred to as "Tornado Alley," struck often, violently, and without mercy. Those just into their first few days and weeks on the trail had nothing to compare them to. The wet spring of 1849 gave a lot of the emigrants reason to complain, as Niles Searls did in his May 19, 1849, entry: "heavy rains,— The wagons were often imbedded in the loose murky earth to their hubs. Tongues were broken, harness torn, mules lamed, and to all appearances we were nearly shipwrecked. After three hours of hard swearing, we reached the high ground and encamped for the night."[31]

Some diaries reported it rained nearly every day throughout the first three weeks of May, 1849, a wet year to be sure, but not totally unusual for the eastern plains region even today. Searls, on May 21, 1849, continued his lament of the weather. "The wiffletree to our carriage has given out and we were assisting to repair the injury when the storm, accompanied by a gale of wind, overtook us. The violence of the wind was such as to render it almost impossible for a man to retain his equilibrium. The united efforts of those in the carriage were hardly sufficient to keep it from oversetting. Hailstones the size of the end of a man's thumb, driven by the blast, pelted us with unprecedented fury. Our horses and mules, rendered frantic with fear and pain, were with difficulty prevented from making their escape altogether."[32]

J. A. Pritchard likewise reported heavy and nearly continuous rains. Having left Independence on May 2, 1849, he reported showers on May 3; on May 4, he wrote, "It was raining this morning and we did not start to 9 and in 8 miles came to where the Santa Fe road leaves the old Oregon trail. It still continued to rain and the roads became somewhat heavy. Still passing over high rolling prairie we continued till 3 P.M., which brought us to a large creek, called Bool Creek. Just before we reached the creek we found one unfortunate fellow with the tongue broken square off at thonds [hounds?] of his wagon. It had been raining all day & we were wet & chilled by the exposure. We discovered a dead Oak close by and in a few minutes it was converted into a splendid log fire, by which we cooked our supper & got comfortably warm before bedtime. We passed some 70 wagons to day."[33]

Forty-four miles after leaving Independence, the Oregon road, which for most had then become the California road, diverged north and west from the old Santa Fe Trail. Micajah Littleton reported in late May, 1850 that the going proved tough. "Left this morning from the Santife [Santa Fe] Road. Crossed many bad places, creeks & Ravines, one creek 8 miles from where we started from we Bridged done it in one hour. Broke an axeltree which detained us about 3 hours. Rolled on and after a short distance one other wagon Striped a Skein which detained us about an hour. Although you may consider this as Rough a Road as any person may wish — I hope we shall find Better Roads Soon." And then he concluded his entry, "the country is Beautiful in the extreme."[34]

Having reached the vicinity of what is today Topeka, Kansas, the emigrants had to ford or ferry the Kansas River, the biggest obstacle before reaching the Blue River. By leaving from Independence, ferrying the Missouri River could be avoided, but although the Kansas proved nowhere as deep or wide as the Missouri, it still presented a problem in getting across. Near Topeka there were a number of tributaries of the Kansas River, some creeks, and the largest being the Wakaruska, most described as a small river difficult to cross. Josselyn reported on May 6, 1849, "got to the Walkarush [sic] about 10 o'clock and there being several teams ahead of us it took us about three hours to get across."[35]

Littleton described crossing the same point on June 1, 1850, and found the going no faster a year later. "The main fork of the Walkerusha is quite a large stream and about 5 or 6 miles from where we encamped. Its Bank on the South Side is very steep and we had to hold all the waggons going down. The timber about it and in its Bottoms are of a fine growth. The Roads are Stumpy in the Bottom where we broke one waggon tong which detained us some 2 or 3 hours. This evening there was 19 Indians came flying across the Road on a way chase. From the best information they are the Pottowattimas [sic] fighting the pawnees. The Road still bad in all the Ravines."[36]

As we have seen, emigrants reported an Indian presence in the area of the Kansas River ferry. "Several Indians have been prowling around our camp this evening, rendering the precautions of bring in our horses necessary," commented Searls, expressing the almost universal distrust of the emigrants toward the native Americans.[37]

Besides the Indians many emigrants expressed so surprise at the presence of white settlers in the area as well. Though they would have technically been either licensed traders or squatters on Indian land, the whites appeared to have been there some time. "At Cow Creek, is the residence of a Mr. Rogers, one of those semi-barbarians who, from long intercourse with the natives have assimilated themselves to their habits and manner of living,"[38] wrote Niles Searls in describing a white man who had made his home among the transplanted Indians on the plains. Kansas did not organize into an official United States territory until 1854. Some eastern tribes that had been forced from east of the Mississippi River a decade earlier had settled in northeastern Kansas and received aid from both government agency and missionaries. The Potawatomie tribe had been one such transplanted nation, settling in the area around present-day Topeka and tried to assimilate into life on the Great Plains. Some of Amos Josselyn's May, 1849 entries describe what he saw near the Kansas ferriage. "Drove 15 miles to a small creek and camped where there is a wagon shop and black smith shop established by the government for the benefit of the Potawatamie Indians."[39]

Searls also took note of the Potawatomies in his May 23, 1849, journal entry. "Our camp today has been the resort of a large number of Indians with whom many of our company have been trafficking. They are all of the Pottawatomie tribe. This tribe was originally from Wisconsin and some of our passengers were acquainted with many of them in that place. They have here a fine territory and some of them appear to have made considerable advancement in civilized life."[40]

Interaction between the Indians and the large numbers of emigrants passing through their lands must be considered as natural. However the interaction nearly always reflected an air of mistrust, though in fact the Potawatomies offered no threat to the emigrants, even to those that on occasion wandered off by themselves. "We yesterday lost 3 of our mules and in looking for them I got too far from camp and it getting dark before I could get in I lost my way and spent the night in rambling about. I had to move about to keep warm. I tried to sleep two or three times but it was too cold," wrote Amos Josselyn of an experience in Potawatomie territory. "I got into camp about 7 o'clock this morning and found that the mules were in. They were brought in by three Indians who said that they cought some Indians of another tribe driving them off. They wanted $9 for returning them but took five."[41]

A stream that through most of the year it is quite shallow, but in May, is swollen to some extent by spring rains, the Kansas River proved difficult to ford, except by the most resilient swimmers or the foolhardy. Most emigrants chose to be ferried over by a number of operators who could charge whatever the market could bear. Sometimes, depending on the amount of traffic, a wait could last the better part of a day. "Got to the Kansas River about noon, but by the time we got ferried across it was nearly sundown," wrote Amos Josselyn of his experience. "We drove about two miles from the Kansas to Soldier Creek and camped where we intend to stay until we organize into a company large enough to go through. The roads this day were pretty bad."[42]

J. A. Pritchard reached the Kansas River on May 7, 1849, making a decision on which ferry to use and reporting on his encounter with the Indians of the area. "We had to travel 16 miles to the upper ferry or 3 to the lower ferry. What we lost on this side by travelling to the upper ferry we gained on the other and as nearly all the Emigrants were going to the lower ferry we took the upper one. And one mile before striking the Kansas River is a mission and trading post called Potiwatin. There are several white families living there & some 4 or 5 stores black smith Shop etc. A number of Indians are living in the village. We called a halt of an hour or such a matter in the town and let the boys trade a little. We reached the River about 12 P.M. and crossed at 3 P.M. There was 2 ferry boats one kept by a half breed Indian (Michegan) & the other by a white man."[43]

Searls described crossing the Kansas River in more detail in his May 22, 1849, journal entry. "Reached the ferry of the Kansas this morning and were fortunate in finding an opportunity to commence crossing our wagons immediately. The ferry is owned by two half-breed Indians and the boats, two in number, are worked by the natives. The Kansas, like most of the streams emptying in the Missouri, is walled by high banks of loose, loamy earth which, continually crumbling away and falling into the stream, giving to its waters a muddy turbid appearance. The river is about thirty rods in width and, at the present stage of water, not over five feet in depth in the deepest places."[44]

Once across the Kansas River the emigrants pushed on toward the Blue River junction with the main road leading from St. Joseph and other points above Independence. At 37–40 miles northwest past the Kansas ferry, the emigrant trains looked to strike the Vermilion Creek, halfway to the Big Blue River. The landscape began to change some, and trains continued the process of reorganizing, but the concerns about illness, much warranted, and Indians, mostly without cause, continued to haunt those going to see the elephant. The fear of illness and the fact that it could fell anyone from the green horns to the most hardened veteran of western travels seemed to preoccupy the minds of many of the journal keepers, even when referring to other points. "This trail [toward the Platte] was first laid out by 'Black Harris' our intended guide," wrote Searls on May 24, 1849, adding, "who unfortunately for us died in Independence of Cholera; just before our departure."[45] Two days later he wrote, addressing major fears, "One company from Missouri has lost its captain by Cholera, and several others are at the point of death. They entertain some thoughts of disbanding and returning home. Near us are several comfortable log houses erected by Uncle Sam for the Pottawatomies, and from which they have been driven by the Pawnees. We shall enter the territories of the latter tribe in a day or two and some fears are entertained of trouble with them."[46] Though the Pawnees had apparently earned a reputation, true or false, for being hostile, few emigrants ever actually encountered one of that tribe. That fact did not seem to dim the reputation any. Searls wrote two days later, "Struck camp at an early hour and rolled over an excellent road, through a region still more broken than that passed through yesterday. Not a single Indian has made his appearance since we entered the Pawnee Country. They are unfriendly to the whites and seldom show themselves except as enemies."[47]

As the trains pushed on the shifting of persons from one unit to another, became routine. Despite constitutions, contracts, or well intended pledges by companies from the same community, even families, to stay together till the end, groups came and went, moving from train to train, consolidating and then breaking up when the situation presented something perceived to be better. Josselyn described a typical situation of train reorganization, a process that began almost as soon as the emigrants began jumping-off on the trails and which would continue unabated throughout the journey to California. "In the evening a company of 23 came up. We being 18 strong joined them which made 41, which we considered about strong enough and agreed to push on in the morning. This morning a company of 12 from Stubenville, Ohio joined us making us 53 strong."[48] Early on, strength in numbers seemed to be advantageous. Fifty to one hundred men in a company offered better protection against possible Indian trouble than did ten. It also meant that duties like night guard could be spread out among many. However, later on, that many, staying together and in some form of agreement, would have been unusual.

Despite the youth, vigor, anticipation of both excitement and challenge, many a young man going to see the elephant didn't last long enough to truly appreciate their undertaking. Hardly two weeks after leaving Independence, one of Niles Searls' companions succumbed to cholera, and his journal entries provide both an eloquent and poignant epitaph. "Our patient [Sinclair] has been suddenly taken much worse and in all human probability will soon be called to 'That bourne from which no traveler returns.' Poor fellow! Who that possesses a soul, can look unmoved upon him amid his sufferings. Far from home, and the friends he loves, with few of those kind offices which take from pain its severest pang, his case seems truly distressing. Charlie has been all attention to him since his first attack and, alike regardless of comfort or exposure, has done everything in his power to smooth our new companion's pathway to the grave. I shall take his place tonight in watching over his, apparently dying, pillow."[49]

The next day, he continued, describing the death scene. "Calm and collected, he spoke of his approaching end with out fear or trepidation. His mental faculties were unimpaired up to the last moment of his life and when no longer able to use his voice, he showed conclusively by signs and gestures that he fully comprehended the remarks addressed to him. Gradually yielding to the embrace of the monster, death, he quietly breathed his last at four o'clock P.M. May 30th, aged 23 years. Unable to procure other conveniences we wrapped him in his blankets and with sorrowful hearts consigned him to the 'cold earth' there to remain till the last trumpet shall call him forth to meet the reward of his many virtues. The words of one of my dearest friends were brought most vividly to mind, who in dissuading me from going to the shores of the Pacific, remarked that 'California Gold would cause more bereaved friends and relatives than the late Mexican War.'"[50]

Leaving from Weston/ Fort Leavenworth

Weston, Missouri, lay north of Independence, about midway between Independence and St. Joseph. A bustling town, it grew well because it lay on a great bend of the river with regular steamboat service, and in close proximity to Fort Leavenworth, the premiere military post on the edge of the Great Plains. Economically it did well in proportion to the overland outfitting business it could garner from the two giants to either side of it. Being further up the Missouri, the road to the junction of the main trails at the Blue River was closer, offering a time advantage over Independence. Being a couple of day's journey south of St. Joseph, one could avoid some of the tremendous crowds there and longer waits for ferrying across the Missouri. As one emigrant described her, "Weston is a small town containing about Three Thousand inhabitants situated on the north side of the river."

One of our diarists, Henry Wellenkamp, selected Weston as his jumping-off point, arriving there on April 29, 1850, having come from Washington, Missouri, aboard the steamer *Tuscumbia*. His journal entries tend to be very short and to the point, but provide a good outline of place names and distances from point to point along the way. His entries from May 4 through May 12, outline the progress from Weston to the Blue River, a distance of about 145 miles. "Saturday, May 4, started from Weston via Fort Leavenworth to; Lone Camp, 30 miles, Fork Creek, 22 miles, St. Joseph Fork, 12 miles, Grove Camp, 14 miles, Center Camp, 18 miles, Nag Camp, 22miles, Indian Camp N&W, 18 miles, Sunday, May 12th, [Big] Blue River, 9 miles." May 12th turned out to be a special day for Wellenkamp for other reasons besides just reaching the Blue River. "Celebrated my birthday. Special cigars and games, shooting at targets." And he added, "apprehensive — stories about Indians, etc."[51]

Another gold seeker, John Nevin King, also left from Weston in 1850. A young man and veteran of the Mexican War, having served in Texas and Northern Mexico, he may have been better suited than many others, because he had done some extensive travelling and been exposed to a bit of the spartan life prior to heading off to see the elephant. His letters from Weston give us a better picture of river travel, the town, and particularly the business of signing on with one of the express companies offering organized and all inclusive passage through to California.

"We arrived here yesterday on board steam boat *Kansas* having left St. Louis one week ago yesterday [May 1st]. In travelling up the Missouri you see snags in all directions and during our trip up we were scarcely out of sight of these even for a few minutes. Our passengers are generally a rough, weather beaten looking crowd, still there are some splendid fellows among them. The steamboat *St. Paul* has just passed us loaded down to the guards and crowded with Emigrants. We had quite a pleasant trip considering we had so many passengers on board, 200."[52]

As with most young men out to make their fortunes, anticipation of finally jumping-off on the trek bubbled from every pore. Every day spent in camp, organizing or waiting for supplies, delayed gaining that fortune, and many simply couldn't bear to stand still. "Thursday last (having spent the day previous in town) we concluded to go to Camp, where our expenses would be borne by Messrs. Alexander & Hall, and distance 9 miles from Weston. Our Mess, of whom I gave you a list, started on foot, having placed our Baggage, arms, & ammunition, in one of the hacks. Alexander said if we would wait until next day he would have all the passenger hacks brought in to take us out, but rather than wait for the hacks we preferred walking,"[53] wrote King on May 14, 1850, in a letter to his mother.

Despite not wanting to wait for the company to form up, initial layovers had to be accepted to a degree. Anxiety about all the gold being gone by the time they got there kept the feet moving, even if they weren't actually going anywhere. While they waited, some could find other diversions, tie up last minute details, or gather needed personal effects. In that sense they were no different than modern travelers who drop by the airport terminal shops, to pick up the forgotten antacid or toothbrush.

"Saturday moved from other camp 9 miles over into this one," wrote King describing the rambunctiousness, and restlessness that pervade many of the young men. "Sunday, went to church, distance 1½ miles from Camp where we heard a very good sermon from a Methodist preacher whose name I know not. His text was from Paul's Epistle to the Romans 10th chapter, 9th & 10th verses." Monday — yesterday — went into town to get some Diohrea or Diorhae [diarrhea] medicine my bowels being out of order — spring water not agreeing with them. I did not obtain the medicine but took a glass of good brandy with some Ess [essence] of Peperment [sic] which greatly relieved me — yes it cured me." Concerns about illness tempered everyone, even the most robust. King continued, "Tis reported that the cholera is raging in Saint Louis, all along the river and on the plains. Mr. West one of my mess has a small chest in which are prepared medicines for cholera & everything else with full prescriptions for the use of all."[54]

The jumping-off places like Weston were full of all types of people with all kinds of stories to tell. "We have a passenger in our train, a very old man, worth 60 thousand dollars, and has but one child, who, is of age & in business. He is going out merely to see the gold region and is much for the trip as anything else." While many observations and stories were based on reality and facts, others rose and circulated on any kind of rumor or supposition, multiple re-telling, until many simply defied conventional logic. As King related to his mother, some stories were rather astonishing. "Soon after arriving in town a Team came in, the Teamsters reporting to Alexander that another Teamster had harnessed his 4 mules and hitched them to a Timber wagon and when ready to start the mules became frightened, ran off with the wagon smashing everything — one of the lead mules running against a tree & killing himself instantly the other ran against a sapling and stunned himself badly." Of course, if those mules were like others of that species, with dispositions as reported by other emigrants, that story might not be that far fetched. Stories about Indians, in most cases complete fiction, still sent chills down the spines of many. "A report is circulating that the Pawnee Indians attacked some Emigrants and in the melee 30 on each side was killed, the Indians retreating,"[55] added King in writing to his mother, who no doubt found little comfort when she read her son's letter.

When the trains were finally ready to move off, both anticipation and uncertainty remained. "I will not finish this until we start across the plains when I expect to be able to lay before you the route we will take — as yet Alex & Hall are undecided. We will cross the river here instead of going to St. Joe. That place is crowded with Emigrants. Corn sells here readily at $1.00 per bushel and in some few instances at $1.10 per bushel. Alexander & Hall have some $30,000 invested in their Express."[56]

Leaving from St. Joseph

While Independence could rightfully claim pre-eminence as a jumping-off point for emigrants going to California, by 1849, St. Joseph had made every effort to sell itself as the superior point of departure, and in fact, surpassed its older neighbor to the south. Lying in the bluffs on the east side of a great C shaped bend in the Missouri River, it had both regular steamboat service and could be reached by overland roads from St. Louis and other points east. By virtue of the fact that one could outfit just as completely there and that it lay sixty miles north of Independence, with the advantage of bringing the emigrants 100 miles nearer to the Blue River junction and saving a full week to ten days' trail time, proved its most powerful selling points.

J. Goldsborough Bruff, the fastidious and impeccably organized leader of a company from Washington, D.C., selected St. Joseph to disembark from the steamers and prepare for the overland trek in 1849. The first week of his meticulous journal reflected the routine of emigrants preparing to strike out across the plains and the view of the St. Joseph area seen by everyone who came there. "April 27... At 5 P.M. reached St. Jose[Joseph] — and repaired to the Camp. Regulating matters in Camp, and breaking mules, the latter quite a task for many that had seldom seen a mule. Rousing the camp every morning at 4 o'clock. May 7... As far as we could see, over a great extent of valleys & hills, the country was speckled with the white tents and wagon covers of the emigrants."[57]

Sallie Hester also left from St. Joseph in the year 1849. Like many of the emigrants, her observations of the scene around St. Joseph reflect awe, a true sense of the scope of what the grand migration to see the elephant was all about. On April 27, she wrote, "St. Joe. Here we are at last, safe and sound. We expect to remain here several days, laying in supplies for the trip and waiting our turn to be ferried across the river. As far as eye can reach, so great is the emigration, you see nothing but wagons. This town presents a striking appearance — a vast army of wheels — crowds of men, women and lots of children and last but not least the cattle and horses upon which our lives depend."[58]

Margaret Frink, travelling to California with her husband in 1850, left from St. Joseph. Her diary is most impressive in the scope of its detail, and even more so, in the fact that it presents a woman's voice in a historical event that males so clearly dominated by their sheer numbers. She wrote on April 23, 1850, "We got into St. Joseph at 10 o'clock this morning. The whole country around the town is filled with encampments of California emigrants. This is the head of the emigration at the present time. They have gathered here from the far east and south, to fit out and make final preparations for launching out on the Great Plains, on the other side of the Missouri River. Every house of entertainment in the city is crowded to its full capacity. This has been a backward spring season, and thousands are patiently waiting for the grass to grow. Traveled two miles north of the town and settled into a cabin until the grass should grow on the Kansas and Nebraska prairies, and remained for the next fifteen days. We still lacked something to complete our stock of supplies: for we had neither pickles, potatoes, nor vinegar. The army of emigration was so numerous that the demand for these and many other articles could only with difficulty be fully supplied. Mr. Frink traveled sixteen miles through the farming country searching for pickled cucumbers. I prepared the vegetables and put them up in kegs of apple vinegar; these were our principal defense against that dreadful disease, the scurvy, from which the overland emigration of 1849 had suffered so severely. Not many days had passed before we began to hear frightful tales of Indian depredations on the plains, which had a tendency, at first, to shake the resolution of some members of the party."[59]

Sarah Davis left from St. Joseph, also in 1850. In her clear but simplistic diary she recorded on May 22, "we camped on the black snake hills in Buchanan County in one mile of St Joseph and a pleasanter place I never saw building. I never saw the like and the droves of Catle and mules and the prairie was beautiful." The next day she continued, "we traveled through St. Joseph and then through the Missouri bottom."[60]

While Bruff waited to move his company he continued his preparations which included adding more men. Whereas other emigrants came and went from train to train, company to company with only a nod of acceptance or a tip of the hat good-bye, joining or leaving Bruff's military style operation required an oath. "I had to swear 4 men to the constitution of the company, in accordance with said constitution," he wrote in his journal. However, when looking at the cut of the men he agreed to take on, he realized their acceptance of the by-laws in no way reflected anything like his own commitment to following them or seeing the trek through. "I had intimated, at the meeting which adopted said constitution, how many of the men would regard the obligation about as much as singing pslams [sic] to a dead horse, or whistling jigs for a mile-stone." Completing his list of necessary supplies, he jotted down, "I purchased a common thermometer, the only one left for sale, in St. Jose."[61]

The singular disadvantage of using St. Joseph as a jumping-off point seemed to have been the limited ability of its ferries over the Missouri to keep up with the tremendous demand. At the height of the season, a week, even two, of waiting was not out of the ordinary, though some diarists, like Davis, don't mention delays. That dissuaded some and sent others either up or down the river looking for other ferrying operations to get them across to the Kansas side. As Bruff described it, "There were but two very indifferent scows at the ferry, and these were being plied from the earliest day till midnight, every day; had been so for weeks, and from the mass herd, would continue for several weeks more. From the principal street in St. Jose, down 300 yds. crossing a bridge, to the river bank, was one dense mass of wagons, oxen, and people, and as soon as a wagon entered the scow, the next moved down to the water's edge, and the mass in the rear closed up to the front, affording the opportunity to one or more lucky wagons to fall in the extreme rear, &c. Fighting for precedence was quite common, and a day or two since, 2 teamsters, in one of these disputes, killed each other with pistols. This slow mode of crossing the river, would, I thought, take my train of 14 Company and 2 private wagons, to gradually get into place and cross, in a very disjointed way, about a fortnight." Being as well organized as he was, and to an extreme in comparison to most emigrants, Bruff weighed his options and decided on a different course. "I knew that the opposite site side for a considerable distance was marshy, there were many streams to cross, forage was scarce, and besides there was plenty of Cholera there. Whereas, by going up river, corn &c. could be had, on reasonable terms, a tolerable road laid before us, and lastly, a country of high rolling prairie intervening between the Missouri and Platte rivers."[62]

Many emigrants found the wait at St. Joseph too long, and like Bruff looked elsewhere for a crossing point. The Frinks, who initially traveled alone, composing their mini-train of, "two wagons, one drawn by four horses, a lighter one drawn by two horses, besides two saddle horses for Mr. Frink and myself," also opted to move on. "We were ready to start to-day, and decided that we would travel up along the east side of the Missouri River before attempting to cross over to the west side. Here we again heard alarming and discouraging accounts of deeds of violence and bloodshed that had recently been committed on the plains."[63]

Israel Hale began his overland diary in May, 1849, jumping off from the area around St. Joseph. Like others he decided not to wait for the crowds at the city ferries to subside and headed north of the city toward the little town of Savannah. On May 6 he wrote, "left St. Joseph for Savanna Landing. Found at the landing about thirty wagons ahead of us waiting to cross. Spent the balance of the day in cooking, cleaning up etc. Got the privilege of using the boats at night by manning them and paying an extra price for crossing. Mine was the thirteenth wagon and was crossed about sun rise."[64]

Between St. Joseph and the mouth of the Platte River, there were a number of ferry operations, some well established with proper equipment, others consisting of nothing more than a scow or raft, capable of hauling a single wagon at the time, set up by some enterprising individual who had the dream of getting rich from the gold rush without going to California. The advantage, and the danger of using one of those operations was that their was not the wait, sometimes of a fortnight; but there was a good chance of being drowned or losing one's kit in an accident by an untrained ferryman.

Franklin Starr, from Alton, Illinois, who went to see the elephant in 1849, leaving from the vicinity of St. Joseph, recorded in his diary a novel approach to avoiding the ferry lines. Having traveled up the Missouri on the steamer *Meridian,* Starr reached his jumping-off point early in the season on Wednesday, March 28, 1849. "We arrived at St. Joseph at 10 o'clock this morning. Landed *opposite* and pitched our tents for the first time on the bank of the river." By landing directly on the Kansas side of the river, apparently with the cooperation of the steamboat captain, he avoided the crowds in St. Joseph and the ferrying. We can only assume he brought most of his travelling equipage with him.

In that same day's entry Starr continued with a nice description of the region. "The country around St. Joseph is beautiful but there is a scarcity of Timber. [likely referring only to the area directly along the river bank, for in the next sentence he states] We are camped in the Bottom which here extends some six miles back from the river and is very heavily Timbered with Cottonwood and some Ash Huckleberry Sycamore Box Elder and Coffee Trees. The jointed Rush grows as thick as it can stand and four or five feet high. Deer and Turkey are tolerable plenty and Parakeets [likely some kind of swallow] are continually screaming overhead. We shall stay here some time, as there is no grass yet for the cattle. Corn is very high and difficult to get. We employ our time getting every thing in readiness for starting and in writing laws for governing the company Electing captains, etc."[65]

Bruff and other emigrants avoided the crowds around St. Joseph by going north to Savannah. He recorded on May 17, "camp'd within a mile of the town of Savannah [13 miles from St. Jose, and 75 from Fort Kearney] in a pleasant oak and walnut grove, close by a handsome farm-house, the proprietor of which, his good lady told me, had gone off some weeks ago, with the Savannah Company for Cala. Here we heard of Duncan's Ferry, so I determined to call and see it and perhaps cross there." Merchants in Savannah, like in St. Joseph, tired to make everything the emigrant needed available to them. On May 18, Bruff, "purchased a very fine new ox wagon, with 3 yoke of large good-looking oxen, for $230, for a commissary wagon."[66]

The Frinks also went north past St. Joseph, writing on May 10, "we left Savannah this morning and drove twenty-three miles up the east bank of the Missouri River." On May 11, they, "drove twenty-eight miles today to steam called Big Tarchio [Tarkio]," and on May 12, "drove twenty miles to-day." The next day, the Frinks reached a ferrying point they found acceptable. "This day brought us to the crossing of the Missouri River, ten miles below old Fort Kearney, which stands at the mouth of the Platte River. We found a number of wagons waiting to be crossed over in an old fashioned ferryboat. Each party must take its regular turn as registered on the ferry-book. This was known as Bullard's Ferry."[67]

Delays in crossing led to many short tempers. People gripped by impatience to hit the main trail to the gold fields tried to cut into waiting ferry lines, stream crossings, and lines at merchant houses. As Bruff already observed, people shot each other. Some, because of their size or disposition just plainly intimidated fellow travelers to get what they wanted. Justice had nothing to do with anything that was going on at the time, and the wise person knew when to back away from tense situations, as Bruff recorded on May 22, after meeting a man waiting to join up with another company. "Here I saw a member of the Pittsburgh Co. who informed me that there was so much threatening with Bowie knives and revolvers in the Company, and particularly in his mess, that he was afraid of his life, and left them here, some 18 days ago."[68]

Bruff's company finally found what appeared to be a suitable crossing point on the Missouri, about 50 miles above St. Joseph, on May 26. He wrote, "late in the afternoon reached the Ferry, where was quite a neat log & frame house, containing the families of Mr. Duncan and his connections." Two days later, on May 28, the dangers of the swirling Missouri River, to even the experienced ferryman, were made evident in Bruff's record. "The gang detailed for ferrying took over early, a load of oxen, and returned: then took in 4 oxen and a loaded wagon, Six men of the other company, and 8 of ours. On the other side near where they intended to land, the Scow ran on a Sawyer [long snag in the river] capsized & sank, in pretty deep water. Mr. Duncan, the worthy proprietor of the Ferry, steering the boat, was most unfortunately drowned. The wagon and many of the goods were lost; the oxen swam ashore, as did several of the men, at great peril; and the others remained on the Sawyer till relieved by a canoe sent for them —. Left Duncan's crossed at another ferry operated by four men 4 miles up stream."[69] Bruff's party eventually crossed the Missouri much farther north near the mouth of the Platte at the old Fort Kearney ferry.

The Frinks, who had crossed at one of the many independent ferry operations reported on May 14, "We were safely across the wide and muddy colored steam by eleven o'clock this morning." That danger past, new perils to occupy the mind were presented immediately. "Printed circulars have been distributed informing the emigrants of many Indian depredations. Now I begin to think that three men, one woman, and one eleven year old boy, only armed with one gun and one Colt's revolver, are but a small force to defend themselves against many hostile Indian tribes, along a journey of two thousand miles. I had a very strong feeling at the same time that these men would have felt more at ease if there had not been a woman in the party, to be taken care of in case of danger. However, each company was wholly independent of the others, and our wagons became separated from the other trains. We picked out a camping ground on a rolling knoll, so that we could the better defend ourselves in case we were attacked during the night. The first thing I did after we halted was to get out the field telescope, which we carried, to see if I could find any Indians: and sure enough I soon espied a party of them riding on an elevated ridge a long way off. A few minutes later a company of five fine-looking men from Michigan drove up and asked the privilege of camping with us that night. We were more than glad to have our force increase by the addition of a party of such resolute-looking men. I thought Mr. Frink was sleeping too soundly and breathing too heavily, I would arouse him: I could not understand how he could sleep soundly wherein there was so much danger. For my part I did not change my clothing during the entire night, either shoes nor bonnet. In this manner passed our first night on those vast, uninhabited plains."[70]

Of course the danger never materialized. There were few if any Indian depredations and nothing that amounted to a whole tribe being "on the warpath," at least not against the whites, that close to the jumping-off points. There were stories of tribal warfare and individual Indians, some under the influence of alcohol, did make their presence known, did secure and sometimes return loose livestock, and make a nuisance of themselves by begging, but the fear of losing one's scalp to them was exaggerated. Why the stories, rumors of hostile Indian activities, surfaced, one could only suppose. It can as much be blamed on outdated information, stories being told around a campfire for fun, to frighten a tinhorn, or even a bit of calculated maliciousness hoping to turn back competition heading to the gold fields.

Once across the Missouri River from any of the numerous ferriages around St. Joseph, the trains stuck due west toward the Blue River Road and a juncture with the trail coming up from Independence. The Blue River lay about 120 miles, in a due westerly direction, from St. Joseph. Bluffs and some rolling country and a number of small tributary streams that were easily forded unless excessively high from recent rains broke the road west from St. Joseph. Nearly everyone commented on the country being good, well watered and timbered, with reasonable road conditions. The road from St. Joseph to the Blue River ran through Indian reservation lands, and there were lots of comments about seeing Indians for the first time.

Franklin Starr described his first day on the trail to California from the bottoms opposite St. Joseph, on April 25, 1849. "We commenced our journey this morning and moved on to the Wolf River 18 miles. It has been every one for himself today each waggon starting when they got ready. We crossed mosquito creek a small rapid stream 4 miles from Wolf River. The road is hilly but good. The front axle of one waggon got broke today. The crossing at Wolf River is very bad. The river is like the rest of the streams that we have crossed rapid and clear. It is quite small. There are numerous springs along its banks and excellent fish in its waters. The Indians are very thick about here. There is a village of them about three miles above."[71]

Hale commented in his journal on May 9, 1849, "We are 13 miles from St. Joseph. Traveled seven or eight miles to Wolf River. The country is becoming more level but is still some hilly. Saw the first Indian this day. Since we crossed Missouri we find plenty of good spring water at almost every camp. On Wolf River we saw an Indian grave in a tree also a graveyard near the river. After crossing Wolf River we saw some fine land for farming purposes. Last night we stood guard for the first time. This afternoon we saw several Indians. It is said that a large encampment is very near." Besides dealing with first encounters with real Indians, many travelers, if they had not experienced it around the jumping-off points, had first encounters with sickness. "May 10 — Yoked up soon in the morning and were all ready to start when news came that Nathaniel Clark, one of Isaac Herrington's men had the Cholera, when we again turned out the stock. The man Clark died in ten hours from the time he was taken sick. We buried him today and traveled five or six miles."[72]

Davis wrote of similar experiences just after crossing over the Missouri. "We camped on the bluffs 6 miles from St. Joseph and staid a half a day and cooked and washed and then started on and then we had a vary bad time with the Indians," she wrote on May 24. "One of them was drunk and he ordered us off the land we told him we would not go and he then got down from his pony and said we should we also told him if he did not go home we would whip him and then he got in a rage and said whip whip whip god dam you puchall and wanted us to leave and he then wanted some money just one picaune [small coin] and quarter of a dollar." Over the next six days Davis' wagon came into the company of other travelers, which proved, as with most in the early stages of the trek, a confidence builder. "May 25 ... camped with five or six wagons. Next day we got in company with Mr. Right [Wright] and he had ten wagons and fifty men. May 28, we crossed Wolf River. May 29, crossed nimaha [Nemaha] river. May 30, 100 miles from St. Joseph, crost a creek whare their had bin a man robed and six had to be killed. [Indians?]"[73]

Along the Blue River Road to the Platte

In close vicinity to the junction of the Blue (also called Big Blue) and Little Blue Rivers, the trails from St. Joseph and Independence converged. Driving west they encountered the Blue, or Big Blue first. It presented more of an obstacle in that it had to be crossed to get to the Little Blue. Then the emigrants pushed on west to actually fall in along the Little Blue, which led them northwest toward another important juncture with the Platte River in southern Nebraska. If the emigrants thought their route crowded before, then they began to seen the real extent of the number going to see the elephant. And

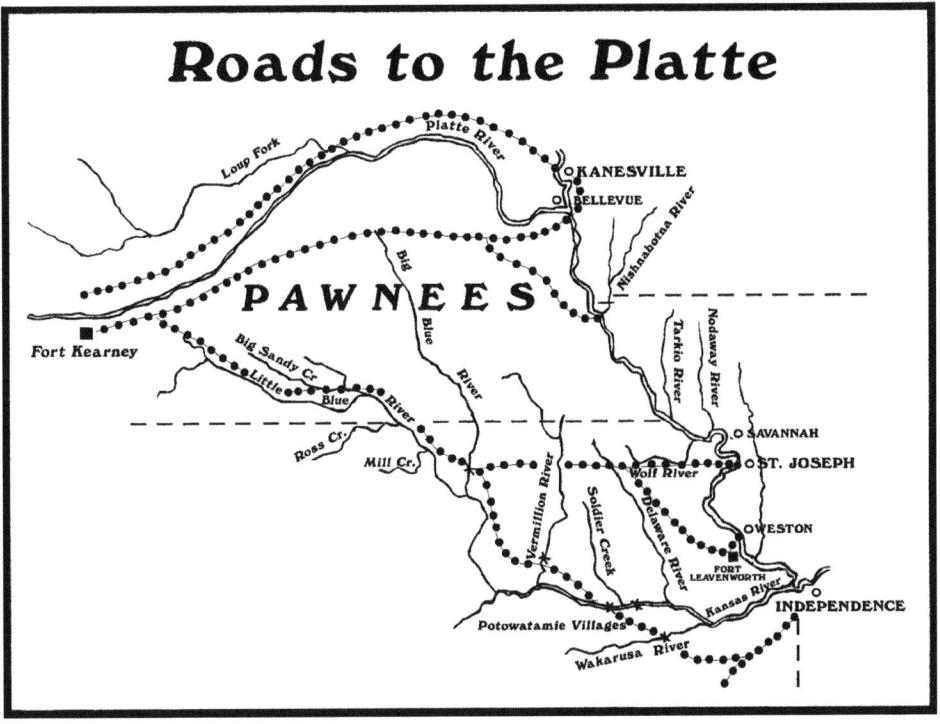

Roads to the Platte — routes from the jumping-off points to Fort Kearney on the Platte.

here the stories of our diarists form both Independence and St. Joseph merge. There are numerous similarities to what they saw, and recorded, like the cool, wet spring weather, but as each had individual experiences, there is a clear variety in how they described the trek along the Blue River toward the Platte. Both actual emigrants and guidebooks reported the distance from first joining the Big Blue to leaving the Little Blue at about 119 miles. The bottom of the Platte lay 26 miles further.

"This day we came to Blue River and crossed and encamped on the west side for the night," wrote Israel Hale on May 15, 1849. "The Blue is near as large as the Maramee [a river near his home] but not so wide. On the bank if this river we saw a quantity of provisions thrown out, such as flour, bacon etc. But this is not the first lot. It is left by persons who have more than their teams can haul." The next day Hale "arrived at the fork of the St. Joseph and Independence Road. Traveled more than twenty miles and encamped in the prairie without wood and water and but little grass. This day we passed some fine country but very little timber or water. We passed several graves during the day and the road is nearly filled with wagons and teams; as many as eight or ten teams in sight at one time, and some of them large. The weather continues cool and threatens rain."[74]

Franklin Starr described the Blue as "the prettiest stream I ever saw about 4 ft. deep and 75 yds over lines with Soft Maple Cottonwood and Willows which branch and divide close to the ground and lean over the water add much to its beauty."[75]

"Passed the Big Blue at 1 o'clock drove 20 miles this day," began Amos Josselyn on the same day as Hale. "At the Blue there is a grave, John Fuller who lost life by the accidental discharge of a gun, buried April 29." The next day Josselyn wrote, "passed junction of St. Joseph and Independence trails at 7:30 o'clock near Battle Creek." Over the next couple of days he, like many, noted the growing size of the emigration. "May 18, passed train of 130 wagons—drove up Little Blue River. May 19, 40 wagons in a train. Camped on little blue with 3–4 other camps in sight."[76]

Niles Searls, who had come up from Independence, had lots to say about the Blue River region, from the weather to the landscape to Indians. "Reached the bank of the Big Blue [36 miles past the Vermilion]. Scarcely a day passes in which it does not storm more or less, in consequence of which we are continually exposed by sleeping on the wet ground," he wrote on May 31, 1849.[77] Three days later he continued in his diary, "Our trail was over an all most entirely level plain, destitute of those eminencies and depressions which have hitherto characterized the greater proportion of the country over which we have traveled. After a few hours travel we found the company would not come to a halt till we reached the banks of the Little Blue. The Little Blue is at this time considerably swollen by the late rains and presents a turbid appearance. Its width is about twenty yards and the banks are covered by Oaks, Elms, Cottonwoods, etc.

"We met a portion of the American Fur Company this morning bound for Mo. They reported having seen a man killed and scalped by the wayside. This is the favorite hunting ground of the Pawnees and a strict guard will be kept up."[78]

As the emigrants began proceeding along the Blue River road they entered Pawnee country. The Pawnees had a reputation that definitely preceded them, earned or not, for being generally a bad encounter for whites. Having heard the stories, everyone had guarded comments. "The country is becoming more broken than formerly. Saw at a distance two Pawnee Indians but none as yet have paid us a visit," wrote Hale on May 17. "Their absence, however, is very acceptable, for they have the name of being a thievish set. Camped at Walnut Creek, we are however several miles from the Little Blue."[79]

Sallie Hester, travelling along the same road in the same week as Hale, expressed a woman's view of the land, life, death, and the native inhabitants. Her words are so important because she tends to elaborate, longer, and in more eloquent terms than most of the male diarists. On May 21, 1849, she wrote, "Camped on the beautiful Blue River 215 miles from St. Joe, with plenty of wood and water and good grazing for our cattle. Our family all in good health. When we left St. Joe my mother had to be lifted in and out of our wagon; now she walks a mile or two without stopping, and gets in and out of the wagons as spry as a young girl. She is perfectly well. We had two deaths in our train within the past week of cholera — young men going West to seek their fortunes. We buried them on the banks of the Blue River, far from home and friends. This is a beautiful spot. The Plains are covered with flowers. We are now in the Pawnee nation — a dangerous and hostile tribe. We are obliged to watch them closely and double our guards at night. They never make their appearance during the day, but skulk around at night, steal cattle and do all the mischief they can. When we camp at night, we form a corral with our wagons and pitch our tents on the outside, and inside of this corral we drive our cattle, with guards stationed on the outside of tents. We have a cooking stove made of sheet iron, a portable table, tin plates and cups, cheap knives and forks [best ones packed away] camp stools, etc. We sleep in our wagons on feather beds; the men who drive for us in the tent. We live on bacon, ham, rice, dried fruits, molasses, packed butter, bread, coffee, tea and milk as we have our own cows. Occasionally some of the men kill an antelope and then we have a feast; and sometimes we have fish on Sunday."[80]

Sarah Davis spent ten days passing along the Blue River road a year later, in 1850, also providing a woman's perspective. She is less detailed than Hester and somewhat more somber, yet had the same feminine eye toward life. Not soon after jumping off, the trials began, as she observed. "May 31, crossed the blue river whare their was a man drowned and one died and to [two] turned back to go home. we then left our company and find another company." The next day, "we crost the quiet creek and then we past nine graves that day and past through phesents [sic] prarie." By the middle of her week she was along the Little Blue and wrote on June 3, 1850, "we crost the big sandy [a tributary creek flowing into the Little Blue from the north] and then had a tremendous thunder sower [shower] it rained till every thing was wet as they could be and still continued to rain till next day."[81]

Like all the emigrants, J. A. Pritchard commented about the scenery and the weather. May 14, 1849, he began, "The little Blue was in full view. Its bottoms are broad and heavily timbered. sweet and refreshing waters, got sight of the first antelope and a few wild Turkeys. loud peels of thunder and fearce [sic] lighting — many of the tents were upset and the men exposed to the storm till their clothing were perfectly saturated."[82]

Writing in his own diary on May 14, 1849, Franklin Starr, also camped on the Little Blue, described the same storm. "We had a thunderstorm accompanied with wind last night. It blew down most all the tents and the tin ware went rattling along and some was never found I was on guard again and got another nice soaking but I was not alone in my trouble for as the tents blew down the inmates crawled out from under them and took to their wagons."[83]

After a couple of weeks on the trail, the road and scenery, began to take on a mundane appearance for some of the emigrants and other simple amusements were sought, and provided, as Israel Hale recounted May 20, 1849. "This morning we left the encampment a little after sunrise, the road heading up the Little Blue. We saw nothing worthy of note except occasionally a hat or cap would appear to take wings and would sometimes go two hundred yards before it could be overtaken, for the wind blew almost a gale. We stopped to noon after ten miles travel and near a small grove of willow trees and within one hundred feet of Little Blue. Foot racing continued during the day or a bare head was the result."[84] If the wind and weather didn't provide a diversion, then insects did. Hale, May 22–49: "For several evenings past we have been troubled with what is called June Bugs. They are a brown or reddish bug about one half inch long. One evening they nearly covered one of our tents," wrote Hale on May 22. He added, "Mosquitoes made their appearance this evening in swarms."[85]

Niles Searls had a similar experience, reporting, "We have been last night and this morning tormented by clouds of beetles. They were so numerous as to almost overpower us. Not a dish could be cooked in which they did not protrude and during a portion of the night might continually be heard the thumping noise occasioned by hundreds of them flying against the tents."[86]

After three or four days for most, the Blue River road ran out and the emigrants prepared to strike out over the plains toward the Platte River bottoms to the north. As Sarah Davis put it so succinctly on June 9, 1850, "we camped on the plains in a butiful [beautiful] place whare their was about fifty wagons in camp and then we left the blue river and came in sight of nebriska."[87]

Hale recounted his departure from the Blue River road on June 4, 1849, writing, "The roads this morning have been heavy, as they are called; that is, they are wet. But we have no reason to complain of roads for they have been dry and solid until yesterday, since we left St. Jo. Our course is still on the left bank of the Blue, and I believe we follow it thirty or forty miles further, after which we leave it to the left and strike for the Platte."[88]

As J. A. Pritchard's company came to the end of the Blue River road, and the congestion caused by the emigration increased, they opted for a change in travel arrangements. "I went to Capt. Fash and told him that I wished to leave his train — not that or any of our company, had any objections to him as capt. but that the train was too large to get along with convenience and speed — to which he agreed and said that there were no objections on his part to our withdrawal," wrote Pritchard on May 15. That evening they were, "Joined by 3 teams form Ill and a wagon with 5 men from Pendleton Co., Kentucky," and the next morning, "shortly after starting we passed the large train of 50 wagons commanded by Capt. Sublett the Old Mountaineer and discoverer of the Sublett or Greenwood cut off. They however, as was the common lot of large companies, had a split that morning — 27 of wagons remained with Sublett, 23 with some Dr. of Mo. By noon we had ascended the little Blue to the point at which we left it — strike across the Platte River. 2 more wagons from Fash's train came up to join and another wagon with men from Ky."[89]

As Franklin Starr departed the Blue River road toward the Platte his concerns suddenly focused more on the company of Indians than reaching the next landmark. "Tuesday, May 15, 1849. Left the little Blue this morning and struck for the Platte. Traveled 18 miles. There was a mist all the forenoon. Crossed several bad branches. About the middle of the afternoon we saw about 3 miles ahead objects what were supposed to be Indians. Not knowing what their intentions might be the Captain ordered the waggons to close up and keep close together and to have the guard so that they could be got readily. They proved to be Sioux and Cheyenne all mounted and armed with each a rifle, spear, scalping knife and so forth. These spears were made of steel the blades about 18 inches long and 1 and ¼ inches wide. There were about half the Indians. A scouting party of 500 warriors were camped on the head of the Little Blue about 5 miles from us. They were after the Pawnees. They were large fine looking men. There [sic] chief's name who was a small man was Little Bear. After accompanying us a short time they left us and as they rode across the Prairie in a fast Gallop with their spears pointed forward over their horses heads they presented a wild and formidable appearance."[90]

Other Roads to the Platte

Those that crossed the Missouri above St. Joseph, moving off from Savannah, like the Frinks and Bruff companies, did not follow the established Blue River road, but cut diagonally across the northeast corner of Kansas into southeastern Nebraska. Finding a ferriage with a shorter wait, thus gaining them time on the rest of the emigrant flood, motivated many of these emigrants, but the availability of grass, vital for the livestock, along the less well traveled trails, also figured in their movements. Though it was not as crowded as the Blue River road, there were still plenty of emigrants moving, finding their way along tracts that while less established still gave some assurance that they would eventually merge with the one great trail along the Platte.

Margaret Frink described in her diary on May 15, 1850, problems involving both the issues of time and grass. "We met a large train of wagons from Ohio and Michigan. The Ohio and Michigan trains who were with us were fitted out with hardy Canadian ponies, small but tough, and capable of enduring greater hardships than ordinary horses. But the drivers were in too big of a hurry to get to California before all the gold was dug out, and traveled too fast. Many of our party being young, inexperienced men, thought it necessary for us to pass all the ox teams and loose cattle on the road, fearing there would be no feed left for our own stock. They would whip up furiously and try to pass every train they overtook. Our own horses, like most of the western horses, were large and had been accustomed all their lives to be fed corn. And now, to get nothing to eat but the scanty new grass on the plains, they could not endure what the sturdy Canadian could, and so after the first week had passed we traveled more slowly."[91]

The Frinks had crossed the Missouri far enough north to totally avoid northeastern Kansas and the Blue River road. Not only did they avoid some congestion, but also they found, "The road along here was in good condition, all the bad streams being bridged." As they approached it, the Platte River valley offered a marvelous vista, which Mrs. Frink set her pen to describe. "Today we traveled about twenty miles, descending the steep bluffs from the high plains, over which we have been marching ever since we crossed the Missouri River, to the low bottom of the Platte River, and coming for the first time to its south bank. A shallow groove, or flat, low valley, from ten to twenty miles wide, has been scooped out of the sandy plains for four hundred miles from the Black Hills to the Missouri. Along each side are broad sandy bluffs, one hundred and fifty feet high. In the bottom of this valley the Platte River has cut out for itself a winding channel from six to ten feet deep and from one to two miles wide. The valley is totally devoid of timber or undergrowth of any kind, except where a few straggling cottonwoods and willow thickets." Beyond the immediate road, Margaret could read in her guidebooks with anticipation about what lay ahead. "Our road from this point follows the south bank of the main stream and of its northern branch for four hundred and fifty miles. Fifty miles beyond it meets the Sweetwater, which leads two hundred miles further to the South Pass."[92]

Bruff's company had also crossed far upstream from St. Joseph, into the southeastern corner of Nebraska, not far from the Platte estuary. His journal entry of June 8, 1849, describes the virgin country he saw, and the expectation of trouble with Indians. "Here were numerous pretty wild flowers, gooseberries, strawberries, onions, and prairie peas. Heard that the Sioux were at war with, and hunting the Pawnees. After dark, a small lean wolf-dog came into camp, exciting my suspicions that some thieving Pawnee might be crawling around to steal mules."

The supposition that the Pawnee might be looking to attack was first carried with a degree of excitement, then almost disappointment. It must be taken for granted that much bravado filled the majority of the young men striking out on the greatest adventure of their lives. To say that a number of them were actually spoiling for a fight with the Indians is proven in Bruff's June 10 entry. "Put the train in motion, at 8 A.M. a young man fell, and a wagon wheel passed over his leg without injuring him. His leg happened to lay in a soft indention of the plain when it occurred. The Pawnees commenced gathering around us; they seem to rise form the earth, on both sides, as far as the eye can distinguish them. I divided my mounted men in two parties, one as an advance guard and the other as a rear guard: and required a man on each side of each wagon, with his gun ready, incase of mischief. I believe the company was a good fighting party; the blackguards, who are generally cowards, were but few. If the Pawnees had made a demonstration, we would most assuredly have made some ponies. But Alas! The great warriors, arabs, and terror of the plains, turned out to be a sadly reduced, starving, contemptible race! They begg'd me for bread, opened their dingy robes, and exhibited their prominent ribs and breastbones. As they were actually starving, famine might drive them to rob and break up some small party, maybe family, in the rear, and we had plenty; so I ordere'd a halt, gave the Indians about a peck of hard bread, half a middling of bacon, and hat full of tobacco."[93]

Two days later Bruff reported they "passed through the deserted Pawnee Village. No regularity in the disposition of the houses here — the trail passes to the left, and close alongside the outer houses, or lodges. In the open space between the huts, are scattered about circular pits, filled with rubbish, and are dangerous to fall into. They were the Indian's granaries. Wooden mortars & pestles, muscle-shells, mats — old & new, worn out moccasins, dried herbs, willow sticks & poles, bones of animals, deer horns, pieces of saddle trees, &c scattered around. An ox-wagon, with a family, camp'd near us, they were quarreling all night about a stray ox. Rain, thunder & lightning."[94]

The Frinks, passing through the same region the year following Bruff, took similar defensive precautions against the Pawnee, whose reputation as fierce plains fighters, no doubt created by some guides who had crossed their territory earlier in the decade, had yet to be replaced by the truth that most of them had been reduced to the status of beggars. She explained in her May 19, 1850, entry, "along the Platte. Here the whole earth as far as the eye can reach, is naked and bare except that a thin growth of grass partly hides the sandy ground. Thinking it prudent to organize our forces for protection against the Indians, and to insure the safety of our stock at night, something of a military system was adopted, with proper officers. In case of an attack by Indians, each man was expected to be at his appointed post. Mr. Frink was elected captain. Four men were to be detailed every night to sand guard over the horses, and bring them in the next morning."[95]

The next day the Frink party apparently passed the same village Bruff had described a year before. "May 20, 1850... We had with us some guidebooks (Frémont's and Palmer's) from which we learned that to day we would pass the village of the Pawnee Indians, who had the name of being very warlike. In anticipation, every gun and pistol was put in good order, and regular military tactics were observed. At ten o'clock we came to the village, but instead of a bloody fight, we took the village without firing a gun. From appearances, the place had not been occupied for years. Our military prowess all disappeared in a twinkling. Up to this time we had seen but a single Indian, and he was a long way off. The tribe had moved north to the Loup Fork of the Platte."[96]

The Indians might cause some limited trouble, pilfering loose livestock, but many travelers found that their draft animals were more threatened by the wildness of the region, and wolves, than the Indian. J. A. Pritchard, who had come up the Blue River road, attested to that point in his diary entry of May 17, 1849. "Last evening we formed our camp regardless of shape there being no one whose duty it was to attend to the forming the company in proper shape. About 10 at night just as the Camp had become quite a large Mountain Woolf made his Debut and brought one of those hideous howls that will startle one from the profoundest sleep — and make him think that one of the Friends of the infernal regions was standing before him. Away went picket ropes and at a single dash about 40 the mules were loosed. Not recovered till morning."[97] As we shall see, nearly every emigrant had something to say about the wolves.

The point Pritchard made about not having someone to set the train in a proper formation reflects a problem common to nearly all the traveling parties. It is true most emigrants signed on with trains, who had captains, and even written constitutions, when they were at the jumping-off points. But once out onto the prairies, the disintegration and reforming process went on continuously. We have seen in numerous early entries numerous travel rearrangements made, including Pritchard's departure from the train of a Captain Fask. If the newly bonded emigrants were wise, they quickly elected someone else to be in charge, only if that new arrangement only lasted a few days. Pritchard nicely describes the process. "It was now apparent to all, that it was indispensable to have a Capt. or commander to the train and that it must be organized with proper rules & restrictions— Thereupon a motion was made to elect a Capt. who should take charge of the company till further regulations could be made. James A. Pritchard elected. The Capt. then made a motion to have one man selected by the members of each wagon to meet at the earliest hour to draft a constitution & by-laws for the farther organization & government of the company."[98]

Eventually all the feeder trails going out from the jumping-off points from Independence, Weston, St. Joseph, and points north up to the Platte River confluence with the Missouri, folded into one great road. The most marvelous description of that folding comes from Margaret Frink who wrote on May 20, 1850, "In the afternoon we came to the junction of the emigrant road from St. Joseph with our road, about twenty-five miles below New Fort Kearney. That road ran westward from St. Joseph to the Blue River and up the Little Blue to its head, where it turned to the northward across the high plains to the Platte. Here the two roads met. Both roads were thickly crowded with emigrants. It was a grand spectacle when we came, for the first time, in view of the vast emigration, slowly winding its way westward over the broad plain. The country was so level that we could see the long trains of white-topped wagons for many miles. The army which had crossed the Missouri River at St. Joseph joined our army, which had crossed the river above Savannah, it appears to me that none of the population had been left behind. It seemed to me that I had never seen so many human beings in all my life before. And when we drew nearer to the vast multitude, and saw them in all manner of vehicles and conveyances, on horse back and on foot, all eagerly driving and hurrying forward, There was a cart drawn by two cows, a cart drawn by one ox, and a man on horseback drove along an ox packed with his provisions and blankets. There was a man with a handcart, another with a wheelbarrow loaded with supplies. And we were not yet two hundred miles from the Missouri River. I thought, in my excitement, that if one-tenth of these teams and these people got ahead of us, there would be nothing left of us in California worth picking up. I was half-frantic over the idea that every blade of grass for miles on each side of the road would be eaten off by the hundreds and thousands of horses, mules, and oxen ahead of us. And worse than all, there would only be a few barrels of gold left for us when we got to California."[99]

Falling in Along the Platte

Reaching the Platte marked the completion of the first leg of the emigrant's journey to see the elephant. True, the Platte represented an important physical landmark, but also by the time they reached the Platte, most emigrants had experienced enough of the trail life to have lost any illusions about the speed or ease of travel. They had by then seen accidents, been battered by the weather, felt the general hardship of self-sustenance, experienced real fear and apprehensions, seen the graves of strangers, and witnessed the deaths of companions. Yet, it can be said that they were nowhere near the nadir of the trip and that they had caught no more than a distant glimpse of the elephant. They carried those things with them to the Platte, but what impressed them the most remained the physical appearance of the new region and the road, which is most clear from reading the diary entries.

"Along the bank of the Platte," wrote J. A. Pritchard on May 18, 1849. "The general course which is nearly from the West to the East — We passed the head of Grand Island — here the river expands in breadth, presenting a surface of water from 1½ to 2 miles wide; it has a strong resemblance of the Missouri river. Although the channel is so broad, and presenting to the eye a volume of water, the stream is nevertheless so shallow that it can be forded without difficulty in many places — The bed of the river is composed of sand — and this is all the time shifting its position and fresh deposits are constantly being made. The banks of the Platte are low and at this time do not rise more than 18 inches or two feet above the surface of the water."[100]

Israel Hale had a similar impression, writing on May 23, 1850, "we came to the bank of the Platte River and followed it up a few miles in a hunt for wood, but were unsuccessful and finally struck camp in the prairie. The Platte River bottom, where we entered it, is most beautiful. It is wide and level, but it is destitute of timber. A man from Prussia [who is with us] says it resembles the valley of the river Rhine, which he always considered the most beautiful spot in the world. Grand Island, I am told, is near one hundred miles in length. It appears to be well timbered, cottonwood."[101] Franklin Starr echoed Hale's sentiments upon seeing the Platte. "There is no timber this side of the Platt but the islands are timbered. The main channel runs this side of Grand Island and is not one fourth of a mile wide. It is rapid and muddy like the Missouri. Grand Island is said to be six miles wide at this place."[102]

Niles Searls entered the Platte bottoms on June 6, 1849. "The descent to the bottom lands of the Platte is by a gradual inclined plain, through the towering points which overlook the whole valley for many miles."[103] The next day he added to his diary, "The Platte at this point is divided by several islands rendering it impossible to estimate its width. Its depth is from one to three feet without any channel."

Having reached the Platte, the routine of trail life would take on some new facets, while other patterns evident from the beginning simply continued. "Mr. Smith died last night and was buried by his brethren of the Masonic Order, assisted by the Odd Fellows at one o'clock P.M. this day," wrote Searls on June 7, 1849. Taking death in its stride he then continued, "We have all been employed in washing. It was my first attempt and for the future I shall more fully appreciate the labors of those by whom this arduous task is performed. The skin was rubbed from my hands long before I had brought my clothing to anything like a right appearance and after all the result seem to be only an equalization of dirt throughout the various articles washed."[104]

On entering the Platte valley, Israel Hale made several important observations, "We still find articles which have been thrown out by emigrants. We have seen two wagons that were left or rather destroyed and judging from the irons and parts left they were of good quality." Taking note that travel along the Platte road went in more than one direction, he added, "We met today five or six wagons from Fort Laramie, which were loaded with robes, furs and the like. They belonged to Mr. Pappin of St. Louis." And, reorganizations continued; "Yesterday our company divided. Five wagons left. They thought our train too large. We now number but eleven wagons and forty men." Hunting for fresh game provided a diversion and supplemented a somewhat mundane diet. "We occasionally see antelope but have not yet seen a buffalo.

Game appears to be very scarce. I have only seen one squirrel. One of our men killed a hare. It was similar to our rabbit, but twice as large."[105]

Two weeks behind Hale's party, Searls had some similar observations. Writing on June 8, 1849, "Our course has been up the south side of the Platte through the bottom, which extends back from the stream a distance of four miles. Near our last encampment we saw several articles which had been abandoned by a pack mule company broken up by dissention in the Company."[106]

The ferocity of the spring storms roaring across the plains seemed to intensify in the openness of the Platte. Searls described one, writing, "We have several times in this trip experienced heavy showers and once or twice have had hail, but all the storms which I ever before experienced were as nothing compared with one we endured this day, just before reaching Fort Kearney. The rain fell in torrents accompanied by a whirlwind and by hail the size of hickory nuts. Two of our carriages were overset by the gale and one of them crushed to atoms. Mules and loose stock were stampeded and ran for hours. Captain Turner, who was on horseback, was struck on the finger by a hailstone, which dislocated the joint. In the short space of ten minutes no less than three inches of hail and rain fell. Our only course was to turn our teams to the leeward and, in the language of the seaman, scud before the gale. At the close of the storm, we again got under way and reached the fort, glad to behold once more the residence of civilized men."[107]

John Nevin King wrote a letter to his family, date June 3, 1850, describing the first leg of his journey from his jumping-off point, Weston, to the Platte valley road. It represents a good summary of probably what a lot of the emigrants saw and experienced. "Everything goes on smoothly and we have passed hundreds of Teams some bound for the Eldorado & some for California. There has been but few deaths among the Emigration of last and the present years judging from the few graves which lie scattered along the roadside. I have counted but 10 & have read all the inscriptions upon any of them. One man came to his death by accidentally shooting himself. [Reported by other emigrants] there has been but little sickness in our Train one case of small pox occurred. A man German named Blum was afflicted — as soon as was discovered he was sent in advance of the train & orders given to proceed without delay to Fort Kearney. The orders were obeyed but upon arriving at the Fort he was not allowed to enter. He is now camped about half a mile from us where he, with the Dr. & two other men who have had the disease will remain until all danger is over & then join us.

"This Indian Territory is the most beautiful country I have ever seen. The Prairie is high and rolling some places very rich others not so rich having a portion of sand mixed. The only objection that can be had to the country is the want of Timber. I have not seen a good body of Timber since I left Missouri."[108]

Leaving from Kanesville/Council Bluffs

Kanesville, approximately on the site of modern Council Bluffs, Iowa, lay as the most northern of the major jumping-off points on the Missouri River, and saw several thousands depart from that environ. Some crossed the Missouri directly opposite Kanesville, landing them in Nebraska north of the Platte River, while some ventured about twenty miles south toward Plattsmouth, Nebraska, and crossed to land on the south bank of the Platte and join the majority of emigrants. Fewer emigrants traveled west along the north bank of the Platte, which had been blazed by Mormon migration. They encountered different physical obstacle, but saw the Nebraska territory from much the same perspective as those on the south bank. By the time they were as far west as Fort Kearney, wagon trains on both banks could easily see, and routinely traveled parallel to each other. In reality, whichever bank one choose to follow west, both would eventually merge near the first great milestone of the trek, Fort Laramie. William Edmundson of Oskaloosa, Iowa, and Caleb Booth of Farmington, Iowa, took the trail along the north bank, while Lucena Parsons, a native of New York, accompanying her husband, George Washington Parsons, swung south. All left from around Kanesville in 1850.

William Edmundson described Kanesville as he saw it on May 27, 1850. "It is the headquarters of the Mormans [sic] in Iowa and Situated about 4 miles from the Missouri River near the lower end of the Council Bluffs at a place formerly Called Indian Hollow. A. W. Hildreth from Highland County, Ohio, Settled here in 1839 and built a Sawmill within the present limits of the Town. The Potawatamie mills on Musketoe Creek are in 2 miles of this place. They were built for The Indians some years ago by the U. S. government. Kanesville contains 5 to 6 hundred inhabitants. They do a flourishing business in the mercantile line Owing Chiefly to the California emigration. The Frontier Guardian a weekly Newspaper is published here Elder Orson Hyde Editor. We camped 2 miles below the Town."[109]

Caleb Booth, a 24-year-old young man, who had joined a company consisting of, "Mr. Hinds, his wife and three children, James Thomas, Alexander Hastings, George Gardner, and myself," arrived at his jumping-off point on May 21, 1850. He wrote, "passed through Kanesville, a small village thronged with California teams laying in provisions &c. for a trip to California, this being the last town and only some 10 or 12 miles from where we cross the Missouri River."[110]

The organization of trains, securing ferriage over the river, and completing the acquisition of supplies, and repairs occupied the time of the emigrants at Kanesville, the same as at the other jumping-off points. "Last evening Mr. Hyde from Kanesville came down & organized us in a company of 50 wagons under the command of Captain Foote & this morning we are repairing as fast as possible to the ferry," wrote Lucena Parsons on June 13, 1850. Her remark about going as fast as possible to the ferry I think is indicative of the fact that her company's starting date was rather late in the season. Starting for California much after June 15 could prove dangerous for getting through the mountains at the other end of the trek. She continued, "We are crossing at Martins ferry 2 miles above Bethlehem. There is as much as both ferries can do, as there are some 700 teams yet to cross. They go in companies of 100 & are divided into companies of 50 & 10 & have captains over each division. All armed with rifles & muskets. Weather very hot. We are in 2 companies of 50 waggons. Our chief captain's name is Wall, & the captain of our 10 is named Maughn. Very fine men."[111]

Caleb Booth's party did not wait long to get past Kanesville and across the Missouri. On May 22, 1850, the day after arriving in Kanesville, he wrote, "Encamped on the bottoms of the Mo. Numerous California teams all about. Some of the men drunk, others cursing. Traveled 3 miles to the river and stopped for the night. This river is about 400 yds. wide. The water very muddy. Boats ply here, all of which are poor things."[112] The preceding quote contains a couple of interesting points. Young Caleb's comments on the drinking and cursing, I believe, reflect that fact that he came from a strongly religious background. That belief can be reinforced by comments made from the beginning of his diary about not travelling on any Sabbath days. Two days before arriving in Kanesville, May 19, 1850, which fell on a Sunday that year, he wrote, "Sabbath. Notwithstanding, most of the teams are traveling, little regarding *that when* in pursuit of gold."[113]

The second point, regarding the boats, is insightful. The fact that there were a number of them, and all perceived to be "poor things," or in bad condition, points out how locals with even a modicum of river knowledge and a bit of business savvy could make a lot of money fast, getting the hordes of emigrants over that 400 yards of muddy water. Booth's party crossed in one of those boats the next day. "We pulled the wagons in by hand and crammed the cattle into boats by themselves. After being delayed several hours from the wind and rain and a huddle of teams, we succeeded in crossing. Fare 75 cents per wagon, 25 per yoke of cattle."[114]

After three days near Kanesville, Edmundson recalled, "A sufficient number of Teams having arrived during the day we joined them and organized into a company amounting in all of 50 men and 2 women."[115] It is worth noting here that Edmundson's ratio of men to women would not have been at all unusual. Other diarists, even the women who went and wrote of the experience, comment on the scarcity of the female sex on the trails. While some trains did have substantial numbers of "family" units, many more had no women at all. It is quite true that "going to see the elephant" attracted a vast majority of young, male adventurers, and while many of them may have been married, it proved an exception when a wife agreed to willingly make the dangerous trek, even more so if there were small children.

Chores, dealing with the everyday facts of life and preparations continued. "The women are washing & baking to start Monday. It takes a great deal of fixing to get started where there is so much order observed. Each captain looks to his own division," Lucena wrote on June 15. The next day she added, "to day it is very hot & sultry & there are some complaining of the headache. I have the sick headache to day. This afternoon we had preaching in front of the camp."[116]

The organization of trains around Kanesville held no more integrity than at any of the other jumping-off points. Companies expanded or shrank daily as the necessities of the individual emigrants, on how to move or stay emerged. "Fell in with a company of 15 wagons including ours and consisting of 61 yoke of cattle. We made a fine appearance while traveling on together,"[117] wrote Caleb Booth. People hurried to get started and patience proved a virtue in short supply. Delays of all kinds compounded the problem. "We started about noon. We were delayed in waiting for some muskets which our captain went back to Kanesville & got. These were distributed among those that were destitute of them,"[118] recorded Lucena Parsons on June 17, 1850. Edmundson recalled just one day after his train had ferried the Missouri, "Some of the wagons being out of order, it became necessary to stay till the afternoon in order to have them repaired, upon which 26 of our company left us and went ahead."[119]

As the case with those crossing the Missouri further south at St. Joseph, the emigrants almost always immediately encountered Indians. "Crossed the river at St. Francis, or Trader's Point, landing at Bellevue where The Agency for the Pawnees, Ottoes & Omahas is located," Edmundson wrote on May 31, 1850. "An Indian School under the direction of the Presbyterian church is established about a mile from the agency under the Superintendence of the Rev. Wm. McKinney; here the traveler may be said to commence his journey across the Plains; The School or Mission being the last Settlement till we reach Fort Laramie a distance of 522 miles."[120] Edmundson knew the exact mileage that lay before him because he had "procured a Mormon guide Book at Kanesville in which places and distances are laid down with great accuracy."[121]

Lucena Parsons encountered Native Americans on a person to person basis shortly after ferrying the Missouri on June 14. "I had the pleasure of giving the chief of the Otoe tribe a loaf of bread, for which he was very thankful. He is a very fine looking man. He is called by his people the Buffalo chief." The next day, "There was an Indian chief visiting my tent to day. I gave him some dinner & he gave me a knife. This is rare for them to give anything away."[122]

Indians near the ferry crossings and the missions had been reduced to a dependent status and sadly reflected the condition resulting from close contact with the whites and their government. As Edmundson recalled, "A few Indians camped with us having followed us al the afternoon for the purpose of Begging."[123] Booth described them similarly saying, "Saw several Indians, some of the Pawnee tribe and some of the other tribes. They have collected along the road to beg and steal from the emigrants."[124]

The first major obstacle for those travelling north of the Platte lay at the Elkhorn River, a tributary about twenty miles west of the Missouri River crossing. Booth described it as a "very crooked stream, 25 to 30 yards wide." He reported that they, "pulled the wagons into the boat but swam the cattle," before continuing on to their campground.[125] William Edmundson crossed at the same ferry a week after Booth crossed but he described the Elkhorn as being 150 yards wide.[126] There are a couple of possible explanations for the drastic variation in the width of the river. The stream might have been swollen from rains when Edmundson crossed, making the river appear much wider, or one of the two diarists had a bad eye for judging distance.

Four days after crossing the Elkhorn, the Loup Fork or River, the next tributary of the Platte, flowing in from the northwest had to be dealt with. Booth arrived at it on May 28, 1850, and wrote in his diary, "Crossed the Loup Fork of the Platte. Ferried the wagons about half across and then pulled them with cattle. The stream is 20 to 30 yds wide. Encamped on its bank. See Indians almost every day, but none today."[127] The implication of ferrying the wagons only part of the way across leaves some question about the ferry operation. However, when Edmundson arrived there on June 6, 1850, he may have explained part of the problem. "Started at 8 o'clock and went 11 miles to the Ferry on the Loup Fork. The Ferrymen were gone and the Boat sunk. We attempted to raise it but found it so much damaged as to be unfit for use. We then took the road up the Loup Fork to the Ford which is 48 miles from the Ferry."[128] Three days later they arrived at the ford and as Edmundson described it, "we forded by laying poles across the tops of our wagon Beds and pilling the loads on the top then taking the wagons across by hand the river is here about 300 yards wide about three feet deep very rapid and full of quick sand. We commenced crossing about 11 o'clock A.M. and finished crossing about sundown camping on the western bank of the river."[129]

Though fording or ferrying tributaries of the Platte hindered travel a bit on the north bank of the Platte, those, like Lucena Parsons, who had swung to the more heavily traveled trail on the south bank were dealing with much more than keeping their feet dry. "This morning we had a powerful rain," wrote Parsons on June 19, 1850. "It commenced to rain just as we all had breakfast ready. We were obliged to lay over till near noon. This afternoon we past the grave of a man that died the 15th of the dreaded cholera. His name is Warren." For the next three days, Parsons' entries briefly chronicle distances and begin with a pleasant observation, but ultimately dissolve quickly into a chronicle of death. "June 20. Traveled over a beautiful country. Past 6 graves all made within 5 days & all died of the cholera. We met some waggons on the back trace. They had lost some of their friends with the cholera. This afternoon past 2 more graves, they seem to be of the same company as the 6 who died. Went 18 miles today. Very warm. June 21. We have been obliged to stop this morning to bury 2 of our company, the first to die with cholera. One man by the name of Brown & a small child. We have several more sick in the company. We have made 15 miles to day & have been in sight of the Platte River. We encamped to night on the banks of Salt creek. Our company came up with another child dead. They buried it at twilight on the bank of the stream. Very hot. June 22. This morning we have buried 3 more children who had the cholera, they all belonged to one family. We went about one mile then crosst [sic] Salt Creek. Traveled very late. The worst time we have had since we left the Missouri. Several sick. Damp and everything wet with very little fire in camp."[130]

Cholera is a disease caused by enterotoxin produced by gram-negative bacillus, *Vibrio comma* (*Cholera*), when present in the small intestines. Outbreaks of Asian Cholera had hit American cities throughout the antebellum period, so it presented as neither a medical unknown nor totally unexpected epidemic. It had been reported in St. Louis and other major staging areas for the gold seekers and traveled up to the jumping-off points on the river steamers. On the trails the disease was transmitted through food and water shared by families and in fecal matter contamination caused by poor hygiene, the general lack of bathing, hand washing, and disposal of human waste common to the mode of transport. It presented suddenly, with severe gastrointestinal symptoms, acute watery diarrhea, heavy vomiting, and rapid dehydration that quickly put victims flat on their back and eventually into systemic shock. The primary treatment is to administer salt and replace water quickly to maintain proper blood chemistry. Today that can be done with a common sodium chloride intravenous solution. Of course they didn't have that medical technology then and very few understood the importance of fluid replacement. Remedies along the trail consisted of medicines like peppermint syrup to settle the churning, knotted stomach, fluids by mouth, what they could keep down, cooling to reduce fever, and rest, which meant the train often had to lay over. After onset it could kill a perfectly healthy young man in two to three days and a small child in less than twenty-four hours. Some died in as little as ten hours after onset. It devastated some families and trains, and left many in a fearful state, waiting, wondering, if it would take them or their companions away. Some trains broke up out of fear, rightfully so, that close proximity to those who came down with the cholera could doom even the healthiest.

Lucena Parsons' diary continued blending a tale of misery with insightful, hopeful glimpses of the prairie. "June 23… Last night visited a very sick boy, son of the first man that died. This morning started early. Past some beautiful country. All it wants to make it delightful is a little of the arts of civilization. Rained nearly all day. The boy that was sick died about noon to day on the way coming. These are hard times for us but harder for the sick. Nothing for their relief at all it seems. Still it rains. Very hot. June 24. Last evening there was 3 more died out of the same family. One was a young lady & there was another child. The 3 are buried together 2 Spoffords & one Brown. Staid here all day, did up there washing. Had a meeting in the afternoon to consider whether it is best to travel in such large company or not. We are to remain, as we are a short time longer & then split if the sickness still continues. Past 5 graves to day of people who had died in another company. June 25 ... detained some 2 hours this morning by the first 50 of our company. The road is very muddy as it rains every day. This morning the mother of the 5 children that have died was taken sick & died at evening."[131]

We know from the accounts of other diarists jumping off from Independence and St. Joseph, that cholera struck down many going to see the elephant in 1849 as well as 1850. But as a widespread epidemic sweeping the plains, universally hitting everyone, it did not. Diarists moving along the north bank of the Platte reported very little sickness resembling cholera. Those who left early, at the beginning of May, seem to have out paced it. Smaller trains that either lost contact with, or intentionally stayed at some distance from the larger trains, usually because of the shortage of grass, not the fear of the disease, seem to have escaped it too. When it did strike a large train, with a few hundred people corralled at night, sharing fire, food, and water supply, like Lucena Parsons,' cholera left a trail of misery.

Still they persevered and it rained. "We had a fine place to camp, it pleases so well I call it Pleasant point in memory of my native home. We made 8 miles today through rain & mud. We had a dreadful time. It rained hard & some went to bed without their supper," Parsons wrote on June 25, 1850. She continued, "June 26 ... past 6 graves & it seems very melancholy to pass so many new graves. The sick in our company are getting better. Met 5 government waggons, they are from Fort Carny & are after lumber. We have not seen an Indian since the first night after we started from the river. Roads very crooked. Camped on the prairie without wood or water. June 27 ... met 2 teams from Salt Lake. They said they met the first emigrants at the mountain pass. June 28 ... staid here all day for the purpose of having a general wash as wood & water are plenty here. We have some very sick in camp to day & one woman, Mrs. Crandall, was immersed twice to day. It seemed to do her good."[132]

Dipping a woman in a stream of cool water to break a fever? A sense of desperation must have gripped those trains in which the disease raged. Doctors did accompany some of the trains and even if one was not present, advice could be sought from another train either in front or behind. Without a trained medical confirmation, one can only suppose how many other maladies, that took life, were diagnosed as cholera, but in reality could have been something else. Food poisoning, forms of dysentery, other than cholera, respiratory infections like pneumonia, even tick bites or a ruptured appendix might have presented, taken a life, and been labeled as the dread cholera.

"We had the hardest thunder storm last night I have witnessed in some years," began Parsons' entry on June 29, 1850. "A little before we stopt [*sic*] at noon there was a woman by the name of Beal died. She was buried on the banks of the Clearwater, a fine stream about 10 miles from where we came on the bottoms. They immersed 3 in this stream for the cholera. Met the Salt Lake mail, they said they met 8000 teams when they got to Fort Laramee. Since that they have not kept count. June 30 ... some hard slews. Platte River, the bottoms are from 8 to 10 miles wide. The river is about ½ mile wide here & runs rapid, the water very rily. I find plenty of wild flowers here, roses in abundance. Mrs. Crandalls daughter died today. She is of the family who have buried so many. She was buried this evening beside 4 others on the bank of the river. They were some who had died of another company."[133]

On July 1, Parsons' train passed the Pawnee town that Bruff and Davis described earlier. Consumed with the death around her, she had not mentioned, or likely seen any Indians since initially crossing the Missouri, a fortnight before. "Traveled some 7 miles & came to an Indian town. It contains some 200 wigwams. They are made under ground, laid up with sticks & covered with earth. Some of them are large & show ingenuity. The inmates have all deserted them & gone on a hunt. There are immense beds of sun flowers in this region. Past 8 graves to day."[134]

Fort Kearney

By the time Fort Kearney was reached all the trails from the various jumping-off points had fused into one, except for those travelling the north bank of the Platte. After the initial hardships and variety of experiences in getting to that point, the merging of trains probably gave a greater sense of strength, if only in the sheer number of visible wagons. The fort presented the appearance of some civilization and help if needed, and a place to contemplate and even turn back if the desire was there. All the emigrants viewed the fort with a sense of gladness and wrote descriptions of it, some in detail. J. A. Pritchard reached the outpost on May 18, 1849, fairly early in the travel season. "At noon we reached Fort Kerney [one of a variety of spellings]. Passed through the place and stopped to graze & rest a couple of hours — Here we found a military post established — and some 80 or 90 dragoons posted here. Also a kind of Post office establishment which gave us an opportunity of sending back letters. The fort is about 12 miles above the head of Grand Island, and the houses are built of adobe or sun dried brick."[135]

Franklin Starr saw it at about the same time, writing on May 17, 1849, "Passed Fort Childs [the first name for the Kearney outpost] which is just established." He concluded, "There is no proper fort built yet but they have a circular saw running with which they are sawing lumber."[136]

"We arrived a what is called Fort Kearny," wrote Israel Hale a week later on May 24, 1849. "It consists of a number of rudely constructed huts (it will not offend our great men to give them that name) built of sods or turfs from the prairie, laid up after the manner of laying bricks; the roofs are covered with the same kind of material. Some of them have glass windows and very decent looking doors, the principal thing that denotes civilization. They have two fields fenced in with the same kind of material. They have also had a store, blacksmith shop and wagon shop. These compose the fort, which is situated near the banks of the Platte, opposite Grand Island. We left several persons at the fort trying to sell a part of their loading. Some sold their wagons for one-quarter what they cost and put their loading in another wagon and joined teams. The wagons are, generally speaking, entirely too heavy for so long a trip. The Platte at this place is as wide as the Mississippi at St. Louis and as muddy as the Missouri, and within one or two feet of the top of its banks."[137]

Amos Josselyn made it to the fort by May 23, 1849, but he was more concerned with repairs that could possibly be obtained there. "Passed Fort Kearny [also referred to by early emigrants as Fort Childs], weather cold and windy, roads level but very tough. In driving out of the correle [sic] one team started too soon and ran against the wagon ahead of it and pulled the spindle off of the axletree. We then turned our teams out again and sent a man back to Fort Kearny for an axletree, and on his way to the Fort he found one in the road that had either been lost or thrown away. As soon as he had returned, we went to work and got it in by 3 o'clock.[138]

Josselyn, like many of the emigrants, did take the opportunity in passing Fort Kearney to post a letter, dated May 22, 1849, to his wife. There were few places along the trail to send a letter back home with any assurance that it might actually reach its destination. Fort Kearney was one of those few. He wrote, giving his wife assurance and relaying news that he had himself just received from acquaintances moving along the trail. "Lippett passed us, (he travels with pack mules) and told us McCadden was dead and that he had died with the Cholera, and that there had been a great many deaths since we left. (this was at Rice's 9 miles from Independence) McCadden's company layed for 12 to14 days and wanted us today there and wait for him but we were too anxious to be moving to lay in one place so long, and it is a fine thing that we did move for some of us might have been sick if we had stayed as there was a great many encamped there, & Lippitt tells us that there was about 40 deaths at that place. But you must not be uneasy when you hear of so many dying at Independence & near there for we are some distance from there & I have heard of no sickness on the road and we are all in first rate health and I think there is not much danger of getting sick for we have plenty of exercise in the pure air of these high planes. We have seen no Indians since we left the Kansas River. The soldiers here [200] are under the command of Major Rough [Ruff]. We met four wagons today loaded with Furs from Fort Laramie and they say that the Roads are just as good all the way as they are along here."[139]

Niles Searls saw the fort two weeks after Hale on June 8, 1849. "Fort Kearney was selected as a location for the troops of the United States about one year since. It stands upon a slight eminence in the bottom nearly one mile from the river and is at present occupied by two hundred soldiers. The buildings with a single exception, are temporary structures, the walls composed of sods three feet square, roofed over with brush and earth. Others are either in course of erection or about to be so, of wood and brick. Several enclosures have been made this spring and sowed with grain. There are no settlers here except a family of Mormons who keep a boarding house and with whom a large number of our men made an excellent supper of bread, milk, fresh butter, doughnuts and all the little et ceteras so acceptable to those precluded of them for nearly a month."[140] Searls' party loitered an extra day around the fort, not uncommon for many that had been on the trail that long and needed a break. "At the fort we saw a Pawnee squaw and boy who had been taken by the troops from the Sioux into whose hands they fell in a late battle and by whom they were about to be burnt when rescued. After partaking of a hearty breakfast at the Mormon house, we again took leave of civilized society. Near the fort I saw a man planting corn in the open plain."[141] The march of civilization continued.

The inscrutable Bruff arrived at Kearney on June 17, 1849, and made his presence known to those in charge. "I visited the Fort after breakfast and was most kindly received by Colonel Bonneville, Lieuts. Boots & Davis, &c. This place is as yet merely the site of an intended fort; it has some adobe embankments, quarters—&c. of adobe & frame, and a number of tents & sheds. Is on the bank of the Platte, where Grand Island makes a narrow branch of the river between it and the shore. They had, somehow, at the Fort got a rumor of my death, by Cholera, and knew no better till my card was handed the commandant by the 2 men I sent ahead." For many companies, Kearney provided a convenient site to reorganize things. "Held a meeting of the Company, and equalized the private baggage—disgarding [discarding] a great deal of superfluous weight. Sold a wagon to the Sutler for $30—and the Ambulance to the Officers for $50. A perfectly useless article, except to encourage lazy men to ride—Forge, Anvil, bellows, some lead & iron, we sold to a Mormon family here for $32.[142]

Those passing Fort Kearney a year later in 1850 did not notice a lot of improvements or were not impressed enough with the facilities to even take time to describe it. Samuel Jamison arrived early in the 1850 travel season, writing on May 11, "passed fort Kearny. Left several letters. Wood very scarce. Some of the men had to use Buffalo chips to cook their diner. Very cold, ice on the buckits [sic] this morning as thick as glass."[143]

"During the day we passed New Fort Kearney, a small United States military station near the bank of the river, the walls of which were constructed largely of sods cut out in large blocks, and laid up as adobes are laid in California," wrote Margaret Frink on May 21, 1850. "This is the first human habitation we have seen since crossing the Missouri, two hundred miles distance. From that point we have been steadily climbing up hill, the altitude here being 2,150 feet, 1,200 feet higher than Bullard's Ferry."[144]

Sarah Davis reached the fort on June 10, 1850, and wrote, "I saw one sand lizard that day we passed at fort carney three hundred and thirty five miles and it seemed good to see a house again. The next day she reflected on some of the bad habits she observed near the military outpost. "We left fort carney and traveled on we traveled on the bottom of the river at fort carney thare was some men in encampment that sold liquor to the soldiers and they were fiend[fined] and to[two] of them taken to the forte and confined and the rest of their liquor turned out of the casque."[145]

Lucena Parsons' party continued to push on toward Fort Kearney during the first week of July, 1850. Her diary entries continued to be short and somewhat morbid. "July 2... Reached the foot of Grand Island at noon. Here we stopt & buried a girl, daughter of Capt. Coon. She died before reaching this point. July 3... Past 6 graves, they most all died between 15 & 28 of June. There seems to be some division in our company. Some of them are so slow & some go too fast. Some sick. July 4 ... we overtook our company & found the Captains ox was gone. We had to stop again & wate [sic] for them to go back & look for it. We were in hearing of cannon at old Fort Carny. July 5... This afternoon saw 2 waggons on the return. They had been as far as Fort Larimee & were sick & their company went on. July 6... Past 9 graves 5 of them were children. July 7... Traveled 7 miles & reached Fort Carny at 11. It is a pleasant place on the river. They have 450 soldiers there now, cultivate some land & have fine gardens. There are some 8 houses built of wood, they get their timber from as far as the Missouri River. Overtook 25 government waggons bound for Larimee loaded with provisions. They have 125 yoke of oxen & carry 60 hundred pounds to waggon. Past 5 graves, one of them an Indian grave. He was buried in a sitting posture. The tribe here is the Pawnees."[146]

58   Part I • From the Banks of the Missouri to Fort Laramie

Fort Kearney to the Platte Fork

For the vast majority of those headed west Fort Kearney had been a brief but welcome respite after, for some, a month on the trail. The next great milestone on the trek to see the elephant lay 96–100 miles from Kearney, the forks of the Platte River. With decent weather that took about five days. The road between Kearney and where the Platte forks, where northern and southern channels merged into the single great river, lay relatively flat and sandy. As Niles Searls expressed on June 10, 1849. "The bottom is almost entirely level with scarcely a single ravin[e] or slough to obstruct the travelers' progress."[147] Emigrants in general wrote of the monotony of the road and scenery and complained about the shortages of grass and fuel caused by too many emigrants occupying the same space at the same time. J. A. Pritchard said it succinctly when he wrote, "We are passing vast numbers of emigrant wagons now every day."[148] Hale continued, "this evening we have somehow got into a perfect nest of emigrants. If I was to guess I should say there was one thousand head of cattle within a mile of camp."[149]

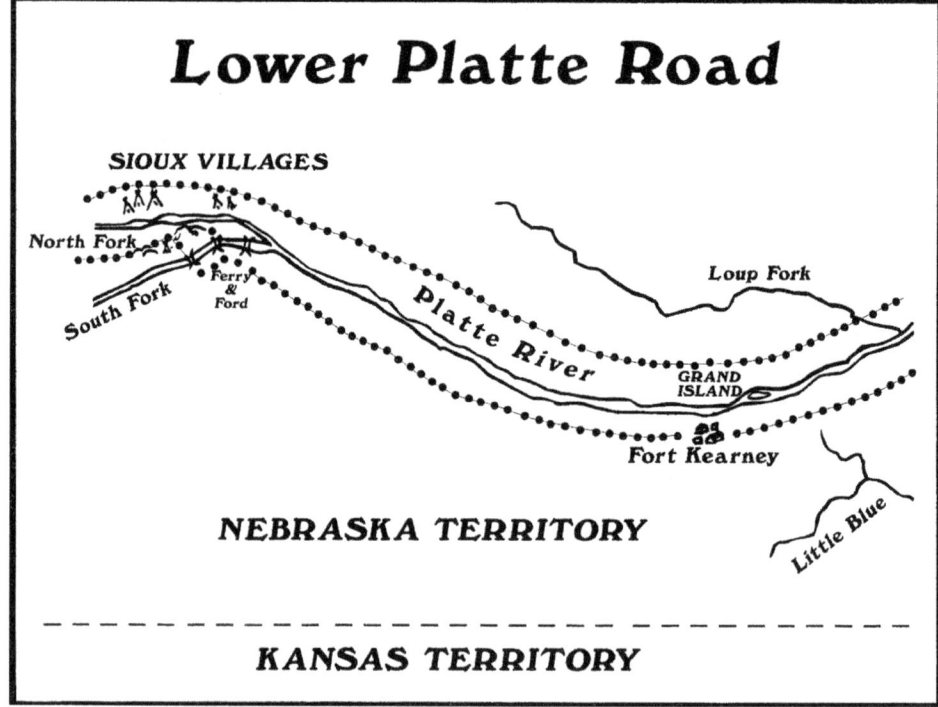

Lower Platte Road — roads from Fort Kearney to Ash Hollow on the North Platte.

Everyone complained about the weather. For most crossing the plains in the month of June, in either 1849 or 1850, they encountered the fast moving thunderstorms typical of south central Nebraska that time of year. But, as could be expected, there were curiosities that caught the emigrant's eye, and unfortunately for many, sickness and death in a variety of forms continued to follow the trains.

Not far from Kearney, Pritchard wrote on May 21, 1849, "The grass was becoming short and indifferent. Had to depend tonight for fuel upon some willow brush which was procured from an island. Here we met several Mountain trappers with their wagons heavily ladened with bails of furs and Buffalo skins. This presented a good opportunity of sending back letters to the states which we all gladly embraced. Their price for carrying the letters was only 25 cents which to us was a small consideration."[150]

One day after he left Fort Kearney heading toward the forks of the Platte, Israel Hale had plenty to complain about. He began his May 25, 1849, diary entry, "Last night the thunder roared, the lightening flashed an almost constant flare, the rain fell in torrents and the wind blew so hard that a man could not walk without staggering." Typical of plains thunderstorms, it rose late in the afternoon. "This storm commenced before sundown and continued until late in the night. The result was the rain blew into our wagons, the ground was soon over shoe in water and nearly every tent was blown down. Every man of our number wished for a more comfortable lodging place, if they did not wish themselves at home. This morning the wind continued to blow and the thermometer stood at thirty-six degrees in the wagon and out of the wind, within four degrees of freezing cold. Could a citizen of Manchester have seen our company this morning after we had started and had not discovered the teams, we should undoubtedly have been taken for Creoles of the country. For almost every man was wrapped in a blanket whether he had on an overcoat or not."[151]

Amos Josselyn wrote of the same storm as Hale, making a diary entry on that same date, May 25, 1849. "It rained and stormed all night verry hard, the hardest I ever saw. It sounded like one continued roar of thunder and verry cold. Some of the guards say that there was hail, but I supposed they were mistaken, but the raindrops came with such violence that they were taken for hail. So cold that we suffered with the cold though we had our overcoats on and walking, the wind blew so hard that it was hard work to walk against it and keep up with the wagons. The next day the weather clear and pleasant."[152]

Those familiar with weather patterns on the Great Plains know that conditions can change rapidly, even hourly. Following the horrendous downpours of the thunderstorms, the road could temporarily become a quagmire, then a day later, be dry and dusty. The heavy, wet road could be frustrating to travel on and fatiguing on both men and animals, as Israel Hale discussed in his May 27, 1849 entry. "Sunday. Contrary to my wishes we left our camp at the usual time once more. It has the appearance of clear weather. It has also turned warm, although we had a hard frost this morning. Having lost several pieces of days by rain and bad weather as well as bad roads is the cause of our traveling today and the fear of a rise in the South Fork may be called another cause. Nevertheless, our men and stock are both much fatigued. Some of our oxen are poor and ready to give out, and it would surely have been good policy to have lain by for the day. I discovered this afternoon the ground where there was no grass had the appearance of having been covered with flour. It looked as the ground would after a flour bag had been shaken. I took a little lump and tasted it and found it was salty. This country very much resembles the salt marshes on the Atlantic Coast."[153]

Amos Josselyn described another serious problem caused by the violent thunderstorms. "Last night we had a verry severe storm of wind, rain and hail. More severe than any we have yet had and at this time it is raining and blowing hard. Last night our cattle got off and strayed away. Several of the men are starting out in search of them. About a dozen of the cattle have been found, two of ours and 9 or 10 more. It is still storming and the men have concluded not to search for the cattle until the storm is over."[154]

Rain pounded the plains through late May in 1849. "Last night we had another dreary night," wrote Israel Hale. "It was my turn to stand guard from eight to half past eleven o'clock. Just as I had got into the wagon a storm came up. The wind blew very hard and the rain fell fast, and for a long time every tent in the train was prostrate with the earth. Some went into their wagons, some under them and others attempted to take shelter under their tent cloths and blankets. In the morning the scene was amusing. Almost every one was giving a history of his troubles on the previous night. When the tents fell, they were generally abandoned together with their contents. And in the morning hats were either filled with water or were laying in the water."[155]

The curiosity of the Platte river valley being without timber forced emigrants to improvise. Hale described the shortage of fuel. "We drove about ten miles and stopped near the river for the balance of the day, having good grass, plenty of water and wood by packing it from the island. It appears that most of these sloughs can be forded with a horse which appears the only chance for the emigrants to get fuel in the absence of chips, (dried buffalo dung) which, are becoming scarce. It is said that the number of wagons that have passed before us exceeds nineteen hundred. This accounts for the scarcity of chips."[156] It seems from the reports that an unseasonable cold front had passed over the plains in late May, 1849. On May 26, Israel Hale commented on the desperate search for fuel. "Good grass but no wood. We made our fire of almost everything: some chips, some brush, some pieces of ox yokes, boxes etc.,"[157] J. A. Pritchard, moving with his party along the Platte, wrote in his diary on May 26, "we passed a broken down wagon which the boys gathered up for cooking purposes."[158]

Fort Kearney to the Platte Fork

The Platte valley offered eastern emigrants an opportunity to hunt game never before seen by them. Large herds of buffalo and antelope still roamed the plains, and though the vast emigrant trains generally frightened then away, brief encounters were recorded. "This afternoon a large number of antelope were to be seen. A number of our party gave chase to them but to no effect. I never saw an animal that can run with the same speed, grace, ease and elegance of these Antelope When hotly pursued on our best horses they fled almost with the fleetness of the wind," wrote J. A. Pritchard of his party's first attempt at taking one on May 26, 1849.[159] Hale may have seen the same herd, writing the next day on May 27. "I saw a drove of antelope today and saw two men on horseback take a run after them. You may be sure the antelope won the race."[160]

Large numbers of wolves also roamed the plains and Pritchard complained of them. "Our mules were kept in a constant state of alarm by the Woolfs [sic] that were prowling around our camp that night. Here I will just remark that a woolf will frighten mules equally as bad as an Indian who appears in their midst — and discovers to them a Buffalo rug with the wrong side out — And the only way to keep them from being stampeded is to be in their midst and talking to them all the time."[161] "I saw today a gray or white wolf lying near the road," wrote Israel Hale. "It was as large as a common sized dog. Whether it was an old one or not, I am not able to say."[162]

After struggling to calm his mules during the evening howling and prowling, Pritchard had an opportunity to see the cause of his and many emigrants' consternation up close. On May 25, 1849, he wrote, "I saw today a village of Woolfs. These prairie or Mountain woolfs are very large — larger than our largest dogs in the States— They are of a grayish yellow — with sharp peaked ears big heads and long drooping tails— I found one of their dens and came very near catching some of the Puppys— that lay on the outside sunning them-selves— I saw some 40 or 50 old ones setting around. I dismounted and looked into the holes. It was a thoughtless thing in me to be down on the ground alone amongst perhaps four of the largest size of these ferocious animals of the Plains— And if I had caught one of their young and it had raised a cry for help I would have perhaps been devoured instantly — All wild animals — however cowardly they may be on ordinary occasions, will fight most furiously for their young."[163]

On a smaller scale, the prairie dog, whose kingdom began not far west of Fort Kearney and extended for some distance on both sides of the Platte, enchanted nearly everyone. "This evening we came into the prairie dog country. I saw one today and there is one of their towns in sight of our camp. I saw one, it is true, but it was so much injured by shooting and not full grown that I cannot give an accurate description of it," wrote Israel Hale.[164] It is worth noting here that though the prairie dogs presented themselves as harmless, good-natured rodents, many of the young men amused themselves along the trail by taking pot shots at the animals, as obviously referenced by Hale. "We passed through a village of Prairie Dogs this afternoon," chronicled Niles Searls on his first encounter with them. "The first intimation which we had of our proximity to these pigmy barkers was the observing of a small animal in the trail, bearing a close resemblance to the rat, though considerably larger in size than that animal."[165]

J. A. Pritchard gave a marvelously detailed description of a dog town in his diary, writing, "Rode through a number of dog towns— Their towns cover an area of several acres & some times they are one fourth of mile in diameter. They burrow in the ground — dig out large holes and throw up oval shaped mounds of from 4 to 6 feet in diameter and from 1 to 2 feet high. It is extremely dangerous to ride through those towns on horse back at full step. They are the size of the largest, kind of ground hogs in our country. They are rather shy and cunning in their appearance."[166]

Caleb Booth, travelling the trail on the north bank of the Platte, also encountered prairie dogs. "Passed through the City of Dogs today. They resembled a woodchuck in shape and color. Are about the size of a cat."[167] Also on the north side, William Edmundson observed the furry little community writing on June 12, 1850, "This day we passed through several Towns of Prairie-Dogs. They bear some resemblance to the Gopher are of a yellowish gray color and are about the size of a small rabbit. They live on the Prairie grass." The next day he added, "a great many Dog-Towns deserted most probably on account of the inhabitants having consumed all the grass in their vicinity which compelled them to seek a new location."[168]

Bruff, whose company moved along the Platte a month behind emigrants Hale, Pritchard, and Josselyn, simply stated that both wolves and prairie dogs were numerous. But for game on a much larger scale, a chance to get a substantial supply of fresh meat, the emigrant could challenge the buffalo. And challenge is exactly what Bruff wrote of when he described the danger of taking on the leviathan of the Great Plains. "The casualties of buffalo hunting are very common," he wrote on June 26, 1849. "Men charg'd by wounded bulls, unhorsed & many badly hurt — the horses generally running off with the band of buffaloes, for the Indians to pick up hereafter. Lots of rifles and pistols lost, as well as horses: and many poor fellow, after a hard day's hunt, on an empty stomach, unhorsed some distance from camp, has a long & tiresome walk, after night, to his own, or the nearest camp he can make. And some have been lost for days at the imminent risk of their lives."[169] Hale drew a similar conclusion that many saw buffalo but few actually got to eat any. "We have passed today a great many buffalo heads or skulls, as well as other buffalo bones which shows that somebody has plenty of fresh meat, but it has not been our good fortune to get any as yet."[170]

Often, the further back along the trail the emigrants found themselves, either from a late start, slow pace of travel, or just normal delays, the more the game had been dispersed by the crowd in front of them. Sallie Hester, about a week behind Pritchard and Hale, reported, "Game is scarce; a few antelope in sight. Roads bad."[171] However, the dispersed animals then might re-cross the main trail along the Platte giving even later emigrants a chance to hunt.

Not only did an emigrant's position along the trail at a given time, or within a specific company or group of trains, dictate whether or not he might see game, but also impacted whether or not he had exposure to rampaging illnesses. Those diarists that had passed through Fort Kearney by mid May, 1849, mention nothing of cholera. But it seems that those reaching Kearney at the end of May and through June saw plenty of it.

Israel Hale's party must have been in front of the cholera outbreaks, but he complained, "The cold weather for some days past has given a great number of our emigrants bad colds, attended with coughs. It has that effect on myself and at night when in the corral, I can hear a dozen persons coughing at a time. With the exception of colds our company is in good health."[172] In contrast, writing a week later from about the same place, "Our tent is now pitched on the beautiful Platte River, 315 miles form St. Joe. The cholera is raging," lamented Sallie Hester on June 3, 1849. "A great many deaths; graves everywhere." Then she added, "We as a company are all in good health."[173]

J. Goldsborough Bruff passed along the south bank of the Platte beyond Kearney in late June, 1849. For several days he chronicled his progress, personal encounters and the death that had swept many from the trail in front of him. He wrote the specifics on every crude grave marker he passed. "Graves close to camp, C. H. Cornwell of Waukeshow, Wis: Died June 10 1849, Aged 26 Years. and J. A. Parks, Died June 4, 1849, Aged 34 Years, from Pontotoc, Miss. A Mississippi and Missouri Ox-train co. passed us. I dined with Capt. McNulty commanding a New York Company called the Colony Guards. Here I was treated to superior strong coffee. A New Orleans ox train company close by. Mosquitoes numerous and annoying. More grave markers: Lemuel Lee of Vandalian, Ill. Died June 3, 1849, at 4 P.M. Aged 64 Years: Died of prostration consequent upon Cholera after an illness of 2 weeks. Captain Pleasant Gray, of Juntsville, Walker Co. Texas: Died June 9, 1849, of Cholera, After an illness of 3 days, Aged 43 years."[174]

With bad weather, an often wet road, shortages of fuel and grass, and often having to go three or even four miles off the main trail to escape overcrowded campgrounds, it is not surprising that people grew sullen, impatient and downright angry. "A considerable uneasiness and discontent has prevailed among our passengers for several days, owing in a great measure to our slow progress," wrote Niles Searls on June 13, 1849, as they pushed along the Platte between Fort Kearney and the forks. "All sorts of abuse has been awarded to Captain Turner, some blaming him for not going faster, others for travelling at all during the continuance of the present bad state of the roads. Our baggage train has been heavily laden and the unprecedented rainy weather has rendered our progress slow and toilsome. Captain Turner resolved to lighten up by destroying everything not essential to our comfort. Liquors to a large amount were turned out, and extra articles of various kind broken up, after which a meeting was called in the Corral at which Captain Turner explained his views and intentions, at the same time, requesting each mess to carry their bedding in their carriage till our arrival at Fort Laramie, at which point it is probable we may pack through, leaving the baggage to come on at leisure. Captain Turner's request was cheerfully acceded to."[175]

Sometimes disputes, real or imaged, as tempers and patience grew short, turned to real anger, that could not be talked through in a meeting. Young and brash gold seekers sought immediate satisfaction with their fists and whatever else they could lay hands on, as J. A. Pritchard recounted on May 23, 1849, after two men in his company got into a fight. "Some unpleasant words passed where upon Hodges struck Hamline & knocked him down — and was beating him severely — when the cry of fight was given — I was the first who got there — and pulled Hodges off of Hamline — when knives and pistols were drawn — I caught Hamline — just in the act of stabbing Hodges with a large Bouy [Bowie] — Knife — and in the effort to arrest the stroke I received a slight cut myself about one and a half inches long across my right arm — Other men interfered by this time, and the combatants were finely separated — Hamline received a very bad cut on his upper lip done when Hodges first struck him — Hodges withdrew from the mess next morning & we left him on the road side with his mule & goods & chattels — and what became of him I know not."[176]

But a spirit of cooperation also existed among many of the emigrants as another passage from Pritchard's diary indicates. "McNeely found two stray cattle and tied them to the back of his wagon. The gentlemen owning them came up to claim them and offered $5 for their return. McNeely wanted $10. 5 disinterested men decided $5 was enough. It is a well known fact that every Emigrants stock is liable to go a stray — as they have no other pasturage than the wide, and unbounded domain, which is equally free and accessible to all. And the common practice amongst the Emigrants is to catch for and assist each other to protect their stock without the hope of fee or reward."[177]

Those passing the trail between Kearney and the Platte forks in 1850 found much that had been seen by those a year ahead of them, but in some cases it was worse. In a letter to his mother, in 1850, John Nevin King gave a marvelous description of the trek along the Platte, comparing it to the land he had seen while serving in the army during the Mexican War. "After passing fort Kearney we have been traveling along the Platte River, the country resembling that along the Rio Grande in Mexico. The Platte is very much like the Rio Grande. Tis somewhat wider, the current not quite so strong as the

Rio Grande, but the color and taste are the same. The Platte is not quite so crooked either."[178]

Samuel Jamison's train had gone by Kearney early in May, 1850. Like so many other companies, it went through one of the frequent reorganizations. On May 13, 1850, he recorded, "Tangaman's train left us this morning. We was sorry for it but it could not be helped. We had to aim to fast to keep up. We made a division in our company to day. Kesler, Simpson and Howe left by taking out their Shares. We put nine shares into one wagon. Disturbed in the night by something supposed to be a wolf." Over the next couple of days, Jamison summarized in his economy of words a typical emigrant routine along the Platte. "Seen Tangaman's old mule lying dead [in reference to his former traveling companion], passed one grave, shot a duck, used small willow brush for fire. Had to dig a hole in a Slu for water. Howe and Armstong went buffalo hunting, passed one grave and three wagons. Mules in one of them Scarde [sic] run around and broke a wagon tung [tongue]. Had to go 2 miles for water and wood."[179]

Margaret Frink's party passed Kearney on May 21, 1850, and the next day she wrote of a new adventure. "After we started this morning, there was great excitement over a buffalo chase, opposite the head of Grand Island in Platte River. Some of our men partook of the excitement. As far as we could see, every one that was on horseback went flying in the direction of the buffalo. Every man took up the hunt. I really could not blame the men very much, though the chase was bad for the horses. The animation and excitement of the moment beat anything I ever saw, and I would not, for a good deal, have missed the sight of that great chase over the grand plain. Some one brought us a piece of buffalo steak, so glad we were not without a share of the prize. Fire-wood is scarce, there being none except along the river bank. Every stray piece we find we pick up and carry with us."[180] Unfortunately the excitement and the prospect of fresh meat did not last too long. In her next entry, dated May 23, 1850, she lamented, "to our disappointment, we have seen only the small herd that came in sight yesterday. There are hundreds of thousands of them on these plains; but the emigration has frightened them to the right and to the left, away from the road, so that they are seldom seen. We often pass the bones and skulls in great numbers, where they have been killed by the Indians."[181]

Jamison recounted his own buffalo hunting experience and the thrill of a long chase on May 17, 1850. "Came on 6 buffalo. Howe and myself took after them on horseback. Run them about 3 miles and Howe shot one of them once with a rifle and four times with a revolver. It then lay down and died. We then went to and cut off the rounds of the hind quarters and took them back to the wagon."[182]

The valley of the Platte, often described as being pretty flat, hardly ever got commended for being straight. The trail markers often attempted to straighten the route by cutting across bends, passing some distance from the main channel. When the trail did this, the emigrants often had problems getting water. "The road often leaves the river to cross a large bend, and does not reach it again at camping time," recalled Margaret Frink. "In such cases, the only resource for water is by digging wells a few feet deep. But the well water is usually muddy and warm. The soil is a kind of sandy loam, through which the river water makes its way, under the entire bottom."[183] Still, another emigrant, John Birney Hill, summed up the stretch along the Platte saying, "From 10 miles the other side of Ft. Kearney, to where we are now 100 miles west of the Ft. the road is the levelest & nicest that I have ever seen in any country, it is sandy."[184] Though the trail proved fairly easy going at that point on the trek, Margaret Frink thought the Platte "road is a little monotonous. The scenery does not change much. The river has a winding course, and contains many islands. Some are little more than sand bars, others are covered with low willows."[185]

Although out of sight of the river, the emigrants rarely left sight of their fellow gold seekers, crowded true, but also reassuring for some. "Today the line of white wagons reaches out to the front and to the rear farther than we can see. Among such an army, we have little fear of trouble from Indians," Frink concluded.[186] John Hill thought it an unusual day on the trail when he observed, "only about 150 wagons at one sight."[187] Lack of good camping sites, and grazing, proved the greatest problem for the emigrants, with so much crowding along the trail. Often, they traveled several miles off the main trail in the evenings to find comfortable surroundings away from their fellow gold seekers.

Besides finding the road along the Platte monotonous, Margaret Frink found the trek an endless string of sometimes grueling chores. Though many emigrants took note of each passing Sunday, the Sabbath, in their diaries, as a customary day of rest, few ever had the opportunity to observe it, no matter how spiritually inclined they might be. "This is the day of rest," wrote Frink, "but there is not much rest crossing the plains. If our camp is at a place where there is neither grass nor water, we are compelled to travel on until we find them. And in camp there is no end of necessary work. Wagons, harness, and clothing have to be mended, washing to be done, animals to be changed on the pasture and guarded, innumerable small things to be looked after. There is no time for reading, and there are neither newspapers nor letters to read. We have not hear from home since we left, nearly two months ago, and do not expect to until we arrive at Sutter's Fort, three months hence."[188]

Sarah Davis passed Kearney in mid June, 1850. By then the plains weather had heated up and all the discomforts of summer and the wave of cholera had caught up with them. She wrote, beginning June 12, "We are now 26 miles from the forte and encamped on the plum creek. The musketoes [sic] were so bad they had like to eat us up. June 13 ... we traveled for eighteen miles that day and camped on the plat river I saw twelve graves to day it seemed like a grave yard almost to me. We traveled about ten miles farther we past thirteen graves. June 14 ... we have past six graves to day. We past twelve more and one grave that they had not put the body in yet."[189] For some, the raging gold fever subsided quickly in the anguish, doubt, and hard times, after only the first month on the trail. Davis recounted the next day, "we past five or six wagons a goin back. They were home sick besides being sick for they were sick."[190]

Mica Littleton passed Kearney only a couple of days behind Davis and echoed many of the same concerns and fears, from a supply of fuel to the scourge of cholera. "Left the Fort this morning ½ past 6. No timber except on the Islands. They say it is some distance to where we can get wood again. The wood is hard to get here, have to ride on a horse across the Slough and pack it over green, cotton wood, the river is Shallow and quick Sand in the bed of the river as bad as Missouri River," Littleton wrote on June 18, 1850. He continued, "we had the first Serious accident Since we left Independence. A young man from Tennessee Mr. Carroll J. Haines who was putting his mule out to grass got him self tangled in the bridle and larriette [sic] and the mule being wild and ungovernable whirled with him and Kicked him on the leg and Broke it about 5 or 6 inches above the knee. 3 or 4 Doctors now fixing to Set his leg. Poor fellow, how he will have to suffer."[191]

There were doctors along with a number of trains, as several diarists make reference to either being in the company of a physician or knowing that one traveled in a nearby company. It could be supposed that they too were going to see El Dorado, and found plenty of medicine in need of practicing as they went along. William Frush recalled fetching a doctor on the night of June 1, 1850. "Camp 22 miles above Fort. John Gidin of Shelby Co. Mo. take with Colera. After dark I went for Dr. Brown at his camp. Took him to see him in night were he encamped and I was awake much during the night. Night rainy & stormy. I lay outside tent all night in rain. Next morning I breakfasted with Dr. Brown and took him to see patient again. Dr. charged $2."[192]

Like Sarah Davis had observed, Littleton noted that some people just gave out as both the number of miles and grave markers along the Platte increased. He recorded on June 19, 1850, "met three waggons returning to the States. Passed 4 fresh graves today." Littleton recorded the names he found on markers along the trail and on that same day he passed that of probably one of the oldest men going to see the elephant. "John Caplinger Died June 1st from Ceder City Mo. aged 74 years." The next day Littleton recorded meeting, "14 waggons returning to the States. Say they are returning for the want of grass. Have past the graves of 21 today. It appears here the cholera has been fatal enough to discourage the bravest heart."[193]

For some turning back came as a matter of necessity, not of choice. William Frush recalled seeing people put in hopeless situations, not knowing which way to go or who to turn to for help. About 75 miles west of Fort Kearney he described a pitiable scene. "3 or four died on the road in this days travel said of Colera. One, ½ mile from this camp left wife and 9 children helpless. They had not moved when I left."[194]

On June 21, 1850, Littleton took names from 23 grave markers, but the next day reported seeing only eight, but added, "I find that there are many very many that are buried off from the road from ¼ to a mile. Some with no head board so we cannot tell who they are." One grave caught his eye and left a chill in him. "I passed one today that appeared to be a woman poor creature. Her skirts and dress lay some 15 feet from her grave as though She had dropped them to go to be. Her Skirts both lay in Side of her dress. Her bed a few yards further and her Pillows and blankets all with some other clothing lay around like it had been only a few hours Since she was buried, a Sad spectacle. It caused deep emotions to thrill in my bosom to look on the Sad Sight but Sooner or later we all have to render up an account to our God." That same day he recorded a marker bearing, "Mary V. Simmons June 15th aged 2 years Franklin Co. Mo,"[195] proving all ages, very old and very young went to see the elephant.

Lucena Parsons' company traveled yet another month behind Davis, making the trek along the Platte in early to mid July, 1850. Death had not only preceded her train but, evident from the number of markers she counted, still, in other insidious forms, accompanied it. Her writing is most melancholy. "There seems to be a sameness in the make of the country," she began on July 8, 1850, just past Kearney. "Past 6 graves. Campted with Footes. They are sick. July 9... Our cattle still lame & we are not able to go far in a day. Camp on Plum creek [noted by Davis the month before.] They had buried a boy of Lovells. He fell from the waggon & broke his leg & died soon after. This is the second child that has broke a leg and died soon after. They [Foote's company] have buried 7 & have some more very sick. Past them and went on. Past 7 graves. July 10... Traveled 16 miles. Past 13 graves."

Over the next two days Parsons observed some of the bounty, good and bad, provided by nature on the plains, but always came back in her writing to counting graves and the lamentable events that took lives in other ways. "July 11 ... we finally had to camp without wood but we found some buffalo chips which answer very well to boil tea & coffee. We see some elk, buffalow, deer & antelope. Past 18 graves to day there seems to have a great many died in June & mostly of cholera. We had the most musketoes we have had. They were very troublesome. July 12 ... traveled slow on account of sick cattle. We were looking for a place to water when a little boy of Captain Maughns, 3 years of age, fell from the waggon. The 2 wheels run over his stomach & he died in about an hour. While stopping the other company past us. This is the first death in our 10. Saw three buffalow feeding on the bottoms. While stopping we found 30 head of sheep some one had left. We brought them on. Traveled 10 miles, found water by digging. Cattle some better. Past 6 graves."[196]

Then, things began to look up for Parsons' company. She continued, "July 13... Past on 3 miles to Ash creek & camped to wash & bake. Past 12 graves to day. Health of the emigrants seems to be better. July 14... Formerly the emigrants have found flood wood here but there is none this year on account of the high water this spring. There was preaching this afternoon & several baptized in the branch of the river. July 15... We are now in buffalow region as they are seen by the thousands. Traveled 12 miles. Past 13 graves. Some of our company killed 3 buffalow. There are large amounts of prickly pears & mushroom here, these look like the ones in the east. July 16 ... past 3 graves. Met 3 teams from Fort Laramie. We have seen hundreds of buffalow to day. They seem to care very little about us, they will hardly move for the firing of a gun. There is also plenty of deer, elk, Antelope & wolves of the largest kind. Generally camp now in good health."[197]

For most parties that had to endure it, the cholera had done its worst by the time most trains had reached the forks of the Platte. Outbreaks continued much farther up the trail, true, but most emigrants, who had seen it raging literally since the jumping-off points, noted a subsidence in its occurrence. But it left an impact on those who survived it, and like with so many other emigrants, the subject of cholera found its way into John Nevin King's thoughts and words. In a letter to his mother he recalled, "We have had 3 deaths from Cholera & one from Diarrhea since we past the Fort, and one young man by name of Ramsey is now very low but likely to recover. Last season the Cholera raged worse among the emigrants between Forts Kearney and Laramie than on any other portion of the route across the plains. Last season report says that there was hardly a case of Cholera on the north side of the Platte."

King went on to describe one of those strange twists of fate and tragedy not totally uncommon on the road to see the elephant. "The two who died first were Felix & William Allen, sons of Col. Allen of Wisconsin Platte County. One was 17 and the other 20 years of age. The next one that died was in the same mess and from the same place. His name was Walker, he was sent out by Col. Allen to take charge of his sons, the Col. paying his passage."

Then King wrote of his own frightening brush with death. "I was taken suddenly ill after finishing my letter at Fort Kearney and Vomited nearly all day. I took medicine in time & had I not done so my bowels would have been deranged & I judge I should have had the Cholera. I spoke of being frightened when the Cholera broke out. Yes and I could not help thinking of the young Allens all night (as they died within 20 steps of me) & in the morning I had a Diarrhea. You know Diarrhea & Vomiting are the first symptoms of Cholera. Nothing but pure fright affected me. I have been informed here by persons who were in Saint Louis all last season during the Cholera that hundreds died there of fright." His conclusion, "Tis awful when you see an acquaintance at noon well and in the enjoyment of health and learn in the evening that he is a corpse."[198]

The Fork of the Platte

One hundred miles after leaving Fort Kearney, the main trail on the south bank of the Platte struck the fork between the South Platte, which rose to the south and west in what is today Colorado, and the North Platte, flowing from the north and west, along which the trail to California continued toward Fort Laramie and South Pass in the Rocky Mountains. However, most emigrants continued along the south bank of what had become the South Platte, for several days and miles further, looking for the best, meaning least dangerous, place to ford.

J. A. Pritchard described how he saw the forks of the Platte on May 23, 1849. "We are now about opposite the junction of the North and South Platte. Meantime we passed the Cincinnati Train, a joint stock association of 50 members. They had 8 mules to the wagon. Our course is now up the South fork of the Platte and along its bottom. The men procured wood by fording across to an Island. We found vegetation greener and grass better on the South fork than it was on the main river. The river here is three-fourths mile wide — The bluffs are much more gentle and sloping than they are on the main river."[199]

Israel Hale, about a week behind Pritchard hardly noticed the geographic landmark but expressed other concerns. "We were informed this morning that we had passed the mouth of the South Platte. If such is the case we passed it unnoticed," he wrote on June 1, 1849. "The bluffs have nearly disappeared. We could drove our wagons up at almost any point. Our greatest anxiety now is, how we are to cross the South fork. Yesterday some of our men killed a buffalo. They killed it so far from the wagons that they brought in but little. I did not get any. We passed a prairie dog town, but I think the inhabitants have gone on a visit, perhaps to avoid receiving company. I have not seen the first live one yet. We saw several trains on the other side of the river. They are supposed to be Mormons. Traveling on the plains in cold and rainy weather is very disagreeable. Several of our men have been out hunting since morning and we look for a feast of buffalo meat. One of them however returned soon: his horse threw him and put his arm out of place."[200]

Niles Searls' express company arrived a fortnight after Hale and though he took little notice of the geography the wildlife did catch his attention. "Reached the forks of Platte about 10 A.M. and kept up south side of south fork. Ascended a beautiful eminence near the river and engraved our names together with those of our friends upon the hard chalky earth. We caught sight of an enormous wolf and were all dismounted and loading our guns when by the accidental discharge of a rifle in the hands of a passenger, Jo [his horse] was shot in the hip and will, as I think, die of the wound. [If necessary] we shall shoot him to prevent his destruction by the wolves."[201]

Two days later, still along the South Fork of the Platte, Searls had an interesting encounter with a buffalo. "We saw four buffalo crossing the bottom toward the hills about noon and in company with Dr. Spears, I immediately commenced a pursuit and were soon alongside our game. After discharging the contents of my rifle into the body of one of them without bringing him down, I dropped the gun and advanced on him again with a large rifle pistol. Owing to the largeness of the percussion cap it slipped from the tube and my pistol missed fire. Both of the Doctor's holsters also missed, and, after running some distance, we finally gave up the chase. Returning to near the spot where I supposed I had left the gun, I searched in vain for it and was at length compelled to return to camp, minus buffalo and minus gun."[202]

Bruff reached the forks on June 24, 1849, and though imperious in describing the weather, geographical landscape, flora and fauna, he had other, more gentlemanly, things on his mind. "I dined & supped with Capt. McNulty commanding a New York Compy [company] called the Colony Guards." Many bands of goldseekers gave their parties special, military sounding, or humorous names. "Here I was treated to superior strong coffee. A New Orleans Ox train compy close by, among whom I found an old acquaintance, formerly of Washington, and several ladies." In closing he added, "A delightful cool spring near us. Clay bluffs ahead, on the left, & half a mile below, on the right, are the forks of the Platte."[203]

Margaret Frink and her husband reached the forks of the Platte in late May, 1850. She had apparently heard some bad stories about the crossing, but had other things to lament as well. "To-morrow will bring us to the South Fork, which we are told we must ford. From what we have seen of the river so far, it looks rather dangerous to cross, and we have some apprehensions of difficulty. But it may not be so bad when we come to it. If we get safely over, we expect to reach more interesting country to travel through." Having thoroughly read her guidebooks, Margaret knew exactly where she was going. "The South Fork heads in a southwest direction from here, among the highest peaks of the Rocky Mountains. Our road will lead us up the North Fork of the Platte, and up its main branch, the Sweetwater, to the South Pass."[204]

Those who passed the forks in 1849 did not mention seeing any significant number of grave markers, but those passing in 1850 saw more. Sarah Davis did not even note the geographic landmark but recalled on the day she would have passed the forks, "the men all went in a swimen and I sow and wash their was three large white wolfs atacked a cow and calf they then surrounded the cow and would have killer her but whilst they ware eating their kill a mr crous shot one and he droped down and he thought he was dead but he rose again and run of [f] I saw thirteen graves to day."[205]

Littleton likewise saw reaching the fork as a minor event writing only that, "we came to where the road forks one goes to the river and the other takes up the bluff. I suppose this right hand road goes to the lower ford of the South fork of the Platte." There were other distractions. "I saw some of our Passengers after 2 buffaloe. They were coming in the direction where I was with 4 or 5 others. One of the men Shot one which did not run more than 100 yards till he fell dead. He was not very fat being a Bull but he was good. I took a hearty diner of the liver and expect to have several good meals more from our part of it. We have passed 13 graves today."[206]

Near the forks of the Platte Samuel Jamison found some diversions from the routine trail life, writing on May 18–19, 1850, in his normal economy of words, "Stopped at a small stream which we found to have a great many fish. We made a brush net and swept some of the holes and got a fine mess of fish." His traveling companion went hunting and he reported, "Armstrong got to close, the buffalo turned on him, and tore his horse very bad. Stewart and the Doctor sowed up the wound." The next day he recorded something many would find rather amazing, if not downright disgusting, but probably not too extraordinary for a young, single man, living on a wilderness trail. "Sunday lay by. I done my first washing today." We can only assume that he brought numerous changes of undergarments and clothing, for he had been moving along in the mud and dust for over a month at that point. We may also suppose that the elements, weather, and often muddy river water deterred even the most sanitary minded. Necessity proved the mother of invention on the trails and Jamison even managed the luxury of a glass of ice water as a reward for his layover and bout with cleanliness. "We had a very heavy hale Storm to day it hailed so hard that we gathered a bucket full of hale to make Ice water for our water is very bad here."[207]

On reaching the fork of the Platte, Lucena Parsons took no notice of it but wrote, "Still we are journeying on & in good spirits." It is entirely possible that many diarists missed noting the Platte forks because their road, one of many broad tracks back from the riverbank, took them over the low bluffs beyond sight of the merging channels. Other thoughts took precedent in her journal. "We have some fine times with all our troubles. We have made 18 miles to day over a very dry country. There seems to be plenty of saleratus, salt & large beds of prickly pear & some smart weed [stinging like nettles] on this these bottoms. Past 19 graves, most of them from Missouri, they died in June & all are young men between 20 & 30 years of age."[208]

Lucena Parsons found that although things were improving within her own train that death had left its visage on the plains too great to ignore. The next day, July 18, 1850, she wrote, "We have past some 12 graves & I am told there is a burying ground near here of 300 graves. If so it must be a general camping ground for near these I find the most graves. I see some painful sights where the wolves have taken up the dead & torn their garments in pieces & in some instances the skulls & jaw bones are strewed over the ground."[209]

The day before reaching the major ford over the South Platte, Mica Littleton recorded a single day's list of names from grave markers along the main trail. He prefaced his entry of June 24, 1850, by saying, "there is nothing remarkable on today's travel." Then he began to recount the toll, a stark and singular eulogy to those along a stretch of trail 24 miles long, who had gone to see the elephant. "We have passed 30 graves today. Sad reflection and I know there [are] many we do not see I think we do not See more than 2 thirds that are buried in this bottom. The names of what I have are as follows:

> I Q Smith died June 11th Sentry Co. Mo.
> John Duncan June 14th age 27 Scott Co. Va.
> Wm K Gunter June 12th age 26 of Mo.
> Geo. Frey June 10th age 23 of Phila. Pa.
> James Lofftis June 8th age 67 Henry Co. Mo.
> John Thomas June 12 age 40 Armstrong Co. Pa.
> Issac Moore June 16th age 37 Ray Co. Mo.
> I. P. Box June 7th age 39 Polk Co. Mo.
> W C Reeves June 10th age 22 Cape Gerardeau Mo.
> James West June 8th age 50 Pulasky Co. Mo
> W. P. Lamb June 15th age 46
> A Wilmoth June 14th age 36 Carroll Co. Ark.
> Capt. Wm C Halley June 23 age 46 of Chariton Co. Mo.
> W B Hays June 10th age 40 Dade Co. Mo.
> Mary Barclay June 10th
> I M Belcher June 10th
> M Wadleyonleet June 10th
> I. L. Knapp June 10th
> T. Wheeler June 10th
> P A Gettings June 4th Dave Co. Ind.
> Aidy Chrisman June 11th
> M V Venable June 11th Davis Co. Ind.
> M. F. Pinkston June 11th age 27 Davis Co. Mo.
> Elizabeth Hendrix June 11th age 21
> Robt. Burcherd June 19th age 19 Osage Mo.
> W. Gapen June 13th
> and 3 without boards. This is all I Saw."[210]

Crossing the South Fork of the Platte to Ash Hollow

Once past the forks of the Platte, emigrants began considering where to ford the southern branch. There were in fact many options, for at least three major fording areas existed, the lower, middle, and upper fords as they were called. Mileage to each area varied but ranged from about four miles past the forks to the lower ford up to 25 miles past the forks to the upper ford. A determining factor would have been the depth of the river channel, whether it had rained recently, or how informed the emigrants were from either their guidebooks or the scouts employed by many trains. Whichever ford the emigrants choose, they understood they were going to get a little wet and hopefully do no major harm to themselves or their belongings. Once over the South Platte, the next major landmark lay at Ash Hollow on the south bank of the North Platte, the point from which everyone set his or her sights on Fort Laramie. Depending where the emigrants forded, Ash Hollow could be 20 miles or 40 miles, depending how far up the South Platte they had gone before crossing.

J. A. Pritchard's party pushed on to the upper ford on the South Platte, reaching it on May 26, 1849. "reached the ford—15 miles distance—3 P.M. we were all safely landed across the river—not withstanding the great number of teams ahead of us—The river here is one mile wide—with a bottom composed of quick sand. The sand breaks under the wagon-wheels and it jars worse than if it was passing over the roughest kind of frozen ground. We were compelled to put two teams to each wagon in order to pull through. If the wagon is permitted to stand for one minute they bury down in the sand holes in the bed of the river. There was a Frenchman there who acted as pilot—his charge was a tin full of sugar & coffee to the wagon—which was generally given—I watch the crossing of one train whilst the boys were doubling on the teams—And when the next started I put in after them with 4 of our wagons and made the crossing in perfect safety."[211]

Some made it across even easier. "This day between twelve and one o'clock we crossed the South Fork of Platte River," wrote Israel Hale on June 2, 1849. "It is said we crossed fifteen miles below the old or common crossing place. The water is swift but is not deep. It did not come into our wagon bed. The bottom of the river appears solid and we crossed without trouble and did not double teams, so now the dread is over. We safely landed on the N.W. side of the long-dreaded stream and have now encamped for the night. The water is nearly as muddy as the Missouri, but there is no quicksand as at the other fords."[212]

Amos Josselyn also crossed the South Platte on June 2, 1849, but probably at the low ford. "Left camp at 6 o'clock. Drove 4 miles up the river to a ford; got over by 11:30 o'clock drove 10 miles across to the North Fork. 20 miles further to camp at Ash Hollow."[213] Niles Searls, traveling with the express company to one of the upper fords, didn't take much interest in the crossing, making a short entry in his journal, dated June 19, 1849. "The river at the ferry is about twelve rods in width without any particular channel and at the usual state of water from two to three feet deep. Fording commenced early and without serious mishap concluded at 11 A.M."[214]

Bruff, crossing the Platte a month behind Pritchard, may have been at the same ford, for in his entry he complained about the quicksand. "Early this morning Capt. McNulty tendered me a mule, and I forded the Platte, with them. Found 2 of men with a St. Louis Comp. on crossing. My New York friends got all their train over without accident, except one wagon, which sank so in the sand that they had to leave it for the day. It was about forty yds. from shore, and about 400 below the landing & camp, and contained a sick man. It looked queer to see a man wading down stream, waist deep, in the rapid river, with a pot of coffee in one hand and a plate of bread and meat in the other, going to the wagon, to the relief of his comrade. On the opposite shore could be seen a pointer dog, at the water's edge, howling for his lost master, on this side (12 mules needed to drag wagon out). It was thought that the emigrants had made many semblances of graves which were actually caches of goods."[215]

Margaret Frink crossed the South Platte at one of the busy lower fords only a "few miles" from the juncture of the two forks. Her description of the crossing is both melodramatic and marvelous. "The stream we had now reached was fearful to look at, rushing and boiling and yellow with mud, a mile wide, and in many places of unknown depth. The bed was of quicksand — this was the worst difficulty. But there was no way to do but to ford it. So we started down the bank and into the raging water.

"From a guidebook we had with us, we learned that the proper way to cross the stream was to take a diagonal course, first down the stream, then up again. Accordingly, after driving into the water, we turned down at an angle of forty-five degrees till we had reached the middle of the river; then, turned up stream at the same angle, we arrived safely at the northern bank, nearly opposite our point of entrance.

"Of all the excitement that I ever experienced or thought of, the crossing of that river was the greatest. A great many other wagons and people were crossing at the same time — mule teams, horse teams, ox teams, men on horseback, men wading and struggling against the quicksand and current, many of them with long poles in their hands, feeling their way. Sometimes they would be in shallow water only up to their knees; then, all at once, some unlucky one would plunge in where it was three or four feet deep.

"The deafening noise and halloing that this army of people kept up, made the alarm in the river more intense. The quicksand and the uncertainty of depth of water kept all in a state of anxiety. Our horses would sometimes be in water no more than a foot deep; then, in a moment they would go down up to their collars. On one occasion I was considerably alarmed. Several other wagons, in their haste, had crowded in ahead of us on both sides, and we were compelled to stop for several minutes. Our wagon at once began to settle in the quicksand, and it required the assistance of three or four men lifting at the wheels to enable the horses to pull out.

"Where we crossed, the river was a mile wide, and we were just three-quarters of an hour in getting over. I here date one of the happiest and most thankful moments of my life to have been when we landed safe on the north side. The danger in the crossing consisted in the continual shifting of the sandy bed, so that a safe ford to-day might be a dangerous one to-morrow."[216]

Mica Littleton, also going out in 1850, crossed the South Platte at one of the indeterminate number of fording places, between the better-known middle and upper fords. "June 25, rolled out this morning at about 7 o'clock 5 miles brought us to the Ford on the South Platte. There is a ford 5 miles above but this being more shallow. We crossed here. We are all Safely over except one carriage and one baggage waggon which we left this morning with a very sick man they have not came up yet. One Doctor came up this evening and left him Some better but entertains fears of his recovery. We shall know tomorrow. We have several very sick in camp this evening. I fear our trouble is only commenced. Still I hope for the better, we have only passed 6 graves this morning that I Saw. The Platte here we found a half-mile wide. We go down Stream to cross keeping on the bank of the Bar all along other places Swim horses. The traveler can know this Ford by observing 2 cotton wood trees about one mile below this ford."[217]

Sometimes the various fording places, the ones reported to be better than the others, could be crowded. "Started early & pushed on as fast as possible to reach the ford which we learned from a company of men on the back track was 8 miles ahead. Those men had 4 waggons. They had had some trouble & were going back to Missouri. Reached the ford & found 30 waggons on the ground to cross. There was 80 with ours," wrote Lucena Parsons in July, 1850. "We had good luck & all got over in half a day. I find dry soda on the bank that I can scrape up. This is the south fork of the Platte. The river is shallow & 1 mile wide."[218] Some emigrants were just happy to get across alive, like Sarah Davis. "we corst [crossed] at waddells forde and no one got drowned at all."[219] And for still others, fording the Platte required nothing more than a brief exercise with immodesty. "crossed the platt this afternoon. Howe and Sprankle waded over by taking off their pants."[220]

Once clear of the fords over the South Platte, all the emigrants moved quickly on toward Ash Hollow, a picturesque spot known for its grove of ash trees, where the roads from the various fords converged on the south bank of the North Platte before striking out for Fort Laramie. Depending where the ford had been made, it might be one, two, or three days to Ash Hollow. The scenery began to change but the amazing sights, challenges, and often drudgeries of trail life did not.

"We immediately crossed the bluff to the valley of the N. Fork and followed that up some eight or ten miles and encamped near a slough where we found good grass and water and some wood," recalled Israel Hale after fording the South Platte. "Someone had encamped a short time before us and had left several articles: salt, bread etc. Should any of our friends think of making this trip I would advise them not to load too heavy, also to not buy a cooking stove in the States, for I have had chances to get one almost every day for the last two weeks, and some days two or three. A small hole dug in the ground appears to answer a better purpose than the most approved pattern of cooking stoves for the plains. We found another wagon today that was left at a camp. They worked horses in it I presume. They took out the load and packed it. Some of our men used a part of the bed for a box. The balance was left."[221]

After crossing to the middle ground between the forks of the Platte, many emigrants reported encounters with a new tribe, the true lords of the high plains, the Sioux. "Several Sioux Indians were in camp last evening and appeared friendly," recalled Niles Searls. "They have lately conducted a fortunate hostile expedition against the Pawnees. Two miles from our camp I visited the sepulchre of a Sioux warrior and chief. It consists of a large tent formed of buffalo skins dressed, supported by poles meeting at the apex; in this tent on an elevated bed of wicker work lay the remains of the dead. By his side were his bow and arrow, tobacco, pipe, etc. Immediately under this was the body of another, probably that of his squaw. We also saw near this spot a dead body enveloped in skins and placed in a small wooden frame elevated in a lofty tree."[222]

Along with the Sioux, there seemed to have been plenty of buffalo roaming the land between the Platte forks, for several emigrants wrote about hunting. Logically, as the Sioux were the great hunters of the plains, they were found where the buffalo grazed.

"Last evening I ate some buffalo meat. It was fine. It was sent in by the men who killed the buffalo a day or so since," recounted Israel Hale. Because of the close proximity of a major plains tribe, stories began circulating among the trains about Indian attacks. Hale relayed one of these in his diary as he continued, "It is reported that three or four men have been killed by the Indians, which prevented our men from venturing far from the train. It appears the men have been killed a long time, as it was difficult to tell whether they were white, black or red. They had on hickory shirts and were scalped."[223] In fact none of the diarists experienced any personal threat from the Sioux, and as we shall see, generally wrote in a complimentary tone about them.

The fluid lifestyle of the Sioux, like that of nearly all of the Native American plains societies, meant they moved almost constantly around and along the trails that passed through their territory. Israel Hale referenced that point as he wrote his entry on June 4, 1849. "This is wash day and we are laying by. I killed a snake today, it being the first live one that I have seen since I started. We heard of one thousand Indians being encamped where we crossed the South Fork. Owing to that and the appearance of a storm we tied our cattle. But neither storm nor Indians came. There is more wind in this country than in any place I ever saw. It often, as at present, shakes the wagon so much that I can hardly write."[224]

Crossing over from the south bank of the Platte did not totally end the outbreaks of disease that continued to carry off emigrants. "I have passed 5 or 6 waggons on the North Side laying by till morning. Many Sick in our camp. Our sick man that was taken last night with cholera Mr. Franklin Burley of Macon Co., Tenn is no more, he has gone The way from which travelers never Return. Peace to his ashes on this dreary Spot. I was not present when he died," wrote Mica Littleton, the day after fording the South Platte.[225]

Ash Hollow

J. A. Pritchard, near the head of the emigrant trains going to see the elephant in 1849, reached the site on May 27. He wrote, "we bid adieu to the South Platte. Mounted the Bluffs and struck for Ash hollow on the North Fork, a distance of 22 miles. Struck the head of Ash hollow, so called there are few clumps of Ash trees standing a long a hollow. The North fork of the Platte here bears some resemblance to the main stream — yet the channel is not so wide — the banks are higher and the current much more rapid — We passed several trains today, that had halted to rest their mules, wash their clothing, sun their goods & etc. Among the rest was the Chicago train that passed us soon after we struck the main Platte — They went by us in a trot and said that they were going to beat every body to California."[226]

Israel Hale came through ten days behind Pritchard and wrote lyrically of the place. "Struck Ash Hollow. It is a narrow, sandy valley with low ash trees scattered along its side. We had not driven far when we found considerable underbrush, such as currents, rose bushes and several shrubs that I did not know the name of. The morning was clear, the air was pure and the roses nearly in full bloom, and sent forth a flavour which can better be imagined than described. The air appeared perfectly scented with them and I think if they had named the place the Valley of Roses it would have been a more appropriate name, for there were fifty rose bushes to one ash tree." But the hollow also had elements not so blissful. "The buffalo gnats are and have been very troublesome for several days. They appear to have a particular spite on the eyes and ears."[227]

Two weeks later, Niles Searls, writing on June 20, 1849, gave a nice description. "Ash Hollow. We left camp and descended into the valley rested till 1 o'clock, then resumed the march. The lofty banks on either side of the Valley are surmounted by a few scattering cedars and in the bottom are a number of ashes, which have given name to the pass. A stream runs through its whole length at high water, but it is now lost in the sand in the lower part. Near its mouth is a copious spring of good water."[228]

Bruff reached the hollow late in June, and in an uncharacteristic fashion wrote practically no geographic description of the place. He did take note of the grave markers near the place and as anyone might, left the place in a melancholy mood. "Reached company at Ash Hollow, 140 miles from Ft. Laramie. Graves marked along the way. John Waugh, of Scott Co. Mo. June 17. 1849, Aged 20 Years. Rachel E. Pattison, Aged 18, June 19, 49." And the most poignant read, "John Hoover, died June 18. 49 Aged 12 yrs. Rest in peace, sweet boy, for thy travels are over."[229]

Margaret Frink reached the vicinity of Ash Hollow on the first day of June, 1850, two days after having crossed one of the lower fords of the South Platte. "To-day the bluffs came to the river and cut off our passage along the bank. We had to climb a long hill to go around. We descended to the river again through a deep ravine called Ash Hollow, where Colonel Harney, with a detachment of United States Regulars, had a severe fight with the Sioux, several years ago. The heavy sand and hard climbing begin to tell on the strength of our horses. Feed is often scarce and they suffer in consequence." But the next day she found something better to say about the environs of the hollow and about the ingenuity of her husband. "We remained in camp all day, repairing our small wagon. The hind axle was broken. Mr. Frink had seen a wagon abandoned, near the road at Ash Hollow. He went back with a man to day, and took out the bolts and brought the hind axle and wheels to camp. It was then fitted to the small wagon in place of the old axle, and did very well."[230]

"The country from the South Platte to the North Platte I think is about 20 miles, 17 or 18 miles to the head of ash Hollow and 3 miles from there to the river," wrote Mica Littleton in late June, 1850. He did not like getting into the hollow but once there thought it as nice as others did who had passed through. "From ash Hollow or where we came into it and Strike the head of the Hollow further to the left, although we got down Safe without any mishap, yet it is a Steep bad and crooked place. Where we came to the North Platte at the foot of Ash Hollow the Bluffs are high and the country beautiful. There are 2 little Islands a little above covered with ceders [cedars] the only timber on them."[231]

Sarah Davis had only bittersweet recollections of Ash Hollow. She began on June 23, 1850, "We camped in ash holler. their was a tremendous thunder sawer one role after nother till it killed a horse that was only one rod from our wagon that night Sarah was taken sick we had no super." She continued the next day, "we camped on the north fork of the plat river and sarah was very sick their was one women died in the camp of colera and was buried the next morning when I went to Sarah she was no beter and I soon saw she would die and she did die before noon. o how lonely I felt to think I was all the woman in company and too small babes left in my care it seams to me as if I would be hapy if I only had one woman with me."[232]

Sioux Country Along the North Platte

Past Ash Hollow the emigrants came well into Sioux territory. That tribe had built a formidable reputation, and gained the respect of the whites passing through their country, as is evident in the writings of most of our diarists. "There is a village of the Sioux Indians two miles above the crossing — and

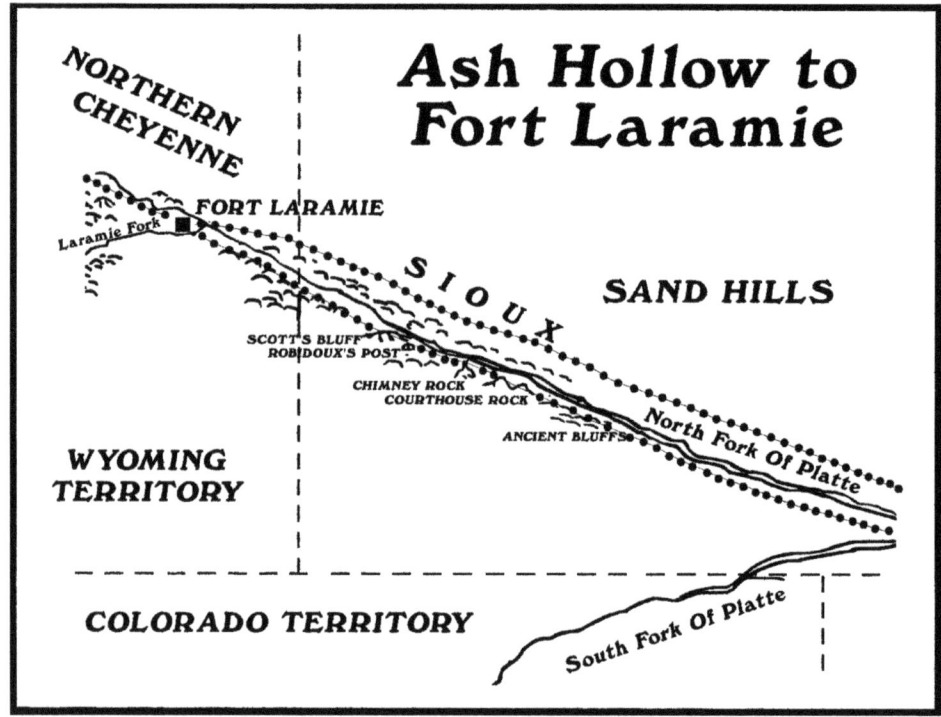

Ash Hollow to Fort Laramie — road along the North Platte to the fort, with landmarks.

some 2 or 300 of them of all sex ages and size were loitering round our wagons pretending to trade mockisons [sic] & skins for something to eat," wrote J. A. Pritchard on May 26, 1850. "The men are large well proportioned & fine looking the women are rather fine looking — The Sioux Indians have never been hostile to the whites — We encamped about one mile above the ford — where we found good grass — There are some ten or a dozen Frenchmen living here in lodges or wigwams — with Squaws for their wives After we had a encamped a large number of the men came round our camp I was not all together pleased with their appearance — So I told the boys about sunset to bring out their Guns and stack them in the center of the corral. After seeing the guns they took very good care to stay away."[233]

"Just below the mouth of Ash hollow there is an Old Indian battle ground. A battle was fought here some 10 years ago between the Sioux and Pawnee tribes,"[234] recounted Franklin Starr, no doubt using information supplied by some fellow emigrant. The tribal conflict continued for another decade at least, as another traveler reported, "The Indians that we hear of were the Sioux. They are at war with the Pawnees and have been down to have a battle, the results I did not learn. I am told that they stole a horse and sold it for a bag of flour and a plug of tobacco, but the owner soon found and redeemed him. I also hear complaints of their taking small articles, such as pans etc. It is said that the Pawnees will kill a man to steal his horse, but that the Sioux will steal a horse but will not kill a man," recalled Israel Hale as he passed through their territory on June 5, 1849.[235]

Two days later, Hale got a close up look at the tribe he had been hearing about and came away somewhat impressed by what he saw. "As we came near the river the bluffs were an uneven ledge of rocks and at the river we found six lodges of the Sioux Indians and some traders. Their lodges were of dressed buffalo skins stretched over about twenty poles and in the shape of an umbrella, but more pointed at the top. The fire is made in the center and a hole on the top fixed on two poles that they can move as occasion may require to keep the wind from blowing the smoke down the chimney. They are much to be preferred to our tents was it not for their weight. These Indians appeared much more comfortably fixed than I expected to see them. They looked clean and were well dressed and had several good horses. I presume they were some of the better class."[236]

Margaret Frink also thought highly of the Sioux. "In the afternoon we passed an Indian encampment numbering seventy tents. They belonged to the Sioux tribe, but were quite friendly. The squaws were much pleased to see the 'white Squaw' in our party, as they called me. I had brought a supply of needles and thread, some of which I gave them. We also had some small mirrors in gilt frames, and a number of trinkets, with which we could buy fish and fresh buffalo, deer, and antelope meat. But money they would not look at."[237]

Other emigrants passing the Sioux in 1850 were not so impressed, but some did report seeing substantial numbers of that tribe. Henry Wellenkamp briefly noted on May 31, 1850, "Many Sioux Indian towns." He reported a couple of days later, "Passed towns of Sioux Indians, 52 wigwams."[238] John Birney Hill wrote of the Sioux, "Saw a good many Indians to day—they are friendly."[239] Mica Littleton, a month behind Wellenkamp, remembered that June 30, 1850, "brought us to the Sioux Village. There are some 4 or 5 hundred of them. They are the greatest beggars I ever Saw."[240] Samuel Jamison echoed that observation. "We encamped for diner at the foot of the hollow at the river on the right hand side of the road in sight of an Indian village. There was about thirty Indians come in to camp while we lay there to beg provisions we gave them some things."[241] Sarah Davis likewise had a lowly impression of the Sioux: "camped on the plat river within a few rods of fifty sue indians we suposed they ware robers for they had a great many horses of the inglish kind and their was a few french with them."[242] Lucena Parsons knew on reaching Ash Hollow that she had reached Sioux territory, but did not happen to see any: "stopt to wash & bake & take on wood to last us over the sand hills which are ahead. We are now in Sous & Sian [Cheyenne] country. There are none of them on the road this year. There are 20 graves in & around this hollow."[243]

Beyond the vicinity of Ash Hollow, Sioux lands extended north and west for a great distance. The road became even sandier than along the lower Platte, and the land began to rise more noticeably. The routine of trail life continued, growing a bit more difficult every day. Samuel Jamison complained, "the road is very sandy since we left Ash hollow it is hard on the mules." And other dangers sprang from the mundane chores like preparing an evening meal. "We had quite a brush this evening with fire which got out from our fire and burnt some of our grass very nigh getting into the wagons."[244]

Israel Hale recalled in his diary on June 8, 1849, a point of interest on the otherwise open plain. "We saw a lone tree something like a mile to the left of the road. In it was an Indian grave." Unfortunately, the point of interest quickly turned to on irrelevancy when the bugs attacked. "We have been very much troubled this afternoon by mosquitoes. They certainly have not been well fed for they are as hungry as wolves." The next day Hale reported seeing an interesting grave marker. "We passed a grave. It was a Mr. Stevens of Boon [Boone] County, Missouri. He died on the sixth and of consumption. He was traveling for his health." However the plague of insects returned. "Soon after we started the mosquitoes made their appearance in swarms. The horse that I was riding appeared half covered with them. They are a large ravenous saucy breed. The wind, however, soon rose and they in a measure disappeared."[245]

Niles Searls also remembered the bugs along the North Platte and wrote an eloquent recounting of the encounter. "We have been annoyed several

Sioux Country Along the North Platte

days with mosquitoes, but until last night were enabled to battle them with some success. They came, however, with the twilight of last evening in myriads, falling like famished tigers upon their prey. A smoke was raised in our tent which for a short period drove them back, but after a pause of a few moments they returned to the charge with renewed vigor. To resist these small shedders of human blood was out of the question. All that could be done was to yield in quiet submission to our fate. Many a hero renowned in history has won his laurels with the loss of less blood than was shed by each of us during this eventful night. We are told we may expect plenty of such martyrdoms for the next two months."[246]

If the mosquitoes did not keep you awake at night, then annoyances from another quarter could. "The wolves howl around camp every night in hordes and each wolf makes as much noise as 5 dogs and probably 500 howl at once,"[247] complained Franklin Starr in his journal on June 2, 1849, just past Ash Hollow.

Lucena Parsons looked wishfully ahead after passing Ash Hollow, writing, "hoping to get through to Larimee in 12 days. Past some fine sights to day among the hills. The water has washed them in all forms. Some resemble pulpits & others look like haystacks. All look fine. Traveled 18 miles. Past 12 graves, one a man of 84 years old. We meet teams most every day, some on the back track, others for the government."[248]

The emigrants had been exposed to the giant thunderstorms, which could often spawn tornadoes, shortly after jumping off onto the Great Plains. On the high plains, with practically no natural barriers or windbreaks, and only the shelter of their frail wagons, the storms of June and July seemed even fiercer. They often developed in the late afternoon heat of the day when heated air on the earth's surface rose and collided with cool air aloft, creating towering cumulus thunderheads. Emigrants from the East were often taken back by the sudden rise and violence of the storms.

"At 4 P.M. I discovered in the southwest a very angry looking cloud arising," wrote Pritchard on May 29, 1849. "I haulted the train, and gave orders to stake the mules, pitch tents as quickly as possible, which was done. The cloud changed rout west-north-west and then bore square down upon us. And at 5 P.M. it commenced raining accompanied with hail and heavy wind — with fearce and vivid flashes of lightening and loud crashing peels of thunder. It raged with increased fury for the space of an hour and a half. Tent pins gave way and tents went by the board nearly all the tents round the camp were blown down and the men exposed to the fury of the storm which raged with such violence that it was impossible for a man to stand erect in it." After the storm, the misery continued. "The storm abated some what in the course of an hour and a half — but the rain continued during the night without intermission. It is still raining this morning with a cold chilling wind from the North. There is scarcely fuel enough in camp this morning to boil a coffeepot and none that we know of to be had in this vicinity. The men's clothing and bedding are perfectly saturated with water and they stand shivering round with cold, no fire nor any thing else to warm them, not so much as a cup of hot coffee."[249]

Niles Searls remembered a similarly violent June storm, writing, "We have several times in this trip experienced heavy showers and once or twice have had hail, but all the storms which I ever before experienced were as nothing compared with one we endured this day. The rain fell in torrents accompanied by a whirlwind and by hail the size of hickory nuts. Two of our carriages were overset by the gale and one of them crushed to atoms. Mules and loose stock were stampeded and ran for hours. Captain Turner who was on horseback, was struck on the finger by a hailstone which dislocated the joint. In the short space of ten minutes no less than three inches of hail and rain fell. Our only course was to turn our teams to the leeward and, in the language of the seaman, scud before the gale."[250]

Amos Josselyn, who no doubt encountered the same storm system sweeping across the plains that Searls described, recalled, "we had indications of a storm all the afternoon: at 4 o'clock it came in earnest, a tremendous hail storm. It lasted about 30 minutes."[251] Though the sandy road tended to drain away the rain well, in places the water could not escape quickly enough, and the trail could become a quagmire. Josselyn remarked on June 8, 1849, "Left camp at 7 o'clock and drove but two miles until we got into the mud up to the axle, and did not get the wagons all through until 12 o'clock. It took 18 yoke of cattle to pull our mules wagon out. It was a mile through the marshy ground."[252]

Landmarks of the Western Plains

Approximately 40 miles up the trail past Ash Hollow, the emigrants began to encounter the geographic landmarks that told them they would soon be leaving the flat grassy plains and passing into the foothills of the Rocky Mountains. These geologic oddities, of sandstone and ancient clay, created by the erosion of wind and water, with names primarily given by semblance to some structure familiar in shape, caught every emigrant's eye, and in all cases, at least a passing mention in the diaries, if not a quite elaborate description. Because of their height above the plain, they could be seen, simultaneously, for long distances from the trails on both sides of the North Platte, and often elicited a side trip of several hours, a break in going to see the elephant, in the otherwise relentless push to reach the gold fields. The first of the landmarks, they encountered in the region of what the emigrants called the Castle Rocks or Ancient Bluff Ruins. Nearby lay the singular natural monument generally known as Courthouse Rock.

In a series of entries, Lucena Parsons referred to the region using the abovementioned reference names. "July 24... Past the Castle rocks this morning, so named by their appearance. We past 13 graves, the graves on this side of Ash hollow have not been disturbed. July 25 ... we have 21 waggons, since we left Ash hollow. We find that small companies get along better where there is a scarcity of grass. There is no wood. This afternoon we past the ancient bluff ruins on the north side of the river. They are infested with rattlesnakes I am told. Past 14 graves. Traveled 22 miles. July 26... Today came in view of a splendid looking sight, like a stone castle. It is 300 feet high & composed of pipe clay [maybe a reference to Chimney Rock]. Past 13 graves."[253]

"About 3 P.M. we came in sight of the Court House rock," wrote J. A. Pritchard on May 29, 1849. "It presents to the eye the appearance of an artificial superstructure. It has a round top with doams [domes] and spires. This Court house rock is about 4 ms to the left of the road. At about the same time we came in sight of the Chimney rock. It has the appearance from here of a house with a tall chimney on the south side. We are now some 15 or 16 miles this side of it. We are now in one of the Platts broadest bottoms, with exelant [excellent] grass."[254]

"I started for the Church or Court House Rock. It is on the south side of the North Fork and about six or seven miles from the road. It is situated on an elevated piece of ground and composed of a soft whitish sandstone," described Israel Hale, on June 10, 1849, of his first encounter with the great landmarks. "It can be cut with any kind of edge tool, even a hoe. It is six hundred feet in length and from thirty to one hundred in width. It is widest in the middle. I would suppose it was two hundred feet high, although it is said to be three hundred. At the top the rock is small. Where you ascend it is not more than two or three feet wide; further west it is six or eight. On the south side and end it is nearly perpendicular. To all appearances it is fast washing away and I believe in time it will be mingled with the balance of the earth in the vicinity. I think it has been larger and much higher than it now is. Hundreds have inscribed their names upon it, and places of residence and date."[255]

Niles Searls, in writing on June 23, 1849, thought the Courthouse Rock closely resembled an actual building he had seen recently. "Encamped at noon just opposite 'Court House' resembling very much the Court House in St. Louis, Mo. Its height is about two hundred feet and is accessible to the top of the dome." From the same vantage, Searls could see, "'Chimney Rock.' When first seen it resembled in a high degree a shot tower, but as we approached nearer, its base appeared gradually enlarging till it seemed like a pyramid."[256]

Margaret Frink wrote in her diary of the illusions of distance, commonly experienced on the plains as her party approached the landmarks. "At three o'clock we came in sight of the famous 'Court-house Rock,' eighteen miles distant, and many miles south of the road. It presents a very imposing appearance. "Chimney Rock" also cam in sight, about thirty miles further on. Our camp at night was made nearly opposite the Court-house Rock, and six miles distant; but the atmosphere was so clear that it did not seem to be more than a mile away. Many persons, thinking they could walk to the rock in a few minutes, would start out on foot to examine it more closely; but after walking an hour, finding it to be as far off as ever, apparently, would give up the attempt."[257]

A day's travel, 20 to 25 miles past Courthouse Rock, depending on which diarist is read, lay Chimney Rock. Pritchard recalled, "We passed this afternoon the chimney rock—it stands about 3 miles to the left of the road—Its elevation is said to be between 250 & 300 feet—Its composition is sand stone or rather sand & clay." He also found that as the land rose, emigrants realized the wagons were a bit too heavy. "A large number of trains had encamped here during a storm. We found this morning where they had been lighting up their loading and throwing away their provisions—They had left Bacon, flour, dried beef, coffee—dried apples, peaches etc. Our boys picked up some of the articles." Also as the land rose, the rate of speed declined. Pritchard decided to check it. "Our boys concluded this morning to carry a surveyors chain, in order to ascertain how fast we were traveling & how far we traveled pr day. They walked by my side all day and carried it against time. Our common gate on firm roads averaged 3 ms pr hour & when the roads were heavy [marshy or sandy] from 2½ to 2¾ miles pr hour."[258]

Franklin Starr's party, just five days behind Pritchard at that point, gave a more elaborate description of nature's grand formation, after making a side trip. "We nooned opposite Chimney rock. I thought that it was not over two miles from us and started to go to it when the teams were hitched up, but found that it was 4. It is a very singular pile. The base is very steep so much so that it would be impossible to climb on some sides. The Chimney is rough and looks as if it would not stand a week. The whole hill and Chimney is composed of a very hard clay or else soft stone and some rock. I climbed up to the base of the Chimney and cut my name among some thousand others, probably it will be cut away in a short time to make room for another."[259] That simply demonstrates that graffiti is not a modern problem.

Israel Hale, who had been greatly impressed by Courthouse Rock, found Chimney Rock even grander. "I then started for the Chimney Rock. While viewing the noble monument at the distance of a mile or two I could not help imagining that it might be the work of some generation long extinct and that it was erected in commemoration of some glorious battle or in memory of some noble chieftain. But on arriving at the spot I could discover no marks of hammer, axe or chisel, no cemented joints by which it should be cemented in one solid mass. It is not then the work of human hands. It must have been a freak of nature to display her art, astonish man with the variety and grandeur of her works and show the power of Deity. It is situated on the south side of the North Fork of the Platte River and two miles from the main road. It has a high bluff on the south, the balance of the boundary is low prairie. It is a soft sandstone with a mixture of small hard stones of different sizes. It resembles an inverted funnel and is two hundred and fifty feet in height. The diameter at its base I would say was five hundred feet. It runs up say one hundred and twenty five feet to a point of forty when the chimney rises one hundred and twenty five feet more holding its size to the top. I was up it as high as the large part. The chimney I presume was never ascended above the large part. I saw many names written on it, some of which were familiar. Like the Court House Rock it appears to be in a rapid state of decay. The rains are washing deep channels in many parts of it. I am very sure it cannot stand many years before large flakes will slide to the ground if all does not come down in a general crash."[260]

Niles Searls, like so many emigrants, saw the Chimney and believed like Hale, that it could not stand much longer. He observed on June 24, 1849, "this being the Sabbath, it was resolved to remain in camp till evening to rest ourselves and animals. We determined to visit Chimney rock situated three miles from our camp. The base of this wonderful object is conical, about one mile in circumference, and so precipitated as to be scarcely accessible. Its height we judged to be about one hundred and fifty feet. From the summit of this cone, the column or Chimney extends upward to an equal distance or from the plain, appears to be not over a few feet, yet when measured proves to be some fifty feet. It is wholly composed of soft sandstone which, yielding to the action of the atmosphere, is gradually decaying and will soon wholly disappear. Our guide informed me that when first visited by him its height was much greater than at present. The whole surface of the rock is covered with the names of individuals who have ascended it for the last few years."[261]

Margaret Frink, who put great store in the guidebooks she carried, came to similar though erroneous beliefs in the rapid decay of the Chimney Rock. "According to Fremont, it was once five hundred feet high, but has been worn down by the winds and rains until it is no more than two hundred and fifty feet in height. It is composed of marl and soft sandstone, which is easily worn away." If that were the true case, as Frémont had first seen it probably not more than a decade earlier, it would have disappeared ten years hence, by 1860. It's still there by the way. Like all the others, she practiced the age-old tradition of travelers and tourists; she concluded her day's diary entry, "Mr. Frink carved our names upon the chimney, where are hundreds of others."[262]

Mica Littleton passed Chimney Rock on July 1, 1850, recording in his journal, "traveled 13 miles [opposite to chimney Rock] this morning. Stopped to Graze 11 o'clk. This chimney Rock is beautiful in appearance. It looks at this distance to be about 150 feet high, is said to be 250 feet. It can be seen from 20 to 25 miles with ease. A few miles west of chimney Rock are a group of Square masses reared up Some 250 feet high resembling the ruins of Some ancient Fortifications there are 5 of them. Some larger and higher than others they present a Huge hill of earth or Rock which could be Seen almost any distance."[263]

Lucena Parsons recorded a similar view. "July 27... Came opposite Chimney Rock which has been in sight since yesterday. It has been seen 30 miles off on a clear day. Three of us went to it. I was struck with amazement at the grandeur of the scene. It is large at the base & then runs up some 300 feet, the last 100 feet is nearly square & in the form of a chimney in the top of a round tower. We found thousands of names engraven in every place up & down its sides. There are similar hills in the vicinity. Some look like churches with spires and others like houses."[264]

J. Goldsborough Bruff remembered Chimney Rock in his journal, but not because he had any interest in describing the scene. Rather, the day, "July 4 ... marshaled the company, fired a feu-dejoi [rifle salute] visited by a squad of our N. York friends, whom we received with military honors, and filed in between 2 wagons, covered over and arranged for dinner; where by request I delivered an address, and at 3 sat down (on the ground) to a sumptuous repast, of pork & beans, buffalo meat, sort of rolls, hard bread, bean soup, & stewed dried apples. Dessert — apple pie. After removal of the tin platters and iron spoons, the medical stores of brandy and port-wine, were used up in drinking a set of regular, and some volunteer toasts. The ladies honored us with their presence on the occasion; and to them we were indebted for several pounds of dried apples, and decent pastry. From this camp Cathedral rock bears W. by S. about 6 miles off. Chimney-Rock W. by N. about 3 miles distance. Numerous graves in the area, most from cholera but one marker read, John Campbell, of Lafayette Co. Mo. Came to his death by the accidental discharge of his gun, while riding with a friend, June 21. 1849. Aged 18 years."[265]

Some emigrants, like Bruff, took note of the landmark, but otherwise did not have a lot to say. Samuel Jamison did not even know what he saw the first time it came into view, writing, "We came in sight of a rock this evening which we do not know the name of. We must be ten miles off. It presents a very beautiful appearance at that distance. I will learn the name hereafter." When he had learned the name he remembered Chimney Rock only for the fact that they had, "diner at chimney rock," and, "got my foot tramped very bad by a mule."[266] Henry Wellenkamp, in his normal economy of words, summed it up best when he wrote, "Tuesday, 4 June, passed Chimney Rock. A grand whim of nature, 300 feet high."[267]

Those traveling along the trail on the north side of the Platte could also see the great landmarks. Caleb Booth, going out in 1850, wrote on June 15, "Still traveling up the Platte. Sometimes on the margin of the river, some-

Chimney Rock, one of the great landmarks along the Platte, by J. Goldsborough Bruff. Reproduced by permission of *The Huntington Library*, San Marino, California.

times 2 or 3 miles back where the river sometimes though not often washes the bluffs. We take up them over the sandhills. Today we passed over what are called the Cobble Hills. Chimney Rock, 20 or 30 miles distant, appears to view, looking more like the spire of a church at so distant a point than a rock." Two days later Booth "Passed Chimney Rock. Though at the distance of 7 miles, it made a fine appearance; looking some like a mud chimney built on the tip top of a clay or sandhill."[268]

Henry Edmundson, also on the north side of the Platte, recorded his initial encounter with the landmarks in his diary, writing on June 24, 1850, "To day at noon we passed some Bluffs on the right of the road, Some of the company ascended them and saw the Chimney Rock a distance of 45 miles." That distance is the farthest any emigrants reported seeing the landmark. "In the afternoon we passed the ancient Bluff ruins. They are high bluffs composed of very soft stone and which from the washing of the rains or other causes have assumed the appearance of Ancient Castles or fortifications." The next day, seeing Chimney Rock from a much closer advantage, Edmundson wrote a brief description and his conclusions about its future. "The chimney Rock commences in the shape of a Cone then running up to a great height something in the form of a chimney from which circumstances it takes its name; Originally it was doubtless one of the largest isolated Rocks or Bluffs so common in the vicinity of the Platte river and being very soft the action of the frost and rain has reduced it to its present shape."[269]

Scotts Bluff

Another day's journey, approximately 25 miles, brought the emigrants to the next great geographic landmark, Scotts Bluff. If the Chimney Rock had been a singular sentinel of the coming foothills and the end of the plains, then Scotts Bluff, to the emigrants, served as a true demarcation line. There were rocks and hills, and springs, and some found timber again, and the fabulous geologic formations continued. "They are sand hills intermixt with rock or a hard substance resembling rock that rise & tower over the other like splendid mansions with numerous chimneys rising to a great height. They are called Scotts Bluffs & extend from Chimney rock to Pony creek, a distance of 30 miles," remembered Lucena Parsons. She added, in the fashion in which she always wrote, "Went 12 miles, past 7 graves."[270]

Franklin Starr recalled his party "traveled 20 miles and camped at a spring on a ridge back of Scotts bluff. The bluffs and the hills are very picturesque resembling ruins and fortifications on every hand. Some hills will rise perpendicular and then have a flat top out of which another shaft rises and some a succession of such shelves and as regular as masons work. Some square some round making the place look like the ruins of a city."[271]

J. A. Pritchard recounted the story of how the bluffs got their name in his diary entry on June 1, 1849. "We were at the point from which the road leaves the river to pass to the left of Scotts bluffs. Scotts bluffs took its name from a man of that name [Hiram], who was a trapper—and in descending the river he was taken sick—and left, by his ungrateful companions to perish—They returned and reported that he had died and that they buried him—The next year his remains were found by some trappers who were passing that way—and with him a journal that gave a full account of the whole transaction—And from that circumstance the bluffs took their name—This bluff is a very large and isolated pile of soft sandstone or rather a calcareous formation of sand and clay. As you are passing it bye and the differences are exhibited—it presents almost every variety of architectural shape that you can imagine, arches, pillars, dome, spire, minaret, temple, gothic castle, a magnificence and grandeur—fair surpassing the constructive efforts of human strength and energy. I involuntarily imagined myself in the midst of the desolate and deserted ruins of vast cities of the Old World, to which Petra, Thebes, Babylon, and Nineveh were but pigmas [pigmies?] in point of grandeur and magnificence."[272]

Besides encountering the "magnificence and grandeur" of Mother Nature, the emigrants also encountered people. "Scott's Bluffs. Here is a trading house kept by a white man who is married to a squaw. The roads were good. We left the river after driving 5 miles. There is a blacksmith shop here also," wrote Amos Josselyn.[273] Niles Searls recorded the handiwork of nature and echoed what Josselyn had seen, writing on June 25, 1849, "Scotts Bluff, like many others which we have passed, is an isolated pile of rocks, resembling on a magnified scale, a combination of all the different styles of architecture. When seen in the distance, it bears a good resemblance to an ancient castle of feudal times. Passing on one-half a mile we encamped near another ravine close by another equally good spring, with plenty of wood for cooking purposes skirting the bluffs. Near this is the house of a Mr. Rubudone [probably Robidoux], a Canadian Frenchman, who has a native wife. Keeps a grocery and a blacksmith shop." Searls also recounted another advantage of reaching Scotts Bluff, adding, "Ascending the range of hills to the west, Laramie Peak, and the black Hills were distinctly visible."[274]

Bruff also recorded seeing the trading post when he passed in early July, 1849. "Camp near Scott's Bluffs, about 1 mile from a trading-post of Rubedeaux's [Robidoux]. This basin, among the singular and romantic bluffs, is a beautiful spot. It appears to extend E. & W. about 5 miles and about 3 miles wide. In a deep gulch lies a cool clear spring and brook. Close by is a group of Indian lodges & tents, surrounding a log cabin, where you can buy whisky for $5 per gallon; and look at the beautiful [probably written in sarcasm] squaws, of the traders. Flour here sells for 10 cents per lb. At. W. end of Bluffs you have the 1st sight of Lariamie peak, about 60 miles off. Beautiful large

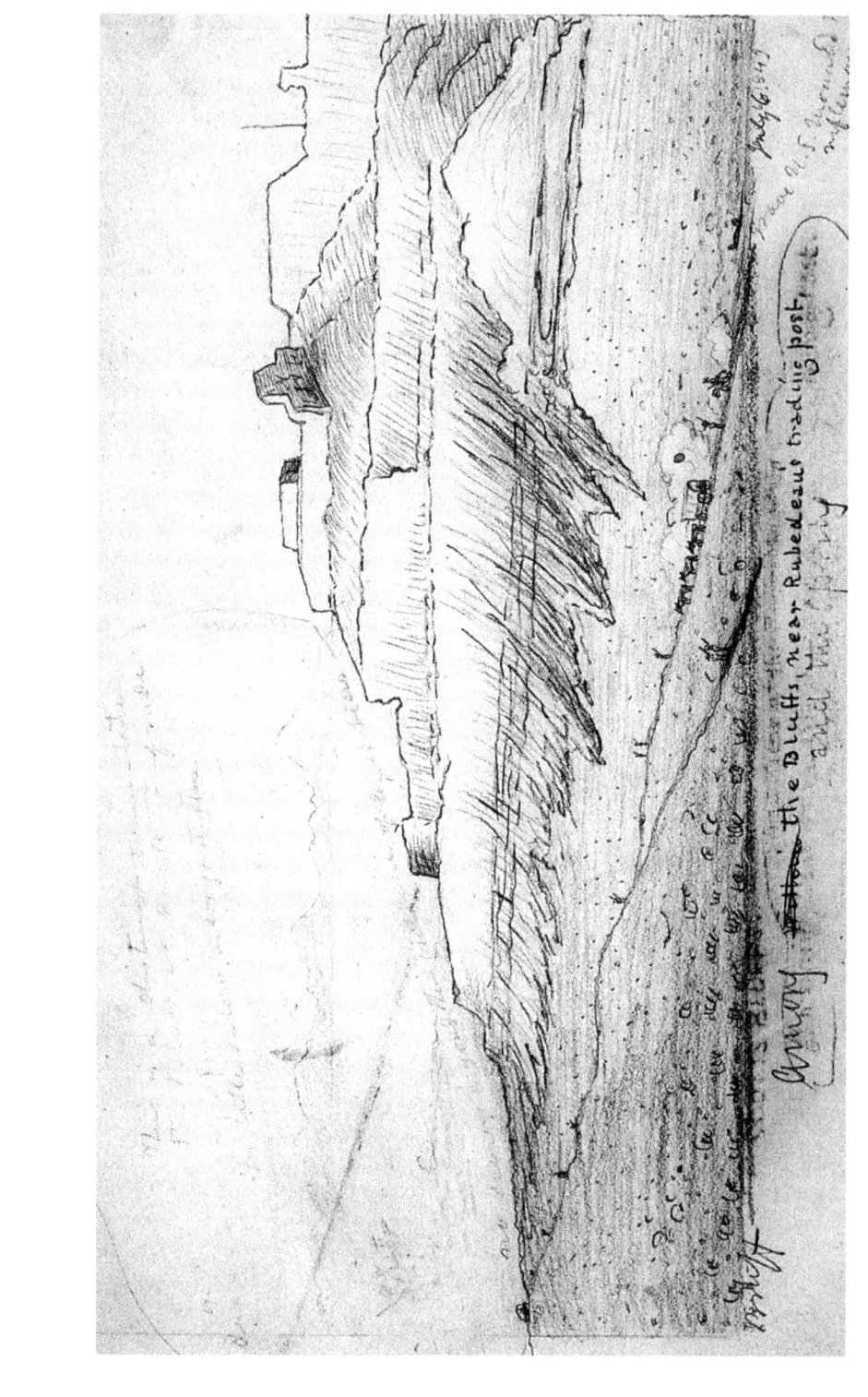

orange colored poppys, and a small animal of the Lemur genus with cheek pouches filled with grass seed. Scattered Sage in the plains. I killed a large rattle snake."[275]

Mica Littleton's party camped near the bluff in early July, 1850. "Now grazing opposite to Scotts Bluffs. In the Valley to the left of the bluffs a Point of mounds with one looking like a large Doam on Some public building. To the right of us the valley or gap behind Scotts bluffs appears to have Sinks for all this Ravines to discharge their water in. Where you come to the first Bluff on the left there is a deep ravine in this and others to your right there are Springs. At this time Some Indians and a blacksmith at those Springs. Passed 9 graves, one Mary Ann McNulty, aged 14."[276]

Sarah Davis did not recall much about the geologic formation of Scotts Bluff but did seem to be concerned about the number of Indians. "June 28 … we nooned near scots bluffs and traveled eighteen miles and then crost the bluffs we crost the bluffs near an Indian viledge they ware [were] siouse indians and some french men among them they had a store and a blacksmith shop their ware plenty of them they ware expecting a fight every night from the crow Indians."[277]

Samuel Jamison passed Scotts Bluff on May 27, 1850. He encountered the same traders, the Robidoux, whom he referred to as French. There are several notable things about his entry that day. First, his party decided to leave their wagons, and secondly, he called the bluffs by a name other than Scotts, for which there is no explanation given. "Lay by and traded with the french for one horse. Made three pack saddles and made a great many repairs. We now will commence to pack. Sold fifty dollars worth of provisions. A great many trains passed this day. Nats [gnats] not so bad as have been. This place is called Smiths Bluffs there is a fine spring here."[278]

Henry Wellenkamp succinctly recalled the main points. "Wednesday, 5 June, to Scott's Bluff and spring. The bluffs are 300 feet high, fine grass on top, here I had the first blue glimpse of Rocky Mountains."[279] Lucena Parsons, writing in her diary near Scotts Bluff, recalled she "met 3 mewl [mule] teams from Fort Larimee. They told us it was 50 miles to the Fort. It seems like home again to met so many on the road. I found the skull of a man by the roadside. I took it on & buried it at the point. There is a blacksmith shop here for the accommodations of emigrants kept by a French man [again, probably Antoine Robidoux, a former trapper]. Here are a number of stick huts & I am told they keep a good assortment of dry goods. The whole 50 waggons met & campt. The rattlesnakes are very thick here."[280]

Opposite: Near Scott's Bluff in western Nebraska, the vicinity of Rubedeau's (Robidoux) trading post, by J. Goldsborough Bruff. Reproduced by permission of *The Huntington Library*, San Marino, California.

On to Fort Laramie

Beyond Scotts Bluff, Fort Laramie lay approximately 50 miles away — two or three days' travel, depending on how tired the teams of animals, and the travelers themselves felt. The landscape of the plains lay much behind them and each new vista brought glimpses of the still distant Rocky Mountains a bit closer. While the landscape changed, dealing with the many variables of trail life and the tremendous array of personalities, and characters, in life and death, did not. Most diarists wrote very little about that span of the trail, but a couple had some significant things to say, if not about the geography, then the continued human interaction. Pritchard described little after leaving Scotts Bluff, recalling only that, "we left camp this morning at 4 A.M. to get a head of the trains that were crouding [crowding] us. The road was heavy and sandy all day, nothing of moment occurred."[281]

Israel Hale saw a tremendous variation in the land, between Scotts Bluff and Laramie, describing an early stretch of trail, writing, "We followed the valley about eight miles and encamped near the head. The bluffs are covered with cedar and is a most beautiful place with good grass and water." The next day he continued, "We drove over a rolling prairie for about twelve miles and turned out at a slough or break. We had to dig the banks before we could cross. This morning we saw some of the peaks of the Rocky Mountains and some who had sharp eyes say they saw snow." Referring to supplies dumped along the trail, Hale added, "Quantities of bacon, beans, etc are still found on the way." He concluded the day's travel by saying, "I have passed some most excellent land today for agricultural purposes, if timber was only at a reasonable distance."[282]

"The country passed over today was generally, sandy and barren, with sand stone. Met 2 wagons, 4 yoke of oxen, each, from Ft. Laramie, bound in to Missouri. An old silver-haired man drove one of them, and lied as though he had followed it all his life," wrote a skeptical J. Goldsborough Bruff. "He told me that he had been 60 miles west of Laramie, where the chief proprietor of the wagons died, it was the last request of the dying man that he would take them and his family back, to Missouri; he said that the widow and children were in one of the wagons. This old sinner told another man, that the cause of his return was, because the Indians, emigrants, & drought, had used up the grass W. of that 300 miles; and to another, he stated that insufficiency of provisions was the cause."[283]

Mica Littleton recalled, "there has been no wood since we left Scotts bluffs. There is some timber on the Islands but a long way to go to it. Passed 9 graves, among them Eliza H. Medley aged 7 years. Sick doing well today except Mr. Tucker he will not live till morning I think." The next day, July 4, 1850, Littleton added, "Our sick man Lewis K. Tucker is no more. He departed this life last night about 10 o'clock P.M. Perfectly resigned he was a member of the M.E. [Methodist Episcopal] Church and expressed his willingness to go (Blessed hope) he was committed to the last resting-place this morning at 6 o'clock. We are now 1½ miles from Fort Laramie. Past 19 graves [three women]."[284] Unlike Bruff, whose party made a point to observe the holiday, Littleton made no mention of any kind of July 4th celebrations.

Though the scourge of cholera along the lower Platte had subsided somewhat, death from disease in the guise of cholera continued to grimly carry off the gold seekers. It caught up with the party of J. Goldsborough Bruff, who had not yet been visited by the dread cholera, while they headed for Fort Laramie. He captured the melancholy of watching a man die and then burying him, in his journal on July 8, 1849. "We moved on, and the train had only gone its length when I was informed that a member, who had, last night complained of indisposition was now dangerously ill. I found the wagon of his messmates standing there, and the Surgeon attending him. The Dr. told me he had all the symptoms of Asiatic cholera. His messmates said that for several days he had complained of indisposition, and had also drank of Slew water, which I had cautioned the men against using. At 11 A.M. he was deranged, saying he was not afraid to die, and requesting his friends to shoot him. At 1 P.M. poor Bishop died, of Cholera. The first casualty in the Company, sudden and astounding, was this very mysterious and fatal visitation. The messmates of the deceased laid him out, sewed him up in his blue blanket, and prepared a bier, formed of his tent poles."

Because of Bruff's fastidiousness, his man got a much more elaborate funeral on the trail then did most. "I had a grave dug in a neighboring ridge, on left of the trail, about 400 yards from it. Dry clay and gravel, and coarse white sandstone on the next hill, afforded slabs to line it with, making a perfect vault. I sat 3 hours in the hot sun, and sculptured a head and foot stone; and filled the letters with blacking from the hub of a wheel. I then organized a funeral procession, men all in clean clothing and uniforms, with music, (a key bugle, flute, violin and accordion) and two and two, with the Stars & stripes over the body, we marched to the measured time of the dirge, deposited the body of our comrade in the grave, an elderly gentleman ran the burial service, and we filled up the grave, erected the stones, and returned to camp."[285]

Bruff's party, after taking most of a day to conduct their funeral, pushed on toward Laramie the next day. Men grew tired, and personalities that had managed to get along for the first seven weeks of the trek began to conflict. Questionable water, food, dust, insects, disease, and death and general hardship all contributed. While some conditions might improve, others got no better or deteriorated. On July 9, 1849, Bruff touched on a variety of the aforementioned issues. "Here plenty of grass, fuel, mosquitoes, flies, and gnats. Biting and stinging insects in the hollow drove them [mules] up on the road, in a great hurry, switching their tails furiously. A guard-sergeant

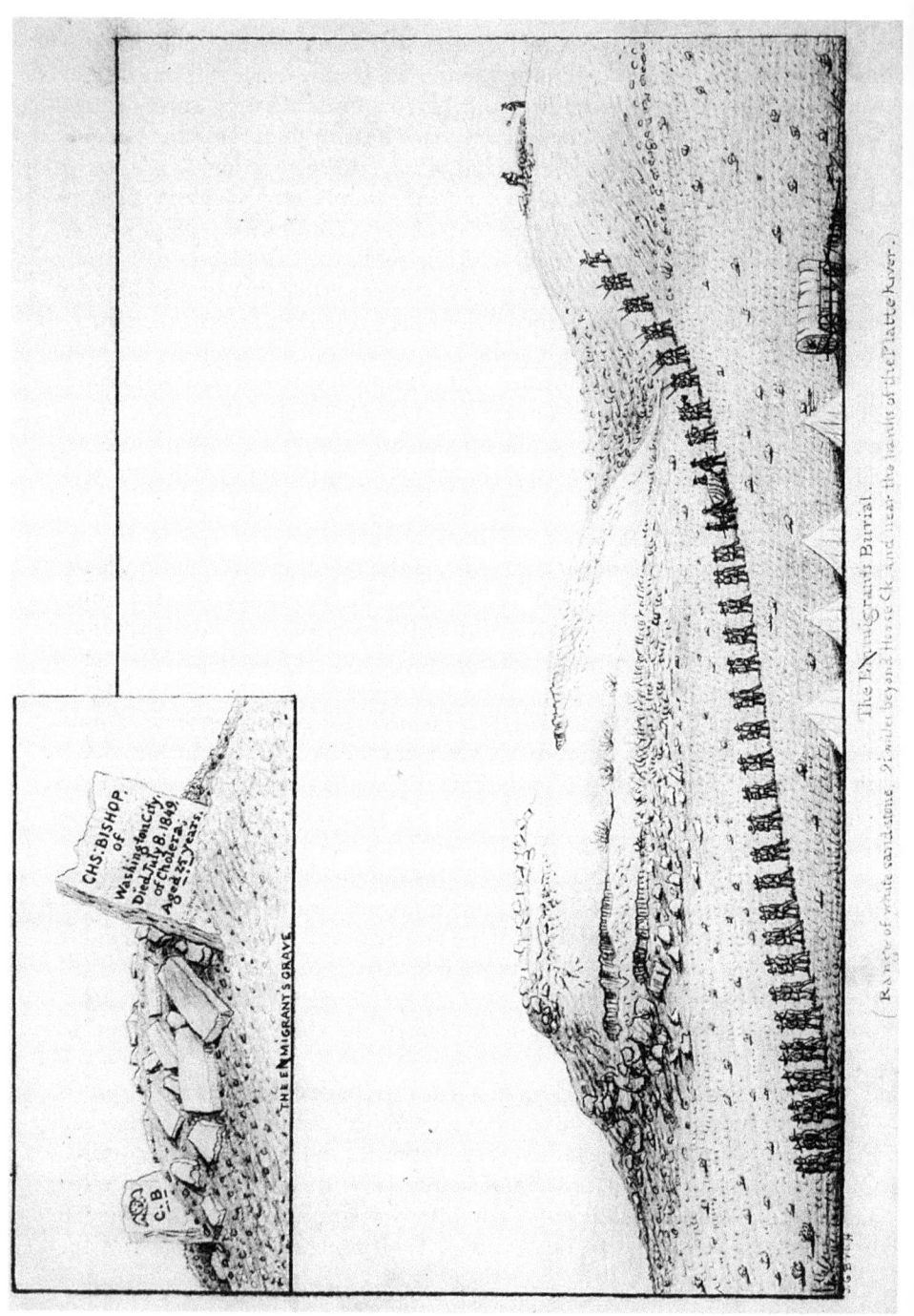

The Emigrants Burial.
(Range of white sandstone 3 miles beyond the sick and near the banks of the Platte River.)

struck one of the men violently in the face, upon which I immediately convened the Company into a drum-head court, tried the offender, broke him of his office, and inflicted 4 extra guards on him," commented Bruff stoically. "The march this forenoon, was exceedingly warm & dusty. The dust here is very annoying, an impallable powder, put in motion by the trains, and blowing directly in our faces." Further, he reflected on what he considered a quirk of human nature. "All the accessible faces of blocks & cliffs, were marked and inscribed with names, initials, & dates. This peculiar vanity has been displayed all along the route, from our frontier down into the valley of the Sacramento. Nothing escapes that can be marked upon. buffalo sculls, stumps, logs, trees, rocks, etc. Even the slab at the heads of graves, are all marked by this propensity of 'pencilling by the way.'"[286]

Shortly before reaching Fort Laramie, John Nevin King wrote a letter to his brother Charles, dated June 11, 1850, and sent it to be posted from there. In it he describes how the express company which he had signed on with faired on its trek along the Platte and provides some important insights into the trip and the mind of a young gold seeker. "I wrote to Father from Fort Kearney & gave him an account of all that occurred up to that time. I informed him that we were all getting along very [well], but since I wrote we have had 3 deaths from Cholera and one Diarrhea, besides having several other cases of sickness which being attended to in due time were cured. Our train has been divided into 4 divisions and our mess was unfortunate enough as to fall into the rear division and I judge we will be some 10 days in California after our first division of the train. For some few days we traveled 20 miles per day until we came to where the road was sandy. Our mules, having nothing now to feed upon but grass, begin to look badly enough and I think that from this and if we average 20 miles per day we will be doing very well. The first division of our train will perhaps go through in 80–85 days and from present appearances will take us about 100. Good grass on this route is scarce. Wood and Water far from Camping grounds. Already we have had to go to bed supperless. Sometime we find Buffalo Chips which are a very good substitute for fuel. Night before last we had to carry water in buckets upward of 3 miles and wood nearly 3, the wood & water being in opposite direction. That evening Buffalo chips are scarce. You might judge they would be when we are behind some 20 or perhaps 40 thousand emigrants and it takes upon an average about 5 bushels for to cook supper & breakfast for twelve persons.

"As soon as we reach Camp it devolves upon me to make the bread & coffee. We are divided into messes of 12 each & one has to help do cooking,

Opposite: The burial of one of Bruff's men. A rather more elaborate ceremony than for the vast majority of emigrants who died along the way. Reproduced by permission of *The Huntington Library*, San Marino, California.

tis not here as twas in Mexico. [Reference to his service in the Mexican War.] There I could always find someone who would do both my cooking and washing for a small compensation but here tis different every person does his own washing & all assist in cooking. While I make bread some grind coffee others bring water, wood, cut and fry meat make coffee, stew dried apples & peaches or make some Mush, Boil rice and one other washing the dishes. I do the making up of the bread & assist in putting up the tent for my share — one Bakes the bread for his share. I have about the easiest to do & I now can make as fair biscuit as you ever tasted. With our rice & mush we eat sugar. I am now very fond of mush, anything for a change. We have plenty to eat and so long as we have I for one cannot complain very much.

"McPike and Strothers Express line has broken up, mules all broken down and passengers all footing it. Jerome Hanson & Smiths proprietors of an other Express line expected to lay in a supply of provisions at Fort Laramie but they found they could not obtain anything & now just for carelessness in not starting with enough they will have to go to Salt Lake for a new supply or go to California upon half rations as reports say they are now on. Brandy sells along the route here at $12.00 per gallon."[287]

Around Fort Laramie

Except for the trading posts at Scotts Bluff, most emigrants hand not seen the home of a white person since leaving Fort Kearney, before arriving at Fort Laramie. Though a grimy looking outpost compared to towns of the East, with their wood and brick houses, green trees and plush fields of grain and grass, most emigrants experienced a sense of relief, if only briefly, when they arrived at Fort Laramie. Most stayed only a few hours, for the crowds of emigrants, as well as the fact that camping facilities and grazing around the fort had long been used up, necessitating that they move on. Fort Laramie provided a logical place for emigrants to make some long put off repairs, reorganize their stock and companies, and make some decisions that would have crucial impact further along the trail.

J. A. Pritchard reached Fort Laramie on June 4, 1849. Though he wrote a brief description of the outpost, his concerns centered on problems within his company. "Fort Laramie is built of adobe or sun-dried brick it is a one story house with several out houses dwellings etc. It is surrounded by high wall — of the same material, and stands immediately on the North banks of Laramie's [Laramie Fork] of the Platte — And it looks more like a place of desolation than like a place for protection — In consequence of the disagreement among several of the members of our company — we were here driven to the necessity of dividing it. The Company in the division split 5 and 3, one wagon each, drew lots for the old mules, split ⅝ of all provisions — The gold washer, gold scales & $75 in money. Disagreement was settled by a jury of three disinterested men from an Ill. company."[288]

Despite the internal conflict and an agreement to divide, Pritchard complained in his journal, "I indignantly rejected the proposition and told Hardesty [one of the instigators of the breakup] that under the circumstances I considered the proposition not only ungentlemanly but dishonorable. I had been at all the trouble of making the outfit I had spent my time and part of my personal funds without one cents charge to the company And not one member of the company had been to one cents expense or one hours trouble, except to put into the Treasury the amount due the company to make the outfit and not only that — that I was doing this thing of separating because Wilkie & Hardesty could not agree with Youell & Stephens — And that Youell, Stephens, Abbott, McNeely, and now Norris, could not agree I remarked to Hardesty. These things being true — I have been induced to use the strong language I have."[289]

Eleven days behind Pritchard, Israel Hale reached Fort Laramie on June 15, 1849, writing one of the best descriptions of the fort and the scene around it. "After a drive of three miles we came to the Laramie River where we raised our wagon beds by means of blocks and crossed the river dry. The river is one hundred and fifty yards wide and where we crossed four feet deep. It had raised from recent rains. The first object of note was Fort John, a short distance from the ford. It is an abandoned fort and from the appearance at the road was nothing but the bare walls which are made of unburnt brick called 'dobaes' [adobe].

"One mile up the river and near the bank stands Fort Laramie. It is also made of the same kind of materials as Fort John but is in tolerable good condition. It is one hundred and forty or fifty feet square and about two stories high. A row of buildings extends round the fort, the wall of the fort forming the outside or one side of the houses. It is now occupied by the American Fur Company. They have a store, blacksmith shop and some other shops all within the walls of the fort. Many emigrants have left their wagons or sold them here for five dollars but they cannot be bought from the fort men for less than from thirty to seventy-five according to quality. It is said that the government have or are about to purchase the fort to establish a military post here for the protection of emigrants and traders. We remained at the fort two or three hours and drove out three miles and encamped on the Platte with wood, water and grass of fair quality. The destruction of property is immense. On the road from the fort I saw a good side saddle left, also a nearly new wagon cut to pieces near our camp. I saw a wagon — tolerable good but heavy — bacon, beans, stoves, chairs, iron wedges, crow bar, soap, lead, ovens and many other articles all laying about in the prairie. They could not use them and they could not carry them, and the only alternative was to leave them."[290]

Sallie Hester passed Laramie within four days of Hale. "Fort Laramie,

Fort Laramie.
(N.E. Angle)

This fort is of adobe, enclosed with a high wall of the same. The entrance is a hole in the wall just large enough for a person to crawl through. The impression you have on entering is that you are in a small town. Men were engaged in all kinds of business from blacksmith up. We stayed here some time looking at everything that was to be seen and enjoying it to the fullest extent after our long tramp. We camped one mile from the fort, where we remained a few days to wash and lighten up."[291]

Niles Searls came to Fort Laramie toward the end of June, 1849, about in the middle of the main wave of migration. He arrived just as the transfer from the American Fur Company to the United States Army, alluded to by Hale who passed the fort three weeks earlier, took place. "The whole country is desolate and rugged presenting a few attractions to the traveler. Laramies Fork, which stream we crossed one mile below the Fort, is a swift running stream with about three feet of water. Fort Laramie stands on the north side of Laramie Fork, a few rods from the stream and one mile south of the Platte. The Fort is constructed of adobes, the various buildings being built around an open Court, of about one-fourth square mile or less area. The buildings are all flat-roofed and covered with earth in the Mexican style. The principal entrance is on the side facing the river. The establishment formerly belonged to the American Fur Company but has just been sold to the government for the sum of 1000 dollars, possession to be given tomorrow. This is the point at which many of the emigrants change other modes of conveyance for pack animals. Wagons are being burnt or sold at prices varying from twenty-five cents to thirty dollars. Articles of almost every description are abandoned on the road. Provisions for sixty days are to be taken and we are promised that within that time we shall reach Sutter's Fort."[292] Searls further commented on the depressing scene around Laramie the next day, writing, "the country around us presents a dreary desolate appearance. The grass being parched with drought." However, he did find something refreshing in the otherwise melancholy landscape. "I bathed in the stream and found the effects beneficial."[293]

J. Goldsborough Bruff arrived in the vicinity of Fort Laramie on July 9, 1849, crossing over to reconnoiter the fort in his military style and make social contacts. "Ford of Laramie River. Here we had to block some of the wagon beds up, to keep the contents dry. About 100 yards over. Several hundred yards back from the river's bank, on the right, stood the old adobe walls of Fort Platte [possibly Fort John, referred to in other diaries], the original post of the fur traders, now in ruin; and looks like an old Castle. Rectangular. After crossing I directed the train to continue, to a Camp of American

Opposite: A contemporary view of Fort Laramie as it appeared in 1849, by J. Goldsborough Bruff. Reproduced by permission of *The Huntington Library*, San Marino, California.

Fur traders & Indians. Here I was welcom'd very kindly, by Mr. Husband — superintendent of the Fur Trading post. He had a letter for me that he had turned over to the Officer at the Fort who was acting as Post Master."[294]

The next day Bruff hobnobbed with the genteel class of Fort Laramie. "I spent the forenoon at the Fort. Major Simons treated me most kindly. Fort Laramie, purchased by our Government, from the American Fur Company is an extensive rectangular structure of adobe. It forms an open area within — houses & balconies against the walls. Heavy portals and watch tower and square bastions at 2 angles, infilading the faces of the main walls. It has suffered much from time and neglect. We bought a small seine here for $10. A very useful article. A nearby trail passes through a burial ground of Traders, and mountaineers. Several picket rectangular enclosures contained one or more graves: several had crosses erected on them, and one, in particular, on the right, containing a single grave, was filled in with buffalo scules [skulls] and deer horns, and also embellished with a rude wooden cross. This I presumed was the grave of some Mountain Nimrod. Other graves near the fort; T. Green. of Cholera, Jackson Co. Mo. 20 June. and Nathan Noland, of Independence, Mo. Aged 47 June 3."[295]

Those passing Fort Laramie in 1850 found a similar scene to those who reached it the year before. Only the emigration seemed to have increased in 1850. Samuel Jamison recorded the statistics he heard from various sources around Laramie in his journal. The accuracy is probably good. Beginning on May 29, he wrote, "traveled 30 miles passed 33 wagons encamped one mile this side of Fort Laramie on the left of the road. There we got the amount of emigrants horses mules oxen wagons: Men 6,582, women 61, children 38, wagons 1,849, horses 6,633, mules 2,268, oxen 1,062, cows 76." The next day, as Jamison's party rested at the fort for a while, he observed, "there had one thousand emigrants passed this day until 12 o'clock. Very heavy hale storm. A great many wagons layed by. A great deal of property destroyed of all kinds."[296]

Margaret Frink and her husband found some brief respite from the trail at Fort Laramie but she had in no way convinced herself of anything but that the best part of going to see the elephant still lay ahead of her. "When we came to the Laramie River, the water was very high, and ran into our wagon. This is a dangerous ford, where a number of persons have been drowned," she reported. "At four o'clock we arrived at the place we have so long been anxious to reach, Fort Laramie. This outpost formerly belonged to the American Fur Company, who built it as a protection against the savages, then very numerous and hostile. After the United States government bought it, they sent regular troops to protect the emigration. As it is not our intention to go by Salt Lake, this is the last human habitation we shall see until we reach Fort Hall, five hundred and thirty miles further on." Then no doubt quoting from her guidebooks, "The altitude of Fort Laramie is four thousand four hundred and seventy feet. This is almost four thousand feet higher than our starting-point. But we are not yet half way up to the highest point of our road, and have traveled not half its length."[297]

William Frush, who had left St. Joseph in pursuit of his brother, caught up with him at Fort Laramie. He spent more time there than most and wrote a number of interesting observations about the place and the people coming and going. "10th June Monday. Rode 6 miles to Fort Laramie — arrived at 7 oclk A.M. Crowded hard and got our Breakfast at 37½ [cents] each. Registered my name and went back on road 3 miles to graze horses. There is a vast quantity of waggons left here. Traders pretend to trade for them but pay nothing. I can buy of them a new waggon of choice for $25. A waggon & 4 set harness cost in States $100. Given for 4 pack saddles, they sell here at $2 a piece. Returned to Fort at night & got supper & lodged in map room. Bought today 2 lbs. coffee 70 cents, 2 lbs. sugar 60 cents, 8 lbs. bacon 90 cents."

Lying by another day, Frush witnessed a little excitement between a man named Smith, his messmate and a third man who apparently had a dispute with Smith's friend. "See 1 pirty [pretty] fight at Fort to day with two men in waggon mess. The 3rd man wanted to make peace & Smith one of the 1st, made for his arm after getting a pistol. His antagonist disarmed him and did not use the weapon but Smith made them run their vary best to get out of his way. The 3rd man he made up with & went on. The other started to the Fort to have the matter settled by court's office."[298]

William Frush waited until June 18, 1850, before his brother arrived. He had left St. Joseph hoping to catch up with him on the trail but apparently unknowingly passed him by. Besides meeting with his brother and other friends, Frush had the chance to meet a bonafide American legend, Kit Carson. "At noon John H. Frush, George Griffith & Wm. & Al Lawson crossed Laramie Fork when I took up with them and passed on 6 miles west of Fort and encamped in Co. with the horse shoe train. Left at Fort in camp with Mr. Metcalf, Kit Carson the celebrated Rocky Mt. guide. His advise to me was to go by the way of Oregon to California as the immense Emigration ahead would destroy all the grass on St. Marey [Mary's or Humboldt] River." Frush also provided some important numbers in his diary, for he apparently went to the recording office and jotted down the figures for the emigration of 1850, up to the date of his entry. "Boys all well. No. of Men up to day passed this Fort; 30,964. Women 439. Children 508. Waggons 7,113. Horses 19,866, Mules 6,470. Oxen 18,238. Cows 2,758."[299] Considering that the emigration would continue to pass Fort Laramie at least through the end of July, those are impressive figures.

Those who had come up the Platte on the north side found it advantageous to cross the North Fork at Fort Laramie and join the emigration that had come up on the south bank. Caleb Booth, one of those traveling the north bank of the Platte, wrote of reaching the vicinity of Fort Laramie on June 20,

1850, and of the flow of emigrants and the reason for crossing there. "Traveled about twelve miles and encamped near the Fort [Laramie]. Numerous companies encamped all about us. The boat at the crossing [from the north bank to the south bank of the Platte] has been cut loose and a new one is building which will soon be done. Between 7 and 8,000 wagons have already passed the Fort. The name of the company & men are taken as are also the number of cattle. Some 200 wagons have gone up this side of the river, but it is said to be impossible to force a passage."[300] That last point referenced the ruggedness of the bluffs on the north side of the river.

Unlike most of the trains passing Laramie, Booth's party stayed a while for some important repairs. During that time he recorded some important observations. "It is reported that seven have died of Cholera at the Fort within a few days," he wrote on June 21, indicating that though the cholera had diminished its attack somewhat it still took opportunity to attack new victims. Still across the Platte from the fort, two days after arriving, and still waiting for the boat to be finished to ferry their wagons over, he continued his diary writing. "For the sake of getting shoes for our cattle we burnt a coal pit last night. We have several smiths in our company and there is a set of tools at the Fort which they can have the use of providing they furnish the coal."[301]

With the boat finally finished, Caleb Booth and his party crossed the Platte on June 23, and arrived at the fort. "Swam our cattle and put off at a pretty late hour," he wrote, referring to getting over the river late in the night. "Fort Laramie is situated on the Laramie River, 2 or 3 miles above its junction with the Platte and about 1 mile from the ferry. The place is full of life at this time as the emigrants are almost continually passing. Between 30 and 40,000 having already registered their names. It consists of an arsenal, hospital, store, blacksmiths shop, several long horse stables, a few private dwellings, tents, &c. A great many wagons are also standing about, many of which the emigrants left and which can be had for little or nothing. There are at present 200 men stationed here, a part of whom are going to Oregon this season."[302]

William Edmundson, who had also come up the north side of the Platte, arrived at Laramie a week behind Booth in 1850. He immediately heard news that likely made him feel much better about his decision to do so. "Arrived opposite Fort Laramie," he wrote on June 29. "Some Emigrants crossed from the Fort who had come up on the South Side of the Platte River who informed us that the Cholera had been very fatal among the emigrants on that rout." When he crossed the next day he described the military units stationed at the fort. "The fort is now occupied by 2 companies of Infantry and one company of Mounted Riflemen under the command of Major Sanderson. An office is kept here in which is registered the name and former residence of each emigrant traveling this rout."[303]

Lucena Parsons, passing toward the end of the migration in 1850, did not reach the area around Laramie until the beginning of August, 1850. She wrote, on August 1, "traveled 15 miles. This brought us to Fort Larimee which we were glad to see as here we crosst the Larimee fork of the Platte. The Fort is built on the Larimee fork some 1½ miles from the river. We had no trouble in fording, though there have been 5 men drowned here this spring in crossing their teams. They were carried down by the current which is very swift even now. We past a camp of Indians to day that have the small pox. They have it very bad & many of them have died. We saw one squaw dead under a blanket & her papoose wailing round her sick." The next day Parsons' company "went to the Fort to get some blacksmithing done but could not — they have so much work. This is a very pretty place to look at, it is so clean. The Fort is command by a Major Anderson [actually Winslow Sanderson] he is a fine man. There are 250 soldiers & some 12 families. They have a sawmill, one public house, one store. They hold goods high & work is also high. They offer for carpenter work 60 a month & find them, & a woman to cook 20 a month. Flour is 18 [dollars] per hundred & whiskey 8 per gallon in the emigrants store. They are now building several fine frame buildings. They say there have [been] 75 thousand pass here this season & some days there were 1500 here. There was some sickness among them & some deaths. There are hundreds of waggons left here which can be bought for a few dollars each from the soldiers. Weather dry and very dusty."[304]

Laying over another day at the fort, Parsons continued in her diary on August 3, "We stopped to let the teams rest here to day & the men went to work & burnt coal to doe their own blacksmithing. They have a bellows & anvil & are now busy preparing to shoe the cattle as their hoofs are wearing out with driving over the gravelly roads. The women are baking, washing, cleaning, & repacking wagons as they do when we stop. We have plenty of good grass & water & are in sight of the Black Hills which we expect to begin to ascend soon after leaving here."[305]

John Nevin King, writing home from the trail just past Fort Laramie, did not have a lot to say about the fort itself, but did have complaints common to many who had signed on with and paid so called express companies, and yet endured real maltreatment and hardship on the trek to Laramie, only the first third of the journey to see the elephant. In a letter dated June 16, 1850, he wrote, "Some few of our Mules have already given out our wagon covers leak and a good many persons have better outfit's than we. Hall has made himself very unpopular. He knows nothing about conducting a train. I have spoken concerning the train being divided. I think as Hall is in the advance he wishes to make pretty good time with his part of the train & we will travel just fast enough to prevent our mules from falling off. I think the whole train is conducted shamefully. When these men who died were taken sick they should have stopped the wagons belonging to the mess & remained until they died or were able to travel. They had the proper medicines administered & in due time, but traveling over the rough ground when passing other Trains brought back the Diarrhea & death was inevitable. Our mess, if any are taken sick intend to stopping. Hall will have no control over us that we are determined upon.

"Tell the boys if the last part of this road is not better than the first they need never think of crossing the plains. We have been in sight of the '*Elephant*' ever since we passed Fort Kearney."[306]

Part II
From Fort Laramie to Fort Hall and Salt Lake City

Into the Black Hills

The next leg of the journey took the emigrants from Fort Laramie to the ferry on the North Fork of the Platte, a distance of roughly 110 miles. At the point of the ferry, the North Fork of the Platte turned abruptly south into the mountains, forcing the emigrants to cross it to continue westward. Between Laramie and the ferry lay the rugged upland country generally called the Black Hills, by the diarists. These are not to be confused with the more famous Black Hills, of the Dakotas, associated with George Armstrong Custer and later Indian Wars with the Sioux and Cheyenne. Those lie north and a bit east of Fort Laramie.

Besides the Black Hills, some emigrants make reference to passing the Red Hills, a geologic oddity of the region. And most record crossing a number of smaller tributaries of the Platte in the region, with names such as Horseshoe Creek, Lafonte Creek, Plum Creek, La Perle, and LaFouche Bois Rivers. More accurately, they were probably crossing the northern edge of the Laramie Mountains, part of the Rocky Mountain Front Range. Most emigrants wrote about seeing Laramie Peak as a constant reference point to their south and west. If there had been any doubt before, in the minds of the emigrants, that the plains lay behind them it disappeared after Laramie. The rising of the now rocky trail grasped everyone's first impression, as they pushed off on the middle leg of the great trek. Summing up the attitude of most of the emigrants, probably better than any other diarists, Samuel Jamison wrote in his journal on June 3, 1850, "a race to the goldfields. Left camp at 6 o'clock traveled prity [sic] fast passed a great many emigrants. Came in sight of snow mountains."[1]

Pritchard left Laramie on June 5, 1849, and at first had variable impressions of the new surroundings ranging from bleak to sublime. "At this point we leave the river and commence crossing what is called the Black Hills. Our route today was over rough broken country, of sandy soil, barren and destitute of vegetation. Reached warm spring, nooned, timber and grass plenty. The face of the country was broken and carpeted with a beautiful coat of grass, besides the hills were covered with beautiful groves of seeder [cedar]

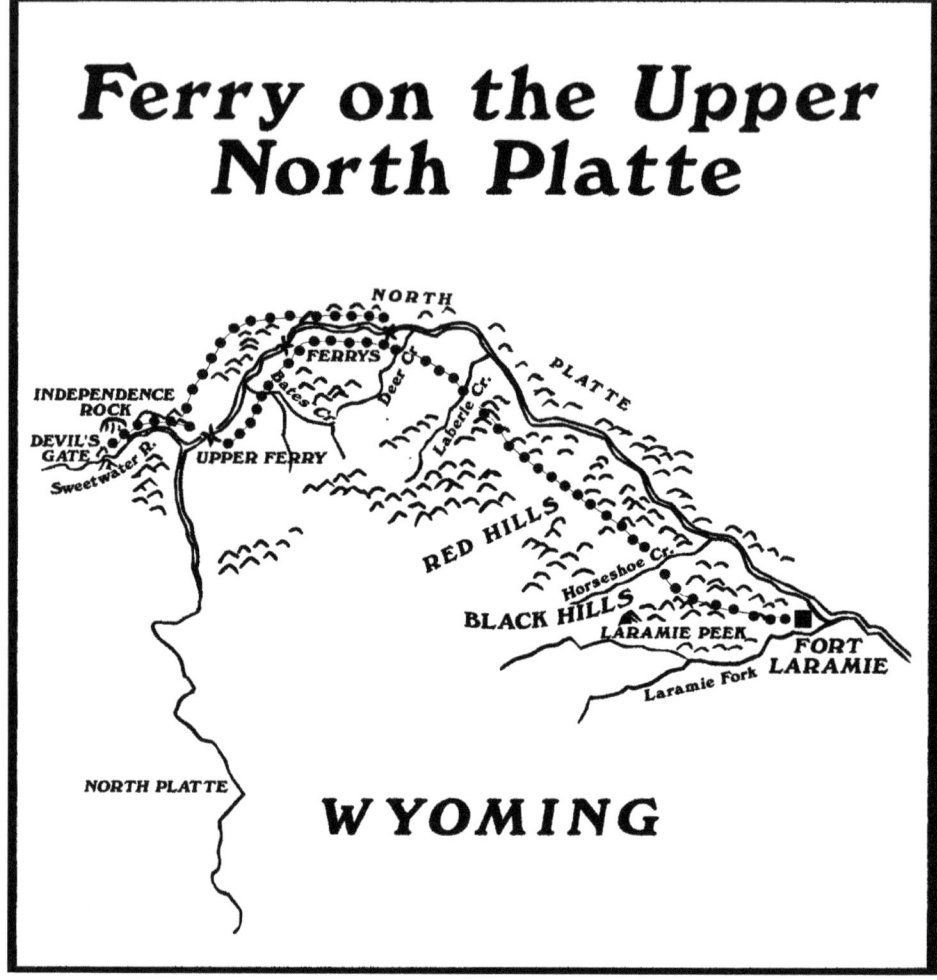

Ferry on the Upper North Platte — route from Fort Laramie to the ferry.

and pine. Just opposite Laramie peak. Upon the whole it was a most picturesque and lively landscape — most beautiful to the Eye — most grateful to the feelings."² The warm spring Pritchard mentioned lay about 12–15 miles west of Laramie (again depending on which diarist recorded the mileage) and was a landmark where emigrants often stopped to camp.

Israel Hale recalled leaving Laramie, writing on June 16, 1849, "This morning we got a late start owing to some of the steers being out. We followed the river [Platte] two or three miles and took across the hill. It was an open rolling prairie with cedar or pine hills in plain view, but no appearance of water until we drove ten or twelve miles, where we found a fine spring about a quarter of a mile to the right of the road. It affords us as much water as Houses Spring of Jefferson County, Missouri. The water however, was warm."[3]

Niles Searls left Fort Laramie on June 29, 1849, and like so many emigrants, "Encamped for noon at 'Warm Spring' twelve miles from Laramie. The spring flows from the base of a high bluff in quantity almost sufficient to turn a mill." While many emigrants stopped at the spring, Searls found that not all were heading west. "We frequently meet with emigrants returning home, even after having reached nearly to the South Pass. Some are deterred by sickness or accident from proceeding farther, others by the reports of the poor feed for stock in the mountains. It was but this morning that I met with an old acquaintance from Lafayette County, Mo., returning to Laramie under the most painful circumstances. A packhorse which had turned his pack and escaped from his owner, ran among their oxen while under headway and stampeded them. They ran with the wagons several miles and ran over three of the company. The former two were so badly injured as to render their recovery hopeless, and my friend Clinton Bledsoe was returning to leave them at the hospital when I saw them. The country through which we have passed has been for the most part more broken and covered with scattered trees, mostly small pines and cedars."[4]

J. Goldsborough Bruff's company left Laramie on July 12, 1849, and he remembered that they "Moved early: The trail is over a hilly, rugged, sand & limestone formation. After going 6 miles saw on the right, on a stony eminence, near trail, a grave, covered with sand stone slabs, and at the head a cedar board, carved with: Mrs. Mildred Moss, wife of D. H. T. Moss, late of Galena, Ill: Died July 7, 1849, Aged 25 years. A stick nailed to the headboard had a white cotton rag attached, like a flag: intended, no doubt, to attract the attention of some acquaintances in the rear. Soon reached the Warm-Spring brook, government wagon & men there, and lime-kilns [likely for making mortar] close by. In the stream noticed the remains of a dead horse, and those singular metamorphosis—horse-hair snakes, in various stages of transformation. Some the worm was only about 2 inches long, with a tail of 10–14 inches of horsehair, others longer. Passed a camp of 5 wagons, one of the party was in a tent dying of Cholera. We moved on among the Black Hills, the road good but tedious, up and down hill. Passed numerous places where emigrants had camped—thickly strewn with discarded effects. At Sun Set passed several dry beds is steams and at dusk corralled on the road, between cliffs and the river."[5]

The fact that emigrants continued to discard material that they had hauled for over 500 miles from the jumping-off points, seemed to still surprise some of the diarists, even though they found it necessary to periodically lighten their own loads, by whatever means fit the situation. Leaving Laramie on June 10, 1850, Margaret Frink recalled, "It was at this camp that we had to leave our cooking stove, which we had found so useful ever since crossing the Missouri. It being light, we had always carried it lashed on the hind end of the wagon. Some careless person, in a hurry, drove his team up too close behind, and the pole of his wagon ran into the stove, smashing and ruining it. After that we had to cook in the open air. We adopted a plan which was very fashionable on the plains. We would excavate a narrow trench in the ground, a foot deep and three feet long, in which we built the fire. The cooking vessels were set over this, and upon trial we found it a very good substitute." After rectifying their camp cooking facilities, the Frinks "traveled fifteen miles, the road was among and over the spurs of the Black Hills, and very rough. Many wagons are being abandoned. Every day we pass good wagons that have been left for any one that might want them. The Black Hills at a distance have a dark and gloomy appearance."[6]

Caleb Booth reflected on the change he noticed in the landscape after leaving Laramie on June 23, 1850. "Now instead of sand hills and prairies with no timber, we have rocky ridges over which pine and cedar are scattered. The land in the valleys & where it is not rocky appears to be sandy and barren. Traveled 14 miles and encamped in a narrow valley between high cliffs of rock. A spring comes out of the hills near by of very warm water and a large quantity."[7]

Mica Littleton struck out from Laramie on July 6, 1850, writing in his journal, "we took the left hand road, several hills one tolerably steep, it is 11 miles where you strike down into a dry gravely creek. Point is the warm Spring a bold spring and good water but warm. There is plenty of wood on the creeks and ravines in this vicinity principally pine and cedar. Grass very thin and much parched. Up there are many pieces of waggons, cooking stoves, etc., left by the way, we have passed 27 graves (two women)."[8]

Diverging from the most heavily traveled route, Lucena Parsons' company left Laramie on August 6, 1850. By doing so she could give a stark contrast to the continuing record of graves kept by Littleton. "Started this morning and concluded to take the river road in preference to the Black Hills on acct of grass which we hear is not plenty on the hills. In 4½ miles we came to a warm spring, next past a lime kiln & then cross Bitter creek, little water in it. Went 16 miles and past 6 graves. The road has been up & down hill all day. Weather very hot and roads dusty."[9] Like Parsons' group, emigrant trains often found, or even blazed for themselves, new or alternative trails parallel to the main, sometimes a few miles off, to optimize their chances of finding more grass, the fuel that propelled their animals, and therefore themselves, toward the gold fields.

"Left camp and started over the Black Hills, sixty miles over the worst road in the world," remembered Sallie Hester in the bluntest of terms after leaving Laramie.[10]

Past the Warm Spring the road continued to undulate over hill and vale as it climbed higher. Following the brief respite from trail life afforded by a visit to Fort Laramie, the human drama in all its various facets continued. Water and grass for their animals led the list of concerns of most emigrants. But the scourge of cholera and the fear it instilled in all, still dogged some of the emigrant trains during both 1849 and 1850. Life on the trail remained totally unpredictable and hardship might come from an unexpected source.

"While nooning a mule kicked C. K. Snyder with both feet in the breast and he fell to the ground lifeless to all appearance. I with several others ran to him — and raised him upon my lap — there was not the slightest appearance of life in him — I rubbed his pulse — bathed his head in water rubbed him with camphor for a considerable length of time before the slightest appearance of life was perceivable — and when we had partially resuscitated him he fainted a way — and it was several minutes before he began to recover from that. But he finally recovered and from which he received no serious injury," recounted J. A. Pritchard of an incident near Warm Spring. Like so many others, Pritchard kept track of the coming and going of his fellow gold seekers. "The Chicago train passed us again but this time on pack mules — It was the same train that had trotted past us on the main Platte. They had broken down their teams, & threw away their wagons at fort Laramie and now were bound to pack to California."[11]

"After descending for several miles, we struck a valley containing good water but destitute of vegetation," recalled Niles Searls, pushing past the Warm Spring. "Our evening's march has been the most toilsome to our mules of any for several days. Our course has been through the very heart of the Black Hills. Ascending one eminence we but gained sight of another more lofty. The vicinity is well supplied with good springs, much better than from all accounts we were led to believe. Game appears abundant, such as antelopes, deer, mountain sheep, etc. Game, however, has not sufficient attraction to allure us out very often, being too much fatigued with traveling to devote any great portion of time to the pleasure of the chase."[12]

Franklin Starr took note in his diary of the many things to be seen along the road through the Black Hills. "The road is lined with different articles thrown away by the Emigrants. Beans Meal Crackers Boxes Trunks Meat and many other things even waggons. The country is swarming with a big black Grasshopper or locust shaped like a cricket without wings. I have seen them marching across the road in countless numbers all going the same course. They feed on the wild sugar as that is almost all that is growing except the trees. There was a horned toad brought into camp this evening. I should certainly have taken it for a lizard. It is chunky and will sit on a person's hand and not attempt to escape."[13]

If the emigrants pushed hard they could be through the Black Hills region in three or four days. But it proved tough going as Searls recalled, continuing in his diary on July 3. "Not a particle of grass has been perceptible for the greatest part of the way. The scanty supply afforded by nature has been nipped to the very earth by the trains in advance of us. Clouds of dust have enveloped us during the day; at times these clouds, raised by the forward wagons and blown by the wind back upon us, we almost suffocating. Reached the Platte towards evening and now appear to have passed the Black Hills."[14]

But others could not push through at that pace. Just one day after leaving Laramie, Mica Littleton's company stopped for a while. "3 or 4 miles brought us to what is called Porters Rock to the left. It is about 10–15 feet high. Plenty of wood and water but grass is Scearce [sic]. Today being the Sabbath we lay by until tomorrow. About 3 or 4 o'clk another one of our train departed this life. Joseph B. Baker of Morgan Co. Ohio. At his burial there was a Hymn Sung a chapter read and a prayer made by Robert Charlton which was good and appropriate."[15]

Several emigrants took note of an unusual change in the nature of the soil as they neared the western fringe of the Black Hills. They referred to the geologic anomaly as the Red Hills. "Nooned on Beaver Creek. Afternoon heavy rain and hail. In the neighborhood of the Red hills," wrote Pritchard on June 7, 1849, marking his third day west of Laramie. "The rain rendered the roads slippery travelling this afternoon." The next day he found "Roads muddy and heavy travelling. Surrounded by craggy hills thrown up to a great height by the up heaving of volcanic eruptions," stating his own geological conclusion. "By night we completed our journey across the Black Hills. Encamped on a fine bold running stream 4 miles this side of the North Fork of the Platte. The Stream is called Fourche Bois River."[16]

Amos Josselyn remembered passing the Red Hills in mid June, 1849. "Came to another creek where we filled our kegs and drove 4 miles over the red hills and encamped, making about 19 miles drive today. The roads for 3 or 4 miles are covered with a red sand that looks just like the dust that gathers about a brick kiln. This day was rather warm for comfort."[17]

And Israel Hale, just a few days behind Josselyn, mentioned the Red Hills in his diary entry dated June 20, 1849. However, his major concerns that day were directed toward the livestock. "Our route this morning was through the valley that contained the red earth. After we left it the ground was rolling. This is a high rolling prairie that is the valley between the mountains. The air is pire [pure] and rather cool until late in the morning and it gets cool long before night. The rains that we had while on the plains have now ceased to fall. The ground is dry and the atmosphere is also dry and clear. I would remark that rains only fall at certain seasons of the year and where the grass is eaten or destroyed it does not grow anymore that year. For the last few days we have traveled through the most barren country that we have seen since we left the States. Our cattle have suffered more for grass and their feet with the gravel in the last four days than they have on the balance of the journey, and it is not done with yet. Some of our men are fearful that one half or more of the cattle will give out and that we will be forced to leave half the wagons, double team, lighten the loads and pursue our journey in that way."[18]

Even J. Goldsborough Bruff, with his tight military organization, found the going through the Black Hills somewhat tough on both his animals and wagons, as well as somewhat crowded. "July 13... Halted here to repair some wagons. Passed camp of Missourians and a company from Lawrenceburg, Pa. Here we sold our 3 yoke of Oxen, as they were tenderfooted, and troublesome. Abandoned the bed of the Ox wagon. Took the running-gear for one of the wagons defective therein, the wheels of which I reserved for spare ones. Here was a Boston pack company."[19] Israel Hale in his diary had alluded to one of the reasons for the constant need to repair wagons. The mountain air, dry and cool, caused the wooden wheels and wagon frames to shrink, causing iron tires and other fittings to sometimes fall off as they bumped over the rough terrain. Rather than attempt to fix the parts, they simply abandoned them. Bruff recalled in his journal having to, "Make fires and re-set some tires,"[20] referring to the practice of shrinking the iron tires on the wooden wagon wheels by a process of heating and cooling the iron to expand and contract it.

Bruff cleared the western edge of the Black Hills on July 15, 1849, and besides recording his observations of the geographic landscape, could not help keeping note of his still active social life. "Moving now over a very rugged and hilly country, red earth and cliffs. The road soon sweeps around the base of a very tall conical hill, crowned with a pile of dingy yellow rock & earth, and resembles much such scenes on the Rhine, a great eminence, with a ruined tower on top. Here we found horn-frogs. Under the shade of some large willows, was a wagon & tent, and a colored man & woman; on going up, I had the pleasure of making the acquaintance of Mr. Pickering & lady, from St. Louis. They had a cow, and most kindly invited to lunch. They had just dined & put away their provisions. Being very hungry & fatigued, I accepted their polite invitation, and had a nice white roll of bread, and a cup of good coffee, with *milk*. Sent the mules down the creek three ms. under guard to graze, as the grass is all gone here."[21]

As Margaret Frink's party pushed through the Black Hills she found little grass and hard going for the animals. Beginning on June 11, 1850, she wrote, "our road keeps on westward up the valley of the North Fork, the river on our right [the south side] and on the left the Black Hills. Laramie Peak twenty-five miles to the south. It is 6,500 feet high. Came to Poplar Creek which is well timbered. The bottom is rich and produces good grass, but it is now nearly all eaten off." The next day the situation did not improve. "17 miles later came to Horseshoe Creek, seven miles beyond that we came again to the bank of the Platte, where we found the feed to be very scarce. The road sometimes follows near the river, then goes over the bluffs, then across deep sand. The hills and bottoms are mostly covered with sagebrush. It grows in dense, tangled thickets, and to break a road through it is hard work for the heaviest and strongest teams. It is about four feet high, with stems two inches thick at the ground, and often matted close together. Very little grass grows among it."[22]

John Birney Hill, not far behind the Frinks in 1850, also commented on seeing Laramie Peak, the quality of the ground, and a treat provided by Mother Nature. "We are laying up to day — resting our Oxen &c. We are within 18 miles of Laramie Peak — it looks like a young Mountain. We saw this peak from Scott's bluff last Wednesday morning. I have not seen any good tillable land; for the last 250 miles back. I think it is rather sandy to produse [produce] well. For the last 4 days, there is plenty of Cedar & Pine on the fluffs. I have hail ice water to day. It fell Friday & drifted in a hollow & did not melt."[23]

Passing through the high country of the Black Hills William Frush recalled seeing the unusual red earth and encountering some new graves. Writing on June 22, 1850, he observed, "vary little water, no grass. 1 mile before and 4½ miles after [reference to a creek bed] drove over red sandy oker land. Drove to spring and noon'd by the grave of Mrs. Cook of Ray Co. Mo. By her grave lay her bed and pillow. The last I got, her husband died before her on the River at Horsecreek. Died June 20th. Lady [no name mentioned] buried left of road to day 2 m. further west." After lunch Frush moved on "to La Prela River. Campt. 1 mile below ford on west side of River fine grass, wood and water. ½ mile East of ford on top of hill N. of road 50 yards the grave of Alex Best, Ill. died 20th June. Our mess and co. of 2 waggons all well. Some slight sickness in our train (Horse Shoe) of 9 waggons."[24]

Caleb Booth also thought the region tough going. Three days out from Laramie, in the middle of the Black Hills, he recalled that "On account of feed being short, hitched up before breakfast and traveled 6 or 7 miles over a rough hilly road. In this distance we passed no less than 7 or 8 graves, the most of which were fresh, having been dug within a very few days. Some say $\frac{1}{10}$ of those who came up on the south side of the Platte died. One man who came that way told me that on one day's travel of 24 miles he passed 36 graves. Cause — Diarrhea or Cholera. Wagon irons & parts of wagons scattered all about the country. Wild sage plenty as back a day or two. Traveled till dark when all were very tired having traveled about 20 miles over hills & hollows."[25]

While most complained of the harsh landscape of the Black Hills, Lucena Parsons' spirits seemed to rise after passing Laramie. "Beautiful country on acct the black hills. We are among them & I like them much. They rise very abrupt & cover the whole country. The reason of their dark appearance is their being covered with low pines. There are large beds of bachelor buttons, marygolds & china oysters (asters) all along this road. They are the same appearance as the tame ones in our eastern gardens. Past 2 graves. We are now getting into a healthier climate. It seems a pity to see the amount of property that is left on this road, wagons & cattle and various things."[26]

She also found nature to be bountiful in that region. "In the last few days we have seen the heads of large buffalows killed by the company before us. We also see many Elk horns by the road side. We found a company campt here & got plenty of buffalow meat from them as they had killed 2 large ones. Went 16 miles over a hilly country, saw no graves. Here are many dry creeks on the banks of which are the finest kind of choke cherries, they are black & sweet. There is another kind of berry sour as currents, they are the bulb berries & are plenty on the banks of these creeks whether with or without water."[27]

Around Deer Creek

Having cleared the Black Hills west of Laramie, the emigrants found the road crossed the Platte tributary called the LaFouche Bois, and then ran close to the main channel again. Within a twenty-five miles radius of the main ferry on the North Platte, operated by the Mormons, the emigrants reached a natural rallying point along the banks of Deer Creek near its confluence with the Platte. Most had had their first real taste of travel in the mountainous region ahead of them and logic told many of them that more unloading and reorganization were needed.

J. A. Pritchard's company passed through the valley of Deer Creek early enough in the 1849 season to still find good grazing and camping. "In five miles we struck Deer Creek [having come from the LaFouche Bois] a fine camping spot. The stream is large & handsome & said to contain an abundance of Fish. The road has been fine to day. By noon we had traveled 15 ms. Here we found in the bend of the river a splendid bottom of blue grass. It was from 12 to 15 inches high and heavily seeded. It resembles very much the blue grass of Ky. The general appearance of the North Platte has naturally changed here. The Channel is not over 150 or 200 yards wide — the water deeper & the current swifter."[28]

Franklin Starr reached the vicinity of Deer Creek on June 14, 1849, needing to rest his oxen. Referring to the previous stretch over the Black Hills, he wrote, "Feed has been very scarce and the cattle have fallen away some having become lame from the wearing away of their hoofs." But the next day he reported, "finding some good Grass we stopped." Taking time to rest and regroup, some of his party went hunting. "Four men went out hunting yesterday up Deer Creek and got back this evening. They brought into camp the skin of a grisely [grizzly] bear and two cubs. They reported having shot the Bear five times before she fell. They also killed a number of Buffalo Antelope Mountain Sheep and Blacktail Deer but it was too far to fetch in any meat."[29]

Starr made no further reference to the bear cubs, but hopefully they were alive and released.

Amos Josselyn, ten days behind Pritchard, also found the area around Deer Creek most pleasant. "We drove 9 miles to Deer Creek and encamped on good grazing," he wrote on June 18, 1849. "Weather clear and pleasant. Here we borrowed a sein belonging to the Government train with which we caught about 4 bushels of fish." But being near the ferrying point, and probably not wanting or being able to afford the ferriage cost, his party set to work on an alternative. "We drove to the river 2 miles above Deer Creek and went to work to make dug-outs to ferry across. We worked all day in company with another company and got three dug-outs into the water by evening."[30]

But despite being only two days behind Josselyn, Israel Hale found no good grazing, writing on June 21, 1849, "we came to the LaFouche Bois and between nine and ten o'clock came once more to the North Fork of the Platte, having traveled eight miles through hills and mountain passes. On arriving at the Platte instead of finding an abundance of green grass, we found the grass thin and nearly dry. After dinner we heard that a ferry was established near and we went up to see. We learned that eight hundred wagons were in waiting at the upper or Mormon ferry and that the cattle were dying there also. But we could not cross at the new ferry, but concluded to try and ferry it on a raft and with wagon beds. We therefore drove up to the place and commenced preparatory to cross on the morrow."[31]

Bruff also encountered the new ferry and its Mormon operators, downstream a few miles from the more established upper ferry, also operated by the Mormons. To put it mildly, Bruff did not think much of the Mormons' business practices. "When near the edge of the Platte, 2 Mormons came up, and desired to cross there, and informing me what companies they had taken over. But I knew what sort of a ferry they had, and that the country, on the other side was a deep sand-drag, and where the proper ferry and conveyance was: And declined. Going on, I found the train halted, and on going back to see what was the matter, found that the Mormons had had the impudence to stop them, to persuade the men to cross there; and the teamster of the lead wagon actually said that he thought the Sense of the company should be taken about it. I order'd him peremptorily to vacate his seat, or drive on at once, and handling a pistol in my belt, told the Mormons to be off, or I'd blow them to blazes."[32]

It is worth noting here that Bruff, like many of his contemporaries, had developed and lived with a distrust of all Mormon people, because of the variations of their religious practices, from mainstream Christianity, such as polygamy. That general distrust had of course led to the widespread persecution of Mormons in Missouri and Illinois during the previous decade, and ultimately the assassination of their founder, Joseph Smith. The fact that the Mormons operated ferries on the western trail only demonstrated the significance of their own trek to Utah under the leadership of Brigham Young, to escape the widespread prejudice, three years prior to the gold rush to California. Whether they had sharp business practices or were simply charging what the market could bear, remained a matter of opinion.

Bruff found the campgrounds around Deer Creek crowded, writing, as they arrived on the evening of July 16, 1849, "passing through hundreds of tents, wagons, camp fires, and people of every age & sex, congregated on its banks." The next morning he had to send his mules seven miles up Deer Creek to find grazing. The lush grass noted by Pritchard had long been devoured. What he observed while his mules grazed appeared to shock and surprise the generally unflappable Bruff.

"The abandonment and destruction of property here at Deer Creek, is extraordinary; true, a great deal is heavy cumbrous, useless articles; A Diving bell and all the apparatus, heavy anvils, iron and steel, forges, bellows, lead, etc. etc. and provisions; bacon in great piles, many chords of it — good meat. Bags of beans, salt, etc etc. Trunks, chests, tools of every description, clothing, tents, tent-poles, harness, etc.

I took advantage of the piles of bacon here, and had all mine trimmed of fat and the rusty exterior and the requisite amount of pounds replaced by choice cuts from the abandoned piles. Was told of a man here, whom a few days ago offered a barrel of sugar for sale, for about treble its cost, price, and unable to obtain that, he poured Spirits of turpentine in it, and burnt it up. The spirit of selfishness had been here beautifully developed. Discarded effects generally rendered useless: Camp utensils & vessels broken, kegs & buckets stove [crushed in] trunks chopped with hatchets, & saws & other tools all broken. A considerable accumulation of ox-chains & yokes."[33]

Along with the tremendous waste, Bruff found American enterprise alive and well. "Trains of ox-wagons hourly coming up, among some of them Mr. Pickering & lady. At Deer Creek there is a camp of 3 wagons & several Missourians, who have 2 wagons heavily laden with Alcohol, for California. This they dilute, and with dried apples, peaches, etc., manufacture all kinds of liquors. They sell a diluted whiskey at 50 cents per pint, and expect that on the route, and in California they will realize a fortune from the proceeds: but I doubt much that they will ever get a gallon of it into California."[34]

Margaret Frink's party reached the camping grounds and ferry in mid June, 1850. "…reached Deer Creek, 13 miles beyond Wood Creek. This is the largest of the many streams running into the Platte above Laramie Fork. Did the washing and during the night a heavy storm of wind came up. For several days past we have been traveling among extensive thickets of sagebrush, or artemisia. It has the odor of turpentine mixed with camphor, which fills the air. A great many emigrants are gathered here and above, preparatory to crossing the river."[35]

William Edmundson, six days travel beyond Fort Laramie, including a single day lay over, arrived in the Deer Creek area around July 8, 1850, writing, "Traveled 8 miles and came to the Platte river which we had not seen for the last 80 miles (here we leave the Black hills). Went 5 miles further and camped on Deer Creek at a celebrated camping place, grass and water scarce but from appearances it has once been abundant in this vicinity."[36]

Mica Littleton, passing from the Black Hills into the valley of the North Platte just a couple of days behind Edmundson, recorded in his diary of only a few references found about African Americans taking part in the gold rush. On July 10, 1850, we wrote, "passed 14 graves among them three women. One more of our train a col. [colored] man did this day of cholera."[37] Like others, mid to late in the travel season, he found the good grass gone around Deer Creek. "No grass but some wood. After crossing Hills and Hollows you come to Fourche Boise River or creek 3½ miles from box Elder [reference to another stream]. Quite a stream plenty of wood and water but no grass, after going over many hills again 4 miles brings you to the North fork of the Platte again. Here you Keep up the bottom of Deer Creek 5 miles. We Struck off about a mile below deer creek to the left to find grass. Plenty of Buffaloe, Elk Deer Antelope mountain Sheep and Sage chickens up the road to deer creek. These mountains on our left look sublime and beautiful. There are plenty of timber on this creek for all the emigrants that may pass here the next 20 years."[38]

Lucena Parsons, a full month behind Littleton, came toward the ferry on the North Platte in mid August. "...box Elder creek. Near her Capt. Maughn lost an ox, it dropped down in its yoke & died. Past 5 graves. Here the men saw a large bear since we got here. There are now several hundred waggons within 30 miles of each other. Feed very poor. Many beaver dams across this river, have seen some beaver. Stopped another day to doctor lame oxen. A company of us went up the river some 2 miles & found the finest kind of black & yellow currants in abundance." [39]

Though Lucena Parsons' grammatical skills were not the best among the diarists, she constructed one of the most beautiful recollections recorded in all the journals. She wrote it at the end of a day of respite from the trail and after finding time to commune with the natural beauty of the American West.

"We spent the day very pleasant in rambling over hills & vallies. At the south mountains reared their black heads & on the north the river glided noiselessly along bringing gladness to man & beast for on its banks they were fed & in the stream they quenched their thirst. We returned at eve laden with plenty of the good things of nature, thankful to the river of all the good things of this wild country & I find comfort though in this wilderness."[40]

Idyllic, but over the next few days, she found again, in the reality of her endeavors to go see the elephant, nature it all its forms, good and bad. "August 14... There have some 10 head of cattle died in our company caused by eating too many choke cherry leaves & the cherries. August 15... Started late this morn on acct of the slothfulness of some of the company we are with. Left them & came on alone, 8 waggons of us. We feel there is no time to be lost. 100 waggons & another 50 waggons campt near here [Deer Creek] In the evening they all met & had a ball. August 16… We staid but were not content. In a whole company of 150 waggons I have no heard of any sickness except a little diarrhea."[41]

Ferry on the Upper Platte

Getting across the Platte proved a challenge. For some it required time and money, for others, backbreaking work and real danger to life and limb, depending on whether or not one used a ferry or chose to get over some other way. Emigrants used a number of crossing points from the upper Mormon ferry to sites twenty miles below that.

Writing on June 10, 1849, J. A. Pritchard described his party's crossing. "At 9 A.M. we reached the Ferry. It was kept by some Mormans [*sic*] from Salt Lake who had come clear there to keep ferry for the season. We found about 175 wagon a head of us & we had to take our turn. We however joined another company of 2 & constructed a raft to cross our wagons on. After several efforts we succeeded in crossing 2 wagons — but we found the current so strong and the raft so heavy and unweilding that we abandoned the project and awaited our turn which came on Wednesday morning. While waiting we spent time washing cloths, shoeing mules, fixing wagons etc. A young man by the name of Brown from Howard Co. Mo. was drown in attempting to swim his stock across the river. Brought the mules in by day-light, put them all together and swam them over the river before the sun rose — it being the best time to swim animals at this point — we crossed all safe."[42]

Amos Josselyn, like Pritchard, did not want to wait on the ferry and decide to have a go at raft building too. "We drove to the river 2 miles above Deer Creek and went to work to make dug-outs to ferry across," he wrote on June 19, 1849. "We worked all day in company with another company and got three dug-outs into the water by evening." Next day, on the 20th, they took the plunge. "Got our dug-outs lashed together and found that they were not sufficient to carry our heaviest wagons, and while a part of us were ferrying the light wagons, the balance went to work at another dug-out, and got it into the water by the middle of the afternoon. We then found our boat sufficient to carry any of our wagons. We got but 10 wagons over today."[43]

Sallie Hester experienced the dangers of fording the swift moving Platte, at one of the Mormon ferries. Even under the best circumstances, crossing could prove fatal. "June 21… Have again struck the Platte and followed it until we came to the ferry. Here we had a great deal of trouble swimming our cattle across, taking our wagons to pieces, unloading and replacing our traps. A number of accidents happened here. A lady and four children were drowned through the carelessness of those in charge of the ferry."[44]

Israel Hale's party, like Josselyn's, improvised its crossing. "The 22nd was a busy day. We obtained a raft ready-made and situated two of the best wagon beds and corked them, fitted them out with oars for boating. The raft was composed of four cottonwood logs with four binders strongly pinned to them. Thus equipped we commenced operations about nine o'clock in the morning. The river was three hundred yards wide and the boats and rafts could make a trip in forty-five minutes, strong as the current was. The raft was towed up by oxen but the boats by manual labor for you may well suppose that a craft of that kind could not go straight across. When we commenced crossing with the boats a company of us swum the cattle over except the four yoke we kept for towing purposes. And a little after sunset we landed the last of the goods on the north side of the river. A few men, however, were left that stopped to swim the towing steers. I was among them which made it about dark when we got across. And just as I expected everything was in confusion. In the evening there was a fire — one just below the wagons on the opposite bank. A tree was on fire and burnt rapidly. In the mountains south we could plainly see a number of signal fires made by the Indians (we are now among the Crows) to call a council or something of the kind and then up and down and across the river were the fires of the emigrants."[45]

The express train carrying Niles Searls reached the crossing area around Deer Creek on July 3, 1849. They decided to avoid the crowded upper ferries and use a combination of rafts and a lower ferry for their passenger carriages. "The river at this point is from ten to twelve feet and can only be crossed by ferrying. Emigrants are crossing from a short distance below us to a point thirty miles above, at every place practicable. The usual method is to prepare some two or three 'Dug Outs,' pin them together by means of cross timbers, thus forming a kind of scow capable of carrying a wagon. The builders, after crossing, sell out to some other company who, in turn do the same to a succeeding one. Our Company has purchased two of these rude machines. The carriages will proceed to the lower ferry in the morning and cross, while the baggage train does the same here. By thus passing over at once, we hope to steal a march on a large portion of those waiting on the south bank. The number of which within thirty miles is estimated even as high as two thousand wagons. The Oregon battalion [a United States Army military unit] with a train of four hundred wagons is encamped seven miles above us. Their numbers have been much reduced by desertion, since leaving Leavenworth." Noting the date, Searls added, "We shall ferry the river tomorrow and also endeavor to exhibit our patriotism in some degree, sufficient at least to show we have not forgotten the 'Glorious 4th.'"[46]

As promised, Searls and his party did not forget the holiday. "The day was ushered in by the discharge of firearms in all directions. Every one was astir betimes and for all I could see the hurrahing was very much the same as in the States. After breakfast we hitched up and rolled down to the ferry, but had to wait till 1 o'clock P.M. before the boat was at liberty. Charles improved the time by preparing a 4th of July dinner. Fresh fish, peach pies, etc., were among the constituents of the repast. At 1 o'clock the cloth was laid — Yes, Cloth, for this time we spread a large piece of canvas upon the ground [on] which we placed our dinner. If the viands were not equally rich with those enjoyed by our friends in the States, they were at least enjoyed with quite as much zest. We have passed the day with reading, chatting, feasting and telling stories. The celebration was continued by few till near morning. The wagons were not all passed over till 11 o'clock at night, but was at last completed without any accident, though we were near being sunk by overloading the boat with passengers."[47]

Franklin Starr's party joined the procession of emigrants using and reusing rafts built by those ahead of them. "There are three rough log canoes lashed together here which some Emigrants have made and left for the use of those behind. There is a flat bottom boat a few miles farther up owned by some Mormons but there is such a crowd waiting to cross that we have concluded to try this. The Platt is not more than one hundred yards wide but deep and swift. The canoes will not bear up a loaded waggon but have to take the load separate. They are hauled across by means of a rope stretched across the river to the middle of which they are fastened. We expect to get over tomorrow. Our cattle have to be taken some five miles toward the mountains to find grass." The next day he described the actual ferrying, writing, "We crossed our provisions in the canoes and dragged the waggons through the water by fasting a rope to the tongue and one to the backend and lashing an empty keg to each wheel to keep them from upsetting. We were not two days crossing. A number of men have been drowned here and above the last week and a great many cattle and horses."[48]

Bruff opted to use the upper ferry on the Platte, arriving there on July 19, 1849, and crossed without incident. "The Ferry-boat here, made and tended by 3 or 4 men, is composed of 8 dugouts or canoes, of cotton wood; and grooved timber pinned over, connecting them and forming a railway to run the wagons on. Several trains of ox-wagons crossed the ferry: the animals are swum across. Crossed the company after dinner, and camped a little above the landing. Paid $1 per wagon for crossing." The next day Bruff's party "Completed some slight repairs and greased all the axles. In the bottom, close to the edge of the river, under the willows, had been a large camp, and in the midst was a hole in the earth, fresh cut, like a grave, and a board with fragments of an inscription, to the memory of XXX died June XXX1849. All the rest obliterated. Over the quondam grave, a board was nailed to a tree, on which was pencilled this inscription: '*The fools are not all dead yet.*'"

Surprisingly, Bruff found in the camps across the Platte "A great many women and children in companies." How many, he did not account; but most trains had very few women, and we don't know his point of reference. Once across, he noted that the reorganization and unloading of the wagon trains continued. "More beans discarded than any other article of provisions—often disagree with the bowels, and are heavy freight. Sheet iron stoves, which every mess of the emigrants had, were gradually dropped, as useless & troublesome. Sugar & liquor are now scarce. A great many parts of wagons & wheels, many trunks and much ironwork, scattered over this campground. An emigrant took a pare of fore wheels, axle, & tongue, and secured a chest on it, to drag on with a yoke of oxen."[49]

Henry Wellenkamp arrived at the main Mormon ferry on Friday, June 14, 1850, and found the line very long. "…to upper Ferry on Platte. Six miles to our left is a high mountain covered with snow. The immense number of emigrants prevented crossing till our turn came. Laid by two days." Therefore, not until Sunday, June 16, did he write, and in something of a surly mood, "Crossed N. Fork of Platte. River turns south in deep mountain canyons and returns no more. Paid $11.00 ferriage. Here are horned toads and wild flax. Took water and entered the ante chamber of Hell; no wood, no water, no grass, but myriad millions of departed souls in the shape of crickets, and stinky water is all. Camped."[50]

Margaret Frink prepared to pass over the North Platte on June 16, 1850, after finding "The water is too deep to ford and the ferry charges are very high. Some are making ferry-boats of their wagon bodies taken off the wheels, and launching in the water, with long ropes to haul them back and forth across the river. In some cases, empty casks are tied to the four corners of the wagon body, to keep it from sinking. This plan is very dangerous in the swift current, and we hear of many persons who have lost their lives in these attempts. Deciding the danger she spoke of was too great, her party waited for the ferry the next day. "A great crowd was waiting to cross the ferry. But by starting early, we were not delayed, and got over by six o'clock. This ferry was established by Kit Carson, the famous hunter and trapper, one of Fremont's guides. There were several ferryboats. The water was deep and swift. The boats were attached to strong ropes stretched across the river, and were driven quickly from shore to shore by the strong current. We paid $5.00 each for our two wagons, and $1.00 each for our seven horses."[51]

On July 9, 1850, William Edmundson's party, following so many others who heard of the crowds at the main ferry, "Went down Deer Creek to its mouth and crossed the Platte river in a boat that had been found and repaired by the emigrants and camped on the North Side opposite the crossing 28 miles below the upper or Mormon Ferry." He noted at his crossing point that, "the water of the Platte river much clearer and the Current more gentle than it is lower down."[52]

Ferrying the upper Platte River above Deer Creek. Bruff's drawing shows the detail of the rafts commonly used. Reproduced by permission of *The Huntington Library*, San Marino, California.

North Platte Ferry to the Sweetwater

Once across the North Platte, and depending on exactly where the emigrants crossed, the next leg of the trek to see the elephant took them west across a fairly dry, barren region, noted for the encrustation of its soils with various salt, alkali, and sodium deposits. The trail took the emigrants toward the Sweetwater River, a tributary of the North Platte that flowed east from its rising point near the continental divide. From the upper ferry on river, the distance was roughly 50 miles; a line of march only broken by the appearance of a place called Willow Springs. Again, as Bruff had observed after crossing, many found need to further reorganize and re-evaluate the situation.

Held up at the ferry for two days, J. A. Pritchard's company struck off toward the Sweetwater on June 13, 1849, giving a marvelous description of the new landscape. "We crossed all safe. Our course was up the river on the north side for about 9 miles. The road there bore to the right across the bluff in the direction of the Sweet water. The road has been heavy and sandy to

Sweetwater Road

Sweetwater Road — route from the North Platte ferry to South Pass and Pacific Springs.

day. The country over which we passed today has been arid & sterile. No vegetation except the wild sagebrush. In 5 miles after leaving the river we came to a mineral lake and mineral spring. At 3 P.M. we struck a dry branch and passing down it some distance we came to a spring & pool of water — strongly impregnated with Sulphur & Alkali. Continued until 7 when we struck a small branch that afforded a scanty supply of water that was impregnated with the carbonate of soda & alkali — we could bearly [barely] use it for coffee.

Had to keep guard with the mules all the time to keep them from swamping in the spotty places—a man would sink to his neck instantly several of the men fell in during the night. I saw 5 head of oxen sunk down to their homes [haunches] the owners pulled them out with ropes around their heads."[53] Apparently what Pritchard encountered in the dry streambeds, or branches as he referred to them, was something like quicksand.

Amos Josselyn glimpsed the rising road ahead of them after crossing the Platte and made a decision. "This morning we lightened our loads by throwing out over 200 lbs. of bacon and ½ bbl of buns, etc." Then, "We left camp at 6¾ o'clock and drove to the Willow Springs, a distance of 28 miles."[54]

Leaving from the Platte for the Sweetwater, Israel Hale had impressions of the road similar to those of Pritchard. He wrote in his diary on June 25, 1849, "In the afternoon we drove thirteen miles over the most barren country that I have seen lately. We also passed several springs, some of alkali, some of sulphur and one of good water, in about ten miles. We encamped about one mile below Willow Spring and near the spring branch. We had no good water, no wood but wild sage and almost no grass at all. Saw quite a number of dead cattle, caused by drinking poisoned water."[55]

Niles Searls found himself across the Platte the day after the Fourth of July, 1849, and wrote a rather melancholy entry in his diary. "The novelty of the trip appears to have worn away, and now many of us long for excitement of some kind and to those who indulge in games of chance, play appears the most natural resort. Large sums are staked and lost. The winners of yesterday become the losers of today." Searls did not indicate whether he counted himself between those two options. And more bad news. "In crossing the river with them an accident occurred which came near proving fatal to the life of 'Chihuahua Bob,' a teamster. He was thrown from a horse while swimming the river and was only saved by being taken from the water in a drowning state by Mr. Wolfe, a passenger."[56]

Moving up the Platte from the lower ferry where his company had crossed the next day, Searls abandoned the carriages for his saddle horse and found a new, if only temporary distraction. "A division of the 'Oregon Battalion' came up this evening and I rode for some distance in their company. The regiment has been fearfully reduced by desertion since leaving the Platte. The mania for going to California has seized the soldiers and they leave in squads of from ten to twelve, taking with them their horses, arms, and provisions."[57]

On July 8, four days after ferrying the Platte, Searls' express company finally turned west toward the Sweetwater. "Leaving the Platte we ascended a long hill for a few miles wound among the barren hills, after which we again descended into the bottom. Clouds of dust enveloped the trail almost suffocating both man and beast. A Strong southwest wind blew the hot sand into our faces until to bear up under its scorching influence was almost impossible.

After buffeting with this American sirocco for several hours, we encamped nearly one mile from the river at the point where it finally leaves the stream."[58]

The next morning found Searls' party rising and, "With early dawn we left camp, pushing ahead with all practical speed in order to reach, if possible, Willow Spring before encamping. With the advancing sun came the same scorching heat that we had experienced for weeks. I fell in company this morning with a Mr. Fox who was scalped by the Indians last summer on the Arkansas River. He was also pierced in several places with spears and left for dead. As might be supposed he is no friend of the natives." Moving on, Searls "Passed the Sulphur Springs and encamped for noon in a small valley through which ran a small stream of water highly impregnated with sulphur, carbonate of soda, etc. After resting a few hours we rolled on three miles to Willow Springs and encamped for the night. The springs there are several and throw off a creek of considerable magnitude. The waters are among the best with which we have met since leaving home. A number of companies are encamped in our vicinity, in one of which are several Ladies. We were treated this evening to a vocal concert from them, which was really entertaining."[59]

Having departed the Platte ferry, Bruff did not have the heat to contend with that Searls wrote about. "July 21... Rain fell in perfect sheet, blinding and appalling lightning, and crashing thunder. In a few seconds from the commencement of this tempest, the hail suddenly descended, like large gravel in immense quantities, thrown down upon us. Then Hailstones of extraordinary size, not only cut and bruised the men, whose faces and hands were bleeding, but it also cut the mules. I thought that in my younger days, in the tropics, and at sea, I had seen some tall storms, but this one beat all my experience. In so brief a period the temperature had fallen about 40 degrees and the hot mountain top, ankle-deep in ice and ice water, in pools, and running down in cataracts through every crevice & gulch. Dead cattle numerous, and several worn-out oxen and cows deserted."[60]

Pritchard passed Willow Spring at mid-day on June 14, 1849, and he wrote appreciatively, "here we took a cool refreshing drink." Not staying long, they pushed on and encountered one of many wonderful geologic anomalies along the trail. "At. 4 P.M. we came to several large lakes of pure salaratus— It was as genuine an article as I ever saw. I gathered several pounds & used it in bread — One of these lakes looked at a distance of 300 yards like a river disgorging itself of ice & with its broken flakes upheaved in all manner of shapes—the water had dried away & the pure genuine double refined salaratus as white as chalk was left on the ground from one to ten inches thick."[61]

Probably a student of human nature equal to, or more so than Searls, Bruff wrote frequently in his diary about the people on the trail. Well educated, like Searls, he may have done so because he felt superior to them, or maybe he simply found that they handled tough situations differently and he felt compelled to comment. "July 22… Last night Capt. Duncan U.S.A. with a man and boy, mounted, came to our camp: and said that he was in search of 4 deserters, from Ft. Laramie, and that one of them was suspected of having ravished an emigrant's wife, in the absence of her husband, and robbed the tent of considerable money; and that they had also stolen a box of Colts' revolvers. I told the Captain of seeing 4 men in dark clothes riding close together on the opposite side of the river, day before yesterday." After relating his assistance to the army officer, Bruff continued, "A party with mule-wagons camped near us: they were packing, and discarding their wagons. We gave them a couple of indifferent common saddles for a fine wagon. And I made a similar bargain with another company. Company busy drying and packing goods, fitting the wagons and cleaning arms. In this extensive bottom, are the vestiges of Camps: Clothes, boots, shoes, hats, lead, iron, tinware, trunks, meat, wheels, axles, wagon-beds, mining tools, etc. A few hundred yards from my camp I saw an object, which reaching, proved to be a very handsome and new Gothic bookcase! It was soon dismembered to boil our coffee kettles."[62]

Having just passed Willow Spring, and looking with anticipation toward making the Sweetwater, some level of anxiety seemed to have infiltrated Niles Searls diary. "Something must be done to relieve us from our present uncomfortable position or we shall soon be compelled to disband and proceed as best we can," he wrote on July 10, 1849. "The only feasible plan appears to be, to destroy baggage. Our wagon masters say that unless this or some other plan is devised they shall leave the train and push on. A number of passengers are preparing to do the same." The conditions along the trail must have been a major contributing factor to his and nearly all the emigrants' growing anxiety, as he described the horrendous scene. "The road for several days' journey has been strewn with dead oxen, some of them have no doubt been poisoned by the impregnated water, but most of them have died with fatigue and heat. In one place was passed eight in a single heap. It was remarked, that a blind man might find his way by the odor of dead oxen."[63]

A fortnight behind Searls in 1849, Bruff's company had turned into the barren expanse moving toward Willow Spring and eventually the Sweetwater, with conditions deteriorating. As a great number of emigrants had preceded him across, it presented an even more brutal sight than Searls had described. "Rolling & broken country. Large isolated masses of gray sand stone scattered about. The road generally good. The hills on the W. side of the creek are bare, blue color, & slate. Seem to contain coal, a few dwarf cedars are here & there seen. The level country is a parched heather [color] and barren. A few dusty sage bushes show that they can live where no other plant can. Passed through a very singular defile called Rock Avenue about 50 ft. wide, and some 200 long. As the Mineral Springs were supposed to be poisonous, I would not allay the mule's thirst at the risk of their lives and they suffered much. At the base of these hills was the "Alkali Swamp & spring," 2 miles from the Defile, and 7½ from the Mineral Spring. The water here — strong lye, was the color of coffee. And piled around were hundreds of dead animals chiefly oxen. Ox gearing lay about in profusion. From Alkali Swamp, to our camp, the road was lined with dead oxen — these all killed by exhaustion and effects of drinking the Alkali water. On the left of the trail, 5 yoke of dead oxen, just as they had fallen in gear: and was told that a stroke of lightning, from the great hailstorm, had killed them."[64]

If the mounds of dead animals were not bad enough, Bruff had to deal with the breakdown of morale in his military, ordered company. No doubt the trail to see the elephant grew harder and harder, and hardship had broken and continued to break a lot of emigrants. "All the bad traits of the men are now well-developed, their true character is shown, untrammeled, unvarnished. Selfishness, hypocrisy, etc. Some, whom at home were thought gentlemen, are now totally unprincipled. All this I was prepared to see and encounter." And the material waste. "Threw away our beans. Passed over a fine smooth road. Rattlesnakes quite numerous, occasionally amuse myself by putting my foot on one, while I deprive him of his rattles; have a pocketfull. Vestiges of women's visit, pieces of calico, a bonnet, etc. Discarding our india-rubber boat [of no use in the present low stage of all the streams], and a very heavy article. A lot of iron implements. 2 large kegs of gun-powder, which we put in a wolf-hole, on a hill, close by, and blew up."[65]

Passing from the Platte ferry to the Sweetwater the following season of 1850, proved no easier for our diarists. Samuel Jamison wrote little of the region, pushing hard to make it across in a day and a half. He stopped overnight at Willow Spring and reported, "here we had the first good water since we left the States."[66] Margaret Frink described her traversing of the region, writing on June 17, "Our road here leaves the Platte, which we have followed for 450 miles, and strikes across to the Sweetwater, fifty miles further west. The space between the rivers is mostly a desert, covered with sagebrush, and producing but little grass. There are pools of alkali water and beds of dried up ponds, crusted with soda or salt, several inches thick. The wheels and horse's hoofs break through the crust as if it were ice. On our left are some high red cliffs, the 'Red Bluffs.' After 20 miles without water camped at Willow Springs; it lies in a deep, narrow gully, where the water is dipped by the cupful to fill the kegs and water vessels. While camped a heavy storm of wind and snow came up."[67]

William Edmundson, like Jamison, pushed hard across to the Sweetwater, reporting a staggering 38 miles in a single day's travel on July 11, 1850. Having crossed 28 miles downstream from the main ferry, they began their trek that day within ten miles of it and "arrived opposite the upper Ferry about noon, went 15 miles further and stopped near sundown at some springs, but the water being represented as poisonous we did not use any of it and concluded to go on to the next water (13 mile) where we arrived about Midnight and camped on a small creek 3 miles below Willow-Springs having traveled 38 miles to day."[68] That distance truly represented the outer limit of endurance for men and animals, considering the harshness of the trail. The next morning, having started early, Edmundson's party "went on to the Willow-Springs where we stopped for breakfast, on reaching the Top of the hill after leaving the Willow-Springs we came in sight of the Sweet-Water Mountains."[69]

Sarah Davis, exactly a month behind the Frinks at that point, described the land beyond the Platte in her diary on July 17, 1850, in her marvelous simplistic style, sans all grammar. "we are now crossing a desert we come to a mineral lake and spring then we came to low land hilly charged with alcholie we then came to a spring and water our catle [probably Willow Spring] and got some super and then traveled all night our catle ware nearly worne out not having any grass since we left the plat nearly fifty miles."[70]

After crossing the Platte ferry, Lucena Parsons' party moved further up river for a couple of days before striking off for the Sweetwater. She recalled as they camped in the evenings, that she "Saw 10 Californians on the return. One of them came to our camp. The news very good from there. They have been there one year, made a fortune & glad to get back home." If the news from the gold fields rang happy in their ears, that of the trail just ahead of them did not. "They say some 200 miles this side of there they found men without food eating their horses & mewls. One young man rather that eat his horse plunged in the river & drowned himself. There are also with the Californians men from Fort Laramie in search of deserters this season."[71]

When Parsons' party moved from the river they found things much as their predecessors had seen things. "came to the oald [old] road again & found this better. Went 2 miles & came to the Rocky avenue where there are high rocks on both sides of the road. It is beautiful. In 2 miles came to a mineral spring & swamps. These are very poisonous & many have lost nearly all their teams by letting them drink the water & eat the grass. In 4 miles more found good water & surrounded by some willows. Have seen many dead oxen & some horses to day." The next morning there was a delay. "This morn found our cattle all gone. The men went back & found them on Willow creek."[72]

The Sweetwater, Independence Rock and the Devil's Gate

Approximately 22 miles after leaving Willow Spring, the emigrants came into the valley of the Sweetwater River. It must have been a sight for eyes made sore from having just passed a fifty-mile stretch of alkali and soda dust.

The Sweetwater rose near the continental divide and the crystal clear runoff coursed through its shallow channel. Ten miles past the point where the road fell in along the Sweetwater's channel lay two important landmarks of the western trail: Independence Rock and the Devil's Gate. Those magnificent monuments of creation drew the attention of every emigrant that passed them, providing a wide variety of descriptions.

J. A. Pritchard's company had pushed hard to reach the rewards of fresh mountain water. On June 15, 1849, he wrote, likely with some pride or bravado, "made 34 miles previous day." But in the end he couldn't resist being the tourist in his diary. "This morning all the curious were clambering to the top of Independence Rock I among the rest. I saw names to the number of several thousand — some graven some painted. It is an isolated elevation composed of masses of granite rock piled one upon another, about one hundred feet high and about one mile in circumference — located on the northern bank of the Sweetwater River. This river is from 60 to 80 feet wide, deep channel, gravelly bed & swift current."[73]

Israel Hale, pushing hard like Pritchard, had started his day at Willow Spring and driven through to Independence Rock on June 26, 1849. His description is, however, quite brief, as he arrived late in the day. "It is a rock about one thousand feet long and one hundred or more high. It is of an oval shape." Unfortunately, Hale had other things on his mind and found no time to do the tourist bit. "This morning we crossed the Sweetwater Creek about one mile above the Rock. Saw many names on the Rock. I had no time to go onto it. One of my steers was sick and as soon as I saw the team over the Sweetwater went back to see him. He was dead. I then returned and followed the train."[74]

Of the diarists we've been following, Sallie Hester reached the landmark on a date actually close to the landmark's namesake. "July 2... Passed Independence Rock. This rock is covered with names." And of course not wanting to be the odd one out, she recalled, "With great difficulty I found a place to cut mine."[75]

Niles Searls must have been relieved somewhat by the condition of the trail on reaching the Sweetwater, but the turmoil within his express company remained a source of agitation. "We reached the Valley of the Sweet-water. Good grass was found in the valley," he began on July 11, 1849. Pleasant enough, but his thoughts and writing quickly turned to the other matter. "A meeting was called and a committee appointed to take into consideration our situation and draft such resolutions as might be thought advisable under the circumstances. After a couple of hours they returned and resolutions to the following effect were offered: That the baggage of each passenger be reduced to seventy-five pounds, including arms, ammunition, bedding, etc, that the number of passengers carriages be reduced to twelve; that a committee of five be appointed to associate with Captain Turner in taking supervision of the train and recommending such measures as they from time to time may think proper; that Mr. Campbell be allowed four mules of his present team and withdraw from the train." Having concluded that train of thought, he added, "The Sweetwater is only three or four rods in width and from two to four feet deep. The water is clear and cool enough for ordinary purposes."[76]

Searls rose early the next day and as he recalled it, "The sacking of baggage commenced this morning at sunrise and was continued till late in the day. Trunks were opened, their contents scattered on the ground. The most choice articles packed in bags and the residue left in confusion upon the ground, or carried off by immigrants encamped around us. Gold was here, merchandise, law and medical libraries, articles of clothing of every description. Ammunition, etc. were abandoned by their possessors. Our teamsters and Mexican herdsmen were soon arrayed in the cast off finery of their unfortunate fellow travelers. I could not but observe the difference of taste between Mexicans and Americans, the latter preferring substantial lasting articles while the former showed their inordinate love of dress by arraying themselves in fine shirts with linen bosoms and other garments of a corresponding character. To look upon the profuse destruction of property was enough to cause a sigh."[77]

After having dealt with the business of casting things off, and later that same day, Searls encountered "Independence Rock. I soon toiled up to the top of this celebrated mass of solid stone and stood with pride upon the spot, years before consecrated to the birth of our National Independence. The rock is nearly a mile in circumference, of an oblong shape, about one hundred feet in height, with a depression in the summit near the center, or rather it resembles two huge mountains thrown together. When seen in the distance it was compared by some of our boys to three elephants lying together, and as, I thought, not inappropriately. The rock lies not over two or three rods from the northern bank of the river."[78]

Bruff found the Sweetwater refreshing to both men and mules, and the rock a wonderful oddity. "July 26... Made an early start and reached Independence Rock by noon, sent the mules across the Sweet Water river [here very shallow], to a wet marsh opposite, under guard, to graze. Company seems in good spirits. Independence Rock at a distance looks like a huge whale." He encountered the same trouble as Hester. "It is painted & marked every way, all over, with names, dates, initials, etc. So that it was with difficulty I could find a place to inscribe on it: 'The Washington City Company July 26, 1849.'" [79]

Those passing in 1850 found the Sweetwater no less refreshing and the rock no less intriguing. Samuel Jamison reached there on June 6. "Encamped for dinner on Sweet water," he wrote. But despite being there fairly early in the season he reported, "no grass no wood." Continuing, "passed Independence Rock which is a natural curiosity. Is six hundred feet long one hundred fifty wide and I cannot say how high this is. A great many names engraved on this rock. Crossed Sweetwater which we had to ford. The Devil's gate is the next curiosity which is seven miles further up."[80]

"We traveled 22 miles and came to the Sweetwater River, up which our road follows for 130 miles to the South Pass," recorded Margaret Frink on June 18, 1850. She added the next day that they "traveled ten miles and came to Independence Rock, a famous landmark in the Sweetwater Valley. The road runs close to it. It received its name from a party of emigrants on their way to Oregon, several years ago, who celebrated the anniversary of the Declaration of Independence at this point, on the Fourth of July. This singular rock is a granite boulder, about nineteen hundred feet long, two hundred feet wide, and one hundred and twenty feet high, standing on a level plain, entirely detached from the mountains near by. The sides and front, to the height of six or eight feet, contain hundreds of names painted with black paint made of gunpowder and bacon grease."[81]

Henry Wellenkamp struck the Sweetwater and saw Independence Rock on the same day that Margaret Frink did. He thought it huge in comparison

Independence Rock and the Sweetwater River, by J. Goldsborough Bruff. Reproduced by permission of *The Huntington Library*, San Marino, California.

to other emigrants. "Tuesday, 18 June, Road very sandy, passed several alkaline lakes of saleratus. Came to a neat river with sweet water. Entered the Rocky Mountains at 10 o'clock A.M. Independence Rock, an immense cupola, or mass of granite or kiesel, 300 feet high, covering 30 acres at the base."[82]

John Birney Hill passed into the valley of the Sweetwater on June 25, 1850, and saw "Thousands of grasshoppers." That impressed him, but then, "At the ford (on the Sweet-water) is the Independent Rock. It is a naked rock — no dirt or grass on it." Though seeing it only a week after Wellenkamp, his estimate of the dimensions was much more modest. "I suppose it is more than 100 ft. high & covers some 4, 5 or 6 acres. This rock; at a distance, looks like a mound. It is quite round. All around this rock the ground is level for some distance."[83]

Sarah Davis found the graffiti on the rock amazing: "we started on and traveled to independance rock and their [there, she had only one way of spelling that word] stoped to noon their is the most names on it I ever saw in my life the rock is completely covered with names as far as I can see and a great many serched out to put theirs their."[84]

Mica Littleton found the last stretch of road before striking the Sweetwater tough going, and had little to say about the rock. "The roads here are Sandy and heavy. 5½ miles more brought us to Sweet Water river a considerable Stream tributary of the Platte. Here is Independence Rock which is quite a curiosity."[85]

Lucena Parsons party did not reach the Sweetwater until late August, 1850, and the weather had begun to change. "Came to Sweet Water river, campt on it & jerked [dried] our meat. We have had two nights of snow & frost." The next morning, August 23, they "Went 6 miles & came to Independence rock. This rock in shape looks at a distance like a steamboat. There are many names on it both painted & chiseled, many done on July 4, 1850, this year."[86]

As most found Independence Rock fascinating, the emigrants marveled at another site just a few miles up the road. J. A. Pritchard recalled seeing it in his June 15, 1849, entry. "...Come to what is called the deavils [devils] gate — it is a singular fissure or cannon [canyon] in the Mountains through which Sweet water forces its way. The fissure is about 30 feet wide and about one half mile through — With vertical walls from 350 to 400 feet high. The range of Mountains was parallel with the river. In ten miles from the Deavils Gate the road leaves the river to cut off a bend. The road is here heavy and sandy."[87]

Franklin Starr, writing on June 21, 1849, had a simple and probably accurate explanation for the phenomenon of Devil's Gate. "We are camped a little below the Devils Gate where the river runs through the hill instead of going a little way around. The gap or gate is just wide enough for the river to run in and the sides are perpendicular to the top. Where the river runs there is a valley and no obstruction to the river at all."[88]

"Came to the Devil's Gate, which is a gap in the mountains where Sweetwater passes through. The rock is said to be four hundred feet high. It is solid rock. The road runs through another gap to the left, but the rock is not perpendicular like the gate," is how Israel Hale described it on June 27, 1849. However, having lost a steer near Independence Rock, he still had concerns. "I saw a great many steers lying dead by the way. We have now lost four in our train. We drove about fifteen miles and encamped on the Sweetwater. The whole earth appears filled with alkali."[89]

Sallie Hester's mileage may have been a little off when she wrote, "Twelve miles from this is Devil's Gate," referring to the distance from Independence Rock where she had just written her name on the crowded surface. Most other emigrants marked the distance between the landmarks at five to seven miles. "It's an opening in the mountains through which the Sweetwater River flows. Several of us climbed this mountain — somewhat perilous for youngsters not over fourteen. We made our way to the very edge of the cliff and looked down. We could hear the water dashing, splashing and roaring as if angry at the small space through which it was forced to pass. We were gone so long that the train was stopped and men sent out in search of us. We made all sorts of promises to remain in sight in the future. John Owens, a son of the minister, my brother John, sister Lottie and myself were the quartet."[90]

Niles Searls could only speculate about the natural wonder. "Five miles above the rock, we approached what is termed the 'Devil's Gate,' a fissure through the mountain, with perpendicular walls on each side of four hundred feet in height; its width is not over thirty feet. The Sweetwater passes through this aperture. It is truly a singular point. How formed or when is a mystery!"[91]

Having left Independence Rock behind, J. Goldsborough Bruff found himself at "3 P.M. on the banks of the Sweet Water just above the 'Devil's Gate.' Some of the boys clambered up the rocks on the N side of the Gate, and reached some cavernous places, where they fired pistols, and threw down rocks, pleased with the reverberation, which was great. I made a careful sketch of this remarkable gorge."[92]

"Five miles above Independence Rock we came to the 'Devil's Gate,' where the river breaks through a spur of the mountains," wrote Margaret Frink in her diary on June 20, 1850. Like other emigrants before her, she gave her own estimations as to size and distances at the landmark. "The gap is 900 feet long, 400 feet high, and 150 feet wide. The road passes through another break a few hundred yards to the left. This opens into another beautiful valley about five miles wide, hemmed in by mountains that rise abruptly form the plains to a height of 1500 to 2000 feet."[93]

Mica Littleton recorded the distance and dimensions of the landmark, writing, "and 5 miles more brought us to the Devil's gate where the creek runs between 2 high rocks they say 400 feet perpendicular."[94] Henry Wellenkamp did not estimate the scale of the sight but knew whom to assign the honors for its creation to. "Nooned and crossed the Sweet Waters and passed the Devil's Gate or a Hellgate that would do honor to Dante. Camped on the Sweet Water this night. Very cold, heard a grand concert of wolves."[95]

Along the Sweetwater

Having passed the Independence Rock and Devil's Gate, the next, and considered by many emigrants the most important landmark on the trail, loomed ahead: the much-noted South Pass over the continental divide. Believing they had reached the summit of the continent, many assumed the route to the gold fields ran downhill the rest of the way. The psychological boost of passing the summit of the Rocky Mountains lifted many spirits, and beyond that landmark they encountered a rivulet called Pacific Springs, so christened by earlier emigrants who likewise believed they were on the downhill slope to the west coast. In reality they were still over a thousand miles from their destinations and if they thought they had seen the elephant, it proved to only be its tail. Most of the diarists marked South Pass as lying between 100 and 105 miles from Independence Rock, along a route that followed the serpentine Sweetwater almost due west. By straightening the trail, cutting across bends in the meandering stream, emigrants found themselves crossing and re-crossing the river numerous times. It proved a tough stretch of road for some, while others seemed to enjoy the mountain scenery.

"In ten miles from the Deavils Gate the road leaves the river to cut off a bend. The road is here heavy and sandy. We crossed during the forenoon several small streams that flow into the Sweetwater. The waters of which were as cold as Ice they were fresh from the melted snow. This afternoon was the first time that we had a view of the Wind River Mountains," recalled J. A. Pritchard on June 16, 1849. The next day the encounters with the rambling river continued. "We left the river this morning soon after we left our camp — and in six miles we struck it again. We watered our mules & in a mile or so we left it again — and struck it in 8 miles where we nooned. When we leave the river we have deep heavy sand to pull through. The grass is good on the Sweetwater but no timber, we find willow brush occasionally. The balance of the time we have to depend on sage bushes for fuel."[96]

Amos Josselyn, having left Independence Rock on the morning of June 25, 1849, called the "Roads tolerable and weather fine" along the Sweetwater. The near constant shuffling of wagons, baggage, and draft animals continued. "Today we traded two mules for two yoke of cattle and got twenty dollars boot money and ten dollars for a harness."[97] Josselyn's mules must have broken down for they were the draft animal of choice for most emigrants hoping to make the trip at a quicker pace. Yokes of oxen traveled at a slower pace than mules, mules had better footing, yet suffered similar problems with their hoofs on rough ground. And of course mules cost more in the initial investment, two or three times the cost per animal.

Some found the main trails either too crowded or too short of grass. While Pritchard had found good grass along the Sweetwater, when Niles Searls passed in mid July, his party felt compelled to divert to a less traveled route. "Crossing the stream, we took a faint trail leading to the right and crossed the river, keep up its northern side in preference to keeping the old route, which leaves the river to the right and follows a valley some distance from the river. We soon passed between two high mountains and again entered the bottom, soon after which we again crossed over to the south side and kept near the bank. This road, though new, is said to be much shorter and the grass is good. The sun shone through the middle of the day with intense heat. We have crossed the Sweetwater five times during the march."[98]

By late July, 1849, the trail along the Sweetwater had seen heavy traffic. Besides the landscape, heat and dust, Bruff had other things to complain about. "I was quite lame from chafe. Here it will be proper to remark that the Company had given me a horse on the frontier, but I preferred walking, to cure me of dyspepsia, which I had had for many years." To this point there has been very little in the diaries regarding problems with personal hygiene. Bruff's entry is rather frank. Considering the lack of bathing and toilet facilities, the amount of sweat, dust, dirt, and grime that must have impregnated clothing, the appearance of chafing, rash, body odors, and other skin irritations must have been nearly universal among the emigrants. But rarely are these problems mentioned in their journals, and quite possibly, those problems were simply too personal to mention in a diary that might have been read by another at some point in time. His own problem aside, Bruff encountered someone else whose problems were even greater as he passed along the Sweetwater. "I recollect having passed an ox-wagon in the road, without cattle, and a female sitting alone, on the tongue, weeping: I asked her the matter, and she informed me that her husband & son had gone ahead some distance to look for a stray pony, and she was afraid they could not get back before night. On inquiring about her oxen, she said they were below, in the river bottom. I would have left her a guard, but other companies were coming along, & I thought her husband would not be so imprudent as to leave his poor wife alone on the road, in this wild country." That evening, Bruff encountered the errant husband and son and offered them a place to sleep for the night.[99]

The next day, Bruff found little improvement. "Hot sun, and a strong breeze blowing the fine sand & dust full in our faces, rendered this one of the disagreeable days, both to man and beast. The large crickets very numerous. On our left rise the rugged, bare, and harsh looking Rattle Snake Mts. The river and road now enters a gorge of the mountains. Perpendicular rock walls from 400 to 600 ft heights on our right. This is very narrow and rugged pass, or canon [canyon], we crossed and re-crossed the stream again, in 1½ miles. Whirlwind of sand blowing through with a fresh breeze. The rocks here, wherever accessible, are marked all over with inscriptions, as usual. Plenty of remains of broken & burnt wagons here, as well as some dead oxen. Wheels, axles, hubs, tires, ox-chains, bows, yokes etc. mark old camping grounds."

Then he encountered the German woman again. "Just before entering the gorge I passed a wagon in the road, with the poor German woman whom I saw and conversed with, alone on the road, yesterday morning and who it seems is the wife of the fellow who slept last night at my camp. She was again sitting on the wagon-tongue weeping, and said that her son was sick in the wagon, and her husband had gone back some distance, and the oxen were several miles below, in a bottom, with no watch over them. This poor women sees hard times indeed; the son will probably die, the Indians or emigrants, some of whom are little better than the savages, (though the emigration, generally, is intelligent & respectable) will carry off their oxen, and finally the husband take care of himself."[100]

Samuel Jamison passed the canyon and multiple fords of the Sweetwater on June 7, 1850, writing in his journal, "crossed Sweet water 3 times. The rocks have a very strange appearance along the road with a great many names engraved on them."[101] Henry Wellenkamp also found the fording of the Sweetwater quite redundant. "Thursday, 20 June, Sandy. Crossed Sweet Water 3 times, camped at noon, laid by. Shortened and lightened our wagons. In every camping place since we left Laramie we found the ruins of abandoned wagons, and articles of every description on the road; the animals began to give out and ½ the emigrants took to packing, that is, carrying their luggage on their backs."[102]

Margaret Frink, passing along the Sweetwater in late June, 1850, near the area Bruff had described, also found dealing with the infinite variables in the human stream of migration, sometimes just didn't make sense. "…Our fellow passenger Mr. Avery left us this morning, concluding he could walk to California sooner than we could get there, at the rate we were traveling. We gave him all the provisions he could carry, and he started, with blankets, clothing, and provisions strapped on his back, to walk 1500 miles to California [just as Wellenkamp so astutely alluded to in the previous entry]. Six miles from camp we came to the canon [canyon] of the Sweet water, and crossed the river by the difficult fords three times in less than a mile."[103]

William Frush thought the Sweetwater initially an attractive river valley. "Thare [there] is a vary pirty [pretty] bottom on this river from Devil's Gate up for 10 miles. 1½ miles wide affords fine grass. It then gets narrow not more than ½ mile to whare [where] road runs through Mts. about 28 miles from D. Gate for particulars on road see Mormon Guide, the table on basin. Lands between Mts. produce nothing but sand and wild sage. This table or valley is 6 to 10 miles wide. On the north side the sweet water Mts. I have not traveled one day for the last 10 that I did not find a number of waggons cut up and many burned by Emigrants in fitting and abandoning them to pack. 25 miles from Devil's Gate & the doom top Mt. [Independence Rock] north of road a sold granite & not a deface or ruff formation on it. Was clean as the rain of time could wash it."[104]

Lucena Parsons reached the Sweetwater in late August, 1850, the bulk of the emigration having gone before her, though they were by far, not alone on the trail. Over three days, beginning on August 24, she wrote little glimpses of trail life along the Sweetwater. "Two grisly bears were seen on top of these hills. There have been many killed by the emigrants some of them weighing from 7 to 15 hundred pounds. There are no buffalow here. The reason of the river being called the Sweet Water is on acct of the saleratus in it. August 25. The game is sage hen & ducks, deer, elk, antelope & hare. The flies and bugs look different from what they did in the east. No Indians on the road since we crosst the north fork of the Platte. We have been in the Crow Indian territory. Crosst the river twice. Saw 6 graves. Crost Sage creek & on the bank saw the grave of a young man dug up & his body nearly eat up by wolves. August 27. Forded the Sweet water 4 times today. Very poor feed it being an old camping ground. The road today past through some very romantick [sic] places [referring to the canyon area earlier described by Bruff]."[105]

Ice Spring

About 40 miles up the Sweetwater, past Devil's Gate, lay another phenomenon of nature that some of the emigrants could add to their list of landmarks, or singular sights that they would never forget. Several wrote nice descriptions, others, in their hurry, only mention it in passing. "…Came to an Ice Spring one of the strangest & most singular phenomenon in the whole trip — and one of the most singular in nature," wrote J. A. Pritchard, having reached the spring on June 16, 1849. "This spring as it is called is, rather a basin surrounded by sand plains — about one mile in length & from 150 to 300 yards wide — but does not all contain Ice. The ice is found about 8 to 10 inches beneath the surface. There is from 4 to 6 inches water above the Ice — and as turf or sod of grass apparently floating on the water — upon which you can walk all over it. You can stand and shake for 2 or 3 rods square. The water above the Ice is pretty strongly impregnated with Alkali — the upper end of the marsh is entirely of that kind of water mixture — though there is good fresh water in spots. To get to the Ice you take a spade or ax & cut away the sod & then strike down & cut it out in Square blocks. The ice is clear & pure entirely free from any Alkali or other unpleasant taste. It is from 4 to 10 inches thick — and as good as any I ever cut from the streams in Kentucky. I filled my water bucket & took it to camp with me."[106]

Franklin Starr's company traveled the road a week behind Pritchard. He recalled the ice spring, writing, "There was a flat meadow where we nooned which has a layer of 6 to 8 inches of Ice about 1 foot under the surface of the ground. The Ice is clear and solid and never melts. The road up the sweet water has been but little hilly but frequently quite sandy."[107]

Israel Hale, two weeks behind Pritchard, hurried past the natural wonder, more concerned in his diary entry with keeping pace with the other emigrants. "We passed the Ice Spring about midway of the distance where we found clear ice by digging from fifteen to twenty inches. The roads have been good but the country barren. As we came near the river we saw a grave that had been robbed by the wolves. Most of the teams are now making a rush for the South Pass, distance thirty-six miles. Two hundred and fifty teams are within eight or ten miles behind and near five hundred between here and Fort Laramie. It is said there are about eight or ten hundred ahead of us."[108]

On the other hand, Niles Searls found the place fascinating. "By eight o'clock we reached one of the greatest curiosities witnessed during our journey. Situated in a narrow vale of several miles in extent is a strip of porous earth, through which on digging to the depth of six inches may be found a layer of sold ice. In some spots it is covered with water, but in most parts the turf may be removed and the ice cut out entirely free from water. The earth throughout the vale is strongly impregnated with alkali, rendering the water almost as unpalatable as lye. Yet the ice appears free from all impregnation of this kind. This ice should be found thus imbedded in the earth in midsummer with the thermometer ranging from seventy to eighty, or even higher, is truly strange. The Mormons have named this place 'Ice Spring.'"[109]

With much of the 1849 migration ahead of him, a full six weeks behind Pritchard, J. Goldsborough Bruff got to see what the preceding emigrants had done to the phenomenon. "...5¾ miles from the last ford, on right, in the low ground, by digging a couple of feet, ice is obtained. The surface is dug up all about by the travelers—as much from curiosity as to obtain so desirable a luxury in a march so dry and thirsty—this is called Ice-Springs."[110]

Margaret Frink recalled passing the ice spring on June 22, 1850, but found it only an extension of a landscape, so wondrous to easterners, that it no longer awed them. "Crossed ford number four on the Sweetwater then crossed a desert of sixteen miles without water. About midway was an extensive marsh, said to be underlaid with ice, but to what depth was not known. Got our first sight of the Wind River range of the Rocky Mountains. A few miles to Sweetwater ford number five. The great number of fords on this stream are made necessary by the crooked course of the river, and the rough nature of the country. Joined a company from Independence, Missouri with emigrants from Kentucky and Indiana."[111]

Lucena Parsons displayed a mood in her diary entries that changed with the difficulty of the road. Of course we don't know the other factors that helped shape her moods, for unfortunately she did not record most of them, but it appears the Sweetwater portion of the road had worn on her, as indicated in the second of the following two day entries. "August 28... Left early came to Ice springs at 10 & here let the teams feed. These springs are on a low swampy spot on the right of the road. Ice may be found here at all times by digging 2 feet. There is lime & alkali in abundance here & many cattle have died suddenly by drinking this water. Many wagons in sight of us. August 29... There are many difficulties to encounter on this road such as sickness, death & a great loss of property. Since we left Fort Laramie we daily pass much abandoned property such as waggons, horses, oxen, cows, chains of the best kind, & stoves, all destroyed."[112]

South Pass and Pacific Springs

Most emigrants were able to pass the Sweetwater segment of the road in four to six days. All pronounced some happiness at having moved beyond it, if only for the fact they had found the multitude of fords monotonous. Henry Wellenkamp summed it up nicely when he recorded that over the last two days along the route, his party "crossed and re-crossed the Sweet Water a dozen times."[113] Once the road left the Sweetwater for the last time, it began a gradual, and for some, an almost imperceptible rise toward the spine of the Rocky Mountains, and a pass that had been discovered nearly three decades earlier, in 1823, by one of the legendary trailblazers of the American West, Jedediah Strong Smith. He called it South Pass, about 12 miles from the last crossing of the Sweetwater, with the Wind River Range standing as a sentinel to the north.

"This forenoon we crossed several tributaries of the Sweet Water River," began Pritchard's marvelous diary entry on June 17, 1849. "In crossing some of which we found Bank of snow from 2 to 20 feet deep. On one of those wintry looking spots, in a clear warm summer day the Boys took quite an exciting game of snow bowling in which a dozen or more took part. We crossed the Sweetwater River at noon, the last time. About 4 P.M. we stood upon the summit level of the Rocky Mountains. Nor could we have told from observation that we had gained such a great elevation had it not been for the knowledge of our geographical position & the imposing land marks to our right, the Wind River Mountains— whose cold, spiral, snow capped summits were raised to such a great elevation — and the very perceptible change in the temperature of the climate. We are now upon the dividing Ridge of to use a more forcible figure, 'the Backbone of the North American continent,' And from which the waters flow in to the Atlantic & Pacific Ocean. The South Pass is about 300 miles distance from Fort Laramie and about 980 miles from Independence. The Plateau of the South Pass is from 15 to 20 miles wide. The Altitude of the South Pass according to some observations is 7490 feet above the level of the sea. The Latitude North is 42 degrees 27 minutes15 seconds. Longitude west 109 degrees 27 minutes 32 seconds. Two miles west of the Pass is the Pacific Springs."[114]

The transition from the Sweetwater to the South Pass took Franklin Starr's party two days. "Crossed the 3 principal forks of the Sweetwater. Snow has been very common along the road during the day. We lay by all the afternoon. We moved yesterday near a spring on top of the mountain which was the coldest water I ever drank. We are now within a few miles of the summit of the South Pass. The Wind River Mountains lay cold and silent off to our right. The country appears like a high rolling prairie." The next morning, June 28, 1849, "We crossed the highest ridge of the pass at half past nine. Nooned at the Pacific Springs which are not as cold as I expected to find them. The road since we rose the hill day before yesterday has been but little hilly. We scarce know when we were on the highest ground of the pass. The west descent is the most steep."[115]

Israel Hale's party also found the snow. "Some of the men, in hunting wood, discovered a lot of snow near our camp. The distance being short, I went to see it. It was about two hundred yards or perhaps more from camp and up the creek. The bank was near two hundred feet long, from thirty to sixty wide and from one to five deep. I then went a little further into a grove of the shaking aspen. It was a very handsome place situated at the foot of a mountain or high cliff of rocks or rather between the creek and mountain. I noticed the appearance of a road once having been cut through the grove, something like twenty feet wide." The next morning Hale's company continued on toward the summit. "We soon came to another creek and once more, and for the last time, crossed the Sweetwater; and immediately after crossing the road led up a steep hill. I have seen a large quantity of snow today, and wind blowing very hard makes it extremely hard. Almost every one have found their overcoats comfortable. The wind continued to blow so hard that it was attended with much difficulty to cook. The water in the river is nearly as cold as ice water and has no bad taste. In two miles we drove through the South Pass. It is nothing more in appearance than a small ridge. We drove to the Pacific Spring."[116]

"In the valley of Wind River we found a vast bank of snow some eight feet deep, and here we indulged in a game of snow balling." Like so many other emigrants, Niles Searls' party found the diversion offered by a snowball fight in the middle of summer irresistible. "The Wind River Mountains are apparently about twenty miles from us on the right and to the west." Camping over, they resumed their march toward the summit on the morning of July 19, 1849. "As we approach the summit the passage gradually becomes compressed and nearer Pacific Spring, it is quite narrow. The summit for several miles is covered with gentle undulations so that the exact point of division is not accurately defined. In leaving this point and descending to the west, it seemed like abandoning the world and all of interest it contained with prospects exceedingly dubious. Pacific Spring, three miles west of the pass, is a large fountain, or rather two of them. The lower one is the principal spring and throws off a large quantity of good water."[117]

J. Goldsborough Bruff's journal entry for August 1, 1849, seems to burst with pride. "South pass of the Rocky Mountains, and threw our banner to the breeze, on this elevated and noble back-bone of Uncle Sam's. Elevation above the Gulf of Mexico, 7,489 feet. The only marks to designate this particular point, are 3 knolls of decripitating white stone, 2 on the left, and one on the right of the trail." But even on the spine of the continent, they could not escape the incipient grime of traveling to see the elephant. "Fine white dust, in heavy clouds, driving in our faces, a great annoyance. The effects on the appearance of the men rather ludicrous, as their beards and hair were in rank luxuriance, in caught a heavy powdering, and 3 dark spots in the face, was all you could recognize of features, eyes and mouth. The effect on the animals was distressing. Every halt the mules had to be cleaned about the head."[118]

Nothing of the passage between the Sweetwater and South Pass had changed by the time the 1850 emigrants arrived, only that some noted the march of progress in the appearance of a post office at the landmark. Samuel Jamison reached the pass on June 10, 1850, in an apparent hurry after having pushed very hard to reach it. "Left camp at 5 o'clock traveled 35 miles passed several branches of the Sweet Water River. Passed over the Summit. Snow Mountains [probable reference to the Wind River Range] very close. Encamped at the paciffich [sic] Spring. Very cold water. Here the water runs to the west. Very swampy to get to camp ground height of Summit 6,700 feet."[119] Henry Wellenkamp, in his usual economy of words did not have much to say about the landmark, recalling primarily that he got sick there. "Sunday, 23 June, Left the Sweet Water. Ascended the South Pass. Passed the summit at 10 o'clock. Got sick with Mountain Fever. Nooned in Pass which is hardly perceptible being so gradual an ascent and descent. Camped at Pacific Springs."[120]

"Today we traveled twenty three miles, crossing the Sweetwater three times," recalled Margaret Frink, writing on June 23, 1850, as they neared the end of the Sweetwater trek. "Camped at the Quaking Asp branch of the Sweetwater" [referenced by Hale a year earlier]. The next day the Frinks' little party found the attainment of the summit at South Pass a reason to really celebrate. "June 24... Five miles further we came to the main and last branch of the stream [Sweetwater], which we had no difficulty in crossing. On the mountains near the road there were deep banks of snow in the gulches. We then traveled up a long, gradual slope, or plain, free of rocks, trees, or gullies, and came at half past eleven o'clock to the summit of the South Pass of

South Pass and Pacific Springs

South Pass, as drawn by Bruff. The width and flatness of the pass through the Rocky Mountains, as recorded by many immigrants, was not exaggerated. Reproduced by permission of *The Huntington Library*, San Marino, California.

the Rocky Mountains. We could hardly realize that we were crossing the great backbone of the North American Continent at an altitude of 7,490 feet. The ascent was so smooth and gentle, and the level ground at the summit so much like a prairie region, that it was not easy to tell when we had reached the exact line of the divide. But it is here that after every shower the little rivulets separate some to flow into the Atlantic, the others into the Pacific. Near the summit, on each side of the road, was an encampment, at one of which the American flag was flying, to mark the private post-office or express office established by Gen. James Estelle, for the accommodation of emigrants wishing to send letters to friends at home. The last post-office on our way was at St. Joseph, on the Missouri River. West of that stream were neither states, counties, cities, towns, villages, or white men's habitations. The two mud forts we had passed were the only signs of civilization. There was an off-hand celebration of our arrival at the summit. Music from a violin with tin-pan accompaniment, contributed to the general merriment of a grand frolic. In the afternoon we spent some time writing letters to our friends, to be sent back by the express. On each letter we paid the express charge of $1.00. Drove on eight miles and encamped for the night at Pacific Springs."[121]

As he neared South Pass, William Frush suddenly took ill and had to delay his crossing of the continental divide. "Campt on Sweetwater at Ford no. 6. This day I was taken with a fever and severe pains in my limbs with shortness of breath as if produced by the want of a proper atmosphere pressure. I suffered much and took medicine during the night." The next day, July 4, 1850, Frush "lay up all day, myself & Hobbs being sick. We boat [both] improved by delay." He did not mention it being a holiday at all. Continuing on the following day, he wrote, "I lay all day in waggon not able to walk or ride my horse. This camp was at snow drift on creek 26 feet deep." Finally recovered somewhat, he wrote on July 6, "traveled 15 m. to day and campt 3 miles of summit of S. Pass east side. I rode horse back all day. Felt vary much waried [weary] at night. This South Pass or gap in the Mt here is a body of tableland & rol[l]ing but not much mountainous. 15 m. wide. The Mts. are white with snow."[122]

William Edmundson had a little more than usual to say, offering in his diary a nice discourse on the geography of the pass. "Crossed the Sweet-Water for the last time. Traveled 12 miles and crossed the dividing ridge between the waters of the Atlantic and the Pacific about 1 O'clock P.M. The South Pass is an elevated Plain about 7000 feet above the level of the Sea. The road passes about 20 miles South of the Wind-River Mountains which rise to the height of 13000 feet and are always covered with Snow. The Colorado, the Yellow-Stone and Lewis's rivers head in these Mountains. After crossing the ridge we went 3 miles and Camped at the Pacific Springs."[123]

Mica Littleton reaching South Pass at the end of July, 1850, after just another grueling day on the trail, could find little good to comment on. "Came to Sweetwater and crossed it the last time. 7 miles we came to 2 mounds passed between them 2½ miles brought us to the Summit of the Mountain. We turned off to the right and went to graze. About one mile west of the 2 mounds which is call the Twin mounds when on the Summit. 3 miles brought us to Pacific Springs which comes out in a Swampy place to the right of the road. Concluded to Stay and rest our Stock and get Something to eat though we had no water and the water in dry Sandy not fit for man or beast being charged with Salt and alkali. In all 28 miles. Our stock much worn out Passed today 13 graves. This appears to be an increase on the last few days."[124]

Lucena Parsons recorded traversing South Pass on August 30, 1850, and like others did not appear overly impressed with the landmark. "We leave the river here & from here to South Pass the road is broad & fine as any turnpike. See snow in the mts & the hollows. Came to Pacific springs. Past 7 graves today. This pass, as it is called, is nothing uncommon in appearance. Its altitude is 7085 feet. Met a company of American soldiers from Oregon on their way to Fort Leavenworth. They all had Spanish mewls [mules]."[125]

Pacific Springs to the Road Fork on Big Sandy

Niles Searls had subtly suggested that crossing the South Pass had become somewhat of a point of no return for him when he wrote, "it seemed like abandoning the world and all of interest it contained with prospects exceedingly dubious." There must have been many emigrants who felt the same way. And all of them, at least those who could read any common emigrants' guide, knew the greatest distance in their trek to see the elephant still lay ahead of

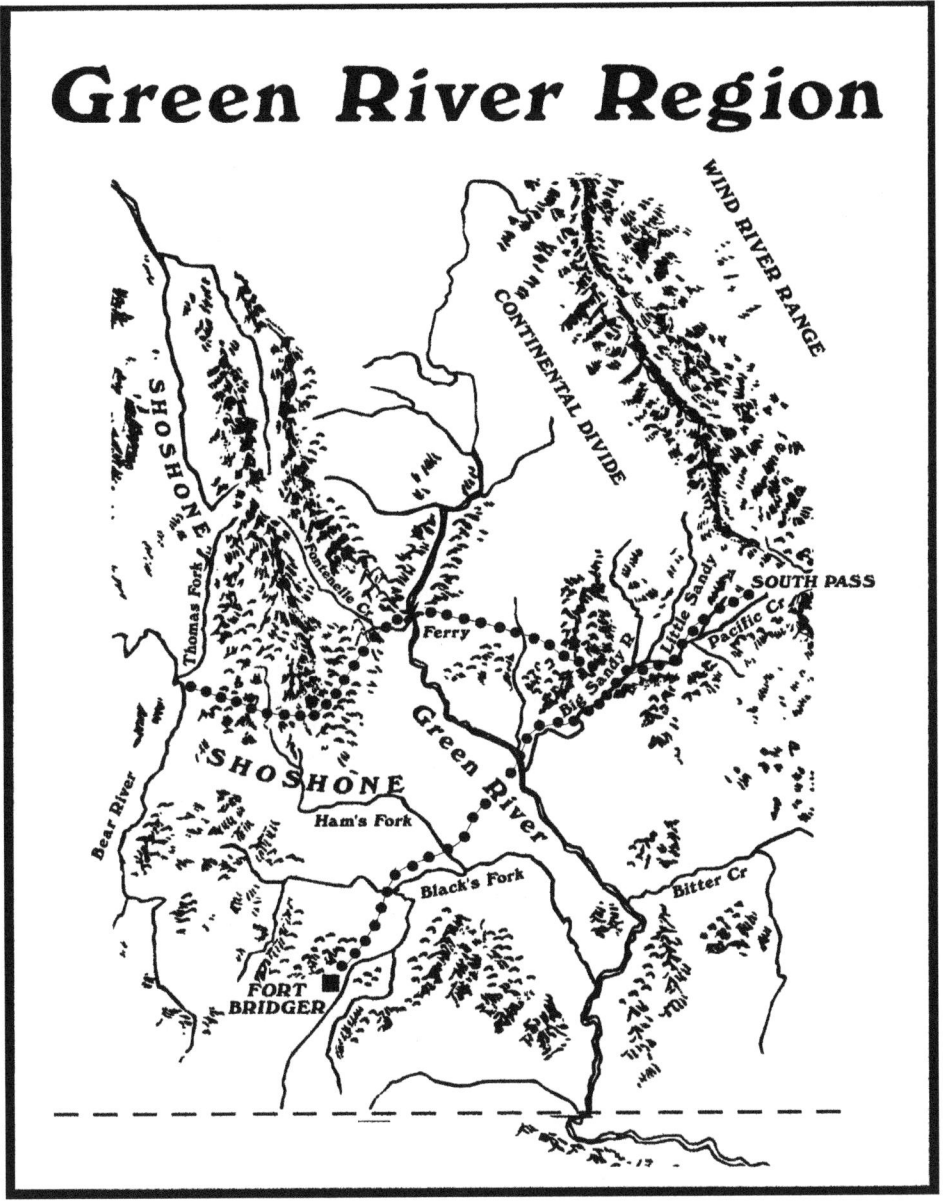

Green River Region — routes from Pacific Springs to the Green River and Fort Bridger.

them. But what lay immediately ahead of them included a crucial choice and potentially another leg of the trek that amounted to approximately 75 miles.

The choice involved which trail they would take after they had passed Pacific Springs. Roughly 15 miles beyond those springs the great trail forked at a site generally called "the parting of the ways." The options at that point were to continue pretty much due west toward the Green River, or veer off to the left, toward the southwest and Salt Lake City. That road followed one the oldest western trails, originally to Oregon, and then substantially used by the Mormons to reach their Deseret. The road due west carried the name Sublette's or Greenwood's Cut-off and saved a hundred miles or more, depending on whom the emigrants were reading distances from. A number of our diarists traded off distance and time, meaning haste, and the general knowledge that the cut-off offered no water, against the older, more established trail, and the loss of several days.

To reach the cut-off, emigrants had to cross three branches of the same river, conveniently named the Little, Dry, and Big Sandy.

J. A. Pritchard left Pacific Springs on June 19, 1849. "We nooned to day at the forks of the road. The left hand of which led to Fort Bridger and to Salt Lake — and the right hand road led to the Sublette or Greenwood cut-off a distance of 19 miles from South Pass. We here took the right road We crossed the little Sandy filled our casks with water."[126]

Franklin Starr spent two days reaching the cut-off and tried to keep which Sandy he had passed in order. "Friday, June 29, Traveled 15 miles crossed the dry Sandy and camped on the Little Sandy. The dry Sandy is a very small stream of Sulphur water. The Little Sandy is about two-thirds the size of the Sweet water. It is now high and muddy. We lay by the after part of the day." The next day Starr continued his Sandy saga in his journal writing "We crossed the Little and Big Sandy and camped on the latter. The Big Sandy is about the size of the Sweet water and is now muddy like the little Sandy."[127]

Amos Josselyn recalled on July 1, 1849, that his party "drove 22¾ miles to the Little Sandy [after leaving Pacific Springs]. We found no water today for our stock. We crossed the Dry Sandy but the water is brackish and not good for stock, though nothing suffered for water as it was cool all day with 2 or 3 showers of rain and hail. The roads excellent. Today I counted 18 head of dead cattle, killed by drinking alkali water. The Stubenville Company remained in camp on Sweetwater to recruit their stock. By their dropping off our company was reduced to 14 men and 4 wagons."[128]

A full month behind Pritchard, Niles Searls' express company encountered the Sandy Rivers in mid July. "Encamped ten miles from Pacific Spring on the 'Dry Sandy,' a beautiful stream without any water except what was obtained by digging wells in the dry sand composing the bed of the stream," he wrote in his journal. "Ten miles from camp we crossed Little Sandy, a fine cold stream running to the southwest. Here we encamped for noon, but found little or no feed. We are on a barren desert. Everything is parched. The wild sage and grease wood (artamosia) being the only tenants of the greater portion of the soil." Writing his entry the following day, Searls reported, "A man was killed a few days since, near us, by a Grizzly Bear. Reached Big Sandy before sunset and shall remain here till tomorrow night. On next day, moving to prepare for crossing a desert region of thirty-five miles, now before us, without wood or water. This desert is on what is called Sublette Cut-off. This cut-off is said to shorten the old route to Fort Hall some sixty miles."[129]

Sallie Hester crossed the region of the Sandy Rivers on July 4, 1849. She did not have anything to say about the holiday or the trilogy of rivers, but she did pass a site called Lee Springs where she "had the pleasure of eating ice." Apparently she had found another phenomenon like the Ice Spring, or a snow bank. Otherwise she remembered, "At this point saw lots of dead cattle left by the emigrants to starve and die. Took a cutoff; had neither wood nor water for fifty-two miles. Traveled in the night."[130]

The Washington City Company, headed by J. Goldsborough Bruff, like all the other emigrant trains had to make a decision shortly after leaving Pacific Springs. According to his diary entry, that decision had been preordained. "August 2... Pacific Springs, fountain source of the Pacific streams. Numerous camps stretch along this stream on both sides. I had resolved at home, on this route, including a 'cut-off,' which would have saved at least 10 day's very bad travel. I called a meeting at 10 A.M. explained its advantages, etc. and it was unanimously resolved to take it. It is call'd by emigrants, very improperly, Soublette's Cut-Off, but was discovered by another mountaineer, Greenwood; and should be called 'Greenwood Cut-Off." Soublette had discovered and traveled a short cut higher up, from near the base of Fremont's Peak, to Fort Hall which is only practicable for mules and probably nearly obliterated."[131]

There is probably little doubt that some of the men in Bruff's company though him something of a petty dictator. He likewise no doubt felt somewhat superior, whether through education or breeding, to most of the men under him. However, periodically in his writing, Bruff seems to demonstrate a real empathy for his men, as appears in a reflective passage he wrote in his diary on August 2, 1849.

"The night clear & delightful; dark misty blue hills around us, full moon and stars shining very brightly; camp all still except the occasional snore of the weary sleeper, or the hearty laugh of the sentinels below, watching the mules grazing, at some joke to while away the hour, had caused their mirth to break upon the stillness of the night. Strange that no wolves have serenaded us to night! Where are they? The men were lively on striking these waters, & sat up some time after supper, spinning yarns, singing, and performing on various instruments of music."[132]

The following day Bruff had much of the usual business to attend to and write about. "...Half way between Pacific Springs and Little Sandy, we crossed the bed of "Dry Sandy, containing pools of Alkali water. Crossed 4 dry sandy ravines, and reached a tank, within 10 paces of the trail, on the right; It was dug square, containing good cool water, with probably a fine clay held in suspension, giving it much the appearance of cream tartar water. The drive fatiguing from heat & dust, though the road is a good one. In the afternoon, 9½ miles to Little Sandy, a northern tributary of the N.E. fork of the Colorado [River]; a beautiful mountain stream, a little brackish, but cooled by the melted snows at its source in the Wind river Mountains. Told of a grave, in the rear, inscribes with the death of Dr.— of St. Louis, died of Cholera. It seems that this was a cache where the aforesaid Doctor, had deposited $500 worth of Medicines, on his way to the Salt Lake settlement. Had sent a Mormon wagon out for it, but found, on reaching it, that some knowing one had abstracted about $200 worth, and left a note to that effect. Snow tipped peaks of the Bear River chain ahead, and on our right and rear those of the Wind River Mts. A mule, at noon, had the cholic badly, but relieved by a dose of lard oil.

There is a Fork in the road 4 or 5 miles before reaching the Little Sandy. The left branch to Fort Bridger, Salt Lake, &c. and the right is the cut-off route. At the Forks of the road, the emigrants had a meeting, when all of them followed me on the Cut-off except 2 ox wagons, who turned off to the left, on the other route. A great many trains have already preceded us on this route — broad & well beaten trail. Counted 46 dead oxen in today's march. Indeed, it is difficult to find a camping ground, destitute of carcasses."[133]

Samuel Jamison came to the region of the Sandy Rivers early, in June, 1850. He found the Big Sandy "a smart stream. Grass and wood plenty. Passed the Junction of the California and Oregon roads this day." He also found that the mostly male migration had temper problems. "Big fight in camp this evening. Sprankle and Gumpers knocked each other prity [pretty] smart. Not much hurt."[134]

"We are now on the borders of the desert region," wrote Margaret Frink as her party passed Pacific Springs. "Between here and the Green River extends a barren plain seventy miles wide, with only two streams and but scanty grass. Started across the first stretch of 21 miles, prepared to travel in the night to avoid the heat and lessen the thirst of our animals. The road was level and good. In ten miles we reached the dry bed of the small creek called Dry Sandy. The violinist played while others sang, and the long night passed off very pleasantly. We reached the first water at Little Sandy."[135]

Sarah Davis remembered the stretch of trail crossing the Sandys in somewhat the manner of Jamison. The heat, dust, lack of water, and general strain on man and beast simply meant that some people just could not get along. In the case she reported in her diary, a wife beater got a taste of frontier justice. "July 28 ... we went on to little sandy distance of twelve miles and their stoped for the day and to grase our catle we had to drive them five miles to grase and whilst the men ware gone with the catle this large train come in one mile of us and camped their a rose a quarel with them and what quareling I never heard the like they were whiping a man for whiping his wife he had whiped her every day since he joined the company and now they thought it was time for them to whip him and they caught him and striped him and took the ox gad [whip] to him and whiped him tremenduous she screamed and hollerd for him till one might have hare him for three miles."[136]

Mica Littleton left Pacific Springs on July 30, 1850. "About 8 miles more brought us to Little Sandy. Here we thought we Should find grass but the emigration has consumed all the grass within 3 and 4 miles of the road, and our Stock very much in want here. At Little Sandy there is not a spear of grass within 4 miles and what there is lies immediately on the creek. Little Sandy is a fine Stream Some 20 or 25 feet wide and 2 feet or more deep running from the mountains. Current rapid Sandy bottom. Here immediately after you cross Sandy if you take Sublette's cut off. You Strikeout to the right west or N. West. If you take the old road you take down Sandy Some miles before you Strike out. 21 of our passengers break off today on their own hook having brought oxen and made some arrangements with the proprietors. 18 miles."[137]

Sublette/Greenwood Cut-Off

Crossing the Big Sandy marked the beginning of the Sublette/Greenwood Cut-off. Some emigrants stayed on the east side and followed it south to join the old trail to Fort Bridger. The distance from the Big Sandy to the Green River via the cut-off, varied with the emigrant's estimates, or what they read in their guidebooks. Most recorded the distance at roughly 50 miles, some more, some less.

"Reached and crossed Big Sandy 7 A.M.— the starting point to cross the Green wood or Sublett's cut-off," explained J. A. Pritchard in his diary on June 20, 1849. "Our intention in the first place to stop and rest the mules till evening— then start and make a night travel a cross this desert of 45 ms— without water as the practice was heretofore been. As the day was cool and we took water for mules and ourselves pushed on. After 7 miles found a pool of rain water and good grass. The general appearance of the face of the country lying between Big Sandy and Green River is level slightly undulated, no timber, but plenty of wild sage— and in places the grass is very good. The road is firm and until you get within 15 miles of Green River, is very fine and easy travelling. From there on to the river the country is cut up very much by deep ravines. We are now 30 miles from big Sandy according to our roadmeter [a measuring device attached to a wagon wheel]. While we were at supper two gentlemen came from the ferry on their way back to meet their trains. They told us that it was still 18 miles to the river. I invited them to dismount and remain with us during the night, as their trains were not near which they did. We divided our scanty meal with them. Covered 37 miles total." The following morning Pritchard explained, "we found our way into the river bottom by a precipitous and difficult decent from the top of a very high bluff. We reached the river at 11 A.M. four miles above the ferry. After resting a few minutes we drove down to the ferry." [138]

Pritchard reported finding a little grass on the cut-off, and so did Franklin Starr, ten days behind him. Starr also wrote candidly about standing guard while on the trail. "We are now at the commencement of Green River Desert which is fifty two miles wide. We therefore lay by a short time to allow the Cattle to rest so as to start on the Desert fresh." The following afternoon they began the trek. "We lay by until 4 o'clock this afternoon and then after having eaten an early supper drove up the Cattle and started for Green River. Our Cattle had to be driven down Big Sandy some four miles to graze and I was on guard last night and with two others went down with them and make up a small fire and lay down and went to sleep as usual for instead of watching we always sleep." But they got caught. "We were awakened about midnight by the Capt. of the Guard who came from camp and was unable to find us our fire having gone out. We answered him and putting more wood on the fire we went to sleep again." After he woke up, Starr found, "the Desert is without water but there is occasionally a little grass therefore as there had been a storm around us during the day and we found the roads quite muddy we stopped after travelling 14 miles to allow the Cattle to pick for a little while and rest."[139]

Like most taking the cut-off in the dead heat of summer, Israel Hale preferred night travel and if possible a non-stop trip requiring an almost Herculean effort. He began the crossing on July 6, 1849. "Last evening at half past five o'clock we started across from Big Sandy to Green River and arrived at Green River between three and four o'clock [the following afternoon?], and instead of the distance being thirty-five miles as Mr. Ware, in his guide calls it, it is fifty-one and three-quarter miles from one river to the other. The first part of the road is good but the last is bad enough to make it up. The dust was terrible and one hill that we came down was long and very bad. We had to drive down ledges of rocks that were two feet perpendicular."[140]

Niles Searls apparently got hold of the same guidebook Hale had been reading and the discrepancy in distance infuriated him. "Were called at 1 A.M. this morning to prepare for our march across the barren plain before us. The road was excellent, with a level country and by 11 o'clock encamped to rest our animals, having made twenty miles of the journey and as we supposed, with only fifteen before us to Green River. The wind commenced blowing a gale about noon, rendering our rolling quite difficult, from the clouds of dust which enveloped us. Having been much on foot, we were all very much fatigued long before night. Our water was exhausted, but still we expected on mounting every hill to behold the river. The mules began to exhibit signs of exhaustion and some were taken from the harness, unable to go farther and pull their loads. At 10 P.M. we had come, according to our roadometer upward of forty miles, yet no signs of any river were found. It was apparent that our guidebooks were erroneous in regard to the distance and in consequence of their blunder we will be compelled to remain without food for man or beast and undergo the parching thirst. For my part, completely exhausted by fatigue, I rolled up in my blankets and was soon dreaming of home and absent friends."[141]

The Washington City Company of J. Goldsborough Bruff "followed a S.S.W. course 6½ miles when we struck Big Sandy, long low banks of sand. A company called the Wolverine Rangers, had been camp'd on the site opposite side of us, in the bottom, just above the road, and had broken up a wagon leaving the sides, etc. for the benefit of our cooks. We also found on their campground several hundred weight of fat bacon, beans, lead, iron, tools, a cast iron stove, etc. Having filled up our water kegs and canteens, at 4 P.M. we left, for the *long drive* variously estimated, from 35 to 55 ms. without water, and in only one spot a little grass; I thought, from the map, that the distance would be found 40 miles, and having water along, and judging that midway grass could be found off to the right, at the base of the hills, a few miles from the trail; and the greater portion of the route level and good. Also, that by the way of Fort Bridger and around, over rugged gorges, down steep hills, and passage of very rough canons, making by that route, at least 15 days longer, and with all its perils, certainly renders this worth the deprivation. A mule in wagon next to rear failed, he had been sick, and we left him to the tender mercy of the wolves. Ox trains rolling along, enveloped in a cloud of dust. Men & oxen suffering much from dust, heat, and sandy trail. Another mule fell, in harness, and finding that plunging the blade of a penknife into his shoulder, created no sensation, we left him also, as a tribute to the lean lank wolves. Dead oxen numerous. Traveled 17 miles rested."

The following morning Bruff's company "started again 4 A.M. Late in the afternoon we arrived at a range of very high and steep clay & sand bluffs, the base of which rests in the bottom of the Green River valley. Looked down on the perilous descent the wagons had to make. This steep decent terminating 'Greenwood's cut-off.' From the crest, down to base, right and left, were fragments of disasters, in the shape of upset wagons, wheels, axles, running gear, sides, bottoms etc. Nothing daunted, we double locked, and each teamster held firmly to the bridle of his lead mules, and led down, in succession, till the whole train reach'd the valley below, about ⅓ mile without accident." Bruff had apparently made his descent at the same place Pritchard had described.

Once down the bluffs, Bruff, unlike Pritchard, did not stop to rest. "We followed the base of these tall heights for some distance, and on a S.S.W. course, generally, for 5 or 6 miles over deep dust irregular small hills, on left side of the river, and then turned down W. to the river; drove in, on its pebbly bottom, hub deep, and rapid, turned down stream about 150 yards to a gravel bank, above water, crossed that in about the same distance, and then across the stream again, obliquely 50 yards to the opposite shore. We drove down the valley ¼ mile and camped, after one of the hardest tramps I ever took, and extremely hard on the mules. Here was another instance of the ignorance and inconvenience of the guide. I was unable to get ahead, or this error would not have occurred. Instead of turning left, some ½ mile to the steep descent, a trail branched straight ahead to the Westward & lead down gently to an old ferry; which if we had taken it, would have saved at least 3 miles, making the cut-off actually but 40 miles. And throwing out the 2 steep descents which are so easily avoided, is a excellent road."[142]

Those going out in 1850, and reading the same guidebooks as those migrating in 1849, saw the cut-off as a good way to make up some valuable time. Crossing the cut-off evolved into something of an endurance race and most parties pushed to the maximum limit of their energies to make the crossing in the shortest possible time, as did Henry Wellenkamp. In two brief entries, for Tuesday and Wednesday, June 25–26, 1850, he laid out the daunting task in the simplest of words. "Laid by til 4 P.M. Prepared for Sublet's Cutoff or Desert, traveled all night, until 3 P.M. This day we arrived nearly exhausted on the Green River. I was dead sick. Covered 45 miles."[143]

Also in June, 1850, Margaret Frink's party opted for the cut-off as well. "The plain is covered with sage-brush and grease-wood," she wrote to begin her two days of entries covering her trek across the cut-off. "On our right commence the foot-hills of the Wind River chain and beyond that the Snowy Mountains rise abruptly and to great height. Traveled six miles came to the Big Sandy. We passed, on the way, the forks of the road, the left hand of which runs southwest to Salt Lake City, two hundred miles distant. We took the right hand road, which is supposed to be shorter, and is known as Sublette's Cut-off. Having now a forty-mile desert to cross without water, we filled our water bottles, containing five gallons each. Traveled during the night 20 miles and stopped at four o'clock in the morning."

After a brief rest they rejoined the march, noting in her diary that they could "see Fremont's Peak rising above all others. A few miles west of its base are the ruins of an old fort built by Captain Bonneville, of the U.S. Army, who explored this region in 1832. There is no water on the desert, but our bottles supplied us with all that we needed. 27 miles brought us to the bluffs on the western edge of the desert." From the following description, no one had revised the guidebooks to show the easier route down that Bruff had mentioned discovering the year before. "The bluffs were high, steep, and rocky, and we had to let the wagons down cautiously with ropes. The narrow gorges we passed down were filled with clouds of blinding dust. At the foot of the bluffs the dust was twelve to twenty inches deep. The river bottom was a plain of dust, crowded with wagons and animals, and thickly populated with emigrants waiting their regular turn to be ferried over. Each of the ferries has a small flatboat rowed with oars."[144]

John Birney Hill marked his July 4th holiday of 1850, by taking the cutoff. "This morning we took or struck the Desert, which is 53 miles wide. The reason why it is called a Desert is because there is no water (plenty of grass) from Big Sandy to Green-River, (except a mudhole, about 10 miles W. of Big Sandy). For about 25 miles W. of Big Sandy the road is level & good—(but I found it very dusty—some 5 or 6 inches deep.) The rest of the road is cut up with deep hollows—very hard on Oxen &c. A steep hill to go down before you get to the River. Nearly all of the Emigrants start across this Desert about 4 O'clock in the evening & travel all night—stop at daylight—eat their breakfast—let their Oxen, Horses &c, eat a little grass, & start on. Oxen have & are Expiring quite fast, We pass 5 or 6 every day."[145]

Sarah Davis took the cut-off in late July, 1850, and like the rest made the desert crossing at night. "…On the big sandy parted with some of our company there some of the best men I ever got acquainted with. I think they went to California and us go on to Oregon." It is quite true that the original destination of the Davis party was to be Oregon. But three weeks after she wrote this entry, they concluded that California held greater promise and they turned toward the gold fields. "we encamped on the big sandy 35 miles of desert traveled all night and come to green river there is a ferry here this river is clear and swift curent the river is thirty rods wide I saw six snake Indians here they cary a white feather with them a sign of pease they look fright full."[146]

Big Sandy to Fort Bridger

Emigrants turning to the left at the Big Sandy forks headed toward Fort Bridger and eventually Salt Lake City on the old road. Whereas most of the diarists going out in 1849 took the Sublette Cut-off, many of the diarists following, particularly in 1850—Josselyn, Jamison, Littleton, Parsons, Edmundson, Davis, and Booth—decided to forgo the cut-off and probably based on their own interpretation of the guidebooks, or having heard the route via Salt Lake City instead of Fort Hall might be shorter or better, began the approximately 82 mile leg to Bridger. Like those taking the cut-off, they began their trek by crossing the Big Sandy but then veered off to the southwest, roughly parallel to the river, and moved toward its confluence with the Green River.

It took Amos Josselyn five days to make the 80 miles, indicative of the sometimes difficult nature of the trail. The terrain undulated a great deal, primarily due to the number of streams, nearly all tributaries of the Green River, 50 miles below where those taking the cut-off encountered it. Each branch had its own valley and set of bluffs that had to be ascended and then descended. Josselyn's chronology is crisp and his diary entries short, beginning on July 2, 1849. "Drove 8¼ miles to the Big Sandy before breakfast. Weather cool and roads excellent. Made 25¼ miles today. July 3 ... drove to Green River 10 miles. We found the river too high to ford, but there is a ferry, kept by Mormons. There is about 20 wagons ahead of us and that being as many as can cross today, we will not get over before tomorrow forenoon. Weather cool and pleasant. Roads excellent. July 4... By 10 o'clock they got ready to cross our wagons but being hindered by wind and rain we did not get over much before night. We however hitched up and drove 8 miles and encamped. July 5... Drove to Black's Fork [tributary of the Green River] and nooned on good camping ground After stopping three hours we drove to Ham's Fork [flowed into Black's Fork] and encamped on first rate ground. July 6... Left Ham's Fork drove to Black's Fork [second time] which we found too high to ford. Consequently we kept to the north side of it and encamped 7 miles from a stream that empties into Black's Fork. July 7... Drove 13 miles to Fort Bridger."[147] Josselyn does not mention stopping at Fort Bridger and offers no description of it.

Samuel Jamison followed the route to Fort Bridger in mid June, 1850, and found things much as Josselyn did the year before. The number of days required to make it to the fort proved the only major difference. June 12 ... traveled 17 miles [from the fork in the trail] to where the road strikes big Sandy and took diner. Left camp at 2 o'clock and traveled 10 miles to green river which is very hard to cross. We had to swim our stalk [stock] over and take our baggage over on the flat [ferry]. They charge one dollar pr horse here for ferriage. Man seen floating dead on the water here to day who had been drowned on the upper road. Could not be ketched. The river here is ten rods wide and deep an nough [enough] to swim a horse."

On June 13, Jamison reported they "traveled 17 miles for diner. Here we struck Blacks fork of Green River. Traveled up the river five miles to the fording. Here we had to get our Baggage taken over on a wagon Box which some of the Indians use as a Boat and swam our Stalk over. This stream is a bout two rods wide very deep."

The next morning, Jamison's party rose early and "Left camp at half past five. Traveled over very sandy road. Crossed 2 small streams which were prity heigh [probably Ham's Fork and Muddy or Cottonwood Creek]. Very heavy hale storm covered the ground about 1 inch deep. Encamped at four o'clock on small but very rapid stream. This was a very hard night on us. Every thing wet and cold." The following day Jamison's party "passed fort Bridger." They stopped only long enough for his friends, "Spotswood & Gumpers" who had been in a camp fight just days earlier, to "swopt horses here with Bridger."[148]

Mica Littleton's company moved along the old Fort Bridger trail a fortnight behind Jamison. Like Jamison's, his party made the 80 or so miles in about three days. "August 1 ... big Sandy a fine large Stream more than 100 feet wide. Here you cross and take out across the hills and about 17½ miles brings you to Big Sandy again but you do not cross it. There is nothing but hills and ravines from where you cross big Sandy until you arrive on its bank again Some bunch grass but not a drop of water the whole distance but the road excellent except a few places. 10 miles from where you strike big Sandy the second time you come to Green River a beautiful mountain Stream about 200 feet wide. Very rapid current clear water with plenty of fish the mountain Trout in it. We caught 2 in our mess which was very fine. Here there is a ferry. 2 miles below there is a good ford when the river is not too high and there is a ford above also. 31½ miles today."

Littleton reported the next day that his party "Rolled out this morning (after Ferrying across the river) about 11 o'clk. Keeping down the river nearly a South course 7 miles. Here you strike out a Southwest course. There are plenty of camping places from the Ferry to where you leave Green River. It is about 16 miles to Blacks fork. A number of Steep hills and some rough road. Neither grass nor water there. There is little fuel here a few willows on the opposite side. 21½ miles today."

On August 3, Littleton again rolled out early. "4 miles brought us to Hams fork a nice little Stream about 30 or 35 feet wide. Good water good grass and willows for fuel." Having crossed Ham's Fork the trail continued along the valley of Black's Fork, to the southwest. Littleton reported passing "several dry creeks" and rambling along an undulating road, sometimes touching the river, sometimes passing over its bluffs. "In all today, about 20 miles."

The road got worse in the final stretch before reaching the fort, as Littleton described it on August 4. "In 2 miles you will cross Blacks fork again. Keep up the river about 2 miles and cross back again. Here is Some Rough crooked road. You come to Blacks fork again but do not cross it. About 8 miles more you come to Fort Bridger a trading establishment kept by Bridger and Vasquesz. Blacks fork 3 miles above this breaks off into several channels three for 4 you cross before you get to the Fort and one or 2 after you pass the fort. The Fort stands on one of these Islands a beautiful place to live. Here one of our passengers Died after an illness of Some 2 weeks. His name was Adam Thumb died of Tiford [thypoid] fever."[149]

The leg from the Sandy to Fort Bridger had taken Jamison and Littleton about four days. It took Lucena Parsons' party ten days. Much of their original train had left them and their yokes of oxen, slow compared to other draft animals, and even to a man on foot, must have been nearly worn out. Yet she found things of interest along that stretch of trail to write about and took the drudgery of trail life in step. Beginning on September 4, 1850, she recorded a series of entries: "…reached Big Sandy. These rivers are rightly named for look which way you will they are sandy. Here we found several companies of merchants taking goods to Salt Lake. They have 40 waggons, several loads of them stoves. Yesterday the mail going from Fort Bridger to Laramie overtook us. There is a great deal of travel from one fort to another. We are now in the Snake territory of the Indians.

"September 5… Our company left us this morn & went on. We stopt to wate for a cow as many on this journey are obliged to do or lose many of their cattle. At noon there came up 3 waggons & stopt for the night. Wolves very thick here. September 6… Those waggons went on this morning & left us alone again. Rather lonely for one waggon to stop in this dreary place. Saw no one all day, the emigration mostly going up on the old road some 3 miles above here." [I am not sure what road she referenced here, as she was on the "old road." Possibly she referred to the cut-off.]

Then Parsons' party lost two days while they looked for berries and cows. "Sept 7… We went after berries & black currants which are very plenty on the banks of this and nearly all the streams in this reagion. These currants grow as larg as the Inglish cherries at home in the east & are as black as the cherry when ripe. They are sweet & make very good pies. Came home & found the cattle gone. We were in a fine fix so far from help. September 8… The men started at daylight in search of them & found them near where we had left the cow some miles back. They found some one had taken her on so they came back & made preparation to start very early in the morning as there is no use stoping any longer."

Not until September 9 did Parsons reach the Green River, "the most beautiful stream I ever saw. The water is very green & runs very swift over a smooth bottom covered with pebbles. Went 5 miles up the stream & campt. September 10… With the morning we toiled on again. Traveled 15 miles without wood or water, nothing but dry sandy hills. In the eve came to Black Forks." She reported they had made 18 miles that day, for them a major effort and more than they had covered the three previous days. September 11 "…came to Hams Fork, a fine stream & staid her till noon. Made 5½ miles & came to Black Forks a second time. Here we camped in a pretty place with hills on the right & left, all of them green as coperas."

By September 12 Parsons had reached the upper valley of Black's Fork. "Started on again & in 1½ miles crosst Black Forks. After this we found a rough road for 10 miles & no water. Crosst Black Forks the 3[third] time but found no place to camp. Went 2 miles & came to Black Forks for the 4 time & campt. It being an old camp ground we found poor grass." Finally, on September 13, 1850, the goal of finishing the leg to Bridger appeared possible. "By hurrying all day we reached the stream that runs through Bridger & campt 2 miles down the steam. Saw some 200 Indians on horse back riding at full speed." The next day they "traveled 8½ miles & campt on a small creek this side of Fort Bridger. The Fort is composed of 4 log houses & a small enclosure for horses. I think it is a beautiful spot. There are many Indian huts in sight & the land is very rich."[150]

At the Green River

Having reached the western terminus of the Sublette/Greenwood Cutoff, following a grueling 50-mile trek, most emigrants found the meadows of the Green River valley the perfect place to take a rest, refitting the body and spirit of both man and beast. Everyone who wrote of the Green River rallying point had good things to say about it, with the possible exception of the ferry operation there.

"We found there 24 wagons before us—14 of which were crossed by night," recalled J. A. Pritchard on June 22, 1849. "I succeeded in effecting a hire of the boat for the night which was not objected to by those who were ahead of me. We were to furnish the hands to man the boat and pay him $1.50 pr wagon or he would furnish the hands & charge $3.00 pr wagon. I preferred the former as we had men with us that could beat his best hands with ease. We commenced crossing our wagons at 9 o'clock and by 12 we had the whole train over, with all the Baggage. The ferryboat was constructed of 4 small canoes which were roughly rafted together. The ferry is kept by some Frenchmen [more correctly Canadian]—who live in lodges made of skins—and propped up with poles. They have Indian Squaws for wives—in this way they live and trade with the Indians for their Furs & skins etc." Pritchard writing further described the Green River as "a bold rapid stream about 350 to 400 feet wide with a good deal of water for a stream of its size. Boys caught a good many fine fish."[151]

Franklin Starr, arriving on July 3, 1849, remembered, "The hill descending to Green river is the worst we have yet come across being very long steep crooked & rocky. Green River is about the size of the North Platte and more swift. It can usually be forded but now it is to high and is rising." The next morning ushered in a national holiday, but Starr and others at the crossing found little energy to celebrate. "We are still lying here having not been able to cross the river yet as we have to wait until our turn and there are a great many ahead of us. We drive our cattle two or three miles down the river and graze them but there is but poor feed for them and they do not appear to be gaining any. There is a mule train here waiting to cross. A Company of Soldiers accompany them. I believe there destination is Bear River at Fort Hall. There has been some little firing of guns in honor of the Day but the Emigrants are to much worried and worn out to give much exertion." Starr's company did not get across the river until July 6.[152]

Israel Hale's company settled into the Green River valley during the first week in July, 1849. Like everyone else he had to first get across the rapidly flowing river. "We found it too high for fording and the ferry man only charged us seven dollars for setting my wagon over the celebrated Green River, a stream not as large as the Maramee [a river he had lived near back east]." Frankly, seven dollars to ferry a wagon over a river, any river in the

United States, would have been considered price gouging. But then the ferrymen knew they had a monopoly and could charge essentially whatever price they fancied.

Hale also discovered that the Green River valley hardly bore any resemblance to the color in its name. "Of all the poor countries that I have seen this is certainly the poorest. There is little or no grass, no timber — water, but high wind and dust in abundance. Between three and five o'clock we crossed the river, and about the same time swum the cattle over. We found on the west side several half-breed Indians—traders. They bought and sold at their own price. Alkali is still abundant and we find less stock lying dead every day, some from the effect of the poisoned water, others hard driving."[153]

Like other diarists reaching the Green River, Niles Searls would have liked to have a word or two with the authors of the most popular guidebooks. "We descended several dangerous hills, one of them one-half mile in length, and finally, after dragging rather than travelling nine miles, reached the river, making in all fifty-two miles from the Big Sandy. Had the authors of our guidebooks been along during the last few miles, I fear they would have paid dearly for their carelessness or ignorance. The sight of the river, however, a fine, swift stream one hundred and fifty years wide, with pure ice water from the mountain above and a hearty draught at its brink, soon soothed our perturbed feelings and revived our spirits. The channel contains from six to ten feet of water, and is crossed by a ferry established by some Mormons from Salt Lake. The terms for ferrying are $2 per wagon and from sixty to seventy-five are crossed per day. [One can only wonder why Hale paid seven dollars, but probably he used the ferry run by the French half-breed traders and not the Mormons.] The stream is lined with wagons waiting to recruit their teams after their unexpected drive. A number of fine fish (salmon trout) have been caught in the river."[154]

J. Goldsborough Bruff's teamsters had taken the plunge and forded the Green River on arriving, thus avoiding the wait at the ferry. Once over they found it just as advisable to rest themselves and their animals for a while. Bruff found a lot to see and do along the river. "At the Ferry, numerous dead oxen and wrecks of many wagons. Thomas and 2 other mountaineers came into camp. Said that from here to Fr. Hall the grass was plentiful, but beyond that probably scarce. He was from Fr. Bridger and with a party of traders, was speculating in horses. Said he knew Col. Fremont, who was once anxious to employ him. The Missouri whisky cart, got down here, and some of my men obtained Alcohol from it; particularly a party, faction, or clique, who were electioneering very strong to change the Presidency of the Association." Bruff, of course, served as the president, and from his report, he expected problems from the beginning. "When the association was formed, with its constitution, civil officers, etc. for mining purposes, I told them, at home, that it was all of no importance, and would never go into operation in California; well assured in my own mind, that the hardships of the tramp, and its consequent development of bad spirits, and selfishness particularly, would combine to scatter the members, as soon as they struck the Sacramento valley, in all directions."[155]

Pritchard's company decided to regroup and rest, and do a little business at the Green River. Writing in his diary on June 22, 1849, he had some good things to say about the Native Americans he encountered there. "Abbott purchased a horse this morning at the ferry of one of the Frenchmen at $50. We here found quite a number of Indians loitering round the ferry. They had a great number of fine horses and for which they asked a big price. These are the Soshonees [sic] or Snake Indians. They are decidedly the best looking and most intelligent Indians that I ever saw. They possess an affability and suavity of manners not common at all to the Red Men of the forest. Their women are handsome delicate & genteel looking all the circumstances taken into consideration. The Shoshonees are, and, have always been kind and friendly to the Whites." That conclusion may have been reinforced by a visit Pritchard received that very evening before writing his entry.

"This evening the Old Chief of the Soshonee tribe came on from the ferry where he had been stopping for a time and encamped near to us with his family and a party of 25 or 30 men women & children. The Old Chief shook hands with me and said in broken English the he wished to tell me that his people would not disturb anything that belonged to us. He said his people were honest and would not steal. He continued to say that the White people were a big people — had big country — heap of cattle and horses and lived in great big fine houses. And Indians little people. Laying his hand on his breast he said Indians loved white people — white people love Indians etc."[156]

Pritchard not only had a friendly encounter with the Indians at the Green River, but out of the blue added new travelers to his company whose expertise might come in handy in the near future. "Dr. William Thomas of Augusta, Ky came up and asked me if I had any objection to his travelling with us from then on. I told him no, to turn in. Dr. Roach from New York with two wagons asked the same privilege to which I assented. They had been travelling in Capt. Basye's train from the states, and were not altogether satisfied with his way of doing business and prefured [preferred] mine."[157]

Franklin Starr's company had waited at the ferry for two days to get across the Green River. Despite that, part of his group decided to take time for a little recreation. "The greater part of the company hitched up and drove on 6 miles to a small stream some 10 feet wide and camped. There was a tolerable plenty of feed here. Part of the company remained at the river as they wanted to rubber boat but were not willing to bring it along but wanted us to wait until they got through with it which of course we did not do." Bruff also reported bringing along a rubber boat, but had discarded it because of weight. From Starr's brief comments it seems that some of his company, probably some young men, wanted to do a little joy riding on the Green River's current before they also discarded theirs. The next day, Starr added, "We in company with another wagon left the company today and started ahead. There were two other waggons also that left at the same time. The company wished to remain another day and we were anxious to be moving along. Probably we shall not see them again."[158]

Henry Wellenkamp struck the Green River on Thursday, June 27, 1850. He didn't write anything about the river or the scenery or even the Indians and traders. He did, however, conduct some business. "Bought carriage of Wilkinson for $35.00. Paid for ferry $8.00 [he must have used the same one Hale had the year before]. Sold my wagon for $3.00. Left Green River and went to a creek."[159]

Having tumbled down from the steep bluffs of the Green River, the Frinks, reached the end of the cut-off on June 27, 1850, the same day as Wellenkamp. No doubt with some relief, Margaret Frink wrote, "at the Green River ... many of the animals had already been swum across; but the water was high, deep, swift, blue, and cold as ice, heading in the ice mountains on our right. The poor horses were reluctant to venture in. One of our animals utterly refused to swim. The ferryman loath to take him over but at last consented. Mr. Frink taken sick during the day, no longer able to walk, our wagons could not be taken over. The situation was a serious one. I was frightened at feeling we were almost helpless, a thousand miles from civilization."[160]

William Frush's party had also done the Sublette Cut-off and arrived on the Green River on July 11, 1850. "Driving all night we made Green River at 12 o'clock on this day crossed and swam our stock. I drove 5 miles up River to a prong of it and camped. Paid for Ferry of Waggon $7. Horse $1.50. Oxen $2.00. Thare is much Alkali water near the Ferry on both sides and a vary large number of dead stock about it. Stream 100 yards wide vary swift & deep, dangerous to cross. Boats & facilities good business."

Lying over for a day to rest, Frush's opinion of the Green River valley did not improve much. "We lay by all day & discharged our waggon into Griffith's. George is very sick to day. Fever and much pain taken last night. The valley or bottom of this River is poor burnt up ash and sand. Bottom produces but little grass & that only where the ground is wet and the whole surrounded by high steep hills or mountains of sand. It is not fir for any thing. It has been vary much misrepresented. I heard that it was a rich valley. It is not, the fact it is a miserable valley; but good water. There is many Emigrants laying here to day recruiting." Then almost as a footnote he added, "There was many took the Salt Lake Road after crossing the Green River by going down to west side after striking one of the branches 8 miles beyond the Ferry."[161] If they did, it totally negated the point of taking the cut-off, but some may have had second thoughts about proceeding to Fort Hall, having heard the road through Salt Lake might be shorter or better.

Despite the questionable quality of the area, Margaret Frink found the Green River valley a welcome rest stop in late June, 1850. She reported in her diary meeting yet another interesting character. "This morning we heard that a gentleman by the name of Redwine, who had crossed the plains the year previous, was encamped near us with his family. I called at their camp to learn, if possible, something of the road ahead of us; for our guidebooks did not cover this part of the route. Mr. Redwine's reply was that he knew no more about the road than if he had never traveled it; that everything seemed new to him, but he thought it was yet 1,000 miles to California. The Crow Indians call the Green River the Prairie Chicken River, from the quantity of grouse to be found. The Spanish called it Rio Verde."[162]

Laying over for a couple of days to recoup some strength in their animals, the Frinks suddenly found themselves as a cause for further delay. "Mr. Rose and Frink are sick with mountain fever," she began her entry on July 1, 1850. Then travelling companions reorganized again. "Mr. Wand and his company have left their wagons here and made pack saddles, intending to pack their clothing, blankets, provisions, and cooking utensils on their animals, in order to travel faster." And finally, some startling news. "This morning some packers overtook us and brought the alarming tidings that the cholera had appeared on the Platte River, behind us. This was the first that we had heard of its being on the road."[163]

Toward the Bear River Road

Whether emigrants took the Sublette/Greenwood Cut-off, or the Fort Bridger road, eventually they would rejoin those they had left on the Big Sandy, in the valley of the Bear River. The only exception to that would have been if they had continued on to Salt Lake City and used that site as the jumping-off point for the final third of their journey to California. Separated by a mountain ridge from the Green River, which flows in a southerly direction to eventually join the Colorado River, the Bear River flows northward, across the borders of modern southwest Wyoming and northeast Utah, into southeastern Idaho, before looping back to the south and flowing into the Great Salt Lake. The northerly flowing section of the Bear River provided a pathway from Fort Bridger toward Fort Hall, forming a key section of the original route to the Oregon Country. Those emigrants who had gone to Bridger, unless going directly to Salt Lake, as stated, simply continued along the old road. Those emigrants that had taken the cut-off, continued due west from the Green River, over the mountain ridges dividing the two valleys, and joined the old road again. That distance, most emigrants marked at approximately 60 miles, and contained some major climbs and descents. The individual will of each emigrant received a severe test as the trek to see the elephant con-

162   Part II • From Fort Laramie to Fort Hall and Salt Lake City

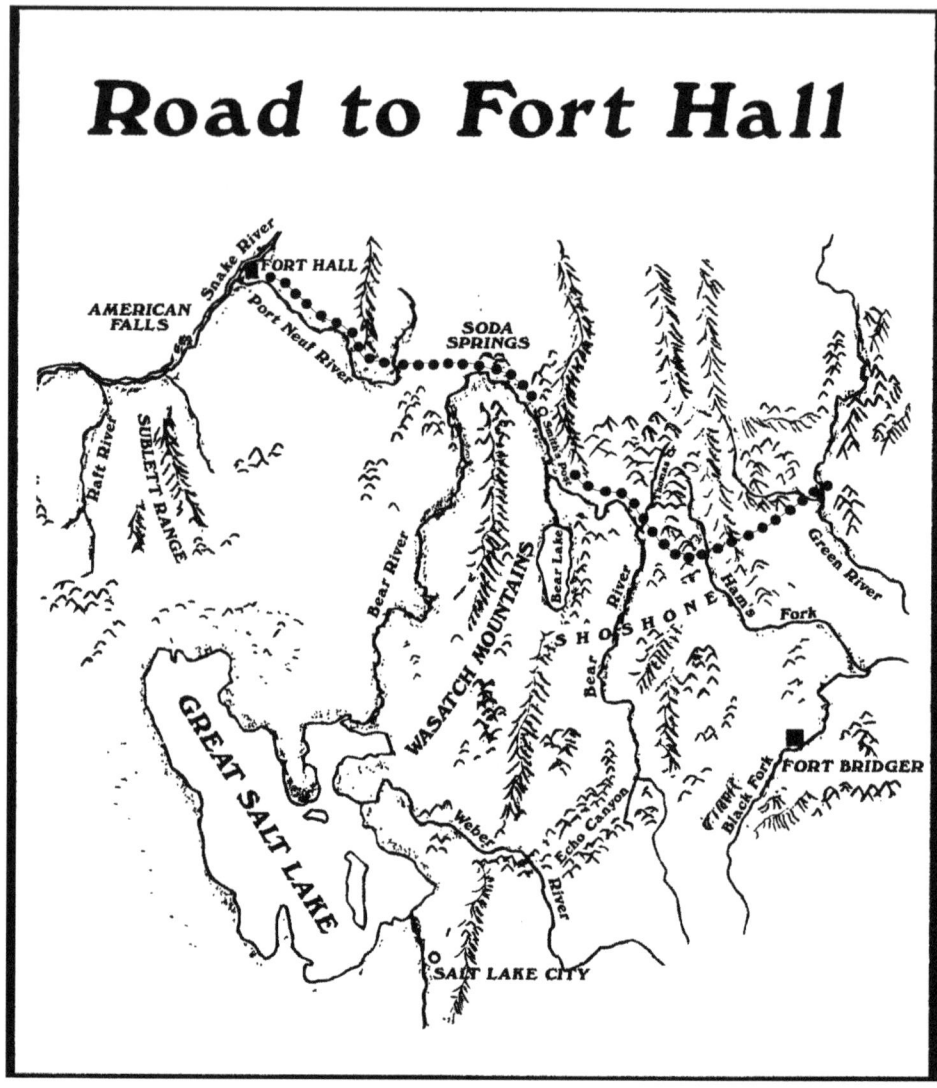

Road to Fort Hall — trails along Bear River to Fort Hall and Hudspeth Cut-off.

tinued but their ability to observe, and interact with fellow emigrants and other characters they met on the way does not seem to have diminished.

"Green willow switches make as poor a fire as anything I ever tried. Buffalo chips are bad enough but willow is worse. Wild sage is good. I had as soon have wild sage for a fire as the common wood used in Missouri. Green or dry it burns well and we often find it of good size; as large or larger than my arm," explained Israel Hale the day after leaving the Green River behind.

"After having encamped for so long a time on the barrens and in the sand, we find it quite a luxury to encamp once more on the green grass and more especially in as handsome a valley and by a fine a creek as this."

The next day, on July 9, 1849, they "drove up Ham's Fork of Green River or Fontinell's Fork [Fontenelle] about four miles. We passed a place where they were burying a man by the name of Merill, of Lexington, Missouri, that was killed by a wagon. We also passed a train of U.S. Troops going to Bear River to build a fort. After that we took to the mountains and traveled through dust ten miles, grass and water tolerable good. About one-fourth of our men are on the sick list and there is much complaint among the trains generally about sickness. We see much of human nature on a trip of this kind; hardly a day passes that a train does not split or a division takes place. In a measure the like has occurred several times in our train. In starting we had more than twenty wagons. It is now reduced to eight."[164]

Franklin Starr had left some of his party at the Green River also and moved on. "Traveled 18 miles and camped on Hams Fork [the Fontenelle]. Our way lay through the mountains which we camped in last night. We have passed some snow and a number of streams made by the melting of the snow. The road has been very hilly. We have fine grass to night for the cattle. There has been a very hard wind blowing from the west for three days." The following day, July 9, 1849, he continued, "We crossed the fork and rose the hill which was very steep. The road is ascending the hill this morning followed the top of a rocky ridge so that on either side of us but few feet from the wagon it was nearly perpendicular. The old road down the hill we descended was so steep that emigrants were obliged to let their wagon down with ropes."[165]

J. A. Pritchard's company had passed the same ridge in front of Starr on June 24, 1849. "Crossed a very high ridge of the mountains. The descent on the west side was so abrupt that we were compelled to let our wagons down in part by attaching ropes and letting the men hold on behind. At the foot of the hill we came to what is called Hams fork of Bear River. [Pritchard had most certainly reached the Fontenelle, or a branch of it and had mistakenly read, or been told it flowed into the Bear River instead of the Green River.] It is about 50 feet wide at this place with a strong current as all these mountain streams have. We had to raise our wagon beds 8 or 10 inches to keep water out" [accomplished by putting wooden blocks between the axle lumbers and the bed].

Then Pritchard proved that despite being on a trail of immense hardships and privations for so many, that there really were good Samaritans to be found along the way. "A Mr. Sidney Smith, Joseph Fiffen, & 3 other from Chiviot, Ohio, in attempting to cross had upset their wagon in the stream & had wet all of their things—and spoilt a great deal of their provisions. They however had succeeded in getting their things out before we got there. I gave them a sack of corn meal which was very acceptably and cheerfully received."[166]

The express company conveying Niles Searls left the Green on June 25, 1849. "Proceeded down from the middle ferry a short distance, then ascending the mountain on the right bade farewell to the Green River. Descending the mountain on the west, we struck Bear Creek [not to be confused with the Bear River still some distance away] and followed it up during the day. Every few days we come across a canvas lodge occupied by some Canadian Frenchman who dignifies his establishment by the name of a trading post, though the title of 'Gambling Hell' would convey a more correct idea of its uses. In general the proprietor is a man who, destitute of character, has wandered off among the Indians; and with a squaw for a wife, lives in all respect like the natives, except that he gambles with the whites. We ascend the mountains through deep ravines from one stream and descend on the opposite side to another. The usual height of these mountains is from one to two thousand feet above the valleys. We are hoping to have better rolling when we reach the Bear River, down which we will descend for a considerable distance." During the night Searls' party "Suffered intolerably from mosquitoes; not even the frosty nights seem to daunt them in the least, but on they come, the foe of man and beast alike."[167]

Bruff's Washington City Company moved off from the Green River on August 7, 1849. He observed some interesting sights as they began their ascent to the west. "On the right of trail, vertical cliffs of a mouse colored sand stone, on the face of which was engraved with a fine-pointed instrument, an Indian diagram, representing 43 rifles, nearly vertical, and a chief and horse, apparently separated from 4 other Indians and a horse laying down, by a stream with a small fork to it. This I accidentally discovered, by going close to the cliff, and at once drew it. Sand hills next to the river. On left of trail, a grave with sandstone slab, engraved thus: Mary, consort of J.M. Fulkerson, Died July 14. 1847. The grave was covered with sand stone slabs, and by the names, it will be seen that the lady is the mother of the youth, buried in the Rattlesnake Pass, miles back which I visited on July 26th. The youth died on the 1st and 13 days after his mother died here."[168]

And there were even more interesting sights, for Bruff to record further along the road to the Bear River. "March of 9 miles, narrow and very crooked ridges, reached the beautiful valley of La Fontenelle a tributary of Green River. The train descended the bluffs, and entered the valley about 1 mile above the French traders camp; and here camped [probably the same that Searls encountered]. I visited the camp of the Frenchmen, composed of conical skin lodges, tents, bush houses, and about 10 blue ox-wagons. Here was a mixture, white women, and squaws & children, of every age and hue. The men were in a tent, playing Monte, on a skin, for silver. Sitting on a Skin, stretched over sticks, to form a seat, was a yellow Indian girl, about 7 years old, dandling an infant, which was nearly white; and another small child was thumping on a common U.S. tenor drum. Indian goods, of every description, mingled with horse-trappings, were scattered around amongst the wagons. In the fine meadow, on the opposite side, was a large band of fat horses & ponies.

"I saw a half-breed woman taking a very young infant by its legs & hands, and plunge it under, head & heels, in the rippling cool stream; it did not squall, probably too much choked to do so. Some squaws were highly roughed with vermilion, and one of the Frenchmen, had several stripes of it, a la sauvage, across his nose & cheeks. About 1½ miles higher up the creek is another camp of these traders, of 4 ordinary canvass tents, 3 skin lodges, & 2 booths. They all have a number of dogs of various kinds. They ask high prices for their horses, few less than $300. These chaps have been sent here by old Bridger, to trade with the emigrants, who have mostly come this way; thus trying to cut off the cut-off folks. Great feats of horsemanship by the French traders, riding at full speed, over plain, stream, ditches, and irregular & elevated places in pursuit of run-away poney." The next day Bruff reported that one of the daredevil riders, "The Frenchman — Thomas was thrown from his horse, had a brick in his hat, at the time [meaning he went over head first], injuring his back and spine much." Bruff also found a new delicacy to eat. "Innumerable large black mice here [probably muskrats], living in holes in the bank of the stream, generally under bushes: they are fat and very soft & silky: not at all shy, probably unacquainted yet with man's destructive propensity, of which I, however, convinced one by knocking it over, roasting & eating it. Found it very tender & sweet."[169]

Pritchard's company took three days to traverse the rough space between the Green and Bear Rivers, arriving at the latter on June 25, 1849. "We descended after crossing the dividing ridge between Green River & Bear River a mountain one mile in length. There was about 200 feet of it over a precipice of stone that we had to take our mules from the wagons & let them down by hand & with rope. After we gained the foot of the hill we crossed a small creek and ascended anther high hill — descended it & struck Bear River valley."[170]

Israel Hale found the hills just as steep, recording his descent to the Bear River road on July 12, 1849. "This morning we drove up a hill and down a mountain, a long and steep one. We then struck a valley which led us to Bear River, a very handsome valley where we encamped. The grass is fine and the alkali abundant. Traveled about ten miles. The water in the wash pan was frozen so hard this morning that it could be turned over without losing its contents."[171]

"This morning we crossed the last ridge of the Bear River Mountains and descend into the Valley of the river having the same name," recorded Niles Searls, in his journal, a fortnight behind Hale. He continued, providing an excellent description of the geography of the area. "The Fort Bridger road unites with the one over which we have come at this point. We are now in the Great Basin, the Bear River emptying into the Salt Lake. Its course here is nearly north and we shall follow its course till it turns to the west and south, a distance of some seventy or eighty miles. The river bottom is several miles in width and abounds in good grass. By taking the cut-off we have gained several days on those who took the old route."

If the emigrants appeared a haggard lot, having reached that far, it could be expected. But Searls might have assumed that United States Army troops on the road at the same time might have fared better. "The Oregon regiment has come up with us this evening. They look as ragged and woe begone as the rest of us. Their guide, a Mr. Wilcox of New York, was shot the other day by an Indian who had brought an express through to the forces from Fort Hall and was returning with them. He was in the wagon with Wilcox at the time and after shooting him, seized a revolver, wounded the teamster, shot a horse, and ran to the river bank where he was overtaken and shot dead by a Lieutenant of the Army. Some suppose that it was a revenge for some former deed that he was murdered."[172]

J. Goldsborough Bruff continued to encounter and describe a marvelous assortment of characters and scenes along the trail after leaving the Green River. First he decided to take a slight detour. "Aug. 9. At 6 a. m. Train in motion. Road winds westerly, over a high ridge, and as our predecessors had all taken a left hand road, along the top of long high ridges, to the left, I took a right hand branch trail, to the right, to ascertain the difference; and found, on striking the valley of 'Smith's fork' that it was much the shortest, though there was a pretty steep but short place in it to ascend." Then amazingly, he reported, "in a narrow swampy passage, with streams, springs, and willows, saw a large cart abandoned, and near it, on the ground, a small piece of apple-pie, and fragments of light wheat bread: I ate the piece of pie, and found it good."

Later in the day, and a bit further along the trail, "On our way down, we passed through an extensive camp, or place where the Indians had had a village, probably last winter. At least 60 willow lodges, in various stages of dilapidation. I here shot 3 grouse, wounded and lost 4 others, and killed 2 prairie dogs, which are very numerous. A number of the red-shouldered hawk flying about, and lighting on bushes. I struck a light & broiled one of the prairie-dogs, and we had a bite." Apparently the pie found on the ground did not fill him up.

Towards late afternoon Bruff caught up with his company and encountered yet another new enclave of mountain traders. "Another detachment of Old Bridger's traders were camped here, and had put up a notice at the branching of the road, for the emigrants to take the left one, as the best. They had horses to sell. Their camp within 200 yds of mine. The trader told me that during the month of June, 3,200 wagons passed through this valley. The chief of this party is named Greenwood, he is a fine tall, well-formed, and handsome fellow about 35 years of age, and dressed in a full suite of smoked deerskin: frock, pantaloons, moccasins, etc. He also has a harem of 3 dark

Shoshonee damsels, two of whom I saw, were as black & ugly as mud. Ox wagons, skin-lodges, tents, squaws, papooses, saddles, etc. as usual."

As darkness fell Bruff ended another eventful day of his trek to see the elephant. "At night, being fine & clear, a party of our musical boys went over to the trader's camp; with a violin, accordion, bugle, etc. and were politely invited into a skin lodge. Our party of a dozen, and the Frenchmen & squaws, all crowded around the interior of the lodge, made it rather uncomfortable. They performed several lively airs, such as 'Dan Tucker,' 'Carry me back to old Virginia,' 'Zip Coon,' Etc. accompanied by singing, which delighted the traders much, and particularly the Indians."[173]

The Washington City Company pushed on the next morning following their night of music and revelry. Bruff found more somber things to write about. "...On the left of the trail, a grave — scratched on a sandstone slab, which was at the head, but is now prostrate & broken: This grave has been opened & filled in again. Died July 21st 1847. Mr. Beverly Appron xxx. 5 miles beyond, Sacred to the memory of Alfred Corum, Who died July 4th, 1849. Aged 22 years. 300 yds further... Margaret Campbell, departed, July 28, 1848, Aged 36 yrs: 4 mos. 23 days. Reached Smith's Spring, the head of a branch, 3 miles below Smith's fork of the Bear River, after a very toilsome & dusty drive, nearly suffocated with dust. Found numerous ox companies here. Passed several dead oxen on the road."[174]

On July 3, 1850, Margaret Frink's small and somewhat ill band departed the Green River. "This morning Mr. Rose was not quite so well. In the afternoon he grew much worse, having a severe attack of mountain fever. At two o'clock a company from Illinois overtook us. I rode on horseback most of the day. We traveled thirteen miles and encamped on Ham's Fork [Fontenelle] which runs southward into Green River. This is a beautiful stream of clear water, in a narrow, grassy valley." The next day ushered in the nation's birthday, but like so many emigrants, a celebration took a lower priority. "Thursday, July 4 ... after going a short distance down stream, turned to the right and climbed up a long narrow spur, to the top of a high mountain. We continued to ascend one after another, until we had reached a great height. This was the Bear River Range of the Rocky Mountains. From this high point the road ran rapidly down, through a long, dusty, rocky ravine, or canon [canyon] to a small valley within three miles of Bear River. Not withstanding our anxiety and fatigue, our dinner, in honor of the national anniversary, was the best we could provide. The last of our potatoes, which had long been saved for the occasion, made it a rare feast." And no doubt using her guidebook as her source, she concluded her entry, "Since crossing the high ridge we had descended, in less than half a day, one thousand eight hundred thirty feet, the elevation of this Fourth-of-July camp being six thousand four hundred feet."[175]

John Birney Hill left the Green River on the afternoon of July 6, 1850, and reached the Bear River on July 11, making the traverse in five days. He reported in his diary seeing, "Plenty of grass & Willow-bushes" and "Wild Sage, from 6 inches to 6 or 7 feet high; Owing to the fertility of the Soil." He also found "thousands of Mountain Squirrels, out here. They resemble the common Gray Squirrel — but they are much less — they live in the ground." He recorded crossing numerous streams, which he did not name, and then finally on the 11th, reached the last ridge before the Bear River valley. "Found a steep long hill to climb — the worst that we have had yet. We are now among the Mountains. This evening we past through a forest of Spruce Pine — these trees are beautiful. Soon after we past through the forest, we went down — as soon as we got down — we had to climb a hill — found it steep to go down — as soon as we got down this hill we were in Bear River Valley, but not close to the river."[176]

Having departed the Green River, William Frush's party worried about losing their stock, apparently to bad water. "George Griffith lost a steer this morning. Mr. Christy also one. We traveled 5 miles further to Hams Fork of Green River. 4 rods wide, 2 ft. deep and campt for the day. Here the company lost 3 more steers. This is a fine valley of grass the best we had for 200 miles, mostly red top. There is a large number of the Snake Indians camped here. We campt with them. They are Intel[l]igent & civil and have a large quantity of fine horses. Thare is a very steep Mountain to ascend & descend 5 miles before you get to this River. We had a vary fine mess of speckled Trout for supper which is plentiful in river."[177]

Sarah Davis began a series of entries on August 1, 1850, in her wonderfully simplistic prose, describing her trek from the Green River to the Bear. "we left green rive and crost over the mountain a distance of thirteen miles we then came to a branch of greene river [probably the La Barge] a butiful [beautiful] stream it is we camped on it and we past some Indians snake Indians August 2 we now are in sight of an Indian town we then came on eight miles and in between too [two] more mountains within an Indian camp their was to [two] more camps insight

"August 3 we then started and traveled on ten miles to good grass was good grass to for it was ne [knee] high to a man we then came to hams fork of greene river a beautiful stream it runs vary swift and is clear as cristal it is a bout three rods wide and has plenty of trout in it. here is an Indian town they swarmed around us it is the snake tribe of Indians who in habit these snow mountains they look fright full

"August 4 layed over to rest catle and wash and bake our men took off one of their wagon covers and sowed them to gether and used it for a sane they had lots of fun here they caught about too [two] thousan fish with big little and all together their is goosebarys here and seatilsey[?] here and some butiful roses and pine in abundance.

"August 5 our catle bein all fresh we then comence to clime the mountains I saw where we had to go before starting as I has the sick head ache vary bad I saw nothin all the four noon. In the afternoon a more butiful sight I never saw the whole mountain was coverd with flowers of every description.

"August 6 we then crost over mountains for six miles and thene come in bare river botom and their we had a runaway our calt [cattle] run and the leader fell down and that stoped them noting got broke we then went on to bare river and nooned."[178]

Henry Wellenkamp made the run between the rivers in just over three days. In his short entries he summed up the trek pretty well. "Crossed several streams. Had fine grass, high hills and snow. Dry sage is the principal fuel which fills all the barren millions of acres from Laramie to Carson River. Along beautiful pine groves, high hills; bad and frequent crossings, animals begin to drop, particularly oxen."[179]

Around Thomas' Fork

Once the emigrants struck the Bear River valley they turned to the north and west and proceeded on toward Fort Hall. Like Fort Laramie in eastern Wyoming, Fort Hall in southeast Idaho stood out as a tiny speck of civilization in the great American wilderness. Like Laramie, Hall had started life as a fur trader's outpost, and in 1849–1850, retained much more of that atmosphere than Laramie. The Hudson's Bay Company had built the outpost and even though the United States had annexed the area, still exercised substantial influence there. Fort Hall lay approximately 150 miles from the point where the emigrants joined the Bear River road, a good week's travel. As with the other stretches of trail the emigrant's had plenty to see and new faces to meet. Thomas's Fork, a tributary of the Bear River, presented the first major obstacle, about six miles after the descent into the Bear River valley.

"Came to Thomas' fork of the Bear River," recalled J. A. Pritchard on June 25, 1849. "We found it too deep to be forded with safety without raising our wagon beds some 15 or 18 inches—so the remainder of the afternoon was spent in cutting down cotton wood trees and cribbing up our wagon beds. We lashed the timbers & beds fast to the Axels of the wagons. We here overtook the mule train of Col. Russell of Mo. who left Independence 15 or 18 days before we did. The Col. had just completed the job of ferrying his train over by converting one of his wagon beds into a boat & pulling it backwards & forward by a rope that was stretched across the stream." Unable to simply drive through the ford, because of the depth, Pritchard's company improvised the next day. "June 26… We commenced by swinging the mules over and then spliced our five chains and made one end fast to the end of the tongue and laid the other across the river and hitched it to a span of mules.

The mules that were suspended to the end of the chain drew the wagon through — this was done in order that the current should not carry the wagon and wheel mules off." Pritchard found the Bear River region so beautiful, he may have briefly considered staying there. "This is the most beautiful valley that I ever beheld. I am sure that the grass cannot be surpassed by any other spot on earth. And if I were to settle anywhere beyond the pales of civilization this should be the spot. What can be more inviting than a bold flowing river, a beautiful valley — and lofty Mountain scenery? Bear River is about 200 feet wide at this point."[180]

Franklin Starr also found the crossing at Thomas's Fork daunting. His party reached it a fortnight after Pritchard. "We crossed Thomas's fork immediately after dinner. It was too high to cross at the usual ford but by going up about a mile we crossed it where it was divided into several slews. It is about 13 yards over and swift and deep. The road at the ford lay between the foot of a steep mountain and Thomas's fork for a short distance and was almost impassable on account of the rocks that lay in it and which had rolled off of the mountain. On Thomas's fork where we crossed there were 4 lodges of Snake Indians."[181]

Israel Hale found the altitude of the Bear River valley region a bit tough to deal with. Having completed the descent from the dividing ridges he remembered in his diary, "We then followed the bottom of the Bear River and near the bluffs. Bear River is not as large as the Maramee, that is not as wide, but deeper. The air in this country appears close and is hard to breathe, and the higher we go the more close the air appears to be. It may be good for weak lungs but it certainly is very hard on them if they are very weak. Violent exercise here would almost force an emigrant to faint, the difficulty of breathing would be so great. This afternoon we followed Bear River Valley a few miles and there took up the valley of another creek [Thomas's Fork]. We drove up this valley to get a good crossing. About 20 miles today."[182]

Upon reaching the Bear River road, Bruff's company also turned north. As long as he commanded the company he could find time to socialize, and in doing so recount some amazing stories. "…banks of the Bear River. Visited a neighboring camp, and a man there told me, that about a week since, an emigrant went out in the Bear river mountains, from this place, to hunt, and was lost; he met some Indians, to whom he gave his rifle to conduct him back to his comrades. Finding them gone, he desired to be conducted to Salt Lake, and off they started, over the mountains for that settlement. At a camp on the Green river, a trader informed me, of another emigrant, near there, also out hunting, no great distance from his camp, when he was beset by a party of Snake Indians, who took his rifle from him, tied him to a tree, and shot him in the back, and killed him. His comrades missing him too long, went on a search, and found him fast to the tree, a corpse. They then got on the Indian trail, and found their camp, and demanded redress. The chief held a counsel, detected the murderer, and had him tied to a tree; and then told the emigrants, that he was at their disposal. The emigrants replied that he had taken the life of one of us all, friends, and that they, the Indians, must punish him, in such manner as should be decreed. The old chief then called the brother of the culprit, and ordered him to cut the offender's throat, which he instantly done; and the emigrants returned, satisfied with the old chief's justice."[183]

However, Bruff still had the business of getting his company through to California and that he also addressed in his writing. "Passed the government Express from Fort Hall, for Fr. Laramie. Moved on to Thomas fork. Found the banks deep and soft, and narrow inclined planes in different places, where the wagons had forded, and worn them in deep bad ruts. Passed a grave, a rude wooden cross, on which was pencilled: 'An Indian Squaw; June 27th. 1849, Kill'd by a fall from a horse, near this place: Calm be her sleep, and sweet her rest. Be kind to the Indian.' Bear river. The stream here is crooked, with many small branches & numerous marshes & slews, and a bottom plain 10 miles broad, on this side. The old mountaineer, Peg Leg Smith, came into camp: he has a cabin on the bank, some distance below, and trades with cattle, whisky, etc. His leg was injured and he out knife & amputated it himself, and afterward dressed, and fortunately recovered."[184]

Interestingly, the Indian burial Bruff described, had been witnessed firsthand by J. A. Pritchard. In his diary entry, dated June 27, 1849, he explained what he saw. "The wife of the Old Chief of whom I have been speaking [noted from the Green River area] was thrown from her horse to day and killed — and a boy who was ridding behind her was also thrown and his arm broken. She was buried according to their custom. She was put into the ground & all of her things were put with her and an equal share of all their provisions. They then shot the horse and put him into the grave for the woman to ride. They then fired a few guns into the grave and put up a most piteous howling, weeping and wailing and in their state of agony departed from the place."[185] It may have been quite possible, that Pritchard penciled in the headboard Bruff read.

A day's journey up the trail from Thomas's Fork, Pritchard had also previously encountered the mountaineer Smith, whose self-amputation Bruff had described. "This old Smith who lives here has a cork leg — a rough looking man he is too. The place is better known as Smith's trading post. A Salt Lake Mormon & wife were here for the purpose of trading with the emigrants. Several Frenchmen [Canadians]."[186]

As Israel Hale's party moved up the Bear River road he would also encounter the mountainman Smith, and have to deal with some sick companions. Writing on July 15, 1849, he recounted, "For the first time since we left St. Joseph we rested on Sunday, or rather rested our teams. The cause of it was that one of the men that belonged to Tindall's wagon was very sick and he could not stand travel. Soon after breakfast was over, Mr. Smith, a mountaineer, came to our camp. Soon after several other persons called in and if I am not mistaken they had a jolly day of it. As for myself, it was wash day with me. Several gangs of Indians called during the day, the more especially about mealtime. These Indians appear to be well off. They are well clad and have large gangs of horses. Some of our men have caught some mountain trout, but they do not bite free. I have not eaten any of them. They are said, however, to be very firm. Bay, our sick man, is not better this evening."

Forced to lay over another day, Hale found out more about Mr. Smith. "Bay, the sick man, is no better, consequently we are forced to lay by today. Smith the mountaineer was down again today and some of our men went home with him to dinner. I had an invitation, but could not conveniently leave. I am told he has a comfortable house, cooking stove, hogs, cattle, cats and also a churn and to complete his equipage, a squaw for a wife. Smith has but one leg and is quite fleshy, a little taller, but very much resembles Esq. Whaite of Bonhomme Township. He is fond of company and treats them on the best he has and in great abundance, almost to wastefulness. He is about fifty-five years of age and has been in the mountains over twenty years and appears as happy as a lord. His squaw is about sixteen, rather bulky than otherwise. She has one child, a boy, and a spoiled child."

With men still too sick to travel, Hale continued to learn about the mountaineer. In his diary he changed his reference from "Mr. Smith" to "Friend Smith." "The sick man, Bay, is very little better. He is unable to be moved. Titus is sick today and we are still laying by. The cattle are getting in fine order, but our camping ground is nearly eaten out and the water is not very good. Friend Smith and the Indians visit us every day, but there is considerable dissatisfaction in camp on account of our laying by. I think we will start tomorrow. Our trip is a laborious one. We are getting very tired, but when the roads are good and we are not troubled with dust, the variety of scenery and natural curiosities serves in a great measure to blunt the fatigue and hardships of our trip. We were all willing to lay by and take a rest, but are now equally as willing to again start on our journey. We are fearful that the grass will become scarce on the Humboldt River and many other places, although Mr. Smith says we are ahead of the time that emigrants usually pass. Mr. Smith says the snow remains on the mountains throughout the year, but that it goes off in the valleys in April or May when the grass puts up and soon furnishes an abundance of food for the stock. I am sure I would not like to spend a winter in these mountains. Game is becoming very scarce. The principal kinds are mountain sheep, antelope and some black tail deer. Occasionally they kill a white bear. The buffalo have left."[187]

Niles Searls, who had offered such a detailed and finely written diary through July 28, 1849, concluded on having reached the Bear River valley that, "Owing to the difficulty in obtaining opportunity to write, I have resolved to write only weekly for the future." To say that Searls' trek to see the elephant had gone very sour gradually became indicative in the progression of his diary entries. The adventure that presented itself on leaving Independence had become a terrible grind of hardship and deprivation for the young lawyer. As a result, his subsequent entry is not made until August 5, well down the road to Fort Hall, and noticeably lacks the literary verve of earlier entries. "Our course down the valley of the Bear River was marked by few circumstances worthy of note. Several streams were crossed; among them Thomas' Fork, a fine stream emptying into the river. We have traveled nearly the whole way in company with the Government train. Dr. White of St. Louis and his family joined our train at the cut-off and will travel in our company the remainder of the way."[188]

Contrary to Searls, Bruff's spirits remained high and he found many circumstances worth writing about as they continued up the Bear River road. "Aug. 12… Panack Indians. They spoke several words of English. Several of the Indians had on blue cloth caps, one wore a teamster's linen frock, with U.S. buttons on it. A party of these chaps: a young man on a very fine poney, a youth and old man on a fat black mule, and a middle-aged squaw on a mare. They offered the squaw to us for a copper powder flask. [Declined.] A man and his wife, with tin pails, went from an adjacent camp, over the plain a mile, to a band of cattle, and returned with their buckets full of milk. A delightful lively scene, and only needed 2 or 3 cottages to complete the picture."[189]

Margaret Frink's party came down into the Bear River valley on July 5, 1850. "…Down the valley of Bear River. Came to a rapid stream called Smith's Fork, issuing from the high mountains on our right and divided into four separate creeks that ran across our road. The second one being very narrow and deep, with perpendicular banks, had been bridged in a novel manner. A log had been split in the center and laid across with the flat side up, at the proper distance to fit the wagon wheels; so that, by using a little care, the wagons could be safely crossed. Drove to the banks of the Bear River. Traveled on to Thomas Fork."[190]

The next morning they "forded Thomas Fork, and turning west, came to a high steep spur that extends to the river. Over this high spur we were compelled to climb. The distance is seven miles and we were five hours crossing. The descent was very long and steep. All the wheels of the wagons were tied fast, and it slid along the ground. At one place the men held it back with ropes and let it down slowly." The tough going on the road in the vicinity of Thomas's Fork prompted Frink to write two days later, "…Sunday. We are remaining in camp today, resting from the severe labors and anxieties of the past week, as far as the pressing duties of camp life on the plains permit us to do so. Wild flax is growing in many places, as thickly as if sowed by the hand of man. Passed a village of Snake River Indians. I visited a lady today at a train which had halted not far from ours—an unusual incident on this journey."[191]

Soda Springs and Steamboat Springs

About mid-way up the trail to Fort Hall, near the point where the Bear River began to turn abruptly to the west and then back to the south, leaving the road, the emigrants encountered another in the series of marvelous geological oddities, that became a true landmark for most of the diarists. Typically, diarists whose entries had become rather spotty as the trail moved west and got more difficult, like Sallie Hester, took a moment to mention them, and give a nice summary of what everyone saw. "...Past Soda Springs. Two miles further on are the Steamboat Springs. They puff and blow and throw the water high in the air. The springs are in the midst of a grove of trees, a beautiful and romantic spot."[192]

"We reached what is called the soda or Beer Springs," wrote J. A. Pritchard on June 29, 1849. "These are so called on account of the acid taste and effervescing gasses contained in these water. It is a place of very great interest. The water is clear and sparkling and in many places thrown several feet in the air. The water is constantly boiling up with a kind of hissing noise. The steam boat Springs are about ½ mile below, the water of it are a little warmer than the others and escapes out of the ground through a crevice or apiture in the stone about the size of a man's head. The effervescing gasses being some what confined beneath the ledges of stone—present this puffing appearance in its efforts to escape. About 6,000 feet above sea level."[193]

Franklin Starr's party reached the unusual springs at the end of the day on July 13, 1849. "Traveled 17 miles. We crossed a small stream just at night and camped among the Soda Springs. We visited several of them after camping and drank of the water. The water requires sugar and acid and then it resembles Soda very much. We also added Ginger and drank a great deal of it." If the natural oddity of seeing the springs were not enough, another human interaction in the middle of the night even topped making homemade ginger ale. "Last night we were awakened by a loud how-de-do repeated continuously in the broken accent of the Indian. We immediately crept out of our tents to see how the land lay and found an Indian and a Squaw who made all the nois [noise]. He was Shoshone and was mounted on horseback. He was probably afraid he would get shot if he undertook to pass without noise. We thought when we first awakened that there was a company of them and as there were but two waggons of us that their intentions might not be very peacable [sic] but after shaking hands He rode on and we retired to our blankets."[194]

Soda Springs and Steamboat Springs

The next morning Starr's party moved on and shortly came to Steamboat Springs. "We had expected to see a very interesting object and were not disappointed. The Spring comes out of the middle of a rock close to the river. The aperture through which the water runs is about 6 inches over and then dashes up and forms something to the height of 3 ft. It comes out in perfect foam and is rather more than blood warm. It tastes like the other Springs in the vicinity. Sometimes it ceases for a moment and then dashes up with renewed violence. Eight or nine feet from it there is a crack in the rock through which the gas rushes making a noise like the escaping of steam from a leak in a boiler."[195]

"We came to the Soda or Beer Springs about three o'clock. There are several of them and each appears to have its own temperature and flavor. I did not see them all; those that I saw boiled like a pot. Some were warmer than others and some sour, while others had a sweetish taste. We drove a mile or so beyond the springs and encamped on the river with good grass and some wood, tolerable convenient," remembered Israel Hale. But then he complained, "For two days we have had no noon spell, which is something that I object to, both on account of men and cattle. Both become fatigued and hungry, and not only that, we do the work in the heat of the day." The following morning they "left Bear River. After a few miles travel we came to another Beer Springs. It did not boil like the others but was rather soaur [sic]. It tasted like the bottled soda of St. Louis shops. We had rather a rough road; a great many rocks in it in places."[196]

"The soda springs six miles east of the cut-off [reference to a trail variation just beyond the site] attracted universal attention," recalled Niles Searls in the first of his weekly entries on August 5, 1849. He provided a wonderfully literate description of the area. "They cover a large extent of country and present many singular phenomena. The waters of them all are kept constantly boiling by the escape of tartaric acid gas. Near them is the steamboat spring, boiling forth from the surface of a rock with a noise resembling that made by the water thrown up by the wheel of a boat. The whole country around is covered with cinders and bears abundant proof of having been subject to volcanic action. Near the forks of the road is an old crater of large extent, now nearly filled up. Around are several smaller ones, varying in depth from four to twenty feet, while the rocks are rent by chasms of fearful depth."

Like Starr, Searls encountered Indians near the springs. "Near the springs we saw a large camp of Shoshones, with whom we had an interesting conversation by means of signs. They exhibited the most friendly feelings, seemed disposed to trade, but preferred rather to get their wants supplied by begging, at which they exhibited great address. Their appearance was fine, many of them possessing an intellectual expression unlooked for by me."[197]

Bruff found the vicinity of the geologic phenomenon a bit smelly and full of Indians, though the two were not related. "A great many skunks here.

Several dead ones about, and live ones running across the plain. A dog chased one and gave us some sport. At 9 A.M. we rolled on. Character of the country very interesting and picturesque to me. Volcanic formations, tufa, etc. Made 10½ miles, and noon'd near the celebrated Soda and Beer Springs. Camps and moving bodies of Shoshonees, in all directions, plenty of fine horses, colts, etc. squaws, papooses, warriors— old & young, dogs, etc. The young men continually begging for *powdree, baaale,* They stand & sit around the messes, while dining, anxiously waiting for a morsel, and picking up every crumb. An old man and a young one, well-mounted, and accoutered with savage finery, having long rifles, quivers, and bows, stood near me, and I took out my book & pencil, to sketch the young man. The elder saw me, rode round, shook his head, frowned, and cried "no schwap!" I must not draw the Indian or at night he would die."

"Soda Springs," continued Bruff. "The water was fine, only needed lemon syrup, to render it perfect soda water. These mineral springs are very numerous, many wells & springs boiling up & shooting jets. After a short rest, we rolled on. Passed the Steamboat spring, named from the resemblance of the sound it gives, to that of a steamboat's paddles, under water. It is a circular tumuli of about 5 ft, diam. and about 3 ft. high; bubbling & jetting clear sparkling water, as the hissing gases escape." [198]

John Birney Hill, who saw the springs in mid July, 1850, also found the water quite drinkable with a little something added. "This morning we had some hills to climb — not bad. This evening we got to the Soda Springs— they are on the W. side of a Cedar grove close to the road; on both sides. These Springs are small pools— the water is continually bubbling and boiling up — put Sugar in this water & it tastes very much like Sweet Beer — this water is quite Sour. Just below these Springs Bear River runs round the point of a Mountain & runs South. Went two miles below the Springs & campt."[199]

"Reached the far-famed Soda Springs and Steamboat Spring, at the big bend of Bear River. At this point the stream — along which for five days we have been traveling northward — suddenly bends to the left around a high steep mountain, and, reversing its course, runs directly southward for one hundred twenty-five miles, to lose itself in the Great Salt Lake. Soda Springs are on the right of the road and boil up form the ground in many places, forming mounds of earth with a little cup or hollow on the top. Some of the mounds are several feet in height, the water bubbling over the top on all sides. By some they are called Beer Springs, from their peculiar tastes. About a mile further on is the Steamboat Spring, on the left of the road near the river. It derives its name from the ebullition of water at regular intervals of about thirty seconds, which produces a sound similar to that of a steamboat. About three feet from the spring is a constant discharge of steam through a small crevice in the rock. The whole country seems to have been curiously formed," wrote Margaret Frink of her encounter with the springs in July, 1850. But even the most marvelous sights that nature could provide could not deter the emigrants from going on to see the elephant. She recounted, "I left the spot reluctantly. But a party of Michigan men, who were at this time traveling with us, claimed that they could neither see nor feel an interest in anything this side of the gold of California."[200]

"Thare [there] is quite a cedar grove here in neighborhood of these Springs," wrote William Frush on encountering the famous springs on the Bear River. "Thare is a number of Indian lodges here trading. This water tastes like soda or beer and boils with much rapidity out of the earth. Thare is a number of them on this mile of road — all near the bank of Bear River. Thare is much appearance of Boiling Springs and volcanic eruptions in this country, much yellow oaker forms by the boiling of those springs that are least impregnated with soda. 4 miles beyond this the roads fork. the right to Fort Hall the left Hudspeths Cut-off. 5 miles on right road good spring. Right road here we campt."[201]

Junction with Hudspeth Cut-Off

Just five or six miles past the Soda Springs on the Fort Hall road, the emigrants found the intersection of another cut-off. Its name stemmed from one of a couple of trailblazers, or mountaineers, and varies with which diarist one reads. That also applies to the spelling of the men's names. Bruff attributed the cut-off's name to Hedgepeth, a variation of the actual spelling, Hudspeth. Others refer to it as Myer's, or Meirs, and as Bruff later explained, some, for the possible lack of knowing exactly whom to credit, simply called it the Emigrant's Cut-Off. What the cut-off did of course, was to strike off across the mountain rim of the Great Basin region in southern Idaho, due west, cutting across the arch made by the original road that went on to Fort Hall that continued on to the northwest before turning to the southwest again. Estimates varied as to how many miles and days could be saved by taking the cut-off, but the road proved a difficult trek by all accounts. Henry Wellenkamp recorded the distance across the cut-off at approximately 125 miles, consuming seven days travel. In comparison, Pritchard, who went through Fort Hall on the more established road reached the same point after recording 195 miles. With reasonable accuracy the Hudspeth then saved 70 miles and possibly three days. The problem with the cut-off for those traveling in 1849 lay in the newness of the route. J. A. Pritchard, near the front edge of the emigrant wave that year, barely mentions the divergence of the road forking and never referred to it as a cut-off. Israel Hale, also going out in 1849, did not mention the cut-off in his diary either, nor did Franklin Starr. Sallie Hester's party took the cut-off, but she gave no descriptions of it in her diary, and even mistakenly called it by the name "Sublet" for another trailblazer and an earlier cut-off.

J. Goldsborough Bruff, a good six weeks behind Pritchard, wrote about encountering the cut-off and his decision. "Aug. 17... I wished to take the Company by the Fort Hall route, knowing of any other, on this course, till about 10 days ago; and finding that Hedgepeth, a mountaineer, had discovered a passage into the Great Basin, through the N.E. corner of the boundary mountains, and that a large number of trains had preceded us on it, and from reliable information, that it was a good road, and much shorter & better than by the way of Fort Hall, and my men were in favor of it. It is known as 'the Emigrants' Cut-off.'"[202]

However, Bruff had planned to see Fort Hall, and so, sent his company across the cut-off while he went on his sightseeing excursion. "Aug. 18... I determined to visit Fort Hall, more to see the mountaineers there, for information about the travel after crossing the pass in the Sierra Nevada, than any thing else. The company gave me an old broke-down bay horse, and offered me 2 men for an escort, one of whom was to be Stinson, the guide, whom I determined to get rid of at Fort Hall. Reached the turn of the river and forks of the road; the left-hand trail, going over Westerly, by an extinct crater, and the right N.W. up a valley, and over a very tall divide, 50 miles to Fort Hall. I did not think, from the nature of the mountains, the company had to go over, that this 'cut-off,' actually could shorten the trip much: and told my men, that in 10 days I would overtake them, on the Humboldt river, which they seemed to think I could not do."[203]

One of the "large number" of emigrant trains preceding Bruff's Washington City Company was Niles Searls' express company which opted to take the cut-off ten days in front of Bruff's men. "We have left the old Fort Hall road to the right, diverging some forty-five miles from the last mentioned place, at a point called the 'Old Crater.' After leaving the old road our course was nearly due west, over a level expanse of country, then up a precipitous mountain, over which we were compelled, from want of water, to travel at midnight. All is now uncertain with regard to the route. The road having been opened this season, no written mark describes it and none have returned to tell of its peculiarities. We are now encamped on a small stream with towering mountains around us. Mr. J. Eastman died of consumption of the lungs. Thus have three out of six composing our mess at starting from Independence been called away by the hand of death."[204]

One week later, on August 12, 1849, Searls made another entry in his diary, one in which he seemed to battle a severe case of melancholy. It represents a marvelous piece of writing about how not only he had broken down, but how probably thousands of others, now coming into a more direct view of the elephant, must have also been breaking down. "Another week has passed, bringing with it the usual routine of fatigue and exposure. How different is the figure now cut by the redoubtable 'Pioneer Line,' from that made at our departure from the abodes of civilized men? How sadly have we been disappointed. Weary months have rolled away, bringing with them the conviction that ours, like the journey of life, has its periods of darkness and doubt. Still we despair not, though present prospects indicate dissolution of our Company before many weeks. Yet with hearts yielding not to despondency, we shall push forward as best we can, fully determined to reach California in the face of every impediment.

"On, on we journeyed, hoping as we toiled up each steep ascent to find the cherished object of our desires in the next valley. Already had we reached the point at which report said was a limpid stream. In the place of cooling waters, we found the parched bed of a mountain torrent without a particle of aught [anything] beside. Around were the jaded teams of numberless emigrants who like ourselves had hoped to find repose from travel. Women bewailing their hard fate and helpless children crying for water, form no pleasant theme for my notes, therefore I dwell not upon this subject."[205]

A year later, the Hudspeth/Myers Cut-off had become better known, but still did not divert everyone from going on to Fort Hall. Margaret Frink's little party passed that point on the trail and she recalled, "The emigration was very thin on this part of the route, the heaviest portion of it having gone by way of the Salt lake road, that turned off a few miles east of the Little Sandy. From Steamboat Spring we came to the forks of the road, the left-hand one, called Myer's Cut-off going westerly over the plains and hills to Raft River, the right-hand one taking a northwest direction, and crossing the northern rim of the Great Salt Lake Basin, to Fort hall, on the Snake River, or Lewis Fork of the Columbia. We have now traveled 1,622 miles from home."[206]

Faced with the proposition of taking the cut-off or not the next day, Frink related how they made their decision. "We decided to take the right hand forks of the road leading to Fort Hall, because of the advice and illustration given us by an old Indian at the Soda Springs. He raised up the bail of a bucket to signify a high mountain and passing his hand over the top, said, This is Myer's Cut-off. Then laying the bail down and passing his hand around it, said, This is the Fort hall road. We were told afterwards that this was correct. Came to a soda pool, on top of a mound five feet high. I dipped a cupful without leaving my seat in the wagon. Tasted like ordinary soda water but it made very light biscuits."[207]

Henry Wellenkamp began his passage of the Hudspeth Cut-off on Thursday, July 4, 1850. His diary entries were brief, and sometimes almost eloquent, and gave some form to the passing of that section of the trail. "July 4th... Passed along a splendid cedar grove, a town of Flathead Indians and passed the most romantic ridge in the world, in pure and clarified air, cool and chaste, and feel more alevated [sic] in spirit than ever at home. After passing Indian town Bear River turns to the left, S.E. in a deep canyon of volcanic mountains and masses 200 to 300 feet high. In fact everything seen is of some terrible volcanic origin. Flax equal to any in the world in the valleys.

Left Ft. Hall road to the right and too Meier cut-off. July 5th... Country equally romantic [in comparison to earlier reference to the Bear River valley]. July 6th... Ascended a gradual mountain gap for 4 miles, narrow and deep. Descended from summit 300 ft. almost perpendicular, no water. July 7th... Mountainous. Camped in pass, fine grass and water. July 8th... Laid over ½ day. Several groves of cottonwood and mighty snows had crushed whole groves. Echo! Singular and grand, repeated 7 times. Descended a beautiful pass, along a little creek to a valley around which snow glaciers majestically arise. Climate mild and pleasant. July 9th... 18 miles across a valley in which 5 swampy crossings gave sport to the 1000's of emigrants; nearly every animal mired down. Camped on foot of snow mount near Ft. Hall road [having completed the cut-off and merged again with the old road]."[208]

On to Fort Hall

Approximately 55 miles beyond the fork in the road at the Hudspeth/Myers Cut-off lay Fort Hall. Having left the Bear River valley behind, the trail made an overland jaunt to the valley of the Port Neuf River, a tributary of the Snake River and eventually the great Columbia River. As had been the case all along the trail, as one train overtook another they shared information that many had not heard. J. A. Pritchard writing on June 30, 1849, recalled, "Two young men belonging to the Howard Co. Mo. train came up to us today & stated that they crossed the line at the 20th of may and that the grass was eaten down to the ground & that the crowd was not yet past Fort Laramie." As he pushed on Pritchard continued to see sights similar to those encountered around Soda Springs. "We saw on our route to day a vast amount of volcanic eruptions evidently showing that the elements had been melted with a heat that was more exciting than pleasant. We arrived at the point where the road commences ascending the ridge that divides the waters of the Great Basin from the waters of the Pacific."

The following morning, July 1, 1849, they "commenced the ascent at 5 A.M. and by 9 we had gained the summit. In many places the hills were very steep. The descent on the west side is rather more gradual. After we reached the valley we came to a large creek one of the forks of the Port Neuf River." Continuing the diary entry, Pritchard captured with pencil on paper one of the truly eloquent statements of trail life. "Today I found several bunches of roses and they brought to mind recollections of the past which were exceedingly pleasant to reflect upon. Not withstanding that I was a way in the midst of an uninhabited wild mountain scenery — weary of a long and fatiguing journey covered with dust and immersed in care & anxiety — still I found that my sensibilities were not so stupefied as to have lost all taste for the beautiful in nature. I geathered [sic] some dozen different kinds of Flowers and made a Bouquet that would bear an honorable comparison to any made by the most fastidious exquisite of the states. They are wild flowers the living Poetry of those wild mountain sceneries."[209]

By July 2, Pritchard's company had reached the vicinity of Fort Hall. "We are today in the valley of several rivers—to wit Port Neuf—Panack & Snake or Lewis' fork of the Columbia River. Fort Hall stands on the left bank of Lewis' fork. It is surrounded by a vast plain, cut through and through with rivers creeks, & sloughs running in every direction. To all appearances one stream runs parallel with another in opposite directions and but a short distance from each other. Traded with the Panacks. I effected a trade with one of them—I gave him a good rifle a good blanket & some ammunition for a very good young horse. The Indians are rather below in size the other Indians that we have seen on our rout, but the most perfectly formed men I ever saw and with all very keen and active—pleasant and rather agreeable in their manners. The women are small sprightly looking & handsome. They own a great number of horses in which they take great delight and some of their horses are very fine. At the lodges were encamped some of the Soshonees and Senikeis [he is not certain of the spelling of that tribal name]."[210]

"Our direction has been north today toward Fort Hall. There is a range of mountains to cross as we are now in the Great Salt Lake basin," wrote Franklin Starr on July 14, 1849. Then there appears an unexplained gap in his diary until the first week in August. It is a therefore only a good assumption that they continued on over the old road and did not take the cut-off.

Like everyone else, Israel Hale's party dragged itself along, quite tired of the up and down tramp through the mountains. Having made the ascent and descent described previously by Pritchard, he wrote in his diary on July 22, 1849, "We had a rough road for some miles. We crossed a creek that the banks were two feet high and so bad we thought best to dig it down. We at last came to the Port Neuf bottom or a large bottom that we supposed to be that, and stopped for diner. Traveled today about seventeen miles, and all hands perfectly willing to stop at any place where water could be got, the fatigue has been so great."[211]

J. Goldsborough Bruff had sent his wagon on over the Hudspeth route while he took a side trip to Fort Hall. His diary entries are mostly a wonderful rambling on about the people he met getting there. "Met Shoshone in various dress. One of those first met, had on a tolerably decent black summer-cloth frock coat, a blue striped cotton shirt, blue nankeen pants, and cotton suspenders, with an old black hat, decorated with a broad red worsted band. The 2nd was attired in deerskin—frock, leggings, & moccasins; and the 3rd wore a very tall straw hat, a tatter'd Marseilles vest, no shirt, & leggings, with moccasins. Reached springs, the source of the Port Neuf River—some of the fountainheads of the great Columbia River."[212]

The following day, as he approached a newly constructed United States

Army post near Fort Hall, he "met a genteel-looking Panak [Indian], well mounted; and the old man offered to guide us to the Cantonment; I enquir'd who commanded the post, and he informed me that it was Col. Andrew Porter, of the Mounted Rifles. Cantonment Loring — as the post is called, is situated 6 miles above Fort Hall, on the Snake River. A quadrangular Picket-Fort is laid off here 330 by 136 feet. The cottonwood logs are laid down, for the commencement of the bastions — intending to build them up of logs, and the curtain — or walls, of picket, or perpendicular logs, close together. At present, the command is sheltered in tents & a few rough sheds. Admirable neatness & discipline observed. Indians, all Panaks, are seen every where. Many of the men wear the common plaid Scotch bonnet, such as sailors use given them by the Hudson Bay Company. Squads of dirty ill-looking squaws, and dirtier papooses, and mounted men are riding or walking in all directions, or squatted outside the camp, looking with great curiosity at everything."[213]

Margaret Frink encountered Indians in the same area Bruff described a year later in July, 1850. "A party of Snake Indians came into the camp begging flour, coffee, and bread, of each of which we gave them a little. Ascend the mountain chain which separates the Great Salt Lake basin from the valley of the Columbia. The road was very rough. This is the road that was followed by Peter Lassen one of the earliest pioneers of California, long before the gold was discovered." If the terrain approaching Fort Hall did not provide adequate challenge for the emigrant, then long nights of swatting did. Frink continued in her diary, "At night we encamped within one mile of Fort hall. Mosquitoes were as thick as flakes in a snowstorm. The poor horses whinnied all night, from their bites, and in the morning the blood was streaming down their sides." But on the brighter side of things, "At our noon camp we found a thicket of wild currant bushes, from which we gathered currants enough to furnish pies for the next two or three days. A great luxury to people who had been without fruit of any kind for three months."[214]

Fort Hall

Those arriving at Fort Hall generally gave some nicely detailed descriptions of the structures and most importantly the people that inhabited them. "Fort Hall is occupied by English traders," recalled J. A. Pritchard. "They pack their goods from Astoria and other trading points on the Pacific coast of Oregon. The buildings are composed of Sun dried brick. They have vast herds of cattle & horses & mules. They milk a great number of cows and make a great deal of butter & cheese. Their stock runs at large on the plains which is covered with fine grass and every evening & morning you'll see several boys on horse back driving up the stock. There are several families living here — Some

French — Some English — and some Americans. It was quite a pleasant sight to see white women & children."[215]

Pritchard took the opportunity of using the Fort Hall supply base to do some important business. As at every outpost on the trail, the trading benefited one side only. "This morning was spent in trading off wagons for pack horses— 3 of our messes concluded to pack from this point. They became frightened at the alarming tales that were told them of the roads from Fort hall to California. Dr. Roach & co. of 9 men from N. York sold their 2 good wagons & harness for one horse. Mullin's mess of Pendleton Co. Ky. sold one wagon and all their spare provisions for one unbroken horse. Harrison sold his wagon & 2 sets of harness for $6. The traders knew that the men were bound to sell at those prices or leave their wagons and therefore, they would give them no more."[216]

Israel Hale saw the place three weeks after Pritchard. "About ten o'clock we arrived at Fort Hall, which I found was built of mud bricks and was one hundred feet square. It was one story high, except the corners which were higher, the walls forming the outside of the rooms, which extended round. It is still occupied by the N.W. Fur Company. I saw one or two fields fenced in with rails. Several Indian lodges stand about the fort. The ground that the fort stands on is very level."[217]

Captain Bruff remembered Fort Hall well and the opportunity to socialize. "I walked back to the Fort, entered the Great Portal, walked across the open square, (well in the center, a wooden structure about 3 feet above ground with a hinged scuttle to it) and up a pair of stairs, to a balcony, and at a door of an upper apartment met Capt. Grant, the former Hudson Bay commander. Grant is a Scotchman, from Canada, a fine looking portly old man, and quite courteous, for an old mountaineer. His wife is an Iroquois woman, good looking, very neat, and polite. She is of course dark skin. Mrs. G. made a pitcher of fine lemonade, and I found it very refreshing. He said that his whiskey was out, and apologized for the deficiency." We could also suppose that Grant simply did not care to offer Bruff, who could come off a bit pompous, a glass.

"Grant made himself rich, no doubt, by trading with the Indians and emigrants with horses, etc. and his store; the latter going to Oregon & California, and this is the first time that the California adventurers by the Northern route, have entered the Great Basin to the South of this, the Emigrant's Cut-off. Grant is permitted, by Col. Porter to retain his old home, and gives him charge of some stores in the lower apartments of the Fort. The old Captain is very English, and anti–Yankee, and puts me much in mind of his great Hudson Bay Chief, Sir George Simpson, who is very polished specimen of a low adventurer suddenly elevated to a great title. Grant in speaking of the Americans, says "your countrymen" and seems to have had his feelings much disturbed, by the exactment of some thousand dollars, by our Officers, for duties on his trade."[218]

Aug. 25th, 1849.

Fort Hall.
Snake River, or Lewis' Fork of the
COLUMBIA.

J.G.Bruff

Fort Hall

John Birney Hill had skipped the Hudspeth cut-off and arrived in the vicinity of Fort Hall on July 18, 1850. "Saw Ft. Towren [Loring] about 3 mi.'s from the road. We got opposite the fort at noon, the road does not go by this fort. Fort Hall is 5 miles from this fort. Ft. Hall is close to Lewis Fork [of Snake River] I might say, it is on the bank of the River. This River Valley (about the Ft's) is rather swampy & is full of Musketoes. We went 2 mi.'s W. of Ft. hall & campt on a large creek. One of the Boys went back to Ft. Hall & bought 3 lbs. of butter — paid 75 cts. per lb. No hills today but a good many mudholes to cross."[219]

Margaret Frink found Fort Hall a delightful place. "Reached a former trading-post of the Hudson's Bay Company, established many years ago, when the English people made claim to all this part of our territory. It was in charge of Captain Grant, a Canadian, who had been here for nine years, and had entertained Colonel Fremont and his party, in September, 1843, while on their way to the mouth of the Columbia River. We stopped here for a short time, and were hospitably received by Captain Grant, Who treated us in a very gentlemanly manner, and formally introduced us to his wife, an Indian woman, of middle age, quite good-looking, and dressed in true American style. He presented us with a supply of fresh lettuce and onions, expressing regret that because of the lateness of the season he had no other varieties to offer us. We did not visit the United States Government post, Fort Hall [Loring], as it was a mile off the road, though it was in full view on our right as we passed along. This is the most northern point of our wearisome journey. Sutter's Fort is still seven hundred miles distance."[220]

"This is one of the finest natural meadows I ever saw," began William Frush's description of the environs of the fort. "Fort Hall is situated on the south bank of Snake or Lewis River and in an immense bottom with but many little cotton wood timber on the River only. There is a post built and belongs to the Hudson Bay Co. Fort Lourin [Loring] 5 miles up Snake River is an American post. Thare is an American Co. trading at the latter place. Owens Rich & Co. and at Fort Hall a Co. belonging to the Hudson Bay Co. who pack all their sup[p]lies from Fort Vancouver. Thare is a number of Indians with them in Fort. They has a large & vary extra number of Horses."[221] William Frush and his brother took Kit Carson's advice and from Fort Hall proceeded on toward Oregon, diverting from the main trail to see the elephant. They would arrive in northern California in 1851.

Opposite: A contemporary view of Fort Hall as it appeared in 1849, by J. Goldsborough Bruff. Reproduced by permission of *The Huntington Library*, San Marino, California.

Fort Bridger to Salt Lake City

Remembering those emigrants who had gone to Fort Bridger, with intent to pass through Salt Lake City on their way to see the elephant, we find them left with approximately 113 miles and five to six days travel before reaching the next outpost of civilization. If those who had gone the other way, up the

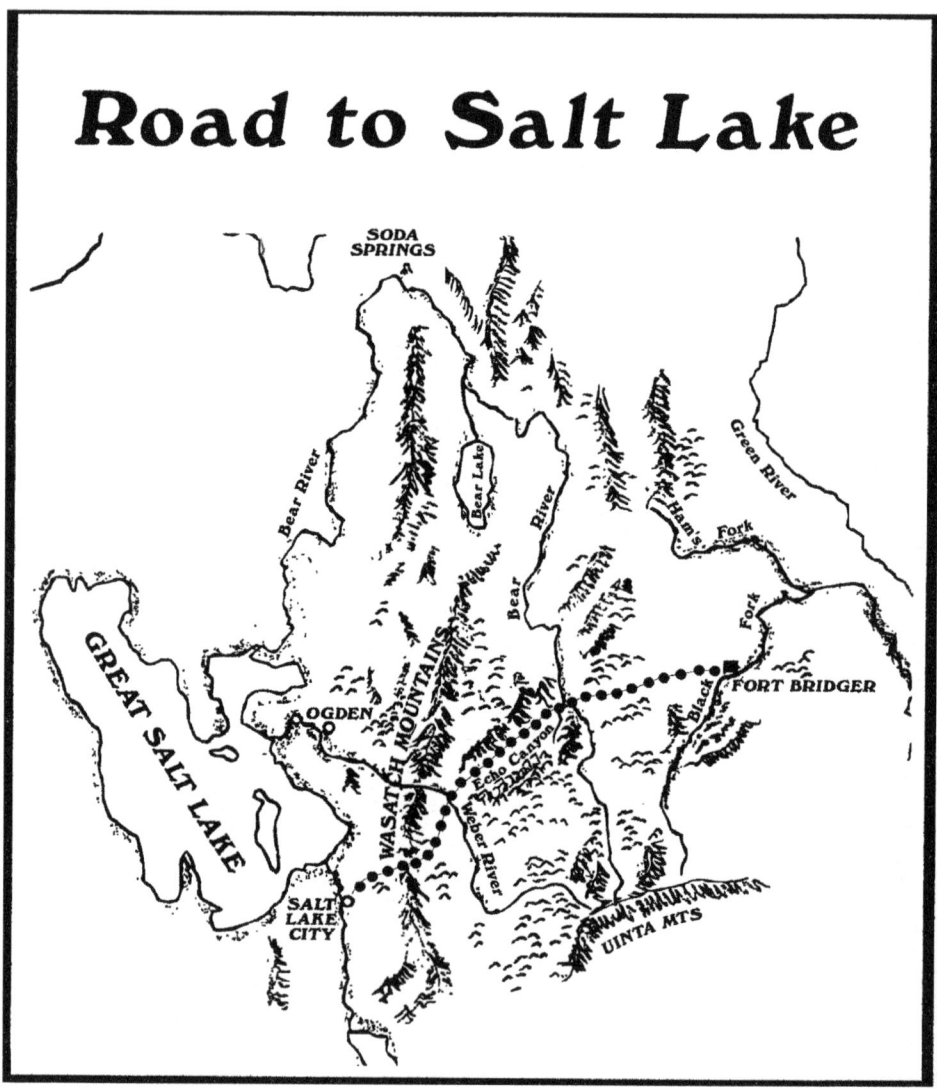

Road to Salt Lake — trail from Fort Bridger to Salt Lake City.

Bear River valley along the Fort Hall road, found numerous natural wonders, those making the trek from Bridger to Salt Lake City found just as many. They also found the road just as difficult, and in some cases, by comparison, more difficult to traverse. Between the two points the emigrants had some high mountain ridges of the Wasatch Range, numerous fords including the Bear and Weber Rivers, tar pits, sulfur springs, and a place called Echo Canyon.

Amos Josselyn passed the leg between Bridger and Salt Lake during the first half of July, 1849. He wrote rather brief entries in his journal but they give a good glimpse of the general progression of the road. Beginning on July 8, he wrote, "drove 19 miles [26 from Bridger] to Sulphur Creek. Roads rough and hilly. Lost an ox today. July 9… We were hindered in fording Bear River which is a very rapid stream. Raised our beds 8 to 10 inches. July10 … drove 25 miles to Echo Creek and camped. July 11 … drove to the Red Fork of the Weber River. The roads were the worst we have had being narrow and crooked and several bad crossings. Drove to the ford which we found pretty deep. We carried our goods over on a raft and lashed the beds fast to the wagons and pulled them through. We got our goods all over and all of the wagons but one. The roads up Weber River are pretty good. July 12 … covered 11¼ miles today over very narrow, crooked and hilly roads. Weather warm and very disagreeable traveling on account of the dust. July 13… 15 miles to a spring on Brown's Creek. Roads narrow, crooked, sidling and mountainous. July 14 … drove 13½ miles to the City of the Great Salt Lake over the worst roads we have yet traveled until we got within five miles of the City. Weather warm and dry."[222]

Samuel Jamison passed the same leg a year later in mid June, 1850. "Passed fort Bridger. Spotswood and Compers swopt horses here with Bridger. Raised the mountains. Still keep raising the mountain the heigst [height] or altitude 700 feet [assumed to be above the altitude of fort Bridger] passed a sulpher or mineral spring encamped on Bear river." The next day Jamison wrote that they lay by, it being Sunday, to rest. But in resting he noted "a great many wagons passing." After the day of rest, Jamison and party continued on toward Salt Lake City. At noon he encountered a landmark noted by many other emigrants called Cache Cave. Writing in his journal, he spelled it "yatch cave. This cave in the Bluff some two or three rods so heig [high] that a man can walk upright in it. Some names engraved in it." And on the same day, not far from the Cache Cave, he encountered "Echo creek. This is a deep revine. The rocks on the right hand side have a Strange appearance. Camped in this ravine Six miles above the Junction of the Kenyin [canyon] & Weber River." Having left the canyon next morning, Jamison "struck wever [Weber] River. Here we had to get our baggage taken over on a raft which is managed by the Mormons and swim stalk [stock] across. Struck the Kenyin [canyon]. Had to cross this stream eleven times bad crossings keep up for thirteen miles."[223]

In late July, 1850, William Edmundson pushed off from Fort Bridger, calculating the distance to Salt Lake, from his guidebook, at 114 miles. Fourteen miles from the fort they had to ford Muddy fork (or creek) "where we saw the Grave of George Tallman a man with whom we were acquainted and who had passed us on the Sweet-Water, he died July 28th [the day before the entry]. This day about noon we crossed the ridge dividing the waters of the Pacific from the Great Basin. We camped at night on Sulphur Creek a branch of the Bear River."

Over the next three days, Edmundson's train pushed on to the Weber River. "July 30th ... we crossed Bear River the largest stream that empties into the Salt Lake. Went 15 miles further and camped on a small creek near Cache Cave. July 31st... Traveled 16 miles to day camped on Echo-creek. A berry resembling the Black-Currant grows here in great quantities. August 1st... Traveled down Echo-creek 5 miles when we came to the Red-fork of Weber River. Here the road forked and a large Guide-Board is placed advising Travelers to take the new or left hand route [no doubt diverting them to the toll gate run by the Mormons] but we kept the Old Mormon road which we afterward understood was much the best."[224]

Mica Littleton left Bridger for Salt Lake on August 5, 1850, a week behind Edmundson. Like many emigrants, he found the natural wonders of the trail impressive. About 20 miles west of Bridger he encountered what he called "Copperas or Soda Spring [not to be confused with the Soda Springs on the Fort Hall road]," and recalled passing the summit of a mountain ridge, the same referred to by Jamison, but at an elevation of "7700 feet." On August 6, they "lay by today. Visited the tar or oil Spring or lakes. They are situated one or 2 about ½ mile South east of the ford. Also a Strong sulphur spring."[225]

The next day Littleton passed Cache Cave but did not stop to look, and on August 8, he reported, "this creek I find is called Echo creek. This is decidedly the worst road we have passed. 16 miles brings you to the mouth of it. There is several Springs on each side of it, plenty of willows for fuel This emties [empties] in to Weber River which runs North. Here the roads fork. The left one goes through a pass where they charge through a tollgate. The one to the right is the old route. The river is about 65 or 70 feet wide very swift and clear water plenty fish in it."[226]

"We started on to salt lake we went back five miles on the road and have not come to the road yet we went on a bout seven miles farther whare [where] we stoped to camp and yet we are not in sight of the road." Sarah Davis' party, made up of a single wagon, with no guide, had gotten lost after leaving Fort Bridger on August 9, 1850: "we started on and traveled some eight miles we then stoped to noon and Zeno and Alick [her husband's name was actually spelled Zeno, and his brother's name was Alex] went to look for the road. I am very lonely and wish we could find the road. we lay by the rest of the day and not founde the road yet."

Two days later, "we still lay here and no hopes of giting a way about four o clock Elic and Edwin came back and they had found the road & how I rejoiced to think they had found the road." The following day, "we started on up the river to find the road and past through plenty of grass nee [knee] high we ware scarecely out of sight of antelope all day." Finally on August 15, "we have now arived at the road and we travel vary fast we have traveled ten miles and stoped to noon on yellow creek not hand some at all their has come up her [here] a man who wants to go with us to salt lake he is sick with the mountain fever and wants to ride in the wagon Elick [one of her variations of Alex] has took him in we have now arived at eco creek a distance of twenty miles." The next day after a trek of 16 miles she reported they finally reached the Weber River.[227]

Lucena Parsons' party probably left Bridger near the back end of the migratory wave of 1850. On September 18, she wrote, "…20 miles past Bridger. One mile south is an oil or tar spring covering several rods. Here are many curious places. At the bottom of this valley are some very singular rocks. It appears sublime to me to see these rocks towering one above the other & lifting their majestic heads here in this solitary spot. Oh, beautiful is the hand of nature. I hate to leave these beauties but must on." Continuing her journal on Sept. 19, she began, "On our way yesterday we passt the Cache Cave in the hills on the right of the road & not far from it. The mouth is a fine arch some 10 feet in height & 20 in width. Many a weary traveler has there left their names. It is not very roomy but is pretty inside, the walls being white & smooth. We crosst Echo creek often while travelling down this canion [canyon]. This morning crosst the Red fork of the Weber."[228]

Once over the Weber the road into Salt Lake City did not improve until practically on the outskirts of the settlement. There were some steep grades as Jamison recalled. "June 19 … highest mountain on the road. Altitude 7,700 feet. At the summit you are in sight of the valley of the Great Salt Lake which is a very beautiful scene. June 20… Came in sight of the city which looked very scaby [scabby]. Every citizen owns one acre and one fourth. There is but one house which makes it very much scattered. Encamped one mile on the west side at the warm springs. This is a very pleasant place to Bathe. The water being about Blood warm. We bathed here several times. Lay by and procured some provisions which we had to pay very high for. Flour cost fifty dollars per hundred, corn meal thirty dollars, barly [barley] twenty dollars pr Bushel, bread fifty dollars per hundred, beef eleven dollars per hundred and very scarce at that."[229]

Mica Littleton made the effort to elaborate in some detail the descent into the city which he made on August 11, 1850, starting from approximately 13 miles out. "Summit of the last high hill. The assent and decent is both very steep crooked and rough. When down you come to the last creek from here down to the Kanyon is the worst road of the whole trip. Crossing the brance [branch] 15 times and some crossings very difficult. From the summit 7½ miles brings you to the mouth of the Kanyon where you come out you find a place almost impassable but others have gone through So can you but it requires great care with teamsters. From here 5 miles will bring you to the City of the Great Salt Lake."

Littleton had an entirely different impression of the city, writing, "this place is situated 5 miles from the mountains where you came out of the Kanyon but only about 2 miles from the nearest mountain and on the east side of the basin and is about 20 miles from Salt Lake. This city is beautifully situated laid off east and west and north and south with Streets 7 rods wide and in wards of from 80, 90 and I believe over 100 acres each. Lot containing 1¼ acres and each Block containing 9 lots with good water leading to every house, lot, block and ward by irrigation there being many mountain Streams coming in from every Kanyon. Peace love Harmony and Hospitality appears to reign Supreme here. After remaining here about 2 hours we rolled out 4 miles. Brought us to the Hot Springs. Quite a curiosity the water is so hot you cannot bear your hand in it more than a few seconds. Present encampment near the Jordan River and on the north route."[230]

William Edmundson hardly bothered to stop in Salt Lake City, writing on August 4, 1850, "reached the City about 11 O'clock A.M. We passed through without stopping crossed the Jordan or Utah outlet on a Toll-Bridge and camped 3 miles from the town." However, his diary has an excellent description of Salt Lake City as it appeared in 1850, and whether it is from his casual observation or a guidebook he did not say. "The city is 22 miles South-East of Salt-Lake on the eastern side of the Valley, on a slightly inclined Plain. It is laid out into 19 Wards, each Ward is divided into Blocks of 10 acres each and each Block is 8 Lots of an Acre and a quarter. The blocks are divided by streets 8 rods wide and a stream of Spring-water from the mountain is conducted through each street throughout the entire length. The dwelling houses are built of Adobe or unburned Brick. They are generally plain but neat and comfortable. They have a State House built of Red SandStone which they procure in the neighboring mountains. The have also a Tithing-House in progress of building of the same material."[231]

If having gotten lost between Bridger and Salt Lake, along with the rough trail were not enough, Sarah Davis' party lost something very important along the way. "Their [there] our catle run a way we thought their was no yuse gardin [guarding] them and all went to bed and the wolfs came and drove them of [off] and killed one of the best cows we [had] though they had him stolen from us in the morning the men took of [off] for them and found them a bout five miles off we then set out for the salt lake valey and Elicks wagon turned over in the mud but still we reached the valey."

Twelve days after leaving Bridger, having taken nearly twice as long as most emigrants, Sarah reached Salt Lake City. "We past through the city of the great salt lake it is a pleasant place here and seams to be improving with great rapidity It seams to have a great deal of vegetation to sell and some rain here we crost the weber river [probably where it flowed into the lake] and stoped."232

Lucena Parsons' party found the road down into Salt Lake as bad as all those other emigrants that had preceded them. But on finally reaching the city, there would be a pause: "…had a very steep mountain to climb. decend & passt down the canion [canyon] that leads into the valley of Salt Lake. While going down this canion we crosst a small creek many times & passt many teams loaded with merchandise that were stalled for this is the worst road we have found yet. Came to the city of Salt Lake in the evening. We shall stop here till spring. Our cattle are tired & so are we & by stoping we shall all rest."233

PART III
FROM FORT HALL AND SALT LAKE CITY TO THE SIERRA NEVADA

Salt Lake City to the City of Rocks

Whether the emigrant in either 1849 or 1850 had reached Fort Hall or Salt Lake City, they had survived to the ⅔ mark of their journey. The distance remaining from either site to the gold fields varied little. And while the main trail to California had split and run to two divergent points, 150 miles apart, as the crow flies, it would eventually merge again in the desert wilderness of northern Nevada along the Humboldt River. In that final third of the trek, the emigrants would come to see the elephant, the nadir of their hardship, face to face.

Beyond the "city of the saints," the next leg of the trail stretched for 190–200 miles, around the north shore of the Great Salt Lake toward a juncture with the road that had passed by Fort Hall, or had been traversed by the Hudspeth Cut-off, at a geological landmark known as the City of Rocks. For most it took at least ten days, with every aspect of privation continuing to increase and the array of natural wonders never ceasing. Moving up the east side of the lake, emigrants had to re-cross two streams they had forded between Bridger and the city. First the Weber River, then the Bear.

Amos Josselyn ran the leg in ten days beginning on July 16, 1849. His diary entries make brief reading, but he kept excellent track of the mileage. On that day they "drove 8 miles to Mr. Baldwin's and encamped." Josselyn gives no identification to the man mentioned. The next day they made 14½ miles, remarking that the weather was "warm and pleasant." July 18, they made 22 miles and "encamped on a small creek 6 miles form Weaver [Weber] River. To cross the creek he recalled, "We had to raise our beds 5 or 6 inches." On July 19, they made another 22 miles, even with "laying by 3½ hours at noon, it being too hot to travail [travel]." The following day, they reached the Bear River, "which we found too high to ford, but we found a man there who had a skiff for carrying goods over. We crossed our goods over in the skiff, and by tying kegs to our wagons we floated them over. By the time we

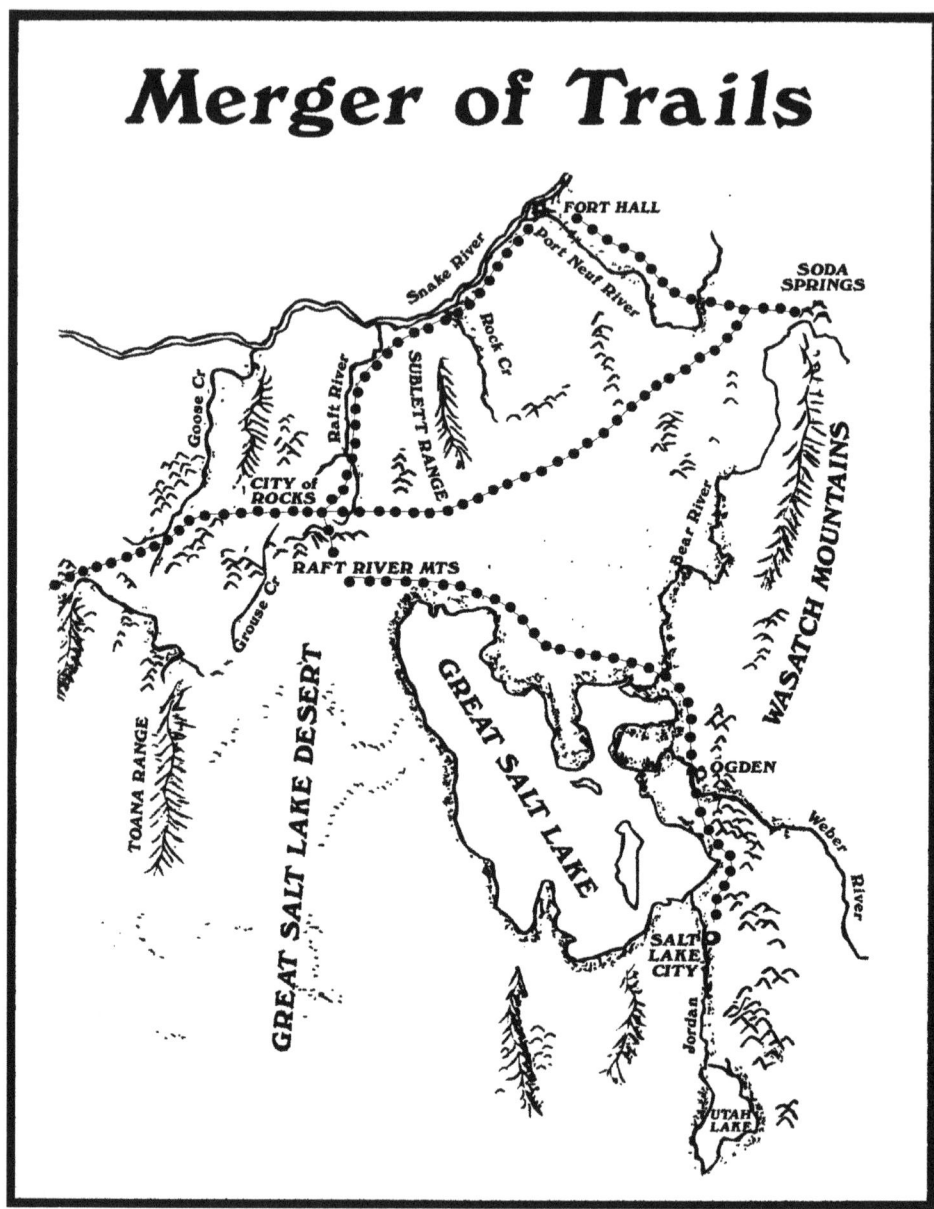

Merger of Trails — routes from Salt Lake City and Fort Hall to the City of Rocks.

got all over it was dark and the waggons being wet we did not pack our goods until morning."[1]

Samuel Jamison departed from Salt Lake City on June 22, 1850, well toward the front edge of the migration. But he had been packing, traveling without wagons, and packers nearly always outpaced the trains pulling loaded wagons with mules and oxen. "…passed the hot springs. This is hot an ough [enough] to scald in a few minutes." Two days later they reached the Weber River where they "poot [put] our packs on the flat and swam our Stalk [stock]. 50 cents pr pack. Crossed several very bad mory [mirey] Swamps. Passed the Boiling Springs. These Springs are so hot that a person cannot bare the hand in it. Making 33 miles." On June 25, they reached the Bear River. "…this we ferried and swam our stalk. One mile and encamp. Making 30 miles." Their pace beat most wagon trains by about ten miles per day.

Caleb Booth, whose journal contained a gap from Fort Laramie on, resumed writing at Salt Lake City on July 28, 1850. Apparently his party needed to re-supply while at the city and he commented somewhat disparagingly about the city's proprietors. "Every nation is coming under Mormon sway. Old J. Smith, the money digger they call Joseph Smith the Prophet. Wheat $5 to $8 per bushel. Flour $25. per hundred; cheese 40 to 50 cents per pound. Pies 50 cents each. Potatoes $4 per bushel. Coffee and sugar 50 cents per pound."

The morning of July 30, Booth's company struck out on the trek around the lake. "Traveled about 13 miles and encamped at Blooming grove. Land good, and considerable under cultivation. Geese thick on the borders of the Lake. A fine looking country. July 31… Traveled about 20 miles and encamped on a beautiful stream a few miles beyond Weber River. Passed through Brownville, a Mormon settlement. Guarded cattle [from the Mormons?]. Cold wind in the night. Mountains and snow near at hand." On August 1, Booth's party "layed by and shod cattle, fished, &c. A few of the Eutah Indians about. A mule train passed us that crossed the Mo. River, May 12. Also a train of mules returned from California." Over the next three days Booth made 37 miles, commenting on seeing lots of good springs but also recording some dissension in his company. "Some dispute this morning about starting. Almost split." They reached the Bear River on August 4, 1850, and he recalled, "for ferrying $5. No fording this season above [probably meaning the river was too high]."[2]

"We have been laying by since the 11th," began Mica Littleton's entry on August 20, 1850, explaining the gap in his diary entries. Apparently his company had decided to take a good long rest for both man and stock, before embarking on the final third of the trek to California. Littleton did not specify why the lay over lasted that long. However, on that day they did finally move off from Salt Lake City, but Littleton's party only drove as far as Blooming Grove and then laid over again the next day. On August 22, the company again moved, first "to Brownsville a Settlement of the east Side of Weber River," a distance of 15 miles from their previous camp, and then 12 more miles making 27 miles for the day, a good average distance.

Moving off again on August 23, Littleton traveled three miles, "to a hot Spring which is Salty with Mineral like Iron. Very hot with Salt oozing out of the earth all around." Seventeen miles more brought them to Box Elder Creek and they camped. The following morning they pushed on. "11 miles you come to bear river. There is no grass at this time from these places [referring to the salt springs] to Bare River. Bear River is a large stream 175 or 200 feet wide Swift current and deep to ford. There is no grass at the ford at this time though there has been grass in many places earlier in the Season."[3]

While at Salt Lake City, Sarah Davis and her husband Zeno decided to divert from their original plans, of going to Oregon, and go with the flow of the gold rush to California. Her diary entry for August 22, 1850, read, "Salt Lake city we lay here half the day and concluded to go to California." Moving out the next day they "traveled 15 miles and past plenty of salt the lake is as salt as brine let it be made as strong as it can be the road is good here and plenty of good water come to a nother mormen settlement [Brownville] whare they was building a mill a saw mill we then went about a mile to the good springs caled bentons mill springs one was salt and the other not." During the next day's travels they "came to a cane break or grass grain rather thick this is caled willow creek we stoped here to put up grass for our catle a cross the desert went twenty miles to day."

On August 25, Sarah recalled they "past more than twenty salt springs the water a bout five feet deep and boiled up in every direction the place it boiled up and spouts as large as a man head and I think of beads their thaught of all colors and shapes the rivers run in every direction." Sarah did not mention crossing the Bear River, but from her description at that point they were either near it or just beyond on the northeastern shore of the lake.[4]

From the Bear River's confluence with the Great Salt Lake to the juncture of the road from Fort Hall, the ground alternated between soggy lowlands and dry, barren, plains broken by an occasional mountain ridge. Jamison lamented encountering one of those soggy places, writing, "crossed Mudy Creek. Bad water — mule got fast in the bridge — fell over — swam out. Creek eight feet wide. 2 miles and springs of good water. No more water for Eighteen miles. Cold & hot springs not good water. Salt & warm. No water for 12 miles." The next two days, Jamison reported alternating between deep, muddy creeks and then stretches of no water for up to 12–15 mile stretches. However his party of packers still made 33 and 30 miles respectively and by June 29, had probably reached the road junction at the City of Rocks although he does not refer to that site in his diary.[5]

Caleb Booth, more than a month behind Jamison's packers, found the northern rim of the lake very dry. He chronicled the gap between the Bear

River and the road junction, beginning a series of brief diary entries on "August 5… Traveled 23 miles on account of poor water and encamped after dark near some warm brakish springs. Very dusty dry country, good grass. August 6… Traveled 12 miles. Encamped by a good spring but some long wet faces before we got there. Horrible thirsty. Hilly country. Last night one of our company lost a cow. August 7… Did not move the wagons. August 8 … traveled 6 miles. Traveled westerly course since crossing Bear River. August 9… Traveled 18 miles. Very dusty. Sage thick. Water scarce. August 10 … the wagon left for better company [but he does not specify whose wagon]. Passed through a large cedar grove at the foot of a mountain. August 11… Sabbath. Remained encamped. The natives are encamped not far off. They come to us to beg and trade. Shoshone tribe. Cold thunder shower in the evening. August 12… Traveled 17 miles. Came in sight of Fort Hall [road]." The following two diary excerpts are a good example of the relative pace set by the emigrants. Jamison, using pack mules, made the passage from the Bear River to the road junction in four days, while Booth's party of ox drawn wagons took eight, counting their layovers.

Mica Littleton recalled the trail between the Bear River and the Fort Hall road for its freestanding pools called sinks. These often formed when creeks, which had been encountered by emigrants earlier in the season, dried up and left ponds in the formerly flowing beds. Writing in late August, 1850 he described his passage. "Sinks. Here there is some grass in the wet part. Water not very good. Sage plenty. The road is deep dust very ugly in dry weather. The water will do to drink but there is but little food. This is a barren country with Sinks in every direction." Three days later, Littleton's party, having made a good pace reached the junction. "5 miles you come to the Steeple Rocks [one of many names for the City of Rocks] that is a narrow place to pass. The old Fort Hall road passes through." [6]

Sarah Davis' little party, consisting of her husband's family and a couple of tag alongs, made the leg from the Bear River to the road junction in six days. They moved along in late August, the Salt Lake basin hot and very dry, except on August 26. "This morning it is raining it seams so pleasant to see it rain as we have not seen it rane since we came in the valey august 27 … we lay buy all day fixen for the desert august 28 … we are not started yet having formed a new acquaintance with mrs crouch this morning I think we will travel to gether to california gold digins." Sarah does not mention the woman's husband but no doubt had to be excited about the prospects of some female companionship. Continuing her entry on the 28th, she wrote, "we left the springs and started over the mountains and first thing we done to help us along was to turn over Elicks wagon were about one hour loading but had nothing broke we then went on and had rufest road we have had atall we had to duble teams twice coming over and them it was vary harde drawing for the catle team yoke august 29 … this day is was vary hot and seams to me as if every thing will perish traveled all night of the 28th and 29th [August] we have now got all most a crost the desert the ground is white with salt all over august 30 ... the men are all tired nearly to death as well as the catle the men are all a sleepe and the catle are a resting themselves the Indians swarm around us and are vary saucy [scary?] august 31 ... we had a harde days travle some of our catle gave out they droped down in the desert september 1 ... since ten this morning is vary colde but the air crisp and clear we are here right in a large canion barely enuf of rume for the wagons to pass each other and varey ruff roads [reached the City of Rocks]."

Fort Hall to the City of Rocks

The distance from Fort Hall to the City of Rocks and the junction with the road from Salt Lake was approximately 110 miles. The route took the emigrants first along the upper Snake or Lewis River and over several of its tributaries, including the Port Neuf and Pannak, and past the American Falls. Roughly 50 miles from the fort the route turned up the valley of the Raft River to near its source, before a short jaunt overland to the point where it intersected the Hudspeth Cut-off, and shortly after that, joined the Salt Lake Road.

J. A. Pritchard's company completed its business and after another parting of the ways by part of its original members, jumped-off on the next leg of their trek on July 3, 1849. "At 3 P.M. we resumed the line of march with our train reduced more than one half. There is no advantage in a large train. It is true that I felt rather unwilling to separate in this remote wilderness from good hearted clever men with whom I had been so intimately connected for such a length of time, and, surrounded by the trying circumstances through which we had passed in a journey of nearly 15 hundred miles—a cross desert, mountain & plain. At the same time I felt relieved [sic] from a heavy task—the charge of so many men & animals. Four miles from Fort Hall struck and crossed the Port Neuf River, 3 miles further the Panack River which is about 120 yds wide with gravely bottom."

Beginning another day of journey on July 4, travel proved most unpleasant. "On the bluffs is a vast level plain covered with wild sage bushes so thick that it is difficult to pass through them on foot. There is no grass, on this plain. Our Fourth of July was spent travelling in the dust—and fighting off Musketooes. Their attacks were more fearce [sic] and determined, and more numerous, along this river than any of the kind I ever witnessed. Wrote a letter to my wife today and forwarded it to California by a packer—whom I thought would beat me in some 15 days. Camped one mile above the great American falls—The musketoes were so bad this evening that they nearly ran our mules crazy. They would break and run and lay down and roll. We cut sagebrush and greasewood & built large fires all round the camp — raised such a smoke that it would suffocate the men & it did no good — And they would pursue & perforate your skin with their proboscises over the hottest fire that you could endure. Frost chilled the Musketoes so that they could not disturb our mules."[7]

Three weeks behind Pritchard, Israel Hale experienced similar discomforts. "Three miles form Port Neuf we came to the Pannack River. It is a clear stream one hundred and twenty yards wide and four or five inches deeper than was convenient for our wagon beds. Soon after we crossed the Pannack, we came to a slough that we had to brush [fill in part of the creek] before we could safely cross it. The mud in the slough was as deep as the river. We then continued down the valley of Snake or Lewis River throughout the day. We traveled on the second bench or bottom and over a country that grew nothing but wild sage, but it produced a quantity of dust. Last night the mosquitoes were more numerous than I have ever seen them and as hungry as wolves. They were not as large as they were further east, but they made it up in numbers."[8]

Once finished with his social call at Fort Hall, J. Goldsborough Bruff pushed on with three travelling companions to catch up with his company that had taken the Hudspeth Cut-off. Leaving the fort on August 25, 1849, he described the country he crossed. "During the afternoon's march, we passed over a perfectly wild country, generally very level, with excellent grass, but much marsh, in narrow stripes. Indications of Indians in all directions. A few miles back, at a very muddy ford of the Panack stream narrow and deep, and locked it with willows, we had some difficulty, but soon splurge through it, with no other disaster than wetting my feet and gun muzzle. After crossing, found relics of an old camp of Indians; & among them an iron dragoon picket. Above us, on the bluffs are remains of several burnt wagons. (Here, no doubt is one of those singular instance of the selfish disposition so oft elicited on these long travels.) The party, intended to abandon their wagons, and pack into California, Grant either did not want, or would only give a very trifling sum for the wagons; so rather than he should get them for so insignificant a sum, or any body have the benefit of them gratuitously, they broke them up and destroyed them."[9]

As noted, mosquitoes inhabiting the Snake/Lewis River valley left an impression on, or more correctly, withdrew blood from, many emigrants. John Birney Hill, passing that section of road in mid July, 1850, recalled, "This morning we crost the creek [Port Neuf] — traveled 3 or 4 miles & come to quite a river [Pannack]. It is 50 yds wide 4 ft. deep — had to raise our wagon-beds. 2 or 3 more watering places we past to day. We are going down Lewis Fork now and generally a mile from the river. This evening we had Millions of Musketoes, & they bit us a few — We slept but little."[10]

The American Falls, between Fort Hall and the confluence of the Raft

River, presented an impressive sight for those emigrants passing by. J. A. Pritchard described the natural wonder in his diary on July 5, 1849. "In one mile from our encampment we passed the great American falls. The fall must be 40 or 50 feet in about 70 or 80 yards. There is not more than from 6 to 10 feet perpendicular fall at any place. The roaring of the waters can be heard for many miles. They rush with great velocity [sic] over and through the vast lumps that lay in massive piles in the channel. There is a solid mass of Black volcanic rock forming a complete abutment on either side of the river. This stone is a composition of volcanic stone, sinder, & smelted oar [ore] of some sort. A thick heavy spray is constantly emitted by the rushing of the waters. To take it all in all, it is a most wonderful & beautiful sight."[11]

"Came to the falls of the Lewis River. They are worthy of note," thought Israel Hale. "The fall of water is from fifty to sixty feet, not perpendicular but from bench to bench until the last where the fall is nearly perpendicular and forms a rainbow." Like nearly everyone else hurrying to see the elephant, Hale moved quickly by. "After passing the fall a few miles, we came to a small creek, sufficiently large, however, to turn a mill, and I have no recollections of ever seeing a better mill seat, the falls was so great. [Probably Beaver Creek, similarly described by other emigrants.] One wagon broke a king bolt at this place. We drove a mile or two and stopped for dinner. If it is a blessing, we have plenty of dust, mosquitoes, and wild sage. To walk in the road the dust is over shoe deep. To walk in the sage is like walking among rough bushes, and the mosquitoes annoy us both day and night. Snow is not as plentiful as formerly. I can see a small quantity of snow from the wagon at this time. The place we neared was worthy of note. It passed through the mountain. It seems to have opened to let the river pass there, being high cliffs on each side. I went over one of them while the wagons went round on the west side. The rocks were black and appeared to have been almost melted. It is, no doubt, the effect of some volcanic eruption. The road passed through several ravines. They were very steep, and a great many holes were worn in the road, especially on the hills. The road led through the mountain like the river. Traveled today about fifteen miles and have river water, wild sage, and poor grass."[12]

Bruff found the American Falls interesting enough to stop and draw them, but other things also caught his attention. "Met 2 Wal-lah-Wah-lah lads, perfectly nude, with fresh salmon, crying out laughingly, 'Schwap, feesh?' With 4 rifle balls we purchased 5 large fresh salmon. Country volcanic, sandy, rocky, and very irregular. A wagon trail in the road, and I picked up an infants fine white flannel undershirt. The 'American Falls' of the Columbia are very pretty cascades, but with more rapids and froth than fall of water at this season. A short distance below, sitting on my horse, I sketched the Falls & scenery."[13]

"In the forenoon we past the American Falls (of Lewis fork). I think the water is running 100 yds. Falls about 40 ft. down at the foot of the falls the water pitches over some 10 or 12 ft. The water is quite rough on the falls—the rock is not smooth, traveled on down the river, till 3 O'clock & stopped," recalled John Birney Hill of his passage. Emigrants up to a bit of sport found the fishing in the region good. "Mr. Ogle caught 48 small fish this evening," added Hill.[14]

"18 miles from Fort Hall, soon came to the American Falls of the Snake River. This stream, which is nine hundred feet wide, is enclosed between high walls of black volcanic rock, and has a fall of fifty feet. Beyond it is a wide plain of black lava, so broken and split with deep chasms that it can hardly be crossed by a man on foot," wrote Margaret Frink, describing the American Falls as she saw them on July 13, 1850. Like Hill, Margaret had a fish story. "We were visited by a party of five Crow Indians, who brought us some fine fish into camp on Beaver Creek."[15]

Along the Snake River, Israel Hale's party had also had an encounter with Indians, or so they thought, and it did not involve fish. "Some few days since, our company came to the conclusion that they would dispense with the cattle guard and it appeared to answer, but this morning five only were in sight of camp. Five more were soon found and by sending men in all directions twenty-one more were driven in. We waited for the balance of the men to return but in vain. Five or six more of us started again. We had not got a mile from camp when we met the captain on his return. He said he could find the cattle, that he had tracked them about four miles but was of the opinion that an Indian had driven them off for they appeared to be in a string, and followed one after the other, and that he plainly saw the track of a horse or of a person with shoes; also the tracks were running back from the river into the mountains, and as he had neither gun nor pistols he thought it best to return to camp for help. We immediately returned to camp and all that could be spared and could bear arms started on the expedition, thinking it highly probable that we should have a skirmish. We had not traveled more than a mile when we saw on the mountain before us the lost cattle coming toward us.

"The mystery is soon explained: the cattle followed a large bridle steer, as a leader, that was, by the by, a great rambler. That shows why they were in a single file; as regards the moccasin track, one of the men had on a pair of moccasins and found the trail and followed before the captain and left the mark of his feet. The cattle soon came up and we returned to camp well satisfied to get our cattle without traveling thirty or forty miles and perhaps then have to fight for them."[16]

Raft River Road

"22 miles from American Falls descended into the bottom of the Raft River. It is a small stream with a smooth strong current and gravely bed. It is at the crossing of this stream that the Oregon and California roads separate," explained Pritchard in his diary on July 6, 1849. "Our course was still up Raft River — 4 ms [miles] found a splendid spring that burst out from the base of the Mts. with fine grass skirting the margins of the spring branch for 400 yds. It had not been discovered by any previous emigrants. This was truly an Oasis in the desert."[17]

Continuing up the Raft, Pritchard found the terrain rugged, but beautiful. "The road was filled with round black stones for 4 or 5 miles which made it bad travelling. Our course was toward the base of the mountains. We struck the north branch of the Raft River up which we continued till noon crossing it and its tributaries several times. We nooned 2 miles up the slope of the ridge that divides the waters that flow into Raft River and Cash Valley." That ridge divided the Raft, Snake, Columbia River system which flowed to Oregon, from the Great Basin in the far northeast corner of Nevada. "Cash Valley is most beautifully surrounded by high mountains — the taller peaks of which are covered with perpetual snows."

Israel Hale started up the Raft river valley, though not quite sure of it. "The creek on which we encamped last night is thought by some to be the Raft River. The road ran up the creek and we followed until noon. There appeared to be a road that ran toward Lewis River that we supposed to be the Oregon Road. Passed two graves today, a man and a woman, one buried in '46 the other in '47. I exchanged the fore wheels of the wagons this morning.

"For the last few days we have had a great deal of wind. The ground is dry as ashes and we are forced to travel in a cloud of dust. Our persons, our wagons and everything about is covered with dust. Water is not plentiful and is warm and bad tasting. Good grass can only be found at times, so that this part of our journey is anything but pleasant, but the worst is still to come. Grass, when we strike the Humboldt, we are told will be very scarce and the water not so good as this and in many places none at all.

"But this is borrowing trouble and I will stop and take a view of the other side. Our cattle are in fair order, our men are mostly in good health and we have a plenty to eat at present and are about two weeks ahead of the time that emigrants generally pass this place, and if no bad luck happens we will, in thirty five or forty days, reach the land that is said to abound in gold now, if, the reports are true and we can reach the place in safety and have common luck, we will be liberally compensated for our toils."[18]

Still not quite sure of his position on the Raft River road, Hale conjectured, then finally concluded he was where he should have been. "We followed up the Raft River, as we supposed it to be, this forenoon past a small spring on the side of the mountain and came to where Hudspeth's Cut-Off came into this road again. The cut-off took out soon after we left Beer Springs; those who took it have not gained very much on us. The road today has been tolerable and we have not been troubled so much with dust. This afternoon the wind has blown very hard and the dust consequently bad in proportion to the wind."[19]

Bruff turned into the Raft River valley on August 28, 1849. "The mountains in our front, (the northern boundary of the Great Basin, and divide between the waters of the Basin and the Columbia — Pacific) were of a soft blue, and in places a flesh-colored tint. The road is a good one, on a S. course. The river here, is a mere brook, and trends round to the S. Willows and reeds mark its sinuous course. The fresh breeze nearly suffocated us with clouds of blinding, stifling dust — right in our faces. We camped on the bank of the stream [head of the Raft river], here a cold brook; and such objects! Such beards & faces! All white with dust, our animals ditto. On halting here, I observed ahead, columns of blue smoke, curling up from nitches in the mountains: probably Digger Indians."[20]

On the trail beyond Fort Hall, Margaret Frink found a woman's work never done. Writing from a point near the Raft River on July 14, 1850, she recalled, "…Sunday, duties of camp life weekly laundry had to be attended to, although the day was excessively warm, the mercury marking one hundred twenty degrees inside our wagon. The dryness of the air, and the high altitude, made the heat more endurable than it would have been in a moist climate at low elevations." Next day they moved on and struck the Raft River. "…traveled down the snake eight miles came to Raft River, a small stream that flowed from mountains on our left. Here the roads fork again the right hand one turning off northwesterly towards Oregon, while we took the left hand one, going south-westerly towards California, leaving Snake River, and traveling up Raft River. Camped on a branch of this stream not far from the junction of the Myer's Cut-off, which we passed near Steamboat Spring."[21]

John Birney Hill found the Raft River road no better or worse than those he had earlier encountered along the trail: "…here the Oregon Road left ours — it goes up the hill — Our road goes up the creek. We had a little rough road in the forenoon — but not bad. In the afternoon it was level & nice. Any quantity of grass on this creek. I did not see only 4 dead Oxen from the forks of the road (on Bear River) to where they come together again (about 7 days travel)." He also had heard about the Hudspeth Cut-off, which he had decided not to take, and adding to his diary entry on July 22, 1850, continued, "I will give you a Synopsis of the Cutoff (from hearsay). [Nice of him to so inform the reader.] From all accounts there is not much difference, in the distance of these roads. The Cut-off has 2 very steep hills to go down. Some say they are the worst hills that they have found yet & the grass is not as good as it is on the Ft. Hall Road. They say there is but very few Musketoes in the Cut-off. About the middle of the Cut-off there is 20 miles without water. Considering every thing, I expect there is not much difference in these roads."[22]

Merger of Fort Hall and Salt Lake Roads at the City of Rocks

Given a number of different names by the emigrants passing it, the City of Rocks stood out as another marvelous geologic anomaly and landmark on the road to California. In a sense, the City of Rocks acted as a funnel or gate through which nearly all the emigrants passed into the Goose Creek/Thousand Springs region of northeastern Nevada, before striking the Humboldt River road which would take them to within striking distance of the Sierras, the gold fields, and the tusks of the elephant.

Pritchard reached the gate on July 8, 1849, referring to the site only as the terminus of the Cash valley. "30 miles from the upper Raft river valley, passed out of the Cash valley. This gorge in the mountains is dangerous to pass on account of the piles of large round stones that lay in the road over which we are compelled to pass. We had to use extreme caution to prevent braking down our wagons — we found one wagon smashed down in the pass. This branch leads out into a small valley entirely surrounded by mts. with a narrow outlet about 30 feet wide with vertical walls from 3 to 500 feet high. The road strikes another valley — and at this point the Salt Lake and Fort hall roads come together again." At that point Pritchard seemed to receive confirmation that he had chosen the best route back on the Big Sandy. "We here overtook a wagon that came by Salt Lake. We had gained from 8 to 10 days on them according to their statement. They stated that provisions were scarce at Salt Lake."[23]

"We took the ridge this morning and left the Raft River. The rise was very gradual, and the descent equally so. Last night, after we encamped, another of my oxen died. He was in fine order this morning. In the afternoon we followed the valley about two miles when the road took through a gap in the mountain. It was narrow but wide enough for a road. We went round one peak and found that the new road from the Salt Lake entered ours about this time," wrote Israel Hale on July 29, 1849.

"The curiosities began to appear. Our entrance into the mountain reminded me of the walls of a city and the many singular shaped rocks of ancient castles, towns etc. The road wound round them and they continued near four miles. They were in almost every imaginable shape. One large round one I noticed had a large cave that projected over sufficiently for one to take shelter under and had a kid of cupola or belfry. Another had a portico similar to a house; some were nearly square. I noticed at the edge of the basin (for I knew of no better name to give it) that there stood a number of small steeples, from ten to fifty feet in height. The mountains around were high and points of rocks pointed still higher. After we got through the rocks, we passed a handsome valley and passed out at another gap on the opposite side. We drove on in quest of water. We drove until dark and encamped without water, wood or anything but grass."[24]

Sallie Hester reached the funnel on August 3, 1849: "...took another cutoff this week called Sublets [actually the Hudspeth]. Struck the Raft River; from thence to Swamp Creek. Passed some beautiful scenery, high cliffs of rocks resembling old ruins or dilapidated buildings."[25]

"...We entered a very extraordinary valley, called the 'City of Castles,' wrote Bruff on August 29, 1849. "A couple of miles long, and probably ½ mile broad, a light grey decripitaiting granite, probably altered by fire in blocks of every size, from that of a barrel to the dimensions of a large dwelling-house; groups, Masses on Masses, and Cliffs; worn, by the action of ages of elementary affluences, into strange and romantic forms. The travelers had marked several large blocks, as their fancy dictated the resemblance to houses, castles, etc. On one was marked with tar, 'NAPOLEON'S CASTLE,' another 'CITY HOTEL.' The outlet of this romantic vale, a very narrow pass, just wide enough for a wagon, and on either side very high, jagged, and thin walls of granite, is called Pinnacle Pass, and the tall rock on the right, the Spire rock. ½ mile down a steep hill the Salt Lake road joins this, the Oregon and California road."[26]

Henry Wellenkamp saw the wonder on Thursday, 11 July, 1850. "Started before sunrise. Wind River mount. Left the valley at 9 and entered the mountains — a grand, natural spectacle presents itself — pyramids, cupolas, elephants, lions, churches, and all kinds of huge and irregular masses of bare granite blocks from 2 to 1500 feet high. A never to be forgotten sight. Met at 11 o'clock the Salt Lake road, 195 miles from Mormon City, said to be 16 days travel from Pacific Springs to this juncture. Fine grass but very bad route. Found a glistening stuff [mica] which nine-tenths pronounce gold."[27]

"During the forenoon we passed through a stone village composed of huge, isolated rocks of various and singular shapes, some resembling cottages, others steeples and domes. It is called the 'City of Rocks,' but I think the name Pyramid City more suitable," concluded Margaret Frink. "It is a sublime, strange, and wonderful scene — one of nature's most interesting works. The Salt Lake road, which turned off between Dry Sandy and Little Sandy, and which we passed on the 26th of June, rejoined our road at this point. The road was very rough. Traveled seven miles. The Goose Creek Indians are said to be warlike and troublesome, but we have not found them so up to this time. Camped in the little valley of Goose Creek."[28]

"We eat dinner in Rock-Town," remembered John Birney Hill. "I call it Rock Town because the naked rock is standing out by themselves— they are of different forms, size & height — At the W. side of these rocks the Road goes between two Mountains of naked rock. There is room for wagons to go between without any trouble. Half past 1 O'clock we come to where the Salt-Lake-Road united with the Ft. Hall road. We are now camped 7 or 8 miles from the junction of the roads—close to Goose Creek."[29]

Mica Littleton likewise suggested a different name for the strange formation of rocks but did not offer much of a description. "5 miles you come to the Steeple Rocks. That is a narrow place to pass. The old Fort hall road passes through and you come into it a little further. Ahead you take down a long hill here and come into a valley. 9 miles you come to goose creek. Here has been good feed water etc."[30]

Goose Creek to the Upper Humboldt River

Seven or eight miles from the City of Rocks, the emigrants struck Goose Creek and a popular and often crowded campground. After ascending that creek for about a day's travel they had to traverse a rugged desert strip to Thousand Springs Creek, and ascend it before jumping once more over a barren stretch into the valley of the Mary's or upper Humboldt River. The length of the Thousand Springs Creek valley bubbled with much geothermal activity and many emigrants referred to it in their diaries as Hot Springs. The distance from Goose Creek to Mary's River was approximately 90 miles, depending on which emigrants' mileage one reads and which tributary of the Humboldt they first encountered.

"...Reached the valley of Goose Creek—found several trains & some packers encamped here. Goose Creek or as it is called by some Rattle Snake River. It is about 30 feet wide with a tolerable abundance of water. The road runs up this creek 22 miles. Crossed over 15 miles of hill into Hot Springs valley. Little to no grass," wrote Pritchard describing the opening stretch of the next leg of the journey. Over the next two days his company pushed south and west along the Thousand Springs Creek toward the Humboldt. "July 10 ... traveled 24 miles through valley dubious grass and water. Surface of ground was covered with an incrustation of Alkaline—we however found a spring of good water. July 11 ... found marsh grass and plenty of ducks, shot 4 which served up a fine dinner. In about 6 ms. we came to the hot springs. These springs boil up in bold streams covering an area of several acres of marshy earth. The water that rises here forms quite a bold running branch for several miles, which sinks in the flats and rises a long in places for some 25 or 30 miles. These waters are all boiling hot and the water runs warm for a mile or so. I put my hand in several places and it would have taken the skin off in less than no time. The water was strongly impregnated with the efflorescence of Alkaline and mixed with a little sulphur. Met six of Bryant's men one of

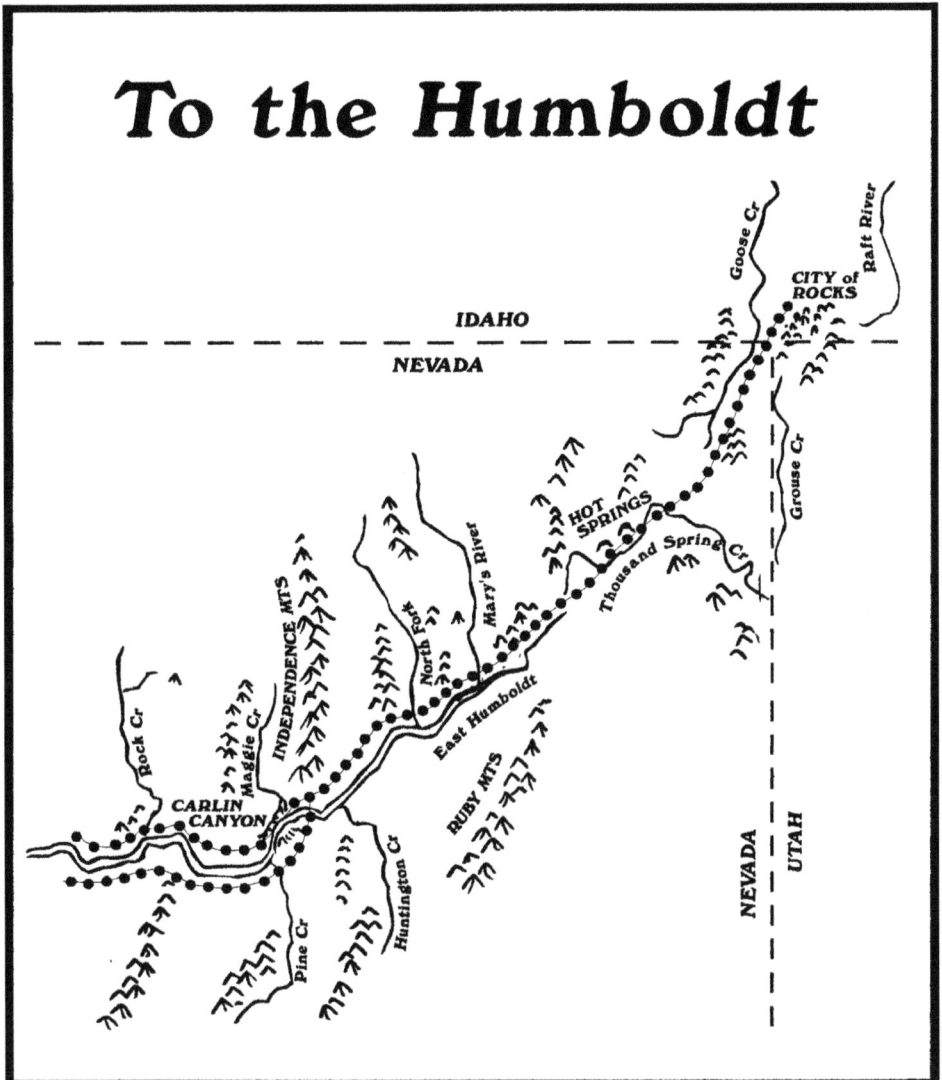

To the Humboldt — City of Rocks to upper Humboldt River and Carlin Canyon.

whom is very sick. Dr. Thomas has agreed to take the sick man in his wagon, and use his mules. Reached the western rim of the Great Basin and struck a small branch one of the tributaries of Mary's River. Grass and water good."[31]

"We then took over the hills to Goose Creek. They were hills indeed, both long and steep," remarked Israel Hale. We passed several springs during the day. They were small but the water was good." The following morning, "We followed Goose Creek this forenoon. The creek is about one rod wide and eight to ten inches deep. The valley is narrow but has posts of good grass; a great many good camping places on it. Several horses were lost last night and I fear they were stolen. I saw ice this morning. There is some fine fish in this creek. In the afternoon we followed up the creek and passed some warm springs. The water, in one, was as warm as I would like to drink coffee."[32]

After laying over a day, Hale continued in his diary on August 2, 1849. "Cattle scattered for miles up and down the valley, the name of which is Hot Springs Valley [also referred to as Thousand Springs]. 16 miles, got water for use by digging. We were indebted to Mr. John Hutson for digging a well, which we gave the name Hutson's well. We followed the Hot Springs Valley eight miles and came to the Springs. There were a dozen or more small springs and all of them nearly boiling hot. They smelt very strong of sulphur and the branch was filled with sediment that resembled rusty iron. About one hundred yards above was a fine cool spring and very deep. The water however was a little brackish. Out drive today has been sixteen or seventeen miles. Hardly a day passes that we do not pass more or less dead cattle, horses or mules and sometimes see all of them in one day. We also see some cattle that have been left from lameness or poison or other sickness."[33]

Sallie Hester's diary entries had become somewhat spotty by August, 1849, but she did remember in her writing passing along the road from Goose Creek to the Humboldt. "Hot Springs, August 18. Camped on a branch of Mary's River, a very disagreeable and unpleasant place on account of the water being so hot. This week some of our company left us, all young men. They were jolly, merry fellows and gave life to our lonely evenings. We all miss them very much. Some had violins, others guitars, and some had fine voices, and they always had a good audience. They were anxious to hurry on without the Sunday stops. Roads are rocky and trying to our wagons, and the dust is horrible. The men wear veils tied over their hats as a protection. When we reach camp at night they are covered with dust from head to heels."[34]

As Bruff proceeded up Goose Creek he noticed the toll of animals increasing. "Dark brown lava Macadamized the road, and the brown dust of it rose in a fine powder. Near the head of 'Goose Creek'—a tributary of the Columbia. Relics of old camps are here numerous; broken wagons; &c. and 1 ox wagon packing. Passed 9 dead oxen, 4 dead mules, and 2 dead horses." Though the days of late August in the Nevada desert are hot and dry, the nights bring a perceptible chill. Bruff recalled, "Arose at break of day with cold, white with frost, and hair again picketed with frost. Plenty of ice in stream. On the left of the road, a stick, with the following notice on it, written in a fair hand.

Public Sale.

Will be sold, on Sunday, 2nd Sept. on the head of Mary's River, Stores, and a lot of merchandize. Emigrants in the rear will do well to be there, as great bargains will be sold. Aug. 29th 1849. Wm. Mullin & Co." Bruff would miss the sale by a few days.

"This is the valley of the Hot Springs," he continued. "Road very deep in dust. Very little good grass, plenty of long dead stuff, sage, and small cedar bushes. The spring at the head of road, first struck on descending a rugged hill, is the source of a Great Basin stream, at this season dry a short distance below the spring. The water we used is from pits dug in the bed of the stream, and is muddy and bad. Passed a grave marked, W. Maxwell, died August 24, 1849, Cholera, Teamster in Pioneer line, Took Cholera on the Platte, then Scurvy; from Independence. Passed to-day 10 dead oxen, 6 dead mules, and 2 dead horses."[35]

Henry Wellenkamp passed the road between Goose Creek and the Humboldt in mid July, 1850. He found a tributary of the creek to be quite refreshing. "Five miles from spring we came to Cold Water or Jar creek, the water being *very* cold in the heat of midsummer temperature 85 degrees." Writing the next day, he shortchanged the valley that he entered. "Up 100 Springs valley. These springs are like wells from 4 to 6 feet diameter and from 10–20 feet deep, of excellent water. Passed at 10 o'clock *boiling springs*. Nooned in tall, dry grass. Sun excessively hot — no water. Here I heard that emigrants suffered from erysipelas [a severe skin inflammation caused by an infection] and a solution of nitrate of silver is in quite a demand as a remedy."[36]

"…Travel up Goose Creek," wrote Margaret Frink, less than a week behind Wellenkamp in 1850. "The road was very rough. Country presents volcanic appearance. Fourteen miles to next water at entrance to Thousand Spring Valley. The spring was beautiful, flowing out form beneath a large rock. Here we traded some gunpowder for an antelope ham, with some Snake Indians. The valley has both hot and cold springs. At the farther end we expect to reach the head of the Humboldt River."[37]

They pushed on. "…Traveled down the Thousand Spring Valley for twenty miles. A party of Indians encamped with us at noon, but gave no signs of being unfriendly. Seldom without company on this part of the journey." On July 21, Margaret encountered one of the strangest sights any emigrant recorded, a naturally occurring laundry with hot water wash, and cold water rinse. "Soon after starting came to springs that were boiling hot. Only five feet from them was another as cold as ice. Here were men engaged in washing their clothing. Their position was such that, after washing a garment in the boiling springs, they could take it by the waistband and fling it across into the cold spring, and vice versa, with perfect ease."[38]

John Birney Hill made the run between Goose Creek and the upper tributaries of the Humboldt in five days, not including one on which they laid over. Beginning on July 25, 1850, he recorded his company's progress. "…come to Goose River; or Creek. This creek is 10 to 12 feet wide. Thousands of Wild Currents [currants] about this branch — they are quite sour —

but they have a pleasant taste. We cooked a pint. The road goes up Goose R. about 18 mi.'s. July 26… It is 13 miles, from where we left Goose River to the next watering place. This 13-mi.'s is hilly—but not bad—No grass—some Cedar. July 27 … we come to quite a large Valley & a Small branch—but the water does not run here. I have seen a good many dead Horses this week. Road level today. July 28… Sunday. Laying up to day. July 29… This morning we Started at an early hour & come to the Boiling Springs. These Springs cover about ¼ of an acre of ground. The water is so hot that it will burn or Scald a person's hand in a very short time. It has an unpleasant smell. Plenty of grass in this valley. July 30… We traveled 3 or 4 miles after dinner to the Branch (this branch runs into Humboldt R.) Any quantity of grass where we are now camped & there is Red clover here to, or it is a Fac-simile, the leaves are not round like tame clover."[39]

Mica Littleton remembered the road from Goose Creek through the Thousand Springs valley as alternating between good and bad. Beginning on August 30, 1850, he wrote, "…you keep up Goose Creek 18 miles. There has been good grass here early, willows for wood and good creek water." Describing the transition space between the valleys he continued, "the road here is Rocky and bad for a short distance and where you cross this stream it is muddy & Banks steep though not high. 13 miles you come to what I shall call Rock Spring [he had entered Thousand Spring Valley]. It is the head of hot Spring Valley. On this road you will find a very rough road full of large rocks. You ascend and descend many hills in this distance. No grass nor water 11 miles down the valley. There are many springs here though I do not like them. They are in such miry places. The valley is wide here—good grass and water can be had every few miles."[40]

Moving on up Thousand Springs Creek, Littleton continued to be disenchanted with the land he crossed. "This valley varies in the Bottom from 1[100] to 600 yards. This part of the country is uninviting to the eye of the traveler and there is much alkalie in all these valleys. You can see it on the ground nearly every place you go, and the last few days we have seen hundreds of dead horses, oxen and mules. This is truly a long and difficult trip on man and beast."[41]

Caleb Booth took six days to make the trek from Goose Creek in mid August, 1850. Like many of the diarists, his entries got shorter as the journey got more difficult and finding the time and energy to write and elaborate on their surroundings waned. "August 14 … traveled up Goose Creek 14 miles, found good grass, also sage and willow. Showers. August 15… Traveled 18 miles and encamped in thousand Spring Valley near a good spring. P.M. Rough road. In passing up Goose Creek for about 19 miles I counted 38 dead animals. Afterward in less than half a mile counted 7 dead ones. August 16… Lost a part of our cattle this morning but after hunting for a few hours we found them. Traveled 10 miles, and encamped where there was but a little

Goose Creek to the Upper Humboldt River

grass and poor water. August 17... This morning found two arrows sticking in the side of one of our oxen. Many clothes thrown away. Passed warm springs. August 18... Sunday. Traveled 15 miles. Encamped in full view of Snow Mountains. Passed a cart, yokes, tool &c. which had been left lately. August 19... Very cold night. Ice formed in pails. Very little if any dew here. Course about S. West. Several of our cattle are lame. Encamped on Canyon Creek, a few miles from Mary's River."[42]

Sarah Davis called Goose Creek "white springs" and reports having laid over there after passing the canyon at the City of Rocks. Though she rarely mentions specific place names in her diary, like other emigrants so often do, probably relying on names in their guidebooks, her progression along the trail can be paralleled from her brief descriptions. But at times, she seems to be in a totally different place. On September 3, 1850, her small company pushed off from the campgrounds on Goose Creek. "...Take over the mountains to the humbolt river September 4 ... traveled 18 miles and came to water and grass September 5 ... traveled 15 miles and found plenty of good grass and water cold as ice [referenced by Wellenkamp] catle are giten fat on this grass I was vary sick all night here with a pane in my breast."[43]

Probably the best way to describe the Davis trek to California would be "wandering" west. On September 6, they seem to have been moving away from Goose Creek, but a distance other emigrants covered in less than a day, took them two. "September 7 ... we past over some of the handsomest land I ever saw in my life the land was completely covered with a thick coat of grass [this indicates they may have not been on the main trail] it looks like a perfect meadow past some five or six boiling springs [indicating they had reached Thousand Springs valley] September 8 ... a butiful morning the sunshines bright and clear as cristal we have past the most butiful sight I ever saw in my life a perfect meadow with ten thousand springs in it a gushing right from the mountain clear and cold some of them large anuff to cary any mill in operation."[44]

From that point they should have been within 60 miles of the upper Humboldt but according to her diary entries they would not reach it for a full week. She reports going to a river that none of the other emigrants encountered by that name. We can only guess at times where she was. "September 9 ... we traveled 25 miles to day we come to Clarks river [?] to day the dust was so bad that it was almost Impossible to travel September 10 ... mr crouch had all of his team stolen buy the Indians and their is truly left helpless we lost one horse the Indian tracks are all over here we have still a vary dusty road it all most sufocates us their is plenty of Indian sign here all the time."[45]

As Israel Hale neared the Humboldt River, in early August, 1849, he seemed to have found more time to write in his diary than anyone else. He wrote about any number of things. He offers some fine insights into trail life as the true nadir of the trip approaches but is not yet evident to so many. "Yesterday when we came to the forks of the road, John Sutton was ahead of the train and took the left hand road and did not get to the train last night. It often happens that a person lost from his train has trouble in finding it again. This is the second Sunday we have not traveled since we left St. Joseph. Our men have scattered throughout the country; some are hunting, some are fishing and some have been hunting John and a few of us have been laying about camp.

"The hunters have killed some hares and birds; the fishermen have caught some fine mountain trout. They are fine indeed in color. They resemble salmon, being of a yellow cast and the water being cold and clear, they have a fine flavor and are hard. A large number of wagons are passing us, but our cattle are resting as well as our men and all will be in better condition for traveling by laying by on Sunday.

"August 6th. We crossed the creek eight or nine times and some of the crossings were bad. A portion of the road through the canyon was very rocky, so taking it altogether it was far from being a good carriage road. I noticed south of us a high mountain, partially covered with snow, which is something that I did not expect to see until we arrived at the Sierra Nevada. I hear about this time of a great number of horses being stolen. One was taken but a short distance from our camp. It is laid to the Indians and probably is, but I think some white men may be at the head of it. Horses are very valuable here. A good horse in order would bring one hundred and fifty dollars and a pony that could be bought in the States for twenty-five would here bring seventy-five or one hundred dollars.

"In passing through the above named canyon, I saw a tolerable large warm spring. It was the handsomest that I ever saw, the bottom was gravel and about as warm as a person would like water to bathe their feet, and perfectly clear. It was sufficiently large for a person to bathe all over.

"We are now coming into Digger Indian country. They are said to be a bad Indian and that they steal horses and cripple cattle so that they cannot be driven, when they get the meat for beef.

"August 7th. In the afternoon about starting time news came round that Bassett was sick and that we would lay by until morning. We dislike laying by for several reasons. We are all anxious to get through and prepare for winter; also that grass is daily becoming more scarce as trains pass us and use it up. And another that there is a possibility of our being caught in the snow should we be forced to lay by much more: and another reason is that butter, milk, fruit and vegetables are luxuries that we are deprived of.

"Horses and mules continue to be stolen almost daily. Six were taken last night from the ground on which we are encamped. One of the mules was regained. They were taken about three hours before daylight. It is said to be four miles to the Humboldt, St. Mary's or Ogden's River (it being known by all three names) where it is necessary to keep close watch on everything that we have. I am almost certain that white men commit depredations on the credit of the Indians, for the horse that was taken from our train a week or so ago passed this place last evening driven or led by a white man and bound for California, but it is doubtful whether the owner ever gets him for we have not a horse in the train that is fit to ride on a trip of the kind and the man that owned him left the train this morning, although he was informed of his horse having passed this place last night.

"Wood continues very scarce through this country. I have no recollection of having seen a tree of any size since we left Fort Hall. We see bushes along the creek in places and sometimes small ones on the hills, but no trees. I think a sage bush is the largest bush that we have passed for near two weeks. How Mr. Benton [a reference to Thomas Hart Benton, a Missouri senator and proponent of western railroad building] intends propelling his locomotive when he gets his railroad completed is more than I can say, for it will certainly be a tedious business to gather sage, for it is short and hard to cut, but when provided would answer a better purpose than anything else that I have seen for the last two hundred miles. However I presume that when that is completed they will load a car or two with fuel and not attempt to procure it in such places as this."[46]

Starting the Humboldt Run

Where exactly the emigrants struck the Humboldt River is open to a lot of interpretation and varies from diary to diary. Most recorded reaching one of the tributaries of the upper Humboldt, Mary's River, after crossing over a ridge approximately 50 miles after leaving the Hot Springs. Another good day's travel beyond Mary's River, they encountered the main North Fork of the Humboldt River and from the point of its confluence, the trail fell in along the main channel and assumed the identity of the Humboldt road. The Humboldt road took the emigrants from northeastern Nevada across roughly 300 miles of desert to west central Nevada, to nearly within sight of the Sierra Nevada Mountains. In Sallie Hester's brief entry on August 20, 1849, she summed up the next major leg of the trek. "Humboldt River. We are now 348 miles from the mines. We expect to travel that distance in three weeks and a half. Water and grass scarce."[47]

At first, the Mary's and upper Humboldt made a fairly good impression on most of the emigrants, because of the available water, grass, and even fish. But shortly the heat, dust, rugged terrain, and unfriendly Indians changed many opinions. "This morning as a pack train was leaving camp they had a loos[e] mule which dropped back a short distance behind and it was instantly seized by a party of Indians who were secreted in the sage brush near the camp and hurried off. They were discovered however by the men 4 or 5 of whom instantly pursued them & in a short distance recovered the mule, but the Indians made their escape," recounted J. A. Pritchard on July 12, 1849. The next morning his company "Struck and crossed the main North Fork of Mary's River. We found the ground on the opposite side to be very marshy & a train had nearly all their wagons & mules mired down. And whilst we were suffocating with dust and heat in the valley the Mountains on either side were covered with snow." Yet, despite complaining of the dust and heat, Pritchard characterized his travel as leisurely, after finding something on the trail. "As I was traveling leisurely a long to day I found a letter in the road written by a young lady who was on a visit to her Aunts in the State of New York. To her father at Independence Mo. Requesting the Old Gentlemen to send her money to purchase a Black Silk dress. She made a great many excuses & many fine speeches. The last one said she that you gave me I want to keep for parties and if I ware [sic] it out on the street it will be so soiled that it won't do for that purpose."[48]

Israel Hale had similar impressions of the Humboldt road to those of Pritchard. "The mountains on each side of the valley are rather high but not rocky. The road is good but a little dusty. The growth of the valley is sage and grass. The margins of the river has in general a strip of willows that shows us its course. We passed an ox last evening that had been killed by the Indians. They had carried off about one half of him, the balance was still laying. It had the appearance of having been killed a day or two but meat will keep in this climate a long time and that without salt. I have eat meat that had been killed from eight to ten days, nor had it been salted and was as good meat as I ever eat in any country. That was on Bear River. This afternoon the road continued in the valley and was good but dusty."[49]

Niles Searls, the young lawyer who had been writing such marvelous daily entries earlier, had resigned himself to only weekly entries at the beginning of August, 1849. By mid August his company had reached the Humboldt and his entry on the 19th of that month illustrated the melancholy which gripped him at that point. "Another week is numbered with the past and finds us toiling down the Humboldt or St. Mary's River. Water, such as it affords, is plentiful and at a few points grass also is abundant, but generally the broad valley is a barren sandy alkaline waste with nothing to relieve its monotony except the ever present and execrable sage brushes, with here and there a fringe of willows along the low banks of the river. Imagine the Erie Canal, increased two or three fold in width, passing through the center of a plain and a fair idea may be obtained of the Humboldt: drink of the waters of that canal, and a Humboldt flavor would probably be appreciated.

"Our men are becoming emaciated and querulous. Luxuries in the way of foods are among the things of memory dear. Rancid bacon with the grease fried out by the hot sun, musty flour, a little pinoles and some sacks of pilot bread, broken and crushed to dust and well coated with alkali, a little coffee without sugar — now constitute our diet. The men need more and must have it or perish. Yet at our present rate of progress, even these supplies must fail long before we can reach California."[50]

J. Goldsborough Bruff, on entering the Humboldt valley caught up with his wagon train that had taken the Hudspeth Cut-off while he went to Fort Hall. In his diary he gave a nice explanation of how the river got its name. "September 3 ... entered a moist flat valley, trending round to the Westward, with springs, and a grassy and willowy rivulet; one of the heads of the Humboldt. This stream was first known by the name of Ogden's river, after a celebrated mountaineer, who first visited it, so they say; afterwards called Mary's river, probably in honor of the Blessed Virgin; and continued by that name, till Col. Fremont re-christened it, in honor of Baron Humboldt. Some travelers adopt the last name, but it is generally called Mary's river.

This valley runs about S.W. Low tableland on each side. Distant mountains in all directions. Passed dead oxen, mules and horses. While breakfasting this morning two miserable, half-clad shivering Indians came into camp. They were armed with full quivers and bows, and very different and inferior to any Indians I had before seen; and was confident they were the Diggeres, who used poisoned arrows. Said to one of them, Digger? He replied with a shake of the head, and downcast look, Shoshonee. But I knew he lied."[51]

Bruff had already observed plenty of waste along the trail, but on the Humboldt that waste of property, animals and even human beings seemed to accelerate. The wide swing from human goodness to evil became evident. "I observed a good wagon standing, with cover, gear, etc. and a card pinned on the side, to this effect: 'August 3, 1849. This wagon and plunder is left for the use of the emigrants: Please don't destroy this wagon, for it might be of great service to some poor Emigrants like ourselves.' signed, Barnet R. Light. Consoling myself with the idea that he had left it for the benefit of 'some poor emigrant' and in this instance it would most certainly be so appropriated. So I took the fore wheels, axle, and tongue, to replace the same parts of one of my wagons, defective therein. Wrecks and fragments of broken up and burnt wagons numerous, of which our cooks avail themselves." The next day, about noon, Bruff encountered the other side. "Passed a grave; Samuel A. Fitzzimmons, died from effects of a wound received from a bowie-knife in the hands of George Symington, Aug: 25th 1849."[52]

Like so many emigrants along the Humboldt, Franklin Starr had close encounters with the Indians. "I was awaken last night by the barking of the dog belonging to the other waggon and raising the bottom of the tent and looking out saw 3 Indians close to the camp. They immediately ran into the willows which every where line the river and in which our Cattle were lying. I got up and stepped to the waggon and got down my rifle and concealing myself in the shade watched for further demonstrations. The bell rattled a few moments and again all was quiet. After waiting some little time I turned in again and was soon asleep.

"In the morning 6 Indians came into camp while we were hitching up our team. I suppose with the expectation of getting something to eat but we were getting scarce of provisions and did not like them about and gave them nothing. While hitching up the train the Cutters came by and one put a knife to one of the Indians throats and another one on the back with an ax. While drawing blood but failed to make him flinch although his face expressed thirst for revenge. One man riding after the train insisted on our giving him a rifle to shoot one of them with but we refused to do so.

"The Indians which came into our camp were much smaller than the Sioux Cheyenne and other tribes that I have seen but looked more intelligent than I had expected. They were active and had a peculiar look. They were slightly dressed in fine skins and were armed with bows and arrows. The arrows were feathered and had a three cornered point on them though some others that I have seen had flint points."[53]

"...Struck the head of the Marays [Mary or Humboldt River] River. This we follow for two hundred and seventy miles," wrote Samuel Jamison on July 1, 1850. The next morning Jamison's pack train "passed a camp that had a man shot by an Indian night before with and [an] arrow while on guard. Crossed several bad Ravines. Crossed Marays River this we had to ferry in a wagon bed and drive our stalk [stock] through. I had to get in to lead them out. We had three places of this kind." Travel conditions did not improve as they pushed on toward the main channel. "Left our gray horse—had the Scours [animal form of diarrhea] got our mules mired very swampy all along this river. Fieryed [a descriptor for it being very hot?] traveled about thirty miles."[54]

Margaret Frink arrived on the Humboldt on July 23, 1850. "This day brought us to the far-famed Humboldt River. We met a party of men with pack mules returning to the Atlantic states. It was a rare thing to see any one going that way. The emigrants were anxious for information. They asked hundreds of questions of the packers. Had they stopped to answer, they would have been kept all summer. They kept their mules going at a rapid gait, and shouted back their answers as long as they could be heard."[55]

Caleb Booth's first few days along the Humboldt passed fairly well except for tales about Indians. "August 20... Encamped on Mary's River, a stream about one rod wide. Saw about 50 antelopes today. Grass good. Cold night. August 21... This morning a train struck our road by a new route from the cutoff, via S. side of Salt Lake 93 miles. Desert." What Booth was describing was one of a number of cut-offs that went around the southern shore of the Great Salt Lake, instead of the northern shore route used by most emigrants. The most noted of the southern cut-offs connecting Salt Lake City with the Humboldt road was Hastings. In a hurry, some emigrants were willing to try any new route that might gain them a few days. The Hastings Cut-off soon earned the reputation of being brutally rough, with trains frequently getting lost or misdirected. William Edmundson took one of the southern cut-offs and found himself backtracking over several days and losing time instead of gaining any. Booth added, second hand, "The Indians on the cutoff were as thick as bees. Several men were killed."[56]

Mica Littleton joined the Humboldt on September 4, 1850, describing in his journal the two main tributaries. "…you come to the principle branch of Mary's river and cross it. It is a fine Stream with plenty fish. 20 miles from the main branch of Marys River you will come to another fine Stream from the North [the North Fork of the Humboldt]. Both together makes quite a river."[57]

"…This morning we met a vary large train comin from the golde digins they ware mormins comin to salt lake we have now come to the humbolte rivere," recorded Sarah Davis on September 15, 1850. Continuing the next day, she wrote, "this travel was vary dusty and harde on the catle one of them droped down in the yoke suficated with dust we have now over taken a great many people and almost every one out of provisions of any kind we solde almost fifty dolars worth of bakin [bacon?] last night." Davis also encountered Indians soon after striking the Humboldt. "September 17 … come to the river again the Indians are vary thick they have killed to [two] men to day and took their ammunition and horses and left them for the buzards they devour them like we would sweete cake we have to have set a strong guarde all the time or we would be killed and may be we will be killed yet we dont no."[58]

The year before, Bruff had also met travelers coming the other way on the trail, like Frink and Davis. Writing on September 5, 1849, he "Found camped near us, a Mormon train of 8 wagons, several women and children, and plenty of stock, among them some very fine California horses, and Mexican equipment. They were from California bound to the Salt lake Settlement. One of the Mormons encamped here had a fine large specimen of crude gold, which he exhibited to one of my men."[59]

Carlin Canyon

By Amos Josselyn's calculations, 41 miles after striking the main channel of the Humboldt, emigrants came to Carlin Canyon, a narrow defile through which the main road passed. They could go through it along the river or take an alternative route over high ground around it, estimated at between ten to twenty miles. It's worth noting that the Humboldt hardly ran any straighter than any other river and the road often moved away from the channel in order to cut across and shorten the distance of a significant bend.

Pritchard arrived at the canyon when the water was too high and went around it. "The road crosses the hills here in consequence of the river's running so near the point of the bluff that we cannot pass round the river road at this present stage of water. After passing through winding ways running to all points of the cumpas [sic] we gained the summit at 10 A.M. We commenced the descent immediately upon arriving at the top of the hill and by noon we had completed the trip across the mountains a distance of 10 ms."

Pritchard found the road difficult and the mood of his company changing. "The soil here is more porous & light than any that I ever before saw. It is not infrequently the case that our mules go out side of the road sink to their knees in dry dirt and almost swamp in dry earth. Several trains that had been pushing hard here came up with us and our boys began to feel alarmed. They thought we were travelling to[o] slow and that all the trains would pass us and that there would be no grass left. By convincing them of the fact that while these men had already broken down their teams by excessively hard driving in order to get a head that we had taken our time for it & taken good care of our teams and still done good travelling."[60]

Amos Josselyn also went around. "Soon after crossing this creek we went over the hills, through a kenyen [canyon] where it was twenty miles before we came to the river again. There was a small spring in the kenyen but there was so many waiting for a chance to water that we drove on. The roads were rough, hilly and dusty and the day hot."[61]

Israel Hale, a month behind Pritchard, opted to take the canyon road. "The road followed the valley this morning about seven miles. It then forked: the right hand led up the mountain, the left followed the river. We took the left. After driving a short distance the river took through a canyon in the mountain. We crossed the river four times and went over several spurs of the mountain and in one place the road ran a short distance in the river. In coming through the canyon we found the passage very narrow in most places and the mountain generally steep.

"Fish in this river are scarce and hard to catch. Our fishermen do not have any luck in fishing. I think Fremont in his writings speaks of the scarcity of fish in the Humboldt. If the whole of California is like the country through which we have and are now traveling, the government has paid dear for the **Whistle**, for on whichever side you cast your eyes beyond this small valley you behold nothing but naked barren mountains, and the mountains beyond and on the top of mountains, and all void or nearly so of vegetation of any kind."[62]

Another month further back, Bruff's Washington City Company also plunged into the canyon. "The road and stream, early this morning's drive, entered a gorge, called the 'Wall defile,' it was a rough and crooked passage, in which we had to ford the river, 4 times in a couple of miles. Passed in the Canon, an abandoned wagon, many wheels, tires, hubs, &c, 1 dead ox and 1 dead horse. The grass dry & scarce. We emerged from the pass, soon forded 'Robin's Creek,' or 'Martin's Fork' of the Humboldt. Had to remain here remainder of afternoon, to repair wagon wheels. Soaked and wrapped them with rags."[63]

John Birney Hill passed through Carlin Canyon on August 2, 1850, describing the multiple fords. "To day, about 11 o'clock we crost the river. Went on 1 or 2 miles & crost again. Then we eat dinner, or took a lunch; as we generally call it. Here the river has a narrow passage between the bluffs. These bluffs are some 4 or 500 ft. high. The road is not bad through this passage, except one short place its sidling. After dinner we crost the river twice more. The bottom after we crost last soon became wider."[64]

Mica Littleton found the canyon passage in early September, 1850. "From the north fork of the Marys river you come to the river and cross it immediately at the junction of the South route from Salt lake and at the head of a kanyon you Keep down the river and cross it in the Kanyon 4 times. Some of the road is a little Steep and rough and Some very dusty. No grass not fit for camping. Past 13 graves yesterday and today most died in August."[65]

William Edmundson's party had taken the road to Salt Lake City, but unlike most of the emigrants, who took the established route around the north shore of the lake, his party had opted to take the Hastings Cut-off, south of the Great Salt Lake. They supposed their heading to be due west with a junction on the Humboldt River road not far from the Sink. But simply put, they got off the dubiously marked Hastings and wandered into the Humboldt valley very near Carlin Canyon. "After going further we came to a river of considerable size which we all supposed to be the Humboldt, not withstanding the notice we had just seen on the road. Soon afterward we were overtaken by some Emigrants who had come by the Northern Route from the Salt-Lake. They informed us that the river down which we were now traveling was Really the Humboldt and that we were now 220 miles above the Sink. Though somewhat disappointed to find ourselves so far from the end of our journey we were glad at being now upon a road of which we had some knowledge."[66]

Dust, Deprivation, Depredation

Over the next 150 miles, every emigrant would experience all of those three. The broad Humboldt valley contained a river with features no one from east of the Rocky Mountains had ever seen or could hardly imagine. It meandered through a sage desert, lacerated by ridges, sand hills, and sloughs, and populated by Native Americans who found no value in friendship with the emigrants, and terminated in a geographic oddity simply known as the "Sink." The road along the Humboldt had nothing to offer as far as the natural amenities one associates with a river, and yet, when they had found their

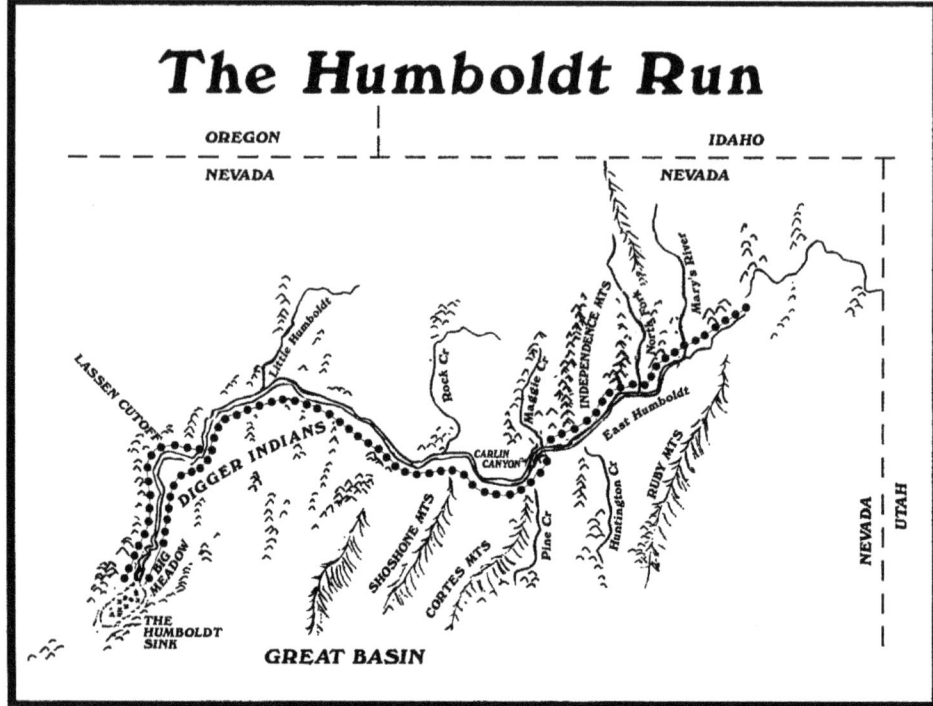

To the Humboldt Run — full course of the Humboldt River to the Sink.

way across that stretch, the worst of the trek remained. They began to see every bit of the elephant, a giant bull with great tusks, about to turn and charge full force. It made no difference if the emigrant went out in 1849 or 1850, every imaginable hardship lay before them and those that could still write about it did. Some of the diarists simply quit. And, on rare occasion, writers saw the bleak landscape as a field of promise, or even something beautiful to behold. Their words alone suffice.

"This morning I found that the guard of a small pack train, had shot one of their own company who had thoughtlessly gone out during the night to re-picket his mules. The guard hailed him when in the act of moving his mule to a fresh place of grass & he answered not. He as hailed by the guard several times but still made no answer. The guard supposing it to be either an Indian or some one stealing a mule fired upon him & the ball took effect and passed through his breast giving him a mortal wound. The fact was the old gentleman was considerably deaf and did not here the guard when he was hailed. He was from Baltimore and by the name of Riddell about 50 years of age. He was still alive this morning but no hope of his recovery. He appeared perfectly composed whilst the certainty of death was before him. He had shipped round a sawmill & a good many other things to operate with when he arrived in California. He had left as I learned from his company a large family behind.

"Shortly after Bryants train left camp this morning a Mr. Bryson of Louisvill[e] Ky one of Bryant's company was taken suddenly sick. He was removed form his mule to an ox wagon that was near at hand — and in 5 minutes thereafter was a dead man. He had not complained any till just at the time. He died with the disease of the heart.

"The bottom of Mary's river has been to-day wide sterile & desolate except just a long the margin of the stream — where in places we find spots of good grass. We have resorted to an artifice that has thus far proven to be beneficial as well as comfortable — and that is to sink a well every noon & evening, we usually dig from 3 to 4 feet and find water after settling that is cool and pleasant tasted. We find no game a long this river except an occasional sage hen or hare & we can rarely get a shot at them."[67] Captain J. A. Pritchard.

"…in company with Mrs. Foshee. Saw our friend Miss Cole today. In the early part of the day we had taken what is called the 'Greenhorn Cut-off,' which requires fifteen miles' travel to gain six miles on our journey. What is called a 'cut-off' is a shorter road across a bend. A 'greenhorn cut-off' is a road which a stranger or new traveler takes believing it to be shorter, but which turns out to be longer than the regular road. There were many such on the plains."[68] Margaret Frink.

"The nights are very cold at this time. I was on guard last night from midnight until morning and found it extremely cold. It was so cold as to freeze in our camp the thickness of window glass, which in Missouri would be called cold weather for the eleventh of August. Our cattle are beginning to fall away. The grass does not possess sufficient nourishment for teams that have so much work to perform, hardships to endure. Having some trouble in gathering our cattle we did not get a very early start. The morning was also rather cool, so much so that an overcoat was no burden, but before ten o'clock the climate changed and it became extremely warm. There was little or no wind and the sun appeared to almost scald. Cattle are stolen almost every day. Night before last about twenty were taken."[69] Israel Hale.

"…Down the river four miles, then came to the mountains, the roughest road we have gone over thus far — a seventeen-mile stretch without water. Mrs. Foshee road [rode] with us today until noon, and took dinner with us, their team not coming up. Our boy Robert took up a horse near the road and got separated from us. I was almost frantic for fear the Indians had caught him, and to increase my agony, a company of packers came along, just starting out to travel all night, who informed us that there were some five hundred Indians encamped very near us. I suffered the agony almost of death in a few minutes. I besought them to turn back and help us look for our lost boy, but they had not time and were on short rations. Just at dark, Aaron came in sight, having the lost boy with him. My joy turned into tears."[70] Margaret Frink.

"Ascended the mountain, had several springs along the route, but no grass, it being very hot and dusty from 2 to 7 inches deep. Laid over at the river. Country all around to the world's end dry as powder, no vegetation, except on the river, and here a complete quagmire. In a complete quagmire our animals give out fast. The river is lined with dead horses, mules and oxen, shattered wagons in every direction. Received for bacon, rice, and meat $2.40."[71] Henry Wellenkamp.

"From 40 to 50 miles back the Indians are very troublesome. Emigrants can not be too watchful as they secrete them selves in the willows and shoot your stock or run them off. They have been robing waggons and has Killed one man. I do hope our Government will see the necessity of placing troops here another Season to protect the lives and property of emigrants."[72] Mica Littleton.

"As there was no grass we did not stop but an hour and then started on. We traveled 5 miles and nooned and 7 in the afternoon. We found but poor grass and indeed there has been but little since the first day we traveled in this river. Instead of being an abundance of grass and fuel as were led to suppose from the guide books there is but very little grass and no fuel but a few willows and sage with an abundance of greasewood and wormwood which will not burn."[73] Franklin Starr.

"It is reported that the men who lost their oxen tracked them up and found all but one: they in possession of ten or twelve Indians, and the men killed seven Indians and took five horses from them. The company was from Jefferson City, Missouri. I give the above as I heard it, but do not vouch for the truth of it. In walking in this valley the ground appears hollow or porous, which is caused by the moles and ground mice. We find this the case in any place where the soil is rich. We are perfectly covered with dust and everything about us in the same situation. How our cattle stand it I am unable to say, for it is often the case that we cannot see oxen or wagon for the dust, consequently have to drive at random."[74] Israel Hale.

"…we are traveling in a southwest direction. The river makes a great bend to the northwest. Sometimes our road runs near it, but often at a distance across the bends. July 30 … today we traveled twenty-five miles. Animals seldom go out of a walk. If they were urged faster, they would soon fall exhausted. July 31 … the valley is rough and covered with sagebrush. A few cottonwoods and low willows grow along the stream, no other timber."[75] Margaret Frink.

"To-day about 1 o'clock we got to where the road tutches [touches] the river. (35 miles from here to where the road strikes the R. [river] again) Today we found the river Valley very wide level & beautiful. A good deal of dust. In the forenoon the roads run S. in the afternoon it run W. I have not seen the first tree on this R. yet. Nothing only willow. I have not seen many dead Oxen, Horses, nor mules, for the last 4 or 5 days. The Swamps along this R. (the Humboldt) are quite miry. In places, a man will mire-down & not half try. The Health of the Emigrants is much better than it was 4 or 5 weeks ago."[76] [He may have been referencing the last outbreaks of cholera he witnessed.] John Birney Hill.

"Still traveling down the Humboldt. Grass has been scarce until today. Though the water is not fit to drink — slough water — we are obliged to use it, for its all we have."[77] Sallie Hester.

"An attempt was made last night about 12 o'clock to stampede our mules & run them off. We were in the habit of picketing some 4 or 5 of our leading mules & herding the others round them. At the time stated some one came dashing through our camp on horse back at full speed. As he passed through the loose mules all took fright and sprang off after him. The guard happened to be in the direction that the mules started and was very prompt & energetick [sic] in arresting their flight. The individual passed through with such spead [sic] that the guard was unable to determine whether it was a white man or an Indian. It was very evident to me that it was an attempt made to frighten off and steal our mules. But their designs were fortunately thwarted by the promptness and vigilance of our guard. I learned next day that a train just above us had a number of their horses and mules stolen that same night. The men took their trail next morning and pursued them some distance & were only fortunate enough to recover a part of their stolen property. It is a common occurrence along her to here [hear] of parties being robed of their animals."[78] J. A. Pritchard.

"Traveled only 10 miles today. Roads dusty heavy and bad. No grass. River bottom very narrow not more than 200 yards wide here. The emigrant Should try to Keep a little hay on hand especially if late in the Season. No grass yet. We are compelled to take it patiently to give our animals time to gather what they can find of willows and grass that has been eat off nearly to the ground — though this place is the best chance for miles back."[79] Mica Littleton.

"Last night it was my turn to stand guard, and from twelve o'clock until daylight I followed our have [half]-famished cattle around the valley in search of grass. I am astonished that they hold up as well as they do. The grass is so dry that it will break as you step upon it. From appearances there has been no rain for months to wet it and there is no dew of a night to even moisten it. But still what little grass there is looks green and must possess great nourishment or our cattle could not subsist. The road left the river and ran through a patch of sage of about ten miles and the dust was from four to six inches deep, when we again came to the river and found a sprinkle of grass.

"I am a little disappointed in not finding swarms of mosquitoes on this river, but as yet we have not been the least troubled with them. I cannot account for it in any other way than, judging from my own feeling, that they cannot stand the dust.

"There is laying a few rods above us a joint stock company from Ohio. They have fell out and divided and fell out again and they agreed to leave it to the Yankees, and I left. Who the Yankees are I do not know, but I have seen enough of this strife to satisfy me that a co-partnership or stock company will not do. The reason is: men do not think alike.

"We are daily getting news from behind and occasionally from ahead, and if one half is true the distress in this great desert, for I can call it nothing else, will be great. We heard by the Parkers [packers?] that the teams that were two and three weeks behind us at the Willow Springs and the Black Hills had no grass at all and that men, women and children were seen sitting by the roadside sadly weeping and lamenting the situation of themselves and teams. Also today we heard a report from ahead that the grass was poor for sixty miles and then we would have to go one hundred and sixty miles with little or no grass and forty five without any water and there was six hundred head of dead cattle between here and the Sink of the river, the supposed distance being one hundred and sixty miles.

"We heard on Bear River that the grass was burned from Fort hall the balance of the route, but we know that a portion of that is false for we have come about four hundred miles from that fort and have seen but very few places that have been burned, and those we presume by accident. However the reports, whether true or false, are well calculated to disturb the peace of the emigrant and cause many a sleepless night."[80] Israel Hale.

"A strong breeze now from the W. annoys us much with the fine dust driven in clouds right in our faces. In a few miles, where the valley spreads out to the left, I saw the government supply train, from Oregon, for Fort Hall, under command of Lt. Hawkins, U.S.A. They had just arrived, and came by the same pass in the Sierra Nevada, as we were steering for. Learnt that the Pitt river (main fork of the Sacramento, its source near the pass) Indians had killed one of his men, and wounded 2 others, and that many of his men had deserted at the forks of the road, where the California branch turns down S. on the Western slope of the Sierra Nevada. I saw a large rattlesnake, alive and writhing, impaled to the ground with a stick, near the trail. Striped snakes numerous."[81] J. Goldsborough Bruff.

"We are now traveling on the south side of the Humboldt River. Camped on a salt plain, found a well. An Arkansas train nearby. We traded pickles and acid with them for tea and sugar. August 3 ... feed is becoming scarcer than ever. Mr. Frink has the men cut a good supply of it with the scythe, and it is then hauled in the wagon for future use. In this hot, dry air, it cures very quickly, adding but little weight to the load. Away form the river, the soil is hard and dry, void of vegetation except sagebrush. It makes a hot fire, from the oil it contains but burns out very soon."[82] Margaret Frink.

"A deep gloom prevails in camp. The men know we must all inevitably starve unless relieved and yet feel like cutting the throat of him who would remind them of it. Upon a hundred and fifty skeletons of mules, we can subsist long enough to scale the great barrier in our way and from the summits of the Sierra Nevada look down upon the Promised Land.

"But what of the sick? How are they to be cared for when the emergency arrives and disorganized, as we must inevitably become, each seek his own safety. God only knows what fate awaits them. We have discussed the question of dividing the train and pushing ahead with the sick and such others as choose to walk, leaving the heavy wagons and remainder of the men to come on at a slower pace, but as usual cannot agree upon any course of action, hence I conclude we shall go on as before.

"The valley of the Humboldt is about five miles in width with mountains two thousand to three thousand feet high and each side barren and desolate they appear."[83] Niles Searls.

"…the Indians are vary thick they have killed to [two] men to day and took their ammunition and horses and left them for the buzzards they devour them like we would sweete cakes we have to have set a strong guarde all the time or we would be killed and may be we will be killed yet we dont no September 18 … we ware all again to be devoured with Indians they surrounded us we thought their was too or three hundred we coulde not tell exactly how many their was but we could see them skulken every whare in the grass mr. hanway shot one or suposed he did."[84] Sarah Davis.

"Here I turned off to the camp of the 'Wolverine Rangers,' an ox company from [Michigan], and conversed with some very respectable & intelligent people, there; several ladies, among who was a Mrs. Chandler, from Boston, whose husband was with her. All well, and looked so. Several camps near them, of 2 and 4 wagons. Heard of many losing their cattle, doubtless by the Indians. Met a man on a mule, going back, in search of cattle belonging to an Ioway company. As the grass was fair, I gave 3 hours nooning, and moved on again. Passed the camps of several small companies, one of them from Wisconsin, had kill'd an ox for meat; several ladies with them, appearing prosperous & happy. River about 60 feet wide, and from 6 ins: to 3 ft. deep here.

"Heard some more Mormon lies, intended to beguile the emigrants down to the Salt Lake Settlement, where they might leave their wagons & oxen, for the benefit of the Mormons. I happened to be wide-awake for these chaps, nearly as far back as Grand Island of the Platte. I found that the whole tenor of their statements, and probably the main reason of their travel back, was to induce emigrants to visit their settlement."[85] J. Goldsborough Bruff.

"The Indians do not show themselves but are on the watch and improve every opportunity to steal Cattle but the Emigrants have learned to be on their guard and shoot them whenever they make their appearance. There is some game in this region such as antelope and hares, sugar hens and prairie dogs but we are too anxious to go ahead and too fatigued to hunt and therefore get note of it. The wolves gave us a fine serenade. They have been scarce for a long time but judging from the noise they must be pretty plenty in the neighborhood."[86] Franklin Starr.

"Remain in camp to recuperate ourselves and animals. Constant travel over rough roads, through suffocating dust, makes a rest welcome whenever we can take it. Have a broken wagon to mend. The heat is sometimes oppressive. The dust is intolerable. Many wear silk handkerchiefs over their faces; others wear goggles. It is a strange looking army."[87] Margaret Frink.

"Crossed the mountains 7 miles and came to the river again. Entered one of the largest bottoms I have ever seen. The road runs 5 miles from the river parallel and 20 miles without water except in one slough. Here are 100 thousand acres of fine wild wheat, also good grass, Buffalo clover etc. Shape of this bottom or flat, delta, all surrounded by high mountains. It would be great for settlement."[88] Henry Wellenkamp.

"...traveled seventeen miles to day we had the best grass I evere saw it looked like a perfect wheete field we then went on a little ways and come to the river their [there] we found a man that had bin killed buy the Indians and his heart taken out he was buried yesterday and their lay a dead Indian it appears he was alone and the Indians came upon him and he shot one an then they shot him he was found with four arows shot in his breast and the Indian found shot under the arm."[89] Sarah Davis.

"Five or ten cattle were stolen last night near our camp. I saw a man from a train camped two or three miles below us that told me they did not guard their stock last night, that their company was large and their young men wanted some sport and concluded to let the Indians steal them to give them an opportunity to go after them and shoot the Indians, and I have no doubt that they thought that they could make a raise of horses from the Indians, as several others had done who had lost oxen, but the Indians were too smart. They did not touch them. These Diggers are a small Indian or rather short and have very few guns but are armed with bows and arrows. They are seldom seen on or near the road, but keep themselves concealed during the day, and in the night leave their ambush and sally forth in search of plunder. It has been their custom to cripple stock in such a way that it would become useless to the owner and they would leave it, when the Indians would return and carry off the meat. But this year they pursue another course. They drive off cattle, horses and mules in large quantities. We have passed several wagons that had lost their stock by the Indians and were unable to pursue their journey in consequence of it.

"It is the opinion of many that either some mountaineers or some of the Mormons are at the head of this business and that they will drive them through some pass in the mountains and eventually return with them to the road one or two hundred miles back and sell them to the emigrants, as they are much needed and would bring large prices. This traffic, it is presumed, could not be carried on without the assistance of white men."[90] Israel Hale.

"The road to-day lay across sand hills striking the river occasionally. The wheels of the wagons will sink from 6 to 10 inches in the sand which makes it very heavy drawing. I had the good fortune to kill a mountain Rabbit both yesterday at noon & this forenoon. They furnish us a feast worth[y] of note. To men completely tired out on Hard crackers, Old bacon & coffee nothing could be finer."[91] J. A. Pritchard.

"Every day I hear of depredations being committed by Indians. They stole a lot of cattle from a company called the Helltown Greasers and I have not heard of them getting them. They stole a lot from one company and they pursued them and found that the cattle had been driven through a narrow pass in the mountain and finally came in sight of them, but in possession of Indians. They had them so fixed in the mountain that they could roll stones down and prevent any person from ascending and there they were, shaking their blankets, hallowing and bidding defiance to the whites, who had lost the cattle, although the cattle were in plain view.

"The water in the river is becoming bad. It is warm and not as clear as it was a few miles back and there is at this place very little current. It is becoming almost like a pond in comparison to what it was near the head. Neither has it increased in size for several days."[92] Israel Hale.

"*Went 25 miles without any water.* Arrived at several sloughs, but the water being so highly impregnated with alkali that it was death to the animals, and had to go 10 miles to get to good water."[93] Henry Wellenkamp.

"Sunday. Got up at 3 o'clock to start. Found two of our mules gone. Hunted until 6 before we found them. Started at 7 and traveled 10 miles without breakfast. Struck the river and encamped. No grass except what we mowed. Lay by the after part of the day. Burnt up two wagons while we stayed."[94] Samuel Jamison.

"We discovered on the flat something like a puzzle. It was a number of little fields that were partially fenced in by laying down sage around them with an occasional gap or gateway. The fields contained about one quarter of an acre. Many were the conjecture of their use. Some thought they were maps of the country made by the Indians, others that they were to give notice of some plan, some one thing and some another, but we finally learned they were for catching rabbits, so the mystery was solved at last. It is raining a little and I have heard it thunder several times. I saw a good wagon that had been left today, also where others had been burned. At our noon camp I saw some rushes of a mammoth size. They were very tall and an inch or more in diameter. The mountains here, like most of the mountains on this river, are round and vary in size and height."[95] Israel Hale.

"Early move. Passed many ox-trains, and 3 dead oxen. Very dusty drive.

A defective wheel caused us to halt at 5¾ miles, and repair. I reconnoitered a point of mountains & bend of the river, for a shorter cut than the traveled trail; ascertained that there was no trail, but the wagons could easily travel it, and plenty of grass: but the company objected, (like all other first travelers, afraid to go off the beaten track) and I did not insist on it. (Ascertained afterward that 8 ox wagons had taken this pass, found a good drive, and excellent grass and water through it.)

"Held a meeting of the company at their very urgent solicitation, and Resolved to send 6 men ahead into California, to make arrangements for meeting us with provisions, &c, &c. I remonstrated, and explained the folly of the measure, but silly counsel prevailed, and I gave them the chance of proving it."[96] J. Goldsborough Bruff.

"It is [the Humboldt] ten to forty yards over and from two to eight feet deep with a slow current. At the head it is a clear rapid stream but did not long contain it. It receives no tributaries below the forks and therefore rather diminishes instead of increasing in size. The valley which is very wide is rich but dry and therefore barren. The grass being confined to the immediate vicinity of the river. There are numerous sloughs near the river some now dry others containing stagnant water. The mountains bordering the valley are round topped and mostly bare of timber. The river is very crooked and would probably measure 1200 miles in length following the crooks. The road follows its entire length some three hundred miles."[97] Franklin Starr.

"Carson boys came up today. Their animals had been suffering from want of feed, and were losing strength every day. Their provisions were also running short, and it was yet 350 miles to Sutter's fort, over bad roads. The long hard journey was not the pleasure trip they had looked for. Some of the company were contrary, and all of them had become, like hundreds of others, much disheartened at the discouraging prospect ahead of them. But we endeavored to put the matter in the best light we could, and render them such little assistance as was in our power. We were able, among other things, to contribute from our reduced stock a supply of those two great luxuries on the plains, acid [vinegar] and sugar, which they fully appreciated. The ground of a dried up lake covered with an incrustation like ice. It is either borax or soda or salt."[98] Margaret Frink.

"It would be a difficult matter to describe our different camps, the similarity is so great on this river ... unless a person was previously instructed in the names of the places, if they have any. Some of the works that I have seen have given names to many of the points they speak of, camping places and the distance between them. But a camping place can be found anywhere where there is grass, and the only art in selecting one is to select good grass and water.

"Where we are traveling we do not know. We suppose, however, on the Humboldt, but the distance to the Sink we have no way of finding out at present. No marks are laid down in any of our guidebooks and we have no person along that is familiar with the route. We suppose that we are between eighty or one hundred miles from the Sink.

"We still find wagons or parts of wagons and dead cattle by the roadside and at old camping places, but we find no provisions thrown away about here. We have a great many that call to stay all night, generally footmen. Some say their teams have given out and some are lost from their trains, others have left their trains; some propose paying, but they are mostly on the begging order and endeavor to pay by telling some great tale respecting the route. We at first entertained these travelers, but we learned that many imposters were on the road and at the present time it takes a very smooth and straight talk to get accommodations in our train.

"Tonight we are to have another feast. We have a sage hen and a duck and with the addition of a little bacon and some crust and other little things to season it, makes us a fine dish. Buffalo, elk and deer or antelope we have not seen for many weeks. It is said that antelope are found in the mountain but they do not show themselves near the road."[99] Israel Hale.

"The faction of bad men in the company, evinced some mutinous conduct, this morning, for being called so early. At 9 A.M. on right of the trail, saw a camp of Missourians, who I was inform'd had bacon to sell. I directed our Commissary to procure 100 lbs., which we paid 15 cts pr lb. for. The Mo. Compy was detained by a lady of their party, in the last stage of consumption. Picked up, in road, this afternoon a piece of paper, on which was written, quite neatly, as follows: 'The magnetic Telegraph Company passed here on Friday Aug. 31st, 1849, at 7 O'clock A.M. All well, come on Boys.' (signed) W. & H. Kilbourn, Edwd Mansfield, H. C. McClure, Thos Jones, J. Vaughan, Jho Banor, Jno. Putman.

"At this camp, we have to cut, dry, and bundle sufficient hay to serve our animals 3 days forage."[100] J. Goldsborough Bruff.

"…Came to the south bank of the river, which here had a westerly course. There was neither bridge nor ferry, and the water was too deep to ford. Some people had made a boat of a large wagon bed, which they had turned bottom upward in the river, with an empty keg lashed under each corner to keep it afloat. A long rope pulled it back and forth. When they finished their crossing, they permitted us to use the boat. We piled our provisions, bedding, cook utensils, hay, and all their stuff, upon it, and after many trips got everything safely across. When I crossed I sat with my feet in the washtub to keep them dry. The horses swam over and the empty wagons were pulled over by long ropes."[101] Margaret Frink.

"We had vary dusty roads to day it was salaratus dust their is plenty of salaratus here and plenty of lie to [lye too] we found an advertisement to be carfull or the Indians would kill us their [there] is plenty of them here we have plenty of good grass to day for the catle we have now arived at camp it is marshey grounde here with here and their a bead of salaratus and a pond of alekelie butiful[beautiful] green grass for the catle."[102] Sarah Davis.

"We should have taken the road that came down on the left side of the river, but we passed it without knowing where it went, for there are many roads that lead off to camps and then return again, but had we taken it we should have saved a great deal of hard pulling. The Humboldt is a long river for one of its size. It varies but little in size from Big River. We have been on is waters sixteen days and have no knowledge when we shall leave it, for we cannot learn the distance to the Sink. The water is getting bad and grass nearly given out. Willows will soon be all that our cattle can get. The low bottom or valley is very narrow at this place, scarcely one quarter of a mile in width.

"Some few days since, a train lost some cattle and thirty men started in pursuit. They divided into companies, most of seven each. One company, however, had but four men in it. This company came across four Indians and walked up towards them intending to take them prisoners, but when they got within bow shot of the Indians they shot their arrows at them and wounded three of the white men: one in the shoulder, one in the forehead, the other in the wrist. The white men killed three Indians and one ran away. I understand that one Indian wounded all three of the men and had two wounds himself and when he found that the white man would catch him, as he had shot all his arrows, he stopped and told the man to shoot him in the head, which he did. The company found their cattle but they had all been killed."[103] Israel Hale.

"Traveled 16 miles along the S. side of the river. Very dusty. Warmer nights. Good grass. Considerable dew in the night along the river. At night dug a well. Saw about fifty Indians. Passed an Indian's scalp hanging beside road. Many sloughs. Expected to lay by today and go back after one of our cattle, but found him dead, having been killed by the Indians. Two horses were also taken by them last night and left a man destitute."[104] Caleb Booth.

"There being no grass where we camped last night we hitched up at 7 o'clock and drove 4 miles to grass and encamped to remain all day. The weather today hot. At 3'oclock the thermometer stood at 106 in the sun and 98 in the shade."[105] Amos Josselyn.

Junction with the Lassen/Myers Cut-off

As the Humboldt made its last great bend to the south, directly toward the Sink, the road forked. According to Amos Josselyn's calculations that fork lay 142 miles down the Humboldt from Carlin Canyon. At the junction, the road diverting from the main route turned off due west, then northwest,

Junction with the Lassen/Myers Cut-off

striking out toward the northwest corner of Nevada, into the very northeastern corner of California, with the target landmark being Goose Lake, which straddles the present California/Oregon border. From Goose Lake, one trail led into Oregon and the other trail turned southwest, then south, along the Pitt River into the northern Sacramento River valleys of California and the hoped for gold fields, but well north of Sacramento and San Francisco. Peter Lassen, who gave his name to the route, owned property, a large ranch, from which he hoped to make a profit by supplying the emigrants spilling into northern California over his route. The distance and hardship proved no less than for those who continued on down the Humboldt.

Like other cut-offs at other places along the way west, the actual name of the diversion could not be agreed upon or had been credited to someone other than the actual discoverer. The Lassen Cut-off provided a case in point. Some refer to it as the Lawson, Myers, Frémont, or even Feather River route. Writing in his diary on September 14, 1849, Bruff explained the naming of the northern pass into California, branching off from the Humboldt Trail, and astutely pronounced it to be wrong. "About 300 miles from 'Lassen's Pass' of the Sierra Nevada. The emigrants have named it 'Lassen's' but it should be "'Myer's Pass'; for J. J. Myers, an old California settler and mountaineer, is the author of this discovery, and he first took (piloted, as the mountaineers say) a Missouri train of emigrants over on it, the opening of this very season; after advertising it, and writing an account of it to the Adjutant General, at Washington; in which he offers to conduct any Government trains over if required. I had determined to take a northern route if practicable, to avoid the long deserts, bad water at Sink of Mary's river, long and heavy sand-drag beyond it, a long and very bad Canon [canyon], and last, tho' not least, a very elevated rugged and dangerous Pass. The aforesaid letter confirmed me: (Lassen followed Myers, having been on a visit to Missouri.)"[106]

Amos Josselyn did not know any of the circumstances relating to the naming of the route. He only knew that his party of packers planned to take what they believed would get them to the gold fields sooner. "Left camp at 6 o'clock and one mile from where we left the old road to make a cut off over to Feather River," he wrote on August 13, 1849. "We understand that three years ago there was some 3 or 4 wagons started through here but could not learn anything about the road. There was 8 wagons started in yesterday led by Magee."[107]

Israel Hale, just a week behind Josselyn, gave contemplation to taking the cut-off. "We met Mr. Green of Franklin County who had been ahead and told us that the route discovered by Mr. Childs [someone else credited for the Lassen Cut-off] was taken by the emigrants and that if we took it we would leave the river in four miles and that by doing so we would cross at the mountain at a lower gap and would find better water and grass than we would by the Sink route and furthermore that we could get to the Sacramento in nine days travel. Having had a history of the route before and hearing that Myers and Hudspeth, two old mountaineers, had taken it we concluded to drive down to the fork of the road there and camp until morning and then take it."[108]

Bruff reached a turn-off on September 18, 1849. Despite what a number of emigrant companies were doing, he knew they were wrong and not yet at "the" cut-off. But he soon set them straight. "Moved early, road generally very dusty, and crooked, following the river bottom; the stream crooked, with numerous islands, all covered with dense growth of willows, reeds, rushes, &c. forded, & soon reached a small bend, where the bottom was narrow, with a high sandy bluff on the right, and a trail ascending the bluff, leading W. along foot of the mountains on an elevated arid plain, and nearly parallel with the mien [main] course of the river, for [16] miles, terminating at the great bend, where the river runs down nearly S. to the 'Sink,' and at the bend the trail branches, the right stretches a Westerly course over the first Desert, on the route we are to take, while the left follows the Humboldt down to the sink, then over, to the Sierra Nevada. Some emigrants had taken this bluff road for the true 'turn off' route, and on ascending to the high plain, I saw their trains, enveloped in a cloud of dust wending their way along the rugged and droughty trail at the base of the mountains. At the foot of the inclined plane, where the trail ascended, was a stick, split at top, and stuck full of notices: and a piece of paper fastened to it, said, 'This is the turn off road.' The emigrants knew that where the road left the river, for the desert, the latter [that is the river] turned S. and as there was a bend here, going S., for only a mile or so, they were at a stand; and a number of trains were halted, awaiting my arrival to set them right. This I did, explaining to them their error; that my odometer registered every inch of the way, and that we had now at least a day's travel to the bend proper; also that this short bend could not answer, nor the description of country, which soon satisfied them."[109]

Franklin Starr's party reached the cut-off on August 16, 1849, but thought better of the old road after a brief encounter on the new. "We took the cut off this morning several trains ahead and some behind. After traveling about 8 miles we met a man riding back in a great hurry who informed us that every body had turned back finding no water. those that had gone in several days and those that were just ahead of us. He was hurrying in hope of preventing his company from taking the road as it was their intention to do so. The trains that were ahead in sight left the road and struck for the river lower down. There they left it and we did the same."[110]

Coming to the fork in July, 1850, Henry Wellenkamp had heard about the route and had a definite opinion. "At this stage of the game the roads fork, the one Lawson [Lassen] Route being finely adapted to perish even Hell. The road runs 3 to 4 miles straight to a high mountain, when some tracks turn to the right or N.E. course. Be sure to take the circle to the left hand, south or southwest. The emigrants had pretty well got through their provisions and commenced fasting. Hundreds hunted 2 or 3 lbs. of flour, bacon etc. Animals dropped down copiously."[111]

William Edmundson had been lost more than once during his trek to see the elephant. On September 8, 1850, he remembered, "This day we traveled 22 miles besides losing about 12 miles by taking the wrong road (probably Lawsons Cutoff) upon which we went about 6 miles and then came back to the road which we had left a short distance ahead of where we turned off. We camped near the river with about 25 men belonging to Woodwards Train from Cincinnati."[112]

The Lassen Route from the Humboldt to Goose Lake

In 1849, three of our diarists, Amos Josselyn, Israel Hale, and J. Goldsborough Bruff, took the Lassen Cut-off. By Josselyn's record, the distance from the turn-off to Goose Lake was 197 miles, which his party covered in 11 days. Each had read the limited literature or been told that the Lassen into northern California could or would save time to the gold fields. They had no doubt also heard that the rest of the road down the Humboldt to the Sink, and the desert that lay after that could not be any worse than what they might face on the Lassen route. None of our diarists going out in 1850 opted to take the cut-off. We may see why.

Amos Josselyn took the cut-off on August 13, 1849. Only a handful of small springs marked the barren route across northwestern Nevada and the Black Rock Desert. Though a small oasis for an individual traveler, the springs with colorful names generally proved woefully inadequate for the droves of emigrants and their teams of animals. "We drove on all day and until one o'clock at night and found no water or grass except a small spring about 14 miles from the river. Here we could not get water for our stock. At 1 o'clock we stopped to let the stock rest."[113]

Israel Hale made the turn off nine days behind Josselyn. "This morning we took the cut-off, if it is one. It takes off at a point where the Humboldt runs south and the cut-off runs a west course to a gap in the mountains. It starts in a valley that extends rather north, and several miles from the road is seen a round mound that appears to be in or near the center of the valley and is eight or ten miles, I should think, from the Humboldt River. By that mound, the bend in the river, etc. the cut-off may be known. We drove through sage about eight or nine miles and then took into the gap or pass in the mountain and after driving in the pass about four miles came to or opposite three springs on our left. But there was so many teams ahead of us we could get no chance to water our cattle.

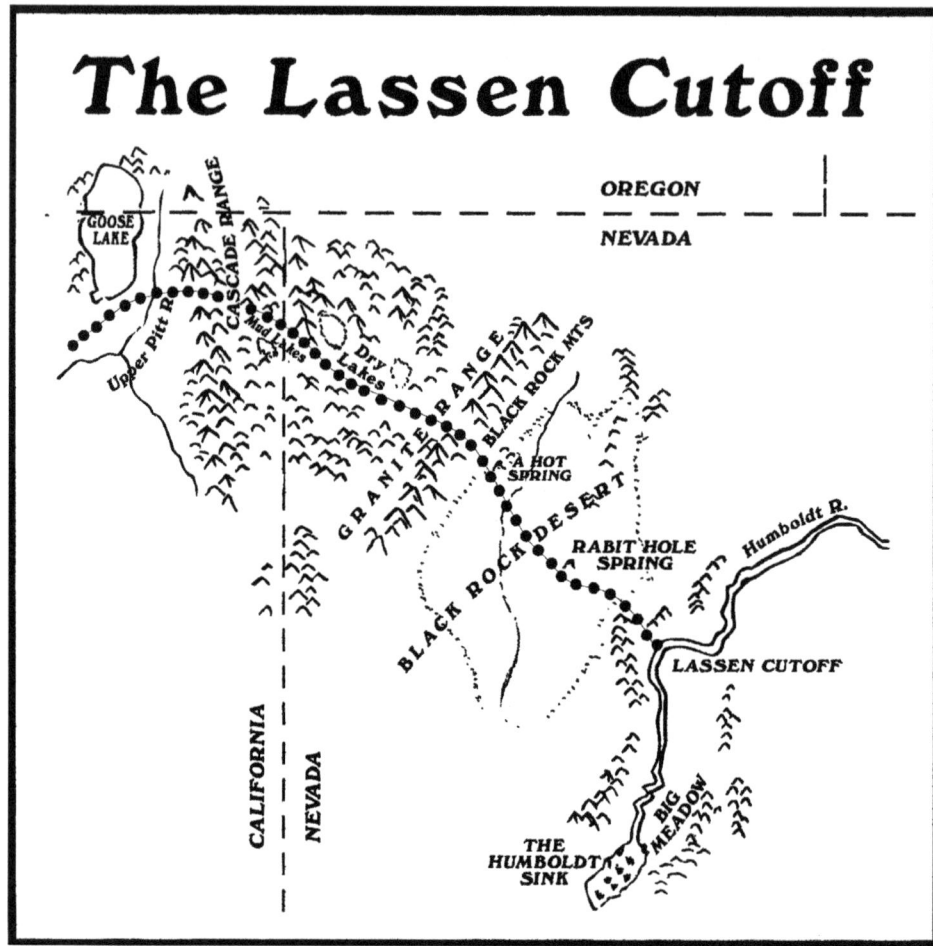

The Lassen Cut-off— route of the Lassen/Myers Cut-off into northern California.

"We started for Rabbit Hole Spring, said by some to be thirteen and by others sixteen miles from the springs in the pass. We arrived at what we supposed to be the spring about ten o'clock at night, but we could not get water there but drove about two miles further where we found some wells that had been dug by the emigrants to get water for stock. We passed a great many dead cattle and as many that were not dead but had given out and had been left to die. We have not seen fifty spears of grass since we took this road and had but one chance for water."[114]

"We reached the 'Forks,' began Bruff's account of the Lassen trek, about a month in the rear of Hale. "The river here makes a short bend to the South — and in 58½ ms.— nearly that course, is lost in the pestilential marshes and alkali pools of the 'Sink.' On the right, about a hundred yds. from the Bend, the Desert route branches off, and in the forks of the road, I observed a red painted barrel standing. I rode up, to examine it. It was a nice new barrel, about the size of a whisky-barrel, iron hoops, and a square hole cut in the head; and neatly painted in black block letters, upon it, 'POST OFFICE.' On looking in, I found it half-full of letters, notes, notices, &c. Near this was a stick and bill-board, also filled with notices. These were chiefly directed to emigrants in the rear, hurrying them along, giving information about the route, telling who had taken this or the southern route, &c. By these I ascertained that a few had taken the Southern road. I inscribed a card and left, here, for the benefit of all whom it might concern, as follows: 'The Washington City Company, Capt. Bruff, pass'd — on the right hand trail, Sept 19th. 2 P.M. 1849.' At the 'turn off' between sand ranges, a new grave, on left of trail: 'Mary Jane McClelland, departed this life, Aug. 18th, 1849, aged 3 yrs. 4 mos.' A single wagon was camped just around the bend of the river.

"Now for the terrible desert! Who's afraid of fire? The first 4 miles was over a plain as level as a marble-tablet, and nearly as smooth; firm, where not cut into by the travel, white, and sun-cracked. Passed on the road since we left the river, 22 dead oxen, and two dead horses, any countless wheels, hubs, tires, and other fragments of wagons; ox-yokes, a bows, chains, &c. Late in the afternoon the ravine road we traveled on, pent up in lofty sterile mountains, mostly naked dark rocks, turned abruptly to the S.W. and became more contracted and rugged, along the bed of what is, in the wet season, a torrent. Men and animals tired, thirsty, and dusty — mules taken to the sp'gs and watered, 13½ miles from the forks to here. There are 3 springs placed here, in this mountain dell."[115]

The first of the important springs was Rabbit Hole Spring. Starting before sunrise, Josselyn recalled, "At. 4 o'clock [A.M.] we drove on and about one mile further on we passed a small spring and if we had stopped long enough we might have got water for our stock but the country looked as though it was watered and we drove on in hopes of getting water and grass, but we found it 20 miles from the spring before we found water." That would have been Black Rock Spring, the second important watering hole by which the emigrants marked each stretch of merciless desert. "We then found warm water and grass. It was between 3 and 4 o'clock P.M. before we got to water, making fifty miles over a barren desert that we drove our stock without water or grass. This day was very warm and both man and beast suffered much for water, but our teams stood it better than any that was on the road. The Newark men left 3 cattle on the road that they could not get along. Milligan then filled a couple of kegs of water and took them on a horse and went back to water the cattle that were left. There was about 50 teams behind us and their stock suffered wonderfully."[116]

"Visited the springs to see what they looked like. These were mere drippings—percolating from small clay cliffs in the hollow slope of the mountain," remarked Bruff, no doubt disappointed but unruffled. "Travelers had dug out hollow reservoirs below each spring, which filling enabled the animals to drink. There was a large drive of oxen there, and others coming up. The selfish proprietors had permitted their animals to crowd in and muddy up the water; and several large steers were standing up to their knees in the larger basin. A few hundred yards higher up the side of the mountain, in a gulch, were other, small springs, of good clear, cool water. Into another elevated valley; then over long high rolls, of brown volcanic detritus and rocks. Fragments of broken wagons numerous. In this pass the formation had every indication of gold-bearing formation. A block of wood, apparently part of an axle, had written on it, 'this is the place of destruction to team.' It lay on the hillside, left of road near by lay several dead oxen, & a broken wagon, yokes &c. Road powder blinding & choking one. I found near an orange clay spur, a well, or tank, of water, and a crowd of thirsty men and animals surrounding it. A few yards to left of this another—similar hole, filled up with dead ox, his hindquarters & legs only sticking out, above ground. Dead oxen thick about here, and stench suffocating. The road here beat perfectly bare of every thing but dust, carcasses, and relics of used up wagons, &c. by innumerable travelers and camps. 16¾ miles from the Springs in Gap to these, the 'Rabbit-Hole Springs' and the Second Desert Stretch.

"Along the edge of this Plateau are a number of springs as they are called, but are actually wells, dug from 3 to 6 feet deep, and from 4 to five feet diameter; containing cool, clear water but a little saline, about half filling the wells. Two of these springs were about 4 feet apart; in one was a dead ox, swelled up so as to fill the hole closely, his hind-legs and tail only above ground. Not far from this was another spring similarly filled. There was scarcely space for the wagons to reach the holes, for the ox carcasses. The ravine was thickly strewn with carcasses. Here, and around the other springs, I counted 82 dead oxen, 2 dead horses, and 1 mule: in an area of $\frac{1}{10}$ of a mile. Of course the effluvia was any thing but agreeable. In the very heart of this Golgotha, was a fresh grave, on the head board of which was this inscription: 'M. De Morst, of Col: Ohio, died Sep. 16th. 1849, Aged 50 years, Of Camp Fever.'[117]

"Before we had our breakfast ready a man from the Black Rock Springs came up and told us we had better hurry and get through the Salt Plain before the heat of the day for if we did not we would see trouble," recounted Israel Hale as his party prepared to make the dash from Rabbit Hole Spring to the next. "We did hurry but it was nine o'clock before we got a start. Our cattle were nearly worn down, having traveled between thirty and forty miles without food and but one sup of water.

"About this time clouds began to appear and shield us from the heat and shocking rays of the sun. The wind began to blow and in a short time it was thick and cloudy and we had a strong wind from the south which to the whole of the dust from drive and oxen. We had a slight sprinkle of rain and we drove on and had just got through the plains as the wind fell and the sun again made its appearance. It was certainly a great blessing sent upon us by the Hand of the Almighty, for if it had continued as warm as it was before the wind raised we could not have come through the plain without losing more or less of our stock, but as it was we came through safe without the loss of a single steer. This plain is from six to eight miles wide. It is covered with a whitish crust and entirely void of vegetation of any kind.

"We came up a small hill and soon were opposite black Rock. The spring is one quarter of a mile from the rock. It is on high ground and runs into a basin from four to six rods square and then runs down hill. The water is hot as it comes out of the spring, but that on the opposite side of the basin is sufficiently cool for oxen to drink without doing them any injury. We are now fairly into the cut-off and through what is called the dry stretch and is called forty-five miles in length this is, from Humboldt to the rock, but if it does not come nearer fifty five than forty five I, for one, am very much mistaken."[118]

"Passed since noon-halt, 103 dead oxen, 3 horses, and 1 mule. Saw also 3 abandoned oxen, lying down, anxiously looking back on the road, in vain, for succor from suffering and a slow death. One of these nearest to the road, I shot, terminating its suffering. The wolves, to-night will finish the others. Passed several pits, dug down to moist clay, where travelers had tried for water; a little more digging, in one place, would have succeeded — near end of this stretch. Around these attempted wells, were a number of dead oxen, chains, yokes, &c. One of these pits was right in the middle of the trail. A little after Sun Set we reached, on our right, a high volcanic promontory, and went over knolls of sand, ravines, volcanic rock, & c. around this extraordinary head-land, ¾ of a mile, a to the "Great Boiling Spring, and a grass valley, a distance of 21 miles from the 'Rabbit Hole Springs,' and terminating the great desert stretch. Some traveler states the entire desert stretch at 40 miles only, a printed Guidebook, some one had, makes it 45 ms. The Mormons said it was 60, but I proved it to be exactly 51¾ miles! Scattered about here, are 150 dead oxen."[119]

Bruff may have had the distance over that first horrible stretch of the Lassen down to the nearest quarter of a mile, but he and the others were in no way past the elephant yet. The emigrants found more desert, the Black Rock Mountain range, canyons, rugged roads, and a landscape wretched from nature lay ahead occasionally interrupted by a brief oasis, for at least three more days, as Amos Josselyn recounted in a series of short entries, beginning August 15, 1849. "[Near base of Black Rock Range] drove 6½ miles to good camping, good water and grass. 16th … drove 15 miles and encamped where there was no water or grass, only what we had in our wagons. We cut grass before we left camp expecting to find none for some distance. Cold nights and hot days. 17th … at 4 o'clock A.M. we hooked up and drove to water and

The vicinity of the Boiling Springs in the Black Rock Desert, by J. Goldsborough Bruff. Bruff's party took the Lassen Cut-off. His drawing captures the hardship of the desert on men and animals. Reproduced by permission of *The Huntington Library*, San Marino, California.

grass. 5 miles. We then lay until 2½ o'clock P.M. drove 12 miles and encamped two miles up a kenyon [canyon]. The roads this afternoon were hilly, being as hard ½ days drive as we have had on the road."[120]

"After breakfast we started for the Hot Springs, five miles further on and passed the Spring in the valley where we herded the cattle last night," wrote Israel Hale after pushing on from Black Rock Spring. "I then saw the springs; they were not so large as the Black Rock Springs, but there are several of them. In one I saw an ox that had been scalded to death, his hind part was in the spring and his forepart on the bank, probably the way he died; his mouth was partially open and his tongue was out. It could but excite pity to look at him. Near another was one lying dead that had been scalded but had been hauled out. Others had got in but were taken out alive, but the hair came off as far as the water came up on them.

"In the valley there are other springs that are equally hot as any that I have seen. I put my hand in one and could not tell any difference from that and any other boiling water. It is said to be one hundred and eighty six degrees of heat."[121]

"This is a very remarkable place," wrote Bruff describing the trail beyond Black Rock Spring. "All volcanic, and in combustion no extraordinary depth below ground. Marshes and plains of poor grass. Streams, of spring rivulets of saline, sulphur, & warm water. The Great Boiling Spring, is like all others I have seen, a raised circular tumola, about 30 feet diameter on top, basin shap'd within, dark bubbling water, overflowing one edge, and received into a circular reservoir, dug some yards lower down, and from that into a 3rd reservoir, in which last it is cool enough to use for ordinary purposes. The Spring is too hot to put your hand in, and the 1st reservoir is quite warm. A grouse had been boiled done in this spring. Coffee also, by immersing the pot containing it."[122]

"This morning our cattle begin to look a little natural. To deprive oxen of water a great length of time has a singular effect. They become much swollen about their eyes and the eyes appear to diminish in size and sink deep in the head and when in this situation a person could scarcely tell his own team by the head, but after they get rest and a good quantity of water and food the swelling goes down and their eyes again get their natural appearance," explained Israel Hale.

"This last drive has been a hard one on both men and cattle. It has been laborious on the men, and the stench arising form the dead cattle, horses and mules on the road and at the camps renders it unpleasant in the extreme: also being deprived of good water is bad on the men as well as the cattle. The spring water is the best that we can get and that when collected in a bucket or can, by standing all night is hardly fit to drink. It has a saltish disagreeable taste and the more you drink the more thirsty you become. We drove eight miles and heard of a spring off to the left at the foot of the mountain. We sent and got a canteen of water. It was cool and well tasting."

Resourceful to the end, the emigrants invented their own version of headlights. "We are travelling after dark. After the moon went down our men would go ahead of the teams and touch a match to a bunch of greasewood bushes that would burn although as green, as will dry oak leaves, which gave us a tolerable light to drive by."[123]

J. Goldsborough Bruff had observed the deterioration of human goodness in some since the beginning. Now toward the end, he still commented on it. "Some of the travelers, among other rascalities, are in the habit of putting up erroneous notices to mislead and distress others. I had the pleasure of correcting some of these statements, and thereby prevented misfortune." And, the scenes of natural wonders, like observations of human nature, never ceased. "From our position at noon across the valley to the N. by W. was a very remarkable resemblance of a castle or fortress, of a white substance, (probably clay) in the face of a brownish hill, resting on a shelf of rock, about ⅓ from the plain; This I sketch'd and named it Fremont's Castle."[124]

"Came into the Salt Valley, where we found good grass and tolerable water, although the grass is mostly dry, but cattle that are hungry eat it very well. We found a large number of wagons encamped, among others a train of the United States Troops. They are on their way from Oregon to meet troops from the States and assist them if necessary on their way to California. If they do not need their assistance they will render such assistance to emigrants as they may need.

"The air here is very close and dry: everything made of wood shrinks terribly. There is scarily [scarcely] a wagon wheel in our train that has a tight tire upon it. The pegs in shoes and boots come loose and the hoe nearly falls to pieces. This has been the case for hundreds of miles back, but I think not to such an extent as at this place."[125]

Five days after leaving the Humboldt road, Amos Josselyn struck that part of the Lassen route through High Rock Canyon country and beyond that, the mud flats of the extreme northwest corner of Nevada. "August 18th ... drove 16 miles up the kenyon. Roads good. 19th ... drove 14½ miles the roads were good with the exception of 2½ miles through a kenyon. Last night was very cold. There was about 2 inches of water in the wash pan and in the morning it was solid. In the middle of the day it was very warm. 20th ... we got to a small mud lake, drove up hill to a spring, 15 miles today. 21st ... drove to the foot of the mountain [range of the Sierra Nevada], making 22 miles today; in the forenoon the roads were rough; in the afternoon they were good."[126]

"Ten miles from Salt Valley we came to High Rock Canyon. The first six miles was an entire up-hill business, for we crossed a mountain that was six miles from the foot to the summit. It was not very steep but a constant drag. The balance of the road to the canyon went through a flat and was very good," recounted Israel Hale, at that point ten days behind Josselyn's pace. Continuing the next day, he wrote, "This morning we started on in the canyon and followed it more than ten miles before we came to the end of it. It is certainly the longest that I ever saw and the most of a curiosity. We passed several fine spots of grass but of coarse quality. The road was good where the passage was wide, but where it was narrow it was rocky. I passed one place that reminded me of Pine Street in New York. The rocks were perpendicular on both sides. The canyon seems to have been formed by nature for a road.

"This afternoon I took a walk to the top of a hill near our camp. I could see nothing but mountains: some appeared to be covered with sage, while others were perfectly bare and all had the appearance so far as I could judge of having suffered by fire. The one that I was on was covered with blackish rock and I saw several pieces of a something that looked like black glass and resembled the thick part of a black junk or Porter battle [?]. Many of the rocks were porous and so light that they would but just sink when put into water.

"I find that the long dry stretch has injured our teams very much. They all appear weak, dull and sluggish and I am fearful that we may lose some of them yet. Some have the hollow horn; for that we bore the horn and put in salt, pepper and water until it runs out of their noses. They have another disease called the hollow tail; for that they split the tail where it is hollow. Two teams left the train this morning in consequence of the steers being weak and sick. We hear sad accounts from the Sink route. It is said to be very sickly and the sickness proves fatal in most cases. It is said that the stench arising form the dead cattle is insufferable and that men die nearly as fast as the cattle."[127] Hale does not identify the source of his information on the "Sink route"—probably others who may have been packing through and changed their course. Whatever the source, it would prove quite accurate.

"At last we made a devious and steep sand descent, among large sage and grease-wood bushes, into a narrow bottom, in which is a brook running through a deep and very rocky gulch, passing through a sort of canyon below into Mud Lake. It is very crooked, and in the wet season is a large rapid stream," estimated Bruff on entering High Rock Canyon. "Thick willows, cedars, &c. Very tall old & new bunch grass here. Near the stream on its western side, was a small dug tank of good cool water, several pools of good water, and a marsh. It was dusk when we reached this, and on a pretty level grassy spot, surrounded by trees and bushes, in this deep narrow vale, stood a tent, a wagon and cart, and a couple of rush bottom'd chairs, by the dying embers of a fire, around which were some cooking utensils, &c. The folks were in the tent and wagon asleep. There cattle grazing about ¼ mile off, and the tinkling of the cowbell sounded very domestic. I was tired, the night cold, and I had no bedding with me but a thin horse blanket, but a couple of clever lads, of the company, Messrs. Truman and Ennis, pressed me to share their bed, which I accepted, and we dozed off the cold night very well."[128]

Pushing on the next morning, Bruff found "the flat grassy basin of the 'Mud Lake.' [This was probably one of a number of basins along the fringe of the canyon country. From his description, it may not be the same "Mud Lake" referenced by Josselyn or Hale as they encountered it after leaving the canyon, not before.] Plenty of tolerable and abundance of dry grass; springs and rills of pretty fair water, some of mineral and hot water, marshes, efflorescence of alkali and salt; grease-wood, and some few green willows. The distance from Grass-Camp to this, per the main road, 14½ miles. Numerous camps here, among them the folks who camped in the deep vale by us last night, a mother and 2 very young children of that party. And here to our astonishment and gratification, I found Mr. Keller and family, who informed me of old Mr. Abbots' death, far back on the Platte. So the silver haired Swiss philosopher found a romantic grave in the wilds of the Platte. One of his little girls knew me, as I rode by, and called me. First time we had met since they left our camp at St. Jose [St. Joseph], and crossed the river there, some time before we started up the Missouri. On a small elevation, surrounded by marsh, is a grave, the board inscribed thus: 'C. H. Bintly, from Yorkshire, England, Died Sep. 9th, 1849, Aged 43 years.'"[129]

"A rugged winding road from Mud Lake to High Rock Canyon," continued Bruff in his entry of September 25, 1849. "While ascending this elevation, I had a fine view around, but the harsh angularly ruptured country close on my right, attracted my attention, and extorted a sketch. All volcanic. (a steep descent of 200 yards, very deep sand, and loose stone. we double locked the wheels, and teamsters and assistants carefully lead the mules, one after the other, slowly, and successfully down on the plateau below.) A mile or so over the head of the basin, bro't us to the entrance of the grand can[y]on—'High Rock Canon,' and 2 miles up in it, we found water holes dug in the bottom of a gulch, on the right hand side, and here camped. Road deep dust but otherwise good. 10¾ miles from Mud Lake Camp. In these deep sheltered gulches, water can almost any where be obtained by digging pits 2 or 3 feet deep, often cool and pure."

"This can[y]on road is quite level and good; the bottom is traversed by a narrow rugged ditch, full of dry cotton wood & willow scrub. In the face of the perpendicular wall on the right side, at base, is a singular cave. (vault 12 ft. high, 35 feet long, and 18 ft. wide) Names and dates scratched all over the outer wall around the mouth of the cave, and numbers within. I wrote the name of the company and date of passing, signed it, and pinned it up in the roof of this grotto. The part of the wall in which this cave is, gave name to the canon: (High Rock) as over the cave it rises in a vast spire, I judge to be 400 feet high: however not over 50 feet higher than the adjoining continuation."[130]

"In this canyon I saw the first trees that I have seen since we left Fort Hall," remembered Israel Hale. "It was quaking aspen or poplar and some of the trees were from four to six inches in diameter. About two miles back we came to a lake. It is near a mile in length and half as wide as it is long. The lake appears to be very shallow and muddy. The water was not more than six inches deep. Snow is beginning to make its appearance again in quantities, which accounts for the cold weather. The nights are very cold and when we get up in the morning we put on our overcoats and wear them until nine or ten o'clock. If we have water standing out at night we have plenty of ice in the morning." [131]

Bruff's Washington City Company had problems to tend with, the nearer they came to the elephant. "Held a meeting to inflict penalties for guard and other delinquencies, and to consider an application from 2 members of the Company, and of a mess who produced much disturbance in the company, and were disposed to do anything but right. This application, respectfully written, from 2 of the most obnoxious men in the company, prayed that we would grant them the 2 lead mules of their wagon, (mediocre animals) 6 days rations of bread, and a full discharge from the company. Some members were opposed to it at first, as a bad precedent, but when I told them how cheaply we should this rid ourselves of these troublesome fellows, and that it must be a peculiar case, expressly for that, and no other occasion, it unanimously passed, with 3 cheers. Such was the company's opinion of the men, and such their joy at the riddance.

"At night the disaffected gang, or 5 of them, stole wine, reserved for medical purposes, and a conceited ass of a fellow, who aspired to command, told them that the company was too large, and it should be divided in 2 separate commands. 2 of these men were the fellows we got rid off with cheers. They turned the bung of the keg down and swore the wine leaked out, though I noticed great laughter & hilarity in their wagons at night."[132]

Israel Hale noticed a declining health among the men he traveled with. Many were broken in spirit and body by the ordeal, and the resiliency and

The Lassen Route from the Humboldt to Goose Lake 243

A precipitous descent, drawn by Bruff in the region of Mud Lake and High Rock Canyon on the Lassen Cut-off. Reproduced by permission of *The Huntington Library*, San Marino, California.

strength of the human body to heal itself faded. "The men too are becoming tired of traveling and want rest. Some are complaining of not feeling well and taking medicine and the sick appear to mend very slowly. But the air is very pure here; the morning was a little cool for comfort without an overcoat. We are now twenty six miles from the summit of the Sierra Nevada."[133]

On September 29, 1849, Bruff's company finally emerged from the canyon country and stumbled into the foothills of the Sierras. "Reached the entrance to the can[y]on. This pass, for trail there was none — was filled with stumps of cotton-wood trees, large, fallen trees, stones and rocks of every size, Dead cattle, broken wagons & carts, wheels, axles, tires, yokes, chains &c &c. testimonials of its difficult character. Trees, principally cotton-wood, and quaken Aspens, grew closely in the can[y]on, were not cut away for travel, and those cut lay where they fell, the tops still green. Thank Jupiter! This incomparable route, was only 2 ms. through! Now we breathe free, A great relief to eyes and feet, Moist and green all around. At this point the trail turns from N.N. W. to a W. course. Then over several low hills, rather stony though not decidedly bad, though somewhat serpentine."[134]

Amos Josselyn commenced his assault on the Sierra Nevada on August

22, 1849. He would see the elephant yet two more days. "After dinner we drove over the mountain. (first crossing of the Sierra Nevada at Fandango Pass, elevation 6,101 feet)." The next day, he added little more than a line to his diary, "the stock being very tired on account of the hard pull up the mountain, we did not start till 3 P.M. Drove 7 miles to a creek." On August 24, Josselyn "drove to Goos[e] Lake 3 miles," completing his journey into northern California.[135]

Israel Hale remembered his last three days on the Lassen in somewhat more detail, but his diary entries also became shorter, either from exhaustion, or anticipation that the trek appeared about over. Writing on September 2, 1849, he recalled, "There is more timber insight of camp than we have seen for months past. The mountain is handsome and the valley is a most beautiful one. The road has been good all day, but since we came into the grass it has been excellent. It is as level as a floor, dry and hard and not dusty." The next morning Hale engaged the Sierras. "Started up the mountain. We drove about one mile and then doubled our teams. We got up without difficulty, although the last mile on the mountain was very steep. We then commenced our descent for the valley below, which might be called handsome. This valley, as well as the flat on the east side of the Sierra Nevada, will in time be cultivated. The quality of the soil, situation of the land, convenience of water and timber all combined, must cause settlements soon to be made. We are encamped in this valley about three miles from the Summit making our drive five miles today."

On September 4, the long haul for Hale from the Missouri must have seemed impossible, yet it was nearly accomplished. "The road, after we struck the timber was a little rocky, but the novelty of traveling in timber made up for the rocks. We had a steep hill to come up and after an hour or so a similar one to go down, when we came to Goose Lake."[136]

By September 30, 1849, Bruff could see the end too. "We pushed to the foot of mountains — the long looked for Sierra Nevada! Over a dusty plain, of white earth, covered with sage and greasewood, on a W.S.W. course. Large timber greeted our eyes, on the mountains ahead. Along base of the mountains; a mud lake [the one referenced by Josselyn and Hale]."

Like a lot of emigrants Bruff thought the Lassen route into northern California would bring them closer to the gold fields than the Humboldt route. Whether they relied on rumors or fact, once they got to Goose Lake they still had a ways to go. "People here much alarmed, and I felt much concern, myself, from a statement, set up in camp, of the distances on the route, on the western side, down to the Settlements. Showing it to be farther than I or any body else ever dreamt of. I felt confident that if followed Fremont's trail in: striking the Valley of the Sacramento in 60 or 70 miles from the Pass, but this shows it to be otherwise! Much scurvy among the emigrants, a little girl's mouth badly effected with it. A man in the Missouri company has the camp fever.

Some of the folks here pointed out a man to me (Symington) who had killed his comrade with a Bowie knife. (probably the one named on the tombboard Fitzzimmons) and that he had also stolen a calf here. Last night the ladies were singing, and some of my boys were performing on musical instruments. The base of the great Sierra Nevada about 6 miles, in a direct line opposite. Patches of snow on some of the highest points."[137]

On to the Sink

The majority of emigrants did not take the Lassen Cut-off and proceeded on about another 60 miles down the Humboldt road to the Sink. The further south they traveled, the river's current grew more stagnant and the water within its banks became more impregnated with alkali. If they could make it to the site called Big Meadow, they could find grass for the animals and enough water to see them along. The strongest, most orderly, and better prepared companies got through, but not without deprivation. Those weakened by the continuing ordeal stumbled on, some making it, just barely, some not at all.

"We had some trouble finding a spot of grass this evening," wrote J. A. Pritchard on July 21, 1849, pushing south toward the Sink. "The ox teams are all failing on account of the scarcity of grass & hot weather. Some of them travel of night and lay by in the day. But this is a bad plan as stock will feed better of a night than they will in the daytime of hot weather. Cattle have never been known to make such time as they have on this expedition. They have traveled from 20 to 30 miles pr day for a distance of 1800 miles."[138]

Pritchard had mules, but they faired little better than those with oxen, for their pace had also been slowed by the deprivation of good grass and water for the animals. Writing on July 23, he recalled, "We were apprehensive from the appearance of things that we were approaching the sink of Mary's river. And we were therefore desirous to give our mules as much time and rest as possible. Having as we know well to cross the great salt desert immediately after leaving the sink. Besides that consideration the weather has been hot, the roads heavy and the grass indifferent, all of which had a direct tendency to pull down and destroy the strength and action of our teams. He added the next day, "It is an alarming and fearful thing to see as we do every day teams broken down by the mismanagement of their owners in this remote wilderness. The teams that alarmed our boys so much a few days since has not been seen since and we learn from packers as they come up that they are falling back every day. Our boys are now becoming convinced that we have been and are still travelling fast enough."[139]

Franklin Starr remembered passing the Lassen Cut-off but associated it with another name, even then infamous among emigrants. "We passed in the afternoon a road leading off to the right over the hills where it is reported to be the road Donners party took. It has been traveled this season and is said to be much higher than the old one." With the known choices at that fork being "bad or worse" Starr proceeded south. "We lay by yesterday for the grass was good and we wished the Cattle to rest a little as we expect food to be very scarce. There was some talk of taking the road to the right but it was thought it might be for the worse and we did not know any thing certain about it. We have seen waggons traveling on the other side of the river which route is said to save in distance."[140]

Unlike most other diarists, as the journey lengthened, Henry Wellenkamp, who had confined his entries to barely a sentence, began to write more, not less, in his diary. He had reported the Lassen Cut-off, then recounted four hard days' travel down the Humboldt toward the Sink before reaching the Big Meadow. "Wednesday 24 July. Endless winding of river along the valley. All marshy and miry, we had to wade and swim to grass, cut and carry to animals. Thursday 25 July. Early in the morning we took a S [south] course to cross a deep and bad slough over dead horses. Turned up a ridge and descended a terrible rough road, all loose cobble stones. Came to river. In the afternoon came to sand bluffs of heavy deep quicksand. Very hot and no vegetation. Friday 26 July. Found Jack, my mule, mired and unable to march, shot him, and toiled our sandy way along. Laid over the afternoon in order to cut grass in the mire, to have some feed for our starving animals. Started midnight. Saturday 27 July. Went 15 miles before we came to river again. Many dead horses on the road, weather excessively hot, clouds of dust, and the odor of carrion, water tepid and highly alkaline, the countless dead oxen, horses, mules and men in it make it a fine flavored soup."[141]

"Some Hungarians passed us today who had eaten nothing for two days. I encouraged them all I could, but the situation looked gloomy to every one of us," wrote Margaret Frink of one of the emigrant groups that disintegrated into a band of desperate beggars. "There was nothing but sand hills as far as we could see, without a spear of herbage. Came to water at ten o'clock at night. Around us was a terrible scene; the earth was strewn with dead horses and cattle. Those on guard duty went to sleep through excessive fatigue, and the horses got to the wagon containing our provisions, and ate all the beans and dried fruit. The animals had had nothing to eat except a short allowance of hay we had hauled with us."[142]

While many emigrants had nothing left by the time they reached the lower Humboldt, a few like Henry Wellenkamp still had a little extra to sell or trade. "Sunday 28 July. Left river early and came to something like a desert. Nooned along the river, no grass at all, dusty and hot, and an evil spirited wind on Platte had taken my hat away so that I suffered severely from the rays of the sun. Bought a sorrel mare from James Noble at $12.50 if she died on the road and $25.00 if she goes through, to be paid in Sacramento City. Sold bacon and rice, $3.50."[143]

Samuel Jamison, rolling south along the Humboldt in mid July, 1850, reported the "road very dusty. Can see the dust rising two or three hundred feet in the air. Met fifty packers returning home from California. Had to swim the river to cut grass with our knives and scarce at that." The next night he reported no grass at all and he had to feed his cattle "willow tops." On July 13, 1850, Jamison reached the Big Meadow. "Traveled 12 miles and good spring water. 6 miles and good grass and water. Here we cut grass to cross the dessert [sic]. We are now within twenty five miles of the sink of Marays or Humboldt River."[144]

"After 20 miles we came to a spring in a deep ravine, where we found many of our former traveling companions," wrote Margaret Frink on August 9, 1850. "It was a pleasant meeting in that desert place. We exchanged congratulations and experiences, each narrating the hardships they had met. During the day we passed many dead animals. Just as the sun was going down we came to a wide tract of marshland covered with course swamp grass, and called the 'big meadows' or Humboldt's meadows. Bought some hay tied up in small bundles for twenty cents."[145]

"Monday 29 July" brought Wellenkamp to the Big Meadow, along with some animal troubles. "Camped last night on low point on river, swam our animals across, started 3 o'clock A.M. Three mules lost while harnessing. Many Indians are about to whom we ascribe the theft. Went along a dry, ashy desert of seeming level riverbank, no vegetation whatever, no green object, only some dry saleratus thorn and sagebrushes. This day shot Charles [one of his horses, we hope]. Balance of animals hardly able to walk. This day saw James Owens, a lone packer, who also abandoned a horse. Sky clear and excessively hot. Passed a dead horse every 20 yards. Camped on the big meadow."[146]

Keeping healthy animals proved to be a real problem that few found the means to deal with. "This morning 2 Indian men and a Boy came to our camp with 2 horses and 2 mules, we talked of claiming them as stolen property but finally let them pass concluding that they were the rightful owners," recounted William Edmundson. "We started and about 10 O'clock met the Owner inquiring for them. They had been stolen the night before. We reached the Big-Meadow after dark where we camped having traveled 30 miles today."[147]

Mica Littleton reached the Big Meadow, about 20 miles above the Sink, on September 18, 1850. "Encamped made hay. Emigrants had better make hay and take water at the upper part of the meadow, as the water is much better and grass as good. This place is I think sickly the water very impure and so much low lands here must make it sickly. This meadow is the only thing for the emigrant. I do not know how any person would get through were it not for this. It lays in sloughs for miles on either side of the river."[148]

Caleb Booth saw the Big Meadow on September 5, 1850, writing in his diary, "Traveled about 12 miles and encamped by the meadow, which is about 12 miles square. Humboldt, being a Catholic, called this St. Mary's River.

Lots of hungry folks all along." The next day he wrote a single line, "Fine weather all the time…" Then his diary contained this note written by another hand: The following day Sabbath, he died of Cholera after a sickness of about ten hours, at the age of 25 years, less 12 days; three weeks before the Company reached the end of their journey. He was buried by his friend and the companion of his travels, Mr. James Thomas of Farmington, Iowa, beside the river of which he speaks so often, St. Mary's, frequently called the Humboldt."[149]

At the Big Meadow

Margaret Frink recalled the Big Meadow being quite crowded. "…all the way, both sides of the road were thickly settled with campers. They are resting and feeding their stock, lightening their wagons, cutting grass and making hay, preparing the best they can for crossing the Humboldt Desert — the worst on all the route — now only two or three days travel ahead. The reports which came from the desert of the loss of horses, mules, and oxen were very distressing and caused much uneasiness. We did not know but that our own animals might meet the same fate. The river is the only water to be had, and there are no brooks, springs, or wells where we first came to it. The river water we found gradually becoming brackish and discolored from the salt and alkali in the soil. The farther we traveled the worse it became. Mixed up with everything nauseous."[150]

Most emigrants used the Big Meadow as a place to lay over, at least a day and more often than not, two or three, to prepare for the ordeal they knew lay ahead. Some found it a refreshing place while others lay by out of sheer necessity.

"The slough where we are camped is a new discovery and our attention was attracted to it by a sighn [sic] put up at the place we leave the old road as a place where plenty of grass could be had," wrote Franklin Starr on August 18, 1849, reaching Big Meadow late in the day. He added in his diary the next day, "We lay by and made hay. There are hundreds of acres of excellent grass here which would cut 1½ pound to the acre [did he mean ton to the acre?]. the best grass to cut is over the slough ½ mile from camp and we have to carry it so far and more than 1 hundred yards through water knee deep, coming through the sludge and rushes which grow very dense and 12 or 15 feet high.

"There are a number of Indians in camp but I do not know what tribe they belong to. The ground between the road and the slough about 100 yards wide for upwards of a mile in length is covered with waggons which are disposed [in] admirable disorder. Each train a little apart from all others. There is an abundance of excellent grass and they are recruiting for the desert ahead and making hay to take along."[151]

"Being now at the Big Meadow, close to the Sink of Humboldt or Margo River and having the *last grass* on this side of the *dreaded desert*, the whole emigration made a halt in order to recruit their animals and make hay to take along into the desert. We ferried a slough, mowed grass, and carried it 1 mile to camp. A grand destruction of wagons, tents, guns, trunks, etc. is going on, many reporting to the last alternative to wit: Pack their bundles on their back. A famine, nearly starvation, among the emigrants. Dead animals are eaten," lamented Henry Wellenkamp on July 30, 1850.

Over the next two days he dealt with a horse gone astray, taking on a new partner, and getting ready to push on. "Lost my mare mysteriously. Laid over and made hay. Took James Owens in company. Obtained my mare again. Paid James Noble $12.50 for mare. Laid over, fixed wagon, gathered hay and made ready." [152]

More than anyone else, Margaret Frink seemed to capture the humanity of the people around her in those desperate days, in that desperate place of no return. "Mr. Clarke's company came up and camped beside us," she wrote on August 11, 1850, beginning to relate a story of amazing faith. "Also part of the Mount Morris company including our lady friend Mrs. Foshee. The Indians had stolen all their horses except two nice ponies. The whole party were now in a sad plight, on short rations, with only two horses, and a lady in the company, whom the young men felt it to be their bounded duty to see safely in California. The young men were willing to walk and carry their own provisions if they could find some one who would take Mrs. Foshee to Sacramento, and accept the two horses for pay. For herself, she had no fear, for she felt sure that God would provide her some way to get there safely, for he had already in a miraculous manner, saved their company from starvation.

"Several days previously, they had just eaten the last food they had. But Mrs. Foshee was not dismayed, and was pleading with the young men not to despair, to still put their trust in God, for she was sure they would be provided for. They had not traveled far that afternoon when one of the young men came across a young cow tied to some willow bushes, with a card fastened to her horns, on which was written the statement that nothing was the matter with the cow, that she was only footsore and not able to travel fast, and that any one in want of provisions would be at liberty to kill her for food. This being their desperate case, they stopped, killed the animal, cut the meat into small strips to dry, and traveled on with lightened hearts. The next day they found a sack of flour with a card attached, on which was written permission to anyone in need of food to appropriate it to his own use. Mrs. Foshee's prediction was fulfilled to the letter. While we were talking the matter over there came into camp the Rev. Mr. Morrow, a Methodist clergyman, to give us notice that he would preach in a tent near by at two o'clock. We had had some previous acquaintance with him, and I suggested to him that here was an opportunity to put in practice the teachings of Jesus Christ, by giving up to Mrs. Foshee his comfortable seat in the passenger carriage he was traveling in. A train to carry passengers across the plains had been fitted out in St. Louis by McPike and Strother, and Mr. Morrow was with them. The situation was fully explained to him. The four young men all that remained of the Mount Morris company offered to give him their only two remaining horses, if he would give his seat in the carriage to Mrs. Foshee. Mr. Morrow consented. Mrs. Foshee sat in her carriage, smiling and happy, ready to continue her journey. At the same time the Rev. Mr. Morrow, riding one of the two horses and leading the other, packed with his clothing, blanket, and provisions, passed out of sight and we saw him no more. The young men had to leave behind the outfit of new clothing, blankets, and comforts with all the little articles which their mothers, sisters, and sweethearts had, with so much care, fitted up for them, as without their horses, they could carry but little save the bare necessities of life. Mr. Bryant, however, carried his pick, with which to dig gold when he got to California."[153]

Unfortunately, the blessings for Mrs. Foshee did not descend on everyone, as Margaret described in her diary the next day. "Many people are passing to-day begging for food. Among the crowds on foot, a Negro woman came tramping along through the heat and dust, carrying a cast iron bake oven on her head, with her provisions and blanket piled on top — all she possessed in the world — bravely pushing on for California." And the following day the report of conditions on the trail ahead got more bleak. "The rumors that came back from there were very distressing — animals dying without number, and people suffering from prolonged thirst."[154]

Some longstanding relationships ended at the Big Meadow. "This morning my Brother David and Myself left the company with whom we had Traveled from home. Went on 5 miles and joined Dr. Bell's Train. Our company being nearly out of Provisions we thought it best to separate," wrote William Edmundson.

Sarah Davis laid over at the Big Meadow in late September, 1850. Though near the end of the travel season, plenty of other emigrants had apparently stopped too. "there is a wagon here that belongs to a nother train it seams they had a fight with the indians seven days ago we are now in the vicinity of the sink I believe I believe their are more than fifty dead horses here but their is plenty of grass her[e] and water and plenty of good wood this eavening we can see smoke in every direction some are Indians and some are emigrants we can see a plenty of fires this day."[155]

The Humbolt Sink

It would be fair to assume that none of the emigrants had ever seen anything like the Humboldt Sink. They had seen rivers of course, great and small, that rose in the hills or mountains, coursed down through valleys that broadened as the channels widened and deepened, until they flowed into some other river, larger and stronger, until eventually reaching the sea. That is what rivers were supposed to do. Not the Humboldt. It had risen in the snow pack of the mountains for certain, but then meandered for 300 miles, growing ever weaker and slower across the wilderness of northern Nevada, before terminating, not in some other great river, or even a great inland sea like Salt Lake. No, the Humboldt dribbled out into a great marshy flat and simply evaporated under the blazing desert sun.

"…By dark we reached the Sink," recalled J. A. Pritchard on July 25, 1849. "Here we found several wells that had been sunk the water in them was barely tolerable. It was so strongly impregnated with Saline & Alkali that we could barely use it. The grass was so indifferent that our mules would not have touched it except in case of starvation. The Sink is a vast plain — over which the water spreads — & gradually sink or looses its self in the sand. It is a vast Quagmire or Marsh of stagnant Saline and Alkali water mixed and emits a most offensive and nauseating effluvia. The sink proper is about 4 or 5 miles wide, & from 12 to 15 in length. It is thickly covered with Bull Rushes. There is nothing of the appearance of Lake about it as you can only see the water about in spots. It therefore has more the appearance of Ponds than a Lake. Taking it all in all, it is one of the most disagreeable and loathsome looking places on the face of the earth."[156]

Niles Searls, already mightily depressed with his experience, thought even less of it than Pritchard. "Sink of the Humboldt — sink of everything that is human and humanizing! We have absolutely used up a good sized river! Have run it in the ground! It is gone! For two hundred miles we have followed the river in all its windings until here, upon a great level sandy waste, its feeble channel spreads out into a shallow lake of a mile across, and is drunk by the thirsty earth and evaporated by the burning heat. The thermometer indicates 140 on this arid plain. I never felt the heat till now, as reclining under the wagon, I look out over an arid, burning waste.

"The whole atmosphere glows like an oven. The water is bitter and nauseous. Off to the southwest, as far as the eye can extend, nothing appears but a level desert. This we must cross! Through its burning sand we must toil! Fate decrees it! A hundred dead animals around us admonish haste. Not a particle of feed for our stock! We only pause here until night, to start for the Carson."[157]

"We traveled 17 miles and camped at the sulphur springs at the lower end of the sink. They are shallow wells containing sulphur water so strong that it would not be drinkable even in coffee, [for] any but Californians. It smells like the washings of a gun barrel!" described Franklin Starr in his diary. "The cattle refuse to drink it. The sink covers nearly the whole width of the valley in high water but now it is not more than 1½ or 2 miles wide and full of islands covered with rushes. The water is covered with Duckweed or some similar plant so that snakes were all over it. It is the very picture of desolation and solitude."[158]

Henry Wellenkamp's party pretty much "ran" by the Sink on Friday, August 2, 1850. "Started ½ past 2 A.M. Went along Humboldt River 15 miles through something like the bottom of an extinct lake, but very dry and hard. At 10 o'clock we arrived at what they call the 'Sink.' Had now come 25 miles. Nooned 2½ hours. Took 11 gallons of bad water and started, however not into the desert as supposed, but along a slough for 8 miles, crossed the same at dark, when we entered the actual desert. Halted and fed at 10 o'clock. Lay down and overslept. 41 miles."[159]

After a four-day lay over the Frink's pushed on toward the Sink. "We had gone but a few miles when we came to a man who was just unhitching his two-horse wagon to abandon it, his horses being unable to haul it any further. Mr. Frink gave him $5.00 for it, and left our cart by the roadside for any one who might want it. We could carry more hay in the wagon, and it was large enough for some of the men to sleep in at night. After this the road turned nearly south, and brought us opposite the end or point of the mountains on our left, on the east side of the river. A broad sandy desert opened and extended beyond them to the east and also to the south, farther than we could see. On the west, forty miles away, we could distinguish the long-looked-for California mountains, the Sierra Nevada, lying in a northwest and southeast direction. They were dark with heavy pine forests. On the plain was neither tree, shrub, nor blade of grass. In a few miles we came to where the river, along which we have been traveling for the last three weeks, spreads out on the level plain, and forms a broad, shallow lake. This lake is called the 'sink of the Humboldt.' One-half of it sinks into the sand, the other half rises into the sky. This is the end of the most miserable river on the face of the earth. The water of the lake, as well as that of the river for the last one hundred miles above, is strong with salt and alkali, and has the color and taste of dirty soapsuds. It is unfit for the use of either animals or human beings; but thousands of both have had to drink it to save life."[160]

Mica Littleton arrived at the Sink on September 19, 1850. This morning we came to the lake which is made by Humboldt River. It is about from 6 to 8 to 9 miles either way. Plenty of small fish in it and I have no doubt but there is large ones and I would here remark that Snakes is more plenty than Grass in all this region. There is a high Flag. Growing all through this bottom where there is water and through this flag there is no mud but where there is no flag there is lots of mud."[161]

Emigrants generally wasted little time at the Sink. If smart they had gathered hay at Big Meadow, and made do with the minimal feed and horrid water at the Sink before striking out across the desert. "…On reaching here we could not so much as find a bunch of wild sage which before had never failed to cook a bite of supper. The boys all retired to their humble couches to take rest without one bite of anything to eat. Dr. Thomas and my-self penetrated as far as we could with safety into the marsh and gathered an armful each of dead and dry Bulrushes. We kindled a fire and held the teakettle over the blaze and broiled a slice of bacon," recollected Pritchard as they rested at the Sink.[162]

"We made our final preparations and crossed the muddy slough expecting to enter the confines of the desert," Frink wrote. "A few miles further we came to the last of the sloughs or bayous, that connect the river with the sink. Here we filled our five-gallon water bottles, and other vessels, it being our last opportunity of doing so. The men waded into the middle of the slough to fill them, hoping the water there might be better than near the bank. We then drove onward until dark, where we stopped for a short time to refresh ourselves and our weary horses. As night came on, the air grew cool and invigorating, which was an advantage."[163]

Sarah Davis recalled meeting emigrant help agents near the Sink. These were men from California, or Salt Lake City who knew how bad the emigrants' condition would be at the sink, and offered supplies, at the right price, of course. "…we met a man that told us their was plenty of flour ahead and meate and coffe we went on then a bout three miles and their we met a train just come in with plenty of provisions here we saw some of the digers [Ute Indians?] they look frightfull and some of their wigwams their was five I think some of them come out to the road and they were stark necked [naked]."[164]

The Truckee Route to the Crest of the Sierras

Two major routes ran from the Sink across the desert to the eastern foothills of the Sierra Nevada Mountains. The routes carried the names of the rivers at which the desert trek terminated, either the Carson or Truckee, also called the Salmon Trout River. The northern or right-hand route lead to the Truckee River and the southern or left hand route to the Carson. Each handled its share of the emigrants and each had proponents and opponents, often depending on what a particular emigrant or party had heard in the environs of the big Meadow or Sink. The distance across either desert stretch had been estimated, or recorded in guidebooks at about 45 miles, which seemed accurate for the Truckee route, but the emigrants recording the actual mileage they traveled on the Carson route generally found it closer to 60. The Truckee route proved to be nearer the mountains and less arduous than the Carson route, but it did deposit the emigrants further north of the primary target in California, Sutter's Fort. They were all at their weakest, and yet they knew

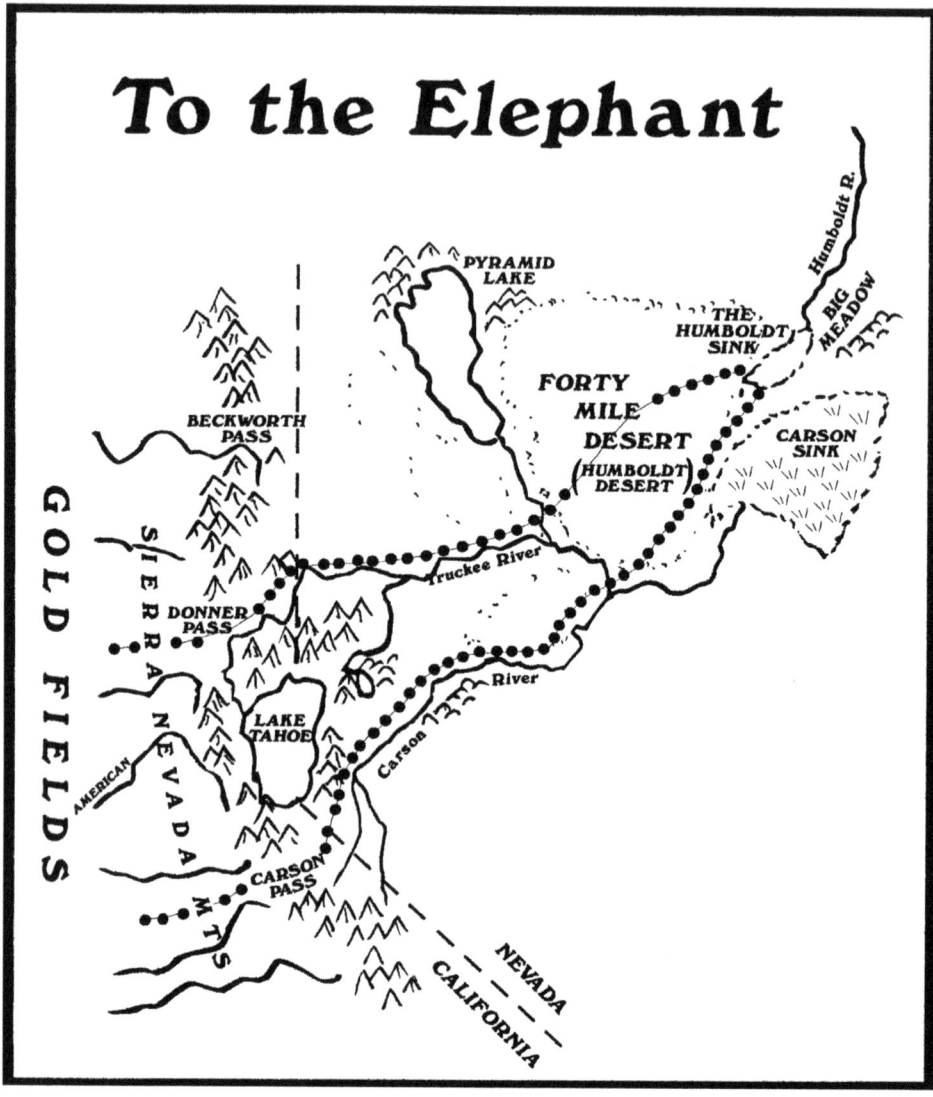

To the Elephant — Carson and Truckee routes from the Sink through the Sierras.

there was no water at all, until they reached the rivers. They were not just seeing the elephant, but standing right beside it.

Late on August 23, 1849, Franklin Starr's party left the Sink. "We did not stop a great while at the sulphur springs but started across the desert about 8 o'clock in the evening after eating our supper and giving the oxen a bit of hay. The road soon forks. The right going to Smokie or Salmon trout river and the left to Carson River. We have concluded to go the old road (Smokie river) and by going ahead and carefully examining the ground we discovered the forks though we could scarcely tell when we were in the road and when out. We appear to be traveling over a flat smooth surface which we entered upon immediately. The surface is smooth and so hard that the waggon makes no impression on it and runs as though it was on a floor."[165]

Sallie Hester's party also took the Truckee route. Departing the area of the Sink on September 4, 1849, she wrote, "Stopped and cut grass for cattle and supplied ourselves with water for the desert. Had a trying time crossing. Several of our cattle gave out, and we left one. Our journey through the desert was from Monday, three o'clock in the afternoon, until Thursday morning at sunrise." As she continued her entry, Sallie Hester constructed one of the great soliloquies of trail life at its nadir.

"The weary journey last night, the mooing of the cattle for water, their exhausted condition, with the cry of 'Another ox down,' the stopping of train to unyoke the poor dying brute, to let him follow at will or stop by the wayside and die, and the weary, weary tramp of men and beast, worn out with heat and famished for water, will never be erased from my memory."[166]

Mica Littleton opted for the Truckee route in late September, 1850. Beginning near the Sink, he recalled, "10 miles more will bring you to the end of the lake. Here is what is called the last Slough. There is 2 routes here. The Carson and the Trucky routs. We take the Trucky rout. The roads appear to cross each other when you are on the east or South side of the river. You cross the last Slough take over the ridge and come down in the bottom and keep around the lake which is on the left, here you take all Right hand roads. The left-hand road keeps down to the left to go the Carson rout. You keep going the Trucky rout around the lake about 10 miles then you take off to the West for 10 or 11 miles then turn more to the South until you come to the boiling Spring. From the Sink there is no water nor no grass. 15 miles you come to the boiling Springs. We left this sink to take the desert at 4 o'clk P.M. Traveled slow and did not reach the Spring until Saturday morning. In coming around the lake you could find in places a little grass but very little. The water will barely do for the Stock to drink but I do not think it good for horses or any thing else as there is much Alkalie in it, this whole country appears to be charged with Salt or Alkalie."[167]

"We reached the Boiling springs at 11 o'clock 25 miles form sulphur springs and half way over the desert. There are a great many wagons lying by at the springs trying to cool water for the cattle. The cattle are suffering form the want of water and we will try and cool enough to be able then to reach Smokie River. The springs are boiling hot and there are a number of them. The largest is a pond 20 ft. long and 10 or 12 broad and although very clear can not see the bottom. I ate bacon boiled in it and it was very well done."[168]

Mica Littleton saw the same natural oddity a year after Starr, and wrote more about it. "This boiling Spring is one of the great wonders of nature of all the wonders I have Seen in my life. I never have beheld one that made such a deep impressions on my mind. It appeared to me when I first Stood and saw the troubled movement of the water (which takes place every 15 minutes and lasts 5) that I was nearly in the presence of the Almighty. The water is extremely hot So much so that when it commences gushing out the Steam rises high up in the air. The water and Steam reminds me of a mud valve under boilers on a Steamboat. The noise not quite so loud. The water when it commences or a little before begins to rise then begins to blubber then begins to blow and the Steam begins to rise. Then let any person stand by and pause for a moment and Say Great are the wonders of Jehovah, and his ways past finding out. There are several Springs all in a line operated on all the Same time but does not run out. One with a blue clay Soft, and blubbers all the time. This water will do for use after it is cooled but I think it is impure. From here you have a good road 13 miles."[169]

Sarah Davis' little band, bringing up the rear of the migration in 1850, left the Sink on September 30, 1850. "...This day all struck the mane desert and now we leave the humbolt in tirely we traveled all night and pas the day we stoped to rest a half our to a time the road were so bad it is a sight to see the distruction of property here." The following day's entry continued to record the rapid pace at which they pushed themselves across the desert, traveling literally around the clock. "This day we traveled all day and all night we come to the boiling spring it is the greatest curiosity I ever saw in my life tis morning we are at salmon trout river [Truckee River?] a bout seven o'clock."[170]

Mica Littleton pushed on from the Boiling Springs. "We left the Spring at 9 o'clk this morning. 13 miles brought us to the Sand plain and 7 miles more to the Trucky or Salmon trout river. This Sand is the worst road we have had on the whole route. Such heavy Sand I never Saw. At the commencement of this Sand off to the left there is some bunch grass. There is also grass in many places between until you get to the river." Having reached the saving waters of the river, Littleton found his party breaking up. "3 or our mess concluded to leave us and pack. Here we divided mules provisions etc. The grass in places is tolerable good but not so good being late in the Season. Crossed the river 6 times today some of them very bad and the road extremely rough. Kept up the right side. There is good grass in many places all along. Some distance here you will find a Bad road. Today we have had the very roughest Kind of a road and Some Steep hills to go up and down 15 miles. You come to the big meadow [valley of the Truckee]. We crossed the river once more today making all together 8 times. This meadow is a beautiful place plenty grass wood and water. Surrounded by mountains."[171]

Sallie Hester, having gone out the year before Littleton, had found the Truckee just as refreshing to reach but just as difficult to cross. "Just at dawn, in the distance, we had a glimpse of Truckee River, and with it the feeling:

Saved at last! Poor cattle; they kept on mooing, even when they stood knee deep in water. The long dreaded desert had been crossed and we are all safe and well. Here we rest Thursday and Friday—green grass and beautiful and the cattle are up to their eyes in it."

But the next day, September 8, 1849, they "Traveled fourteen miles; crossed the Truckee twelve times." And after that, "…made eighteen miles. Crossed the Truckee River ten times. Came near being drowned at one of the crossings. Got frightened and jumped out of the carriage into the water. The current was very swift and carried me some distance down stream."[172]

The valley of the Truckee rose sinuously toward its source at Lake Tahoe and also toward one of the most infamous mountain passes in the annals of the American West. Writing on September 14, 1849, Sallie Hester somberly recalled, "We arrived at the place where the Donner Party perished, having lost their way and being snowed in. Most of them suffered and died from want of food. This was in 1846. Two log cabins, bones of human beings and animals, tops of the trees being cut off the depth of snow, was all that was left to tell the tale of that ill-fated party, their suffering and sorrow. We crossed the summit of the Sierra Nevada. It was night when we reached the top, and never shall I forget our descent to the place where we are now encamped— our tedious march with pine knots blazing in the darkness and the tall, majestic pines towering above our heads. The scene was grand and gloomy beyond description. We could not ride—roads too narrow and rocky—so we trudged along, keeping pace with the wagons as best we could. This another picture engraved upon the tablets of memory. It was a footsore and weary crowd that reached that night our present camping place."[173]

Mica Littleton hurried on, the ridge of the Sierra Nevada clearly in sight, stopping briefly at that spot that had become both a monument and a physical warning to foolhardy emigrants. Writing on September 27, 1850, he reflected on his having survived seeing the elephant and on a party that had not. "Through the pines streams all tributaries of Trucky River. I would remark that nearly all these valleys have some grass. Take off to the right up a little valley where Donner and his company wintered and suffered and Starved So many. When I stood on the Spot and reflected how mesterious [sic] the ways of God, and the fate of so many and being there the Same day of the month 3 years ago, would certainly cause many emotions in my breast although God in his mercy has brought preserved and protected us from all harm on this long and toilsome trip. Here we are encamped. The Stumps are all Standing yet and are 8 to 10 feet high where they cut them from the top of the Snow, Trucky's lake is ½ mile above here. A beautiful lake several miles in length and 1 or more wide."[174]

Over the next two days Littleton's company charged the elephant, climbing to the crest of the Sierra Nevada Mountains. "We begin to ascend the mountain through rocks hills and valley. Small but some Steep and very rough having very large rocks in the road. You wind around however and go on without much danger. 6 miles you reach the Sum[m]it. You can make it all easy enough by taking time. We rolled up with 4 mules in one hour with about 400 pounds in. The decent is also bad and requires care and patience. Here you wind around from hill to vale passing several lakes and steep places with some as rough road as any man ever saw I think. 10 miles and you come down the mountain to Bear River."[175]

The Carson Route Across the Desert

Jumping off from the southern end of the Sink, emigrants taking the Carson route veered left at the fork in the road and pushed off into what became known as the Forty-Mile Desert for a forty hour trek through what diarists analogized as Hell. What they found horrified and tested even the most ardent among them. The fact that so many made it across is a testimony to human drive and spirit in itself.

"Gathered grass and rested the mules till 3 P.M. at which time we intended to commence the much dreaded journey across the 45 mile desert of salt, fire, and I had like to have said Brimstone. The vertical rays of a full sun was so oppressive that we were compelled to place wagons close to gather spread an awning which we made of our Tents from one wagon to another. The forenoon was spent in telling games, cracking jokes, and baking bread etc. to last us a cross the desert. Thus time was whiled away wateing [sic] for the auspicious hour to arrive when we should be relieved from the excruciating tortures of this loathsome & infernal place.

"Our vessels all having been filled with water & all necessary preparation made at the appointed hour we took up the line of march And traveled about ten miles where we struck a large slough in which a number of wells had been sunk which afforded us pretty fair sulphur water. We here threw away the water that we had put in our casks and refilled them. I feed my mules with corn that I had brought with me from the States for this express purpose. Besides I filled a Methuen Duck cloths sack with water that held about 2½ bushels."[176] J. A. Pritchard.

"We are now at the sink of the Humboldt River. The water here is not very good it is alkali by digging into the ground about fifteen inches it will rise very salt. Left camp half past four and started into desert. Spotswood's horse gave out here and we left him. Started at one o'clock [A.M.] traveled 20 miles very sandy and hard on our animals five of which gave out. Left two got three into camp with difficulty. Seen a great many wagons abandoned and horses that had died for want of water and feed. There was a stray horse come into camp while on the desert which we took up and feed that night and found an owner next day. Spotswood went back for the last mule that we left and met a man leading the first. Gave the man four dollars for his trouble."[177] Samuel Jamison.

"Started at 2–3 A.M. Morning glow soon made objects visible. Objects of desolation and destruction, which no pen can describe, wagon on wagon, carcass on carcass, and property, to an amount God only knows. At 7 o'clock halted, fed and made coffee. *Shot pony.* Started at 7 and traveled till 12. Fed and gave our last water. Started at 2 traveled till dark. 25 miles."[178] Henry Wellenkamp.

"Left sink of Humboldt a little before night August 26th and journeyed steadily but slowly all night, and on Monday morning encamped on the barren desert to avoid travel during the excessive heat of the day. I was attacked with a light fever and have only a kind of dreamy recollection of the silence and the heat. Started again at sundown and by 3. A.M. had reached a point within eight or ten miles of the Carson, where we struck deep, loose sand in which the animals floundered for a time and then, overcome by exhaustion, gave up and could be urged no further. A few fell and died in their harness and the rest were turned loose and started for the river. Our passengers soon abandoned the train also and, on foot and as best they could, made their way to the Carson. Five or six of us were sick in the wagons and were perforce compelled to remain. Rogers came out with water in canteens, and eight of the best mules, we were all placed in a single wagon and hauled in."[179] Niles Searls.

"At 8 o'clock P.M. we resumed the line of march & here we struck the desert and traveled till daylight. The road during the night were very good. In 12 ms. we struck Salt creek a most disagreeable place. We crossed this just before the Moon went down. The water of this place is said to kill stock instantly. Covered 35 miles. The boys just dropped down on the ground any where & fell a sleep."[180] J. A. Pritchard.

"For many weeks we had been accustomed to see property abandoned and animals dead or dying. But those scenes were here doubled and trebled. Horses, mules, and oxen, suffering from heat, thirst, and starvation, staggered along until they fell and died on every rod of the way. Both sides of the road for miles were lined with dead animals and abandoned wagons. Around them were strewed yokes, chains, harness, guns, tools, bedding, clothing, cooking-utensils, and many other articles, in utter confusion. The owners had left everything, except what provisions they could carry on their backs, and hurried on to save themselves. In many cases the animals were saved by unhitching them and driving them on to the river. After resting they were taken back to the wagons, which in this way were brought out. But no one stopped to gaze or to help.

"The living procession marched steadily onward, giving little heed to the destruction going on, in their own anxiety to reach a place of safety. In fact, the situation was so desperate that, in most cases, no one could help another. Each had all he could do to save himself and his animals. As we advanced the scene became more dreadful. The heat of the day increased, and the road became heavy with deep sand. The dead animals seemed to become at every step of the way more numerous. They lay so thick on the ground that the carcasses, if placed together, would have reached across many miles of that desert. The stench arising was continuous and terrible. The fault lay, in many cases, with the emigrants themselves. They acted injudiciously. Their fears caused them to drive too fast, in order to get over quickly. Their animals were too weak to be urged in this way. If the people generally had cut grass and made hay at the 'big meadows,' above the sink, as Mr. Frink did, and hauled it with them into the desert and brought a few gallons of water for each animal, traveling slowly and resting often, much of the stock and property that was lost could have been saved, and much distress and suffering avoided."[181] Margaret Frink.

"About 1 O'clock P.M. started on the Desert which commences at the crossing of the Outlet and continues to the Carson River, the distance is said to be 40 miles. We traveled all night and in the morning at sunrise found ourselves about 6 miles from Carson River. Our Teams very tired and the worse part of the Desert before us. We held a consultation and concluded to take the Cattle from the Wagons and send them forward with a party of the company to the river while some of us should remain with the Wagons. This was accordingly done. Four of us remained in the Desert till about sundown when those who had gone ahead in the morning returned with the Teams and we all went to the River.

"The Destruction of property on the Desert during the present season has been immense. At the time we crossed it was estimated that 5 thousand head of Horses, Mules and Oxen were lying dead in a distance of 40 miles; incredible as this statement may see seem it perhaps falls short of the actual number. The destruction of Wagons and other property was in proportion. Our company lost two horses and an another company who traveled with us lost 32 head of Oxen."[182] William Edmundson.

"Just as Aurora's beams began to dawn & scatter her blushing read along the verge of the fare East, and chase away the gloom of a dismal night, and light up the dreary path of weary travelers which lay stretched a cross a place of desolation. We were ready to embrace what to us, seemed to be, an offering of mercy from on high. The rays of the sun, which were shed upon us by the God of day, clear, bright, and beautifully brilliant."[183] J. A. Pritchard.

"The balance of miles being heavy quicksand, animals all giving out, unhitched and sent on to Carson river, myself keeping camp. Men exhausted fell asleep and mules went astray. Pay 25 cents for 1 pint of water; then $2.00 for 1 gallon. Along here 10 miles from desert some men have stationed themselves, carry water to emigrants at $1.00 per gallon and stop and pick up every loose animal around and about, also pair of our mules."[184] Henry Wellenkamp.

"We met a wagon drawn by strong, fresh horses, loaded with barrels of pure sweet water for sale. It has been hauled from a newly discovered spring, four or five miles southeast of the road. Mr. Frink bought a gallon of it, for which he paid $1.00. After the nauseous stuff of the Humboldt sink this spring water was more than an ordinary luxury. We had been thirty-seven hours on that frightful desert."[185] Margaret Frink.

"As we began to approach within 15, 12, 10, 8, 6, and so along miles of the river we found scores of wagons that had been left under the protection of a guard and the teams taken on through to grass for the purpose of recruiting them and then returning for their wagons. It took some of them 3 & 4 days to get through in this way. They had to encounter a black sand that admitted the wheels of the wagons from 6 to 10 inches for the distance of 15 miles before reaching the river. A great number of mules, horses & cattle had been left on the desert unable to get through and many had to abandon their wagons all together in order to get through. From my sack full of water I gave my mules a few swallows occasionally through the day — which kept them revived — And whenever I came a cross a pore fellow who was out I gave him water. The day was oppressively hot and the burning sand reflected the rays of the sun to such a degree that it appeared like suffocation at once. The sight of timber that skirted the river seemed to inspire the men with new life. Our mules were so much exhausted that they would not drink when they got to water. On the opposite side of Carson River we found splendid grass."[186] J. A. Pritchard.

"From last night til this night we had our animals and men on Carson River, myself being with the wagons in the desert. Saw emigrants nearly perishing, frothing at the mouth for want of water. Company returned from Carson at midnight and took our wagons down by 6 o'clock Monday morning."[187] Henry Wellenkamp.

Along the Carson River

The Carson River coursed from the eastern slope of the Sierra Nevada and brought life to those who had endured the desert. Margaret Frink beautifully described it writing, "The Carson River comes close to the south edge of the desert. This stream was named after the famous hunter and explorer, Kit Carson, the guide of Fremont. Its source is one hundred and seventy miles southwest, among the snows and granite of the Sierra Nevada. Its water was clear, cool, and pure, free from salt or alkali, as different from the Humboldt soap-suds is from night."[188]

Though the river must have seemed like paradise after the horrendous desert trek, the path still before the emigrants held some daunting challenges. Many emigrants were worn out and sick from all the deprivation of food, and water and the blistering heat. The road along the Carson ran approximately 75 miles before striking the wall of the Sierras. Though blessed with fresh water, it could at best be described as rugged, with heavy sand, and stretches of desert between the bends of the river.

Captain J. A. Pritchard's company, one of the best prepared from the beginning, claimed to have set a record for the desert passage to the Carson which no other emigrant party, even packers would likely match. "We were just 15 hours crossing from the Slough 5 miles below the Sink to the Carson River. Our time across has not been beaten by any train that have preceded us— nor in all probability will it be. There has been but 3 wagons so far as we have been able to ascertain that have enabled to make the trip clear a cross without leaving their wagons & bring their teams through resting & returning for their wagons. I witnessed a most singular incident this afternoon. It was a lady who came in 12 or 15 miles on horseback in advance of her party to procure water for her husband who was unwell him-self. Besides he had no one to leave in charge of his team. She came in company with several gentlemen who were also going to return. She was a stout robust looking woman about 22 years of age. Her husband was a Dr. his name I did not learn. She borrowed several canteens of men at the river & when I saw her last she had 4 filled with water & swong across her shoulders."[189]

"I am suffering from an attack of what promised to develop into a case of scurvy. Dr. Hutton is down with the same disease. Mr. James died from a like attack the other day and unless we move soon or obtain relief in the way of more suitable food and medicines, a first class cemetery would be a paying investment at this point. A number of our men have left, going ahead on foot," wrote Niles Searls from the Carson after barely surviving the desert.[190]

The Carson River not only provided life giving water, but it lay near enough to the California settlements for traders to make their way over the Sierras and set up shop in the valley to assist, at the highest rate the market could bear, the emigrants. Margaret Frink explained. "By the side of the river, where we came to it, was a collection of dirty tents and cloth shanties called 'Ragtown.' California traders had brought supplies here to sell to the emigrants. Beef was sold at twenty-five cents per pound, bacon $1.00, and flour $2.00 per pound. We bought some beefsteak for breakfast, our first fresh meat since trading with the Goose Creek Indians for antelope ham on the 19th of July. After breakfast we traveled six miles up the Carson River in search of feed for the animals. We were compelled to camp where the grass was very poor."[191]

Samuel Jamison also recalled meeting the traders and like so many emigrants willingly paid high prices for the most basic commodities of life.

"Struck river [Carson] good grass and water. Left camp at 3 o'clock no grass or water for 21 miles. Encamped met two trains of traders from Sacramento city. Asked 150 & 2 dollars for hundred for flour Bacon etc. Moved on 29 miles. Here we found a provision Store we bought 5 lbs. of flour and paid $7.00 for it. We had bread for diner today for the first time in three days."[192]

Henry Wellenkamp also thought the prices gouged a bit but took note of a little charity. "Monday 5 August. Arriving on Carson found a relief Station or Trading Post. Speculating gentlemen from California having with them contributions from the mines, Sacramento and San Francisco. Distributing among the poor emigrants. Otherwise they sold flour at $1.50 to $2.00 per lb., rice $1.50 per lb., beef 25 cents per lb. and one common biscuit at $1.50. Paid for recovery of mule, $10.00, Ferry and water, $30.00, Beef and Kramer [?] $130.00, Crackers $50.00. The Carson River, a handsome stream of clear, good and swift water, lined with large cotton trees etc. The first trees, except pine and cedar since Laramie." The next day Wellenkamp returned to the trading station and referred to it in his diary as, "a Robber's Den."[193]

"Here we found quite a village of Tents a number of Traders having established themselves here temporarily for the purpose of trading with the Emigrants," explained William Edmundson. He did not think their prices were as bad as they could have been. "They were selling Flour at 20 cents per pound which we consider cheap having paid one Dollar a pound at the Big-Meadows. The Carson River is about 30 yards wide much the same size as the Humboldt, it runs into a Lake and sinks, the water is clear and apparently free from Alkali."[194]

After Pritchard's company set its record crossing the desert, they relaxed a bit. "This forenoon was spent by our boys in washing & drying cloths bathing in the river etc. Fine splendid grass from 10 to 24 inches high. We stopped our wagons under some large cotton wood trees that stood immediately on the bank of the river which afforded us a cool pleasant shade. This it itself was a luxury that we have not enjoyed since we passed Fort Hall. The Carson River is about one hundred and twenty feet wide with a strong current and can only be forded in places along here. This river and lake took their name from the famous Kit Carson the Old Mountaineer."[195]

But a year later, and further back in the traveling season, some emigrants did not find the luxury Pritchard described along the Carson. "We remain in camp near the river all day, resting after the severe toil of crossing the desert. We are disappointed not to find the rich pastures that we heard about," wrote Margaret Frink. "Thousands of animals have fed them off. Mr. Frink has had the men cut grass wherever we can find it to take with us. Much of the slope between the mountains and the river is covered with sagebrush."[196]

Emigrants, their fragile wagons, and particularly animals continued to fail even after reaching the Carson. "Wednesday 7 August. Shot 2 more horses, poor animals, my heart bled, but I am determined that they shall not fall to the Indians, or anybody," lamented Henry Wellenkamp. "Went along Carson to a fine camp. Laid over, there being deserts ahead."[197]

"Day very warm — started at 6 P.M. to make a night march across a stretch of 20 miles where we strike the river again," began J. A. Pritchard on July 30, 1849, as they pushed off across one of the desert bends of the Carson. "Wagon broke. With the assistance of my old friend and fellow traveler Jacob Hoover of Ind. I made and put into my wagon a hound [a wooden block between the axle and the bed frame] as good if not better than the original one. It was made of a good tough white oak coupling pole that I had picked up a few days previous. We turned our mules a cross the river to grass & placed a guard over them. We cannot leave them a lone one minute a long this river on account of the Indians (Diggers) who are stealing all the horses mules & cattle that are left unguarded. We can hear of stock being stolen all around us every day and we see the pore fellows trudging a long on foot every day with their packs on their backs. We enjoy frequent bathing in this river which conduces much to our health. The day is spent lounging & napping and talking of our safe & speedy journey a cross the great salt desert. In deed it is with us a matter of general & universal congratulation to think that the greatest barrier that interposed its self to our march to the land of our promise had been subdued and overcome with such ease."[198]

Having reached nearly the same spot, and in direct comparison between diarists in 1849 and 1850, Margaret Frink reported, "horses have little to eat and being in sad condition. Animals were so weak they could hardly walk. We unhitched the horses and sent them to the river. To our great joy, the men had found a fine meadow untouched, there never having been an animal in it. The men took the small wagon to the meadow to fill it with grass. It was a campful of happy people, to know that our half-starved animals had had so good a feed. After dark we were ready to start on a long night journey across another desert."[199]

Henry Wellenkamp aptly described the Carson road in a series of diary entries. "Thursday, 8th August. 16 miles through a desert to the river again. Heavy sand and cobble stones. Friday, 9th August. Another desert — heavy sand. Traveled through the night, got so tired that I fell asleep on the road. Arrived again on Carson at 8 o'clock. Lost my company. We were now entering the Sierra Nevada Mts.—*durchschlangelt*—[Wellenkamp reverting to his native German for that word] snaking, winding, by the river which every 10–20 miles run through a deep canyon. Saturday 10 August. Laid over during the day, started at sundown there being a desert ahead. Traveled over an infernal road, camped midnight in perfect darkness. Made 17 miles."[200]

As succinctly as Wellenkamp described the road along the Carson, Margaret Frink offered the most illuminating description of the emigrants in the last weeks of their trek to see the elephant. "The emigrants are a woe-begone, sorry-looking crowd. The men, with long hair and matted beards, in soiled and ragged clothes, covered with alkali dust, have a half-savage appearance. There are but few women; among these thousands of men, we have not seen more than ten or twelve. The horses, cattle, and mules are getting gaunt, thin, and weak, almost ready to drop in their tracks, as hundreds of them have already done. The hoofs of many cattle wear out, so they can no longer travel, and are left to starve. The once clean, white wagon tops are soiled and tattered, and grimy with two thousand miles of gray dust. Many wagon beds have been cut off short to lighten them, or sawed in two to make carts. The spokes of the wagons left behind have been cut out to make pack saddles. The rickety wheels are often braced up with sticks, the hubs wound with wet rags to keep the spokes in, the tires bound with wire, or wedged with chips of wood, to hold them from dropping off. They go creaking along the dusty roads, seeming ready to fall to pieces, drawn by weary beasts barely able to travel, making up a beggardly-looking caravan, such as never was seen before. The great, splendid trains of fifteen, twenty, or thirty wagons have shrunk to three, four, or at most half a dozen, with three fourths of their animals missing. Their former owners now trudge along on foot, packing on their backs the scant provisions left, with maybe a blanket, or leading skeleton horses that stagger under their light burdens. One of the 'passenger trains' left most of its carriages by the side of the road, the passengers having to finish their journey on foot. One only hope sustains all these unhappy pilgrims, that they will be able to get into California alive, where they can take a rest, and where the gold which they feel skure [secure] of finding will repay them for all their hardships and suffering."[201]

The Elephant — Up the Eastern Wall of the Sierra Nevada

The Carson road terminated at the base of the eastern slope of the Sierra Nevada Mountains, that last great granite barrier before the gold fields. Near the base, emigrants found more traders, a lush mountain valley, the entrance to Carson Canyon, and the point where the road began to go up, and up, and up.

J. A. Pritchard, writing on August 1, 1849, nicely described the transition from the Carson road. "Covered 20 ms. hilly and uneven ground — road very stony & sandy. The bottom where we struck the river this evening is broad and handsome & covered with a luxuriant growth of grasses of the most nutritious qualities. The valley is walled in with high and lofty mountains whose summits are covered with eternal snows and evergreen pine. It is a strange contradiction that winter & summer should stand upon the same spot on earth.

"August 2 ... traveled 8 ms to Pleasant valley. The road leads near the base of the Mountains. We nooned upon a little stream in company with a train from Ohio who had started a cross country with fine Ohio horses nearly all of which had given out & out of 5 or 6 teams that they started with they only had enough fit for services to draw one wagon & a cart that they had made of one of their wagons. The men were all on foot. Six miles further we came to the hot Springs, the temperature of the water was nearly boiling hot. This valley is from 50 to 60 miles long and interspersed with sloughs & marshes. One of our mess being quite unwell the Dr. gave him an Emetic-which produced a very happy effect."[202]

Henry Wellenkamp recorded the transition, writing, "Sunday 11 August. Hunted tire which we lost last night 3 miles from camp. Fixed the wheel and passed through another Desert of 8 miles, nooned in fine grass and traveled 10 miles along Carson. Camped on the base of a grand Glacier. Monday 12 August. Went along the bottom of a beautiful valley, excellent road, grass and ice water. Passed several trading establishments. At 8 o'clock passed several boiling springs at foot of high snow mountains. Pine trees from 3–6 feet diameter, 50 to 60 feet trunk. Weather pleasant but very cold at sunrise."[203]

"We have seen no Indians for several weeks. There are no signs of game, though some of the emigrants have killed sage hens, and it is said there are deer in the mountains. The sage hens resemble prairie chickens, though considerably larger. We never tire of looking at the great mountains we have to climb over," anticipated Margaret Frink in her diary on August 22, 1850. Writing the next day she recalled they "met several gold hunters this side of the mountains [Virginia City, Nevada area]. Two of them had already found gold. The largest piece was thought to weigh [be worth] $4.00."[204]

Making a slow but steady pace, the Frinks pushed up the valley toward Carson Canyon, over three days. "Came into what was called the Carson meadows. We now met many gold hunters, prospectors as they are called. The trading posts became more frequent. Finding at one place some fresh beef just brought over the mountains from California, we bought five pounds for which we paid $1.25. We got within ten miles of the Carson Canyon, and encamped on a beautiful ice-cold rivulet that ran out of the mountains and across our road. There are hot rivulets, too, which burn the mouths of unsuspecting drinkers. The great forest of immense trees come down the steep side of the mountains to the edged of the road."[205]

Samuel Jamison conducted some business at one of the trading posts and figured that his mules were pretty valuable. "Swopt 2 mules for thirty lbs. of flour making the mules worth $20.00 per lb. and the flour worth $1.50 per lb. [he may have meant the mules were 20 lbs. for $1.] Traveled 8 miles to Mormon post. Traded one mule for thirty lbs. beef. Took the George Town

The Elephant—Up the Eastern Wall of the Sierra Nevada 267

road ascended the mountain which is very steep and is about 2 miles high. Very heavily timbered with yellow pine."[206]

"Traveled 5 miles over a low ridge into what is called Carson Valley. Then 12 miles up the Valley and camped near the Mormon Station, having traveled 17 miles to day," wrote William Edmundson describing his trek toward the base of the Sierras. "At this place there is a Log Cabin occupied by Traders. A high Mountain is on our right covered with large Pine Timber. Some Gold-Diggers are said to be at work on the other side of the river."[207]

Sarah Davis also remembered the long valley leading to Carson Canyon and the pines. "…we have past some of the handsomest pine trees I ever saw in my life some of them five feete through and since we had vary hadsome road all day through some pleasant valeys of grass and a handsome creeke"[208]

On August 3, 1849, Pritchard's company prepared for the climb. "Reached the mouth of the canyon that let out from the valley to the top of the Sierra Nevada Mountains. It was certainly one of the grandest and most sublime, picturesque scenery that I ever beheld. Many of these Pine trees will measure 7 & 8 feet in diameter and 200 feet in length. We have just before us now what the emigrants generally call the Elephant. We are resting our teams this after noon in order to give him fair trial in the morning."[209]

"All hands being ready this morning at an early hour we commenced the trying ascent through the Canyon. In about a mile we began to meet and brave the difficulties. We have the river to cross three time, the first and second time it was bridged by falling two large trees a cross and then laying puncheons & poles on them which made a tolerable safe bridge. Forded the third time. The mules fall without great care was taken. The principal obstructions are large piles of granit.l to 300 feet high. These we were compelled to find our way through by circuitous routes. Ascending and descending over steep craggy cliffs and precipices we were compelled to force our wagons through by manual labor. Where we camped for the night we met a family train returning from California to Salt Lake. Part of them were Mormons returning to their People at Mormon City. The balance were families who had immigrated to this country several years since—From the East around Cape Horn. Amongst the rest there was a very intelligent young Lady with one or 2 others in advance of the train who gave as much information with regard to the road & country as any person that it had been our good fortune to meet with."[210]

Niles Searls, who had suffered so much in mind and body for the past seven weeks, could not be sure he would ever see California, despite being so close. But at the end of September, 1849, he could still write, "I breathe more freely. We have traversed the Carson River to the mouth of the worst canyon opening into the valley and that, of course, we turned into to find our way to the Summit. For eight miles we literally climbed and hauled the wagons by ropes and mules over the jagged rocks which in places were higher than the wagons and perpendicular. At the west of the canon, we emerged into Hope Valley — rested a day and then spent another in getting to the first Summit and were caught in a storm of sleet by which forty mules were frozen to death. We are now in camp by snow bank under the 2nd Summit, with a prospect of reaching it tomorrow and looking down on California!

"I am deathly sick and must get better soon or play Moses by looking at the Promised Land and never entering therein. Hutton is dying. Roger is down with scurvy and a score of others are showing the effects of starvation or, what answers the same purpose, the effects of spoiled provisions that do not nourish."[211]

The Frinks began their ascent of the Sierras on August 27, 1850. "...To the mouth of the famous Carson Canyon, where the road turns abruptly to the right, to enter it. This is a great rocky gorge opening into the granite mountain, out of which rushes the west branch of Carson River, foaming, dashing, and tumbling over the huge rocks that have fallen into it from the high cliffs. It was six miles through this canyon over these rocks. The road, if it can be called a road, lay along the river, once or twice crossing it. The river was nothing but a chain of wild cascades. The road was but a track over and among piles of huge rocks. The teams were sometimes taken off and the wagons pried up and raised by levers, to get them over impassable places. At noon we stopped in the canon and took our lunch. Here we met some emigrants, among whom was a lady who had lost or left her husband behind. Their horses had been stolen by the Indians, and he went after them, but never returned. The mother, with seven children, had been brought this far by strangers, and upon them she depended to get through to California. The night was very cold. There was heavy frost in the morning, and ice was formed in the water bucket. In preparation for a still colder climate, we got out our winter clothing to wear." The climb continued all the next day. "We started up the mountain with the small wagon. We first put on four horses, then six. After getting up, we went back for the large wagon. Most of the load was packed on the horses' backs. But still we could not get the large wagon up the steep road."[212]

Wellenkamp began his drive up the mountain gorge, writing on August 3, 1850, "Next day started at sunrise, with a supply of grass, entered and ascended the pass or canyon of the Carson River. Grand, almost sublime! River rushed down in torrents, beating and breaking over ageless granite blocks. High, tall-towering mountains all around, many perpendicular, yet pine in crevices, and on the very top, of exceeding growth, from 1 to 6 and 8 feet in diameter, 100 to 140 feet high. Also shrubbery not yet seen, amongst others Erlen and a great nameless variety. But the road — Eternal Goodness! It is indescribable, over granite blocks the size of a horse and larger. Snow on top of mountains. Passed over steep hills and camped on Carson Bridge.

Noon to two o'clock commenced ascending the Sierra Nevada, ¾ mile having no equal in roughness and steepness. The grand obstacle seems impassable to the wanderer, the steepness is dangerous to a footman and the elevation makes the beholder dizzy, but we ascended. James Owens noted our pass on top of the mountain on a tree. Tall pines grow on these precipices, out of the perpetual snow and granite. Descended and camped in a beautiful valley. At night it froze ice."[213]

Margaret Frink continued to write amazing accounts of the people on the trail in her diary. "Mr. Frink, he got lost, and in his wandering came upon the body of a dead man with a whip in his hand; and he was so much frightened, he did not stop to examine him or find out who he might be. While in camp there came along a man who had lost everything. He had one pint of corn meal left. He was without shoes, and his feet were tied up in rags. I made him a dish of gruel, in to which I put a little butter, with some other nourishing things. Went on to Red Lake, which lies in a valley between the two summits. I went to a trading post near by, and begged some meat for him (shoeless man)."[214]

"After traveling 3 miles we came to a small Lake where the road comes to the Mountain. This lake is by some called the Red-Lake though this name is more generally applied to another Lake on the other side of the Mountain," reported William Edmundson on reaching the landmark high in up the first ridge of the Sierras. "This Mountain is a ridge of the Sierra Nevada and very steep — we crossed it without much difficulty and reached the Valley on the western side in the afternoon where we encamped close to the Red-Lake."[215]

Sarah Davis recounted reaching the high ridge of the Sierras, and expressed a feeling common to all the emigrants. "…we came to cross the sum[m]it and stop her till morning their [there] is plenty of good timber here and pitch pine it is vary colde here and I am giting vary tired of my journey the mountains is covered with snow October 11 … we crost the sierre nevade mountains it was vary steepe we had to duble teams to get up and then had a harde time we founde plenty of snow here and plenty ti[m]bre and plenty rock a litle more to me like we have got over and found a bottom covered with grass."[216]

Pritchard's company kept climbing. "At noon we reached Red Lake, one of the fountainheads of the Carson River. This mountain road is about one mile high and apparently perpendicular. We had to go nearly strait up it winding first to the right & then to the left gaining by gradual approaches. We have to lift our wagons round frequently and make a square tact. Many of the places have such perpendicular falls that if a mule were thrown off or wagon & team they would fall from 50 to 100 feet without touching anything. One of the party started the fore wheel of a new wagon that had been left down this mountain and after running several hundred yards it leaped from one large pile of stone to another and when it struck upon the last its velocity was so great, that it bounded with such force that it touched nothing for several hundred yards — and in its e[a]rial flight — it cleared the tops of some of the tallest Pine trees that grow upon the mountains. We continued the ascent with 14 mules hitched to one wagon and all the men of the train pushing, chocking & holding on & by sunset had succeeded in taking 2 of our wagons to the top."[217]

"We are now about to climb the main ridge of the snowy mountains called the Sierra Nevada," wrote Margaret Frink with probably some degree of trepidation. "From the base to the top the distance is five miles. The snow is from ten to fifteen feet deep. The road was very steep and high, and looked impassable. The road turned to the left and went up slanting which was an advantage. But it was a hard struggle for the weak horses. Though the wagons were nearly empty, we had to stop often and let the animals rest. We tied long ropes to the tongue, and strung them out in front. Four or five men put these ropes over their shoulders and pulled with the horses. Others lifted at the wheels, and when the horses stopped, they held back the wheels to keep the wagon from rolling back. The air is getting lighter at every step and the climb was hard work. We were above where all vegetation grew. It was not far from this place that Col. John C. Fremont and his party of explorers crossed, in February, 1844, six years and six months before we did. He gave the height where he crossed as 9,338 feet above the sea, which is nearly 2,000 feet higher than the summit of the South Pass which we crossed on the 24th day of June. During the night I was seized with a severe chill, the result of over-fatigue, from which I was only relieved by having some rocks heated in the fire, which served to restore warmth."[218]

Samuel Jamison recorded his assault on the elephant, which took three days, beginning on July 19, 1850. "Ascend a very high mountain. Met a train of traders selling flour at $1.50 per lb. pickled pork at $2. Descended the mountain to a very rapid stream that runs down the mountain with about ten feet of fall to the rod then took up the mountain again. This is the Sierra Nevada Mountain. Went up two miles encamped. Two mules gave out — made 25 miles. July 20 ... 1 mile up the mountain. Some very high mountains to cross. July 21... Boyle's mare fell off the bridge into the creek and lost his blanket. We now ascend a very high mountain. One mule gave out near the top. Armstrong begged a piece of raw venison which we eat so and thought it very good. Put the pack on my mule and followed the rest of our company. cot [caught] up in Union valley. Good grass and water."[219]

J. A. Pritchard and company fought the elephant two days to finally reach the summit and begin to see their Promised Land. "Very cold last night grass perfectly white & stiffened with frost. Commenced the ascent of this last high or large mountain at 5 A.M. This mountain or ridge is about 2 miles long. We halted and put all the teams to one wagon. Near the top is a large snow bank. As we gained the summit we were in a region of perpetual snows. After noon we turned our mules down to the right by a small lake. The waters were so cold we could not bathe in it. Its waters were so clear that we could have seen a pocketknife in 10 or 15 feet water.

"August 8 … we are now upon the topmost ridge of the Sierra Nevada Mountains. Language is inadequate to describe the striking contrast between this grand and magnificent Alpine and Elysian Scenery. Nothing in nature I am sure can present Scenery more wild, more rugged, more bold, more grand, more romantic, and picturesquely beautiful, than this mountain scenery."[220]

Henry Wellenkamp wrote of reaching the crest of the Sierras in mid August, 1850. "Wednesday 14 August. Commenced 2nd ascent of Sierra Nevada, a rough winding and turn about road. Passed over a snow bank from 50 to 100 feet deep. 3 hours travel brought us to the steep and keen top, a commanding pinnacle looking over 1000 peaks. All snow capped as far as the eye could reach, one grand chilly waste. At 10 o'clock *highest altitude in my life*. Thursday 15 August. Assumption Day. Descended 8 miles to leak spring and lay over balance of day. Country improving but very rolling, mountains generally lower, but some snow. Weather splendid."[221]

"Our white horse gave out today, he having fallen and hurt himself while he were coming up the one mile mountain," related Margaret Frink as they neared the summit of the Sierras. "He was a favorite horse; and we gave fifty cents a pound for flour to mix in water for him to drink, thinking it would strengthen him; but we only managed to get him as far as Tragedy Springs, where we had to leave him. These springs were named from a tragically affair occurring in 1849, in which two men, intoxicated, got into a fight with each other, in which one of them was killed."[222]

Henry Wellenkamp also found those springs but had a different explanation of what happened there. "After traveling 6 miles we came to a place called Tragedy-Springs from three men having been killed there by the Indians; from an inscription on a tree close by they were killed on the night of the 27th of June 1848. Their names were Daniel Browett, Ezra H. Allen, and Henderson Cox. They are all buried in one Grave under a pile of Stones." Edmundson continued, describing possibly an even greater tragedy, surviving 2,000 miles and then dying on the doorstep of the promised land. "After traveling two miles further we came to a Trading Post about noon where we camped having come 8 miles to day. A young man from Henry County, named Allen Melton died at this place during the night."[223]

Promised Land — Into the Sacramento Valley

From the high ridge of the Sierra Nevada, emigrants looked down onto truly what they considered a Promised Land, in every biblical comparison. Suddenly the elephant they had come so far to see, do battle with, fighting and dying, began to recede from their sight. But they would never forget it.

J. A. Pritchard began his descent, writing, "The road to day has been remarcably [sic] rough & hilly. It runs on the high ridges of the mountains with deep chasms on either side. Camped on a high meadow with many other trains. We found the grass to be of excelant [sic] quality and nearly waist high, we cut and cured all that we wanted in the evening. Made preparations for an early start in order to get the start of the large number of teams that were to leave this camp. The roads have been down hill pretty much & comparatively good all day. We then came on the forks of the road. The left hand leading to Sutters Fort & the right hand to the mills of Coloma. It is 50 miles from this point to the Fort."[224]

For Margaret Frink, her concerns with her fellow humanity never seemed to cease. "We met the barefoot man whom I had given gruel to at Red Lake. He knew our wagon from the name on the side. He told us the most distressing tale. He had left Red Lake by a cut-off through the mountains, only a pathway and he was very weak from having so little to eat. He said he found himself at what he called a cave, by the side of the mountain, where the side of the mountain was rock, straight up and down. He was so weak he could not climb, so he wandered around trying to find a place where he could get over; and in his travels he found five dead men, and several others that were, like himself, looking for a place to climb the mountains, and all weak for want of food. He finally got out with some others, and, by hearing cowbells. He was assisted by the relief committee, sent out from Sacramento to assist suffering emigrants."[225]

Sarah Davis concluded her diary with a couple of brief entries, simplistic and marvelous to the end. "Come to the yuba river it is crowded with stones of all sizes and sorts from a hen ague [egg] to the size of a wagon the water is clear and good October 17 ... we landed in siera nevady city and it is a city to this makes five months since we left home."[226]

"The Summit is crossed!" cried Niles Searls on October 1, 1849. "We are in California! Far away in the haze the dim outlines of the Sacramento Valley are discernible! We are on the down road now and our famished animals may pull us through. We are in the midst of huge pines, so large as to challenge belief. Hutton is dead. Others are worse. I am better — —"[227]

Like Searls and so many others, Samuel Jamison could hardly enjoy the vision of life beyond the elephant for the knot in his stomach. "We are all very weak from want of something to Eat. We sent Howe ahead from here to Georgetown [a mining settlement south of the American River] to get some provisions. We them passed some camps that had been made by the mines. Crossed another stream and ascend a very long mountain. Stopped at the top tied our animals to trees and lay down. Howe came up while we lay here bringing 16 lbs. of flour and 6 lbs. pork. Several men came along that had eat nothing for two days. We gave what we could.

"Traveled up a long mountain and down the same to the Ranch. The timber having a different appearance. It is low and cruby. Traveled to Georgetown. This is a brisk place. Boyle sold his mare for fifty dollars bought some provisions and went 2 miles to grass. No guard to night for the first since we left the states. Divide our cooking utenshails [sic] each man taking a plate, cup and spoon. Sold a mule there for 35 dollars and bought a outfit for the digins costing us 30 dollars."[228]

"This day we reached Dusty Ridge, which was well named. The dust was over our shoe tops. We arrived at Pleasant Valley. There were two or three miners here, but the diggings did not seem to be very rich. We prospected a little for gold, through curiosity, but found none."[229] Those last three words ended the trek of Margaret Frink and her husband, and completely summarized the prospects of the vast majority of those who had gone to see the elephant.

Epilogue

Jon Nevin King wrote a letter to his younger brother James, still back home in Illinois, from California, dated August 28, 1850. It provides a nearly perfect summarization of the trip he made and that of nearly all other emigrants. He had advice to give, and it spoke clearly to all who might listen.

"I was out 98 days from the time I left Weston Missouri until I arrived in Sacramento city and you may be sure I was very well pleased when the trip was accomplished. Just remember when I cross the plains a second time that will be about the time the sun will revolve around the earth. You can form no idea of the trip & my pen is to frail & feeble to attempt a description, suffice is to say that graves, death, rain hail and dust accompany you across. An Express arrived today from the Plains asking for immediate relief. The Cholera is carrying the Emigrants off in great numbers and starvation staring them in the face. There was an immense suffering when I was out; men who had lost all their Animals having been stolen by Indians or died by drinking from Alkali Springs, or worn out with fatigue, to see them marching along with their Blankets, tincup & canteen without provisions, money, or anything else and having to depend upon the generosity of their fellow emigrant to say 'tis hard & then when sick to lie down and die no one about to care or do anything for them. Could people listen to reason and those who are doing well at home stay there, for no person who has ever crossed the plains could ever, (if possessed of any feeling) advise any person to attempt it. Banish from your cranium all such ideas unless you could come by sea."[1]

Notes

Introduction

1. Niles Searls, May 8, 1849. Manuscript. The Bancroft Library, University of California, Berkeley, California. Also see, *The Diary of a Pioneer and Other Papers* (published by the Searls Family, 1940), 7.

Part I. From the Banks of the Missouri to Fort Laramie

1. St. Joseph *Gazette*, February 16, 1849.

2. From a letter written by Mary M. Colby, in Kenneth L. Holmes, ed., *Covered Wagon Women*, 10 vols. (Glendale, CA: Arthur H. Clarke Company, 1983), 2:48–49 Hereafter this work is cited as *CWW*.

3. From a letter by Lucy Rutledge Cooke, Holmes, *CWW* 4:233–234.

4. From a St. Louis edition of an emigrant guide to Oregon, by Captain G. Travault, reprinted in the St. Joseph *Gazette*, March 19, 1847.

5. St. Joseph Gazette, March 3, 1846.

6. *History of Buchanan County*, 645–646.

7. From a letter written by Lucy Rutledge Cooke, *CWW* 4:234–236.

8. From the diary of Elizabeth Dixon Smith, Holmes, *CWW* 1:119.

9. *The Diary of Samuel M. Jamison*, Nevada Historical Society quarterly, volume 10, (Winter 1967), 3–27.

10. Amos Josselyn, April 18–24, 1849. Manuscript, California State Library, Sacramento, California. Also see J. William Barett II, ed., *Overland Journal of Amos Piatt Josselyn: Zanesville, Ohio to the Sacramento Valley April 2, 1849 to September 11, 1849* (Baltimore: Gateway Press, Inc., 1978), 16–17.

11. J. A. Pritchard, April 22, 1849, in, "Diary of a Journey From Kentucky to California in 1849," *Missouri Historical Review*, 18 (1923–1924), 535–545. This article covers Pritchard's diary only up to his departure from Missouri. The rest of his diary is in typescript in the collection of the Western Historical Manuscript Collection, Columbia, Missouri.

12. Pritchard, April 22, 1849, 541.

13. Micajah Littleton, May 11, 1850 "Journal of a Trip Across the Plains from Independence, Missouri to California, May 11, 1850–October 11, 1850." Typescript. California State Library, Sacramento, California.

14. Searls, May 8, 1849, 8.
15. Searls, May 9, 1849, 8–9.
16. Jamison, April 24–25, 1850, 5.
17. Josselyn, April 25–28, 1849, 17.
18. Searls, May 10, 1849, 10.
19. Searls, May 11, 1849, 10–11.
20. Jamison, April 29–30, 1850, 5.
21. Josselyn, May 1, 1849, 18.
22. Jamison, May 6, 1850, 6.
23. Josselyn, May 1, 1849, 18.
24. Searls, May 15, 1849, 12–13.
25. Searls, May 12, 1849, 11–12.
26. Josselyn, May 4–5, 1849, 19.
27. Searls, May 15, 1849, 12–13.
28. Searls, May 17, 1849, 14.

29. Searls, May 17, 1849, 15.
30. Searls, May 21, 1849, 18.
31. Searls, May 19, 1849, 17.
32. Searls, May 21, 1849, 18.
33. Pritchard, May 4, 1849, 542.
34. Littleton, May 31, 1850, 2–3.
35. Josselyn, May 6, 1849, 19.
36. Littleton, June 1, 1850, 3.
37. Searls, May 18, 1849, 16.
38. Searls, May 17, 1849, 15.
39. Josselyn, May 6–9, 1849, 19–20.
40. Searls, May 23, 1849, 19.
41. Josselyn, May 11, 1849, 20.
42. Josselyn, May 6–9, 1849, 19–20.
43. Pritchard, May 7, 1849, 543.
44. Searls, May 22, 1849, 19.
45. Searls, May 24, 1849, 20.
46. Searls, May 26, 1849, 21.
47. Searls, May 29, 1849, 23.
48. Josselyn, May 12–14, 1849, 21.
49. Searls, May 27, 1849, 22.
50. Searls, May 30, 1849, 23.
51. Henry Wellenkamp, April 29–May 12, 1850. *Diary of a Trip from Washington, Missouri to Sacramento, California, April–August, 1850.* Typescript. Western Historical Manuscript Collection, Columbia, Missouri.
52. Letter, John Nevin King to his father, May 8, 1850. From, *John Nevin King: Letters En Route to California*, the King Family Papers, Illinois State Historical Library, microfilm.
53. King; letter to mother, May 14, 1850.
54. Ibid.
55. Ibid.
56. Ibid.
57. J. Goldsborough Bruff, April 27, 1849. Manuscript, the Henry Huntington Library. Also see Georgia Willis Read and Ruth Gaines, eds., *Gold Rush: The Journals, Drawings, and Other Papers of J. Goldsborough Bruff, April 2, 1849–July 20, 1851* (New York: Columbia University Press, 1949), 6. Hereafter this work is cited as *GR*.
58. Sallie Hester, April 27, 1849. "The Diary of a Pioneer Girl," *San Francisco Argonaut*, September 12–19, 1925. Also see, *CWW* 1:236.
59. Margaret A. Frink, April 23, 1850. Microfilm. Yale University Collection of Western Americana, Beinecke Rare Book and Manuscript Library, New Haven, Connecticut. Also see *CWW* 2:74–76.

60. Sarah Davis, May 22, 1850. Microfilm. Yale University Collection of Western Americana, Beinecke Rare Book and Manuscript Library, New Haven, Connecticut. Also see *CWW* 2:174–175.
61. Bruff, May 8, 1849, *GR* 8.
62. Bruff, May 7, 1849, *GR* 7.
63. Frink, May 8, 1850, *CWW* 2:77.
64. Israel F. Hale, May 6, 1849, in "Diary of Trip to California in 1849," *Quarterly of the Society of California Pioneers* 2 (June 30, 1925), 61–130.
65. Franklin Starr, March 28, 1849. "Diary of a Journey to California in the Year 1849." Manuscript. Illinois State Historical Library, Springfield, Illinois, 4–6.
66. Bruff, May 17, 1849, *GR* 10.
67. Frink, May 10–12, 1850, *CWW* 2: 77–78.
68. Bruff, May 22, 1849, *GR* 10–11.
69. Bruff, May 26–28, 1849, *GR* 13–14.
70. Frink, May 14, 1850, *CWW* 2:79–81.
71. Starr, April 25, 1849, 9–11.
72. Hale, May 9–10, 1849, 61–62.
73. Davis, May 24, 1850, *CWW* 2:174–175.
74. Hale, May 15–16, 1849, 62.
75. Starr, May 5, 1849, 15.
76. Josselyn, May 15–20, 1849, 21–22.
77. Searls, May 31, 1849, 24.
78. Searls, June 3, 1849, 25–26.
79. Hale, May 17, 1849, 62.
80. Hester, May 21, 1849, *CWW* 1: 237.
81. Davis, May 31–June 3, 1850, *CWW* 2:175–176.
82. Pritchard, May 14, 1849, 2–3.
83. Starr, May 14, 1849, 21–22.
84. Hale, May 20–21, 1849, 63.
85. Hale, May 22, 1849, 63–64.
86. Searls, June 4, 1849, 26–27.
87. Davis, June 9, 1850, *CWW* 2:176.
88. Hale, May 22, 1849, 63–64.
89. Pritchard, May 15, 1849, 3–4.
90. Starr, May 15, 1849, 23–25.
91. Frink, May 15–16, 1850, *CWW* 2: 81–82.
92. Frink, May 17, 1850, *CWW* 2:82–83.
93. Bruff, June 8, 1849, *GR* 17.
94. Bruff, June 12, 1849, *GR* 19.
95. Frink, May 19, 1849, *CWW* 2:84.
96. Frink, May 20, 1850, *CWW* 2:84–85.
97. Pritchard, May 17, 1849, 5–6.

Notes—Part I

98. Pritchard, May 17, 1849, 5–6.
99. Frink May 20, 1850, *CWW* 2:86–87.
100. Pritchard, May 18, 1849, 6.
101. Hale, May 23, 1849, 64–65.
102. Starr, May 16, 1849, 26.
103. Searls, June 6, 1849, 28.
104. Searls, June 7, 1849, 29.
105. Hale, May 23, 1849, 64–65.
106. Searls, June 8, 1849, 29.
107. Searls, June 8, 1849, 29.
108. King, letter dated June 3, 1850.
109. William Edmundson, May 27, 1850, in "Diary Kept by William Edmundson, of Oskaloosa, While Crossing the Western Plains In 1850," *Annals of Iowa*, 8 (October, 1908): 516–535, 517.
110. Caleb Booth, May 21, 1850. "En Route to California." Microfilm. Yale University Collection of Western Americana, Beinecke Rare Book and Manuscript Library, New Haven, Connecticut, 1–4.
111. Lucena Parsons, June 13, 1850. Manuscript. The Department of Special Collections of the Stanford University Libraries, Stanford, California. Also see *CWW* 2:240
112. Booth, May 22, 1850, 5.
113. Booth, May 19, 1850, 4.
114. Booth, May 23, 1850, 5.
115. Edmundson, May 30, 1850, 517.
116. Parsons, June 15–16, 1850, *CWW* 2:239–240.
117. Booth, May 24, 1850, 5.
118. Parsons, June 17, 1850, *CWW* 2:239–240.
119. Edmundson, June 1, 1850, 518.
120. Edmundson, May 31, 1850, 518.
121. Edmundson, June 3, 1850, 518.
122. Parsons, June 14, 1850, *CWW* 2:239–240.
123. Edmundson, June 3, 1850, 518.
124. Booth, May 24, 1850, 5.
125. Booth, May 24, 1850, 5.
126. Edmundson, June 2, 1850, 518.
127. Booth, May 28, 1850, 6.
128. Edmundson, June 6, 1850, 519.
129. Edmundson, June 9, 1850, 520.
130. Parsons, June 19–22, 1850, *CWW* 2:241–242
131. Parsons, June 23–25, 1850, *CWW* 2:242.
132. Parsons, June 25–28, 1850, *CWW* 2:243.
133. Parsons, June 29–30, 1850, *CWW* 2:244.
134. Parsons, July 1, 1850, *CWW* 2:246.
135. Pritchard, May 18, 1849, 7.
136. Starr, May 17, 1849, 26.
137. Hale, May 24, 1849, 65.
138. Josselyn, May 23–24, 1849, 22–23.
139. Josselyn, letter to his wife, May 22, 1849, 52–53.
140. Searls, June 8, 1849, 30.
141. Searls, June 9, 1849, 30.
142. Bruff, June 17, 1849, 21.
143. Jamison, May 11, 1850, 7.
144. Frink, May 21, 1850, *CWW* 2:87.
145. Davis, June 10, 1850, *CWW* 2:177.
146. Parsons, July 2–3, 1850, 2:246.
147. Searls, June 10, 1849, 30–31.
148. Pritchard, May 26, 1849, 9.
149. Hale, May 26, 1849, 67.
150. Pritchard, May 21, 1849, 10.
151. Hale, May 25, 1849, 66.
152. Josselyn, May 25, 1849, 23.
153. Hale, May 27, 1849, 67.
154. Josselyn, May 30, 1849, 24.
155. Hale, May 30, 1849, 68.
156. Hale, May 25, 1849, 66.
157. Hale, May 26, 1849, 67.
158. Pritchard, May 26, 1849, 8.
159. Pritchard, May 26, 1849, 8.
160. Hale, May 27, 1849, 67.
161. Pritchard, May 22, 1849, 11.
162. Hale, May 26, 1849, 66–67.
163. Pritchard, May 25, 1849, 15.
164. Hale, May 26, 1849, 66–67.
165. Searls, June 10, 1849, 30–31.
166. Pritchard, May 25, 1849, 15.
167. Booth, June 4, 1850, 7.
168. Edmundson, June 12–13, 1850, 520.
169. Bruff, June 26, 1849, *GR* 24.
170. Hale, May 30, 1849, 68.
171. Hester, June 3, 1849, *CWW* 1:237.
172. Hale, May 25, 1849, 66.
173. Hester, June 3, 1849, *CWW* 1:237.
174. Bruff, June 19–25, 1849, *GR* 23–24.
175. Searls, June 13, 1849, 31–32.
176. Pritchard, May 23, 1849, 12.
177. Pritchard, May 22, 1849, 11.
178. King, letter to his mother dated June 16, 1850.
179. Jamison, May 13–15, 1850, 8.
180. Frink, May 22, 1850, *CWW* 2:88.
181. Frink, May 23, 1850, *CWW* 2:88.

182. Jamison, May 17, 1850, 8.
183. Frink, May 22–23, 1850, *CWW* 2: 88–89.
184. John Birney Hill, June 1, 1850. "Journey from St. Joseph to California." Microfilm. Yale University Collection of Western Americana, Beinecke Rare Book and Manuscript Library, New Haven, Connecticut, 3.
185. Frink, May 25, 1850, *CWW* 2:89.
186. Frink, May 22–23, 1850, *CWW* 2: 88–89.
187. Hill, May 31, 1850, 3.
188. Frink, May 26, 1850, *CWW* 2:89–90.
189. Davis, June 12–14, 1850, *CWW* 2: 177.
190. Davis, June 15, 1850, *CWW* 2:178.
191. Littleton, June 18, 1850, 12–13.
192. William Frush, June 1, 1850. Microfilm. Yale University Collection of Western Americana, Beinecke Rare Book and Manuscript Library, New Haven, Connecticut, 11.
193. Littleton, June 19–20, 1850, 13–14.
194. Frush, June 2, 1850, 12.
195. Littleton, June 21–22, 1850, 15–16.
196. Parsons, July 11–12, 1850, *CWW* 2: 247.
197. Parsons, July 13–16, 1850, *CWW* 2:248–249.
198. King, letter to his mother dated June 16, 1850.
199. Pritchard, May 23, 1849, 14–15.
200. Hale, June 1, 1849, 70.
201. Searls, June 15, 1849, 32.
202. Searls, June 17, 1849, 32–33.
203. Bruff, June 24, 1849, *GR* 23.
204. Frink, May 27, 1850, *CWW* 2:90.
205. Davis, June 17, 1850, *CWW* 2:178.
206. Littleton, June 23, 1850, 17.
207. Jamison, May 18–19, 1850, 9.
208. Parsons, July 17, 1850, *CWW* 2: 249.
209. Parsons, July 18, 1850, *CWW* 2: 250.
210. Littleton, June 24, 1850, 18.
211. Pritchard, May 26, 1849, 16.
212. Hale, June 3, 1849, 71.
213. Josselyn, June 2–3, 1849, 24–25.
214. Searls, June 19, 1849, 34.
215. Bruff, June 27, 1849, *GR* 25.
216. Frink, May 28, 1850, *CWW* 2:91–92.
217. Littleton, June 25, 1850, 19.
218. Parsons, July 19, 1850, *CWW* 2: 250.
219. Davis, June 19, 1850 *CWW* 2:178–179
220. Jamison, May 20, 1850, 9.
221. Hale, June 3, 1849, 71.
222. Searls, June 19, 1849, 34.
223. Hale, June 3, 1849, 71.
224. Hale, June 4, 1849, 72.
225. Littleton, June 26, 1850, 19.
226. Pritchard, May 27, 1849, 17.
227. Hale, June 7, 1849, 73–74.
228. Searls, June 20, 1849, 34.
229. Bruff, June 30, 1849, *GR* 27.
230. Frink, June 1–2, 1850, *CWW* 2:94.
231. Littleton, June 27, 1850, 19–20.
232. Davis, June 22, 1850, *CWW* 2: 179–180.
233. Pritchard, May 26, 1849, 16.
234. Starr, June 1, 1849, 49.
235. Hale, June 5, 1849, 72.
236. Hale, June 7, 1849, 74.
237. Frink, June 3, 1850, *CWW* 2:94.
238. Wellenkamp, May 31–June 2, 1850, 2.
239. Hill, June 6, 1850, 4.
240. Littleton, June 30, 1850, 22–23.
241. Jamison, May 21, 1850, 9.
242. Davis, June 25, 1850, *CWW* 2:180.
243. Parsons, July 22, 1850, 2:251–252.
244. Jamison, May 21, 1850, 9.
245. Hale, June 8–9, 1849, 75.
246. Searls, June 22, 1849, 35.
247. Starr, June 2, 1849, 50.
248. Parsons, July 22, 1850, *CWW* 2: 251–252.
249. Pritchard, May 29–30, 1849, 19–20.
250. Searls, June 8, 1849, 29.
251. Josselyn, June 6, 1849, 26.
252. Josselyn, June 8, 1849, 26.
253. Parsons, July 24–26, 1850, *CWW* 2:252–253.
254. Pritchard, May 29, 1849, 19.
255. Hale, June 10, 1849, 76.
256. Searls, June 23, 1849, 35–36.
257. Frink, June 4, 1850, *CWW* 2:95.
258. Pritchard, May 31, 1849,21.
259. Starr, June 4, 1849, 52–53.
260. Hale, June 11, 1849, 77–78.
261. Searls, June 24, 1849, 36.
262. Frink, June 5, 1850, *CWW* 2:95.
263. Littleton, July 1, 1850, 23.

264. Parsons, July 27, 1850, *CWW* 2: 253.
265. Bruff, July 4, 1849, *GR* 29–30.
266. Jamison, May 24, 1850, 10.
267. Wellenkamp, June 4, 1850, 2.
268. Booth, June 15–17, 1850, 10.
269. Edmundson, June 24–25, 1850, 522.
270. Parsons, July 27, 1850, *CWW* 2: 253.
271. Starr, June 5, 1849, 54–55.
272. Pritchard, June 1, 1849, 22–23.
273. Josselyn, June 9, 1849, 26–27.
274. Searls, June 25, 1849, 37. The Robidoux family was French Canadian in origin but had lived in the environs of St. Louis and around St. Joseph, Missouri, before striking out onto the plains and into the Rocky Mountains to establish a far-flung Indian trade business. The keeper of the Scotts Bluff post was probably one of several Robidoux brothers to be in the business.
275. Bruff, July 6–7, 1849, *GR* 30–31.
276. Littleton, July 2, 1850, 24.
277. Davis, June 28, 1850, *CWW* 2:180.
278. Jamison, May 27, 1850, 11.
279. Wellenkamp, June 5, 1850, 3.
280. Parsons, July 29, 1850, *CWW* 2: 254.
281. Pritchard, June 2, 1849, 23.
282. Hale, June 12–13, 1849, 78–79.
283. Bruff, July 7, 1849, *GR* 31.
284. Littleton, July 3–4, 1850, 25.
285. Bruff, July 8, 1849, *GR* 32–33.
286. Bruff, July 9, 1849, *GR* 34–35.
287. King, letter to his brother [Charles] C. S. King, dated June 11, 1850.
288. Pritchard, June 4, 1849, 24–27.
289. Pritchard, June 4, 1849, 26.
290. Hale, June 15, 1849, 80.
291. Hester, June 19, 1849, *CWW* 1: 238.
292. Searls, June 27, 1849, 38.
293. Searls, June 28, 1849, 38–39.
294. Bruff, July 9, 1849, *GR* 35.
295. Bruff, July 10, 1849, *GR* 36–38.
296. Jamison, May 30, 1850, 11.
297. Frink, June 8, 1850, *CWW* 2:96–97.
298. Frush, June 10–11, 1850, 20–21.
299. Frush, June 18, 1850, 26.
300. Booth, June 20, 1850, 11.
301. Booth, June 21–22, 1850, 12.
302. Booth, June 23, 1850, 12.
303. Edmundson, June 29–30, 1850, 522–523.
304. Parsons, August 1–2, 1850, *CWW* 2:255–256.
305. Parsons, August 3, 1850, *CWW* 2: 257.
306. King, letter to his mother from near Fort Laramie, June 16, 1850.

Part II. From Fort Laramie to Fort Hall and Salt Lake City

1. Jamison, June 3, 1850, 12
2. Pritchard, June 5, 1849, 29.
3. Hale, June 16, 1849, 80.
4. Searls, June 29, 1849, 39.
5. Bruff, July 12, 1849, *GR* 40.
6. Frink, June 10, 1850, *CWW* 2:97–98.
7. Booth, June 23, 1850, 13.
8. Littleton, July 6, 1850, 26–27.
9. Parsons, August 6, 1850, 2:257.
10. Hester, June 21, 1849, *CWW* 1:238.
11. Pritchard, June 6, 1849, 29.
12. Searls, July 2, 1849, 40–41.
13. Starr, June 11, 1849, 64.
14. Searls, July 3, 1849, 42.
15. Littleton, July 7, 1850, 28.
16. Pritchard, June 7–8, 1849, 31.
17. Josselyn, June 16, 1849, 29.
18. Hale, June 20, 1849, 81–83.
19. Bruff, July 13, 1849, *GR* 41–43.
20. Bruff, July 14, 1849, *GR* 43.
21. Bruff, July 15, 1849, *GR* 43–44.
22. Frink, June 11–12, 1850, *CWW* 2: 98–99.
23. Hill, June 16, 1850, 5.
24. Frush, June 22, 1850, 30.
25. Booth, June 25, 1850, 13–14.
26. Parsons, August 7, 1850, *CWW* 2: 257.
27. Parsons, August 9–10, 1850, *CWW* 2:258.
28. Pritchard, June 9, 1849, 31.
29. Starr, June 15, 1849, 69–70.
30. Josselyn, June 18–19, 1849, 29.
31. Hale, June 21, 1849, 83.
32. Bruff, July 16, 1849, *GR* 44.
33. Bruff, July 17, 1849, *GR* 45.
34. Bruff, July 17, 1849, *GR* 45.
35. Frink, June 13–15, 1850, *CWW* 2: 99–100

36. Edmundson, July 8, 1850, 523–524.
37. Littleton, July 10, 1850, 29.
38. Littleton, July 11, 1850, 30.
39. Parsons, August 11–12, 1850, *CWW* 2:259.
40. Parsons, August 13, 1850, *CWW* 2:259.
41. Parsons, August 14–16, 1850, *CWW* 2:260.
42. Pritchard, June 10, 1849, 31–32.
43. Josselyn, June 19–20, 1849, 29–30.
44. Hester, June 21, 1849, *CWW* 1:238.
45. Hale, June 22, 1849, 83–84.
46. Searls, July 3, 1849, 42–43.
47. Searls, July 3–4, 1849, 42–43.
48. Starr, July 16–17, 1849, 73–74.
49. Bruff, July 19–20, 1849, *GR* 46–47.
50. Wellenkamp, June 14–16, 1850, 3.
51. Frink, June 16, 1850, *CWW* 2:100.
52. Edmundson, July 9, 1850, 524.
53. Pritchard, June 13, 1849, 32–33.
54. Josselyn, June 23, 1849, 30–31.
55. Hale, June 25, 1849, 85.
56. Searls, July 5, 1849, 43.
57. Searls, July 6, 1849, 44.
58. Searls, July 8, 1849, 45.
59. Searls, July 9, 1849, 46.
60. Bruff, July 21, 1849, *GR* 48.
61. Pritchard, June 14, 1849, 33–34.
62. Bruff, July 22, 1849, *GR* 49–50.
63. Searls, July 10, 1849, 47.
64. Bruff, July 23, 1849, *GR* 50–51.
65. Bruff, July 24, 1849, *GR* 51.
66. Jamison, June 5, 1850, 12.
67. Frink, June 17, 1850, *CWW* 2:101.
68. Edmundson, July 11, 1850, 524.
69. Edmundson, July 12, 1850, 524.
70. Davis, July 17, 1850, 2:183.
71. Parsons, August 18–19, 1850, *CWW* 2:261.
72. Parsons, August 20–21, 1850, *CWW* 2:261–262.
73. Pritchard, June 15, 1849, 34.
74. Hale, June 26–27, 1849, 85.
75. Hester, July 2, 1849, *CWW* 1:239.
76. Searls, July 11, 1849, 47.
77. Searls, July 12, 1849, 48.
78. Searls, July 13, 1849, 49.
79. Bruff, July 26, 1849, *GR* 52–53.
80. Jamison, June 6, 1850, 12.
81. Frink, June 18, 1850, *CWW* 2:101–102.
82. Wellenkamp, June 18, 1850, 3–4.
83. Hill, June 25, 1850, 7.
84. Davis, July 19, 1850, *CWW* 2:184.
85. Littleton, July 22, 1850, 32.
86. Parsons, August 22–23, 1850, *CWW* 2:263.
87. Pritchard, June 15, 1849, 34.
88. Starr, June 21, 1849, 80–81.
89. Hale, June 27, 1849, 85–86.
90. Hester, July 2, 1849, 1:239.
91. Searls, July 13, 1849, 49.
92. Bruff, July 26, 1850, *GR* 52–53.
93. Frink, June 20, 1850, *CWW* 2:102.
94. Littleton, July 22, 1850, 32.
95. Wellenkamp, June 18, 1850, 4.
96. Pritchard, June 16–17, 1849, 34–35.
97. Josselyn, June 25, 1849, 31.
98. Searls, July 15, 1849, 50.
99. Bruff, July 27, 1850, *GR* 54.
100. Bruff, July 27–29, 1850, *GR* 56–57.
101. Jamison, June 7, 1850, 12.
102. Wellenkamp, June 20, 1850, 4.
103. Frink, June 21, 1850, *CWW* 2:103.
104. Frush, July 1, 1850, 38.
105. Parsons, August 24–26, 1850, *CWW* 2:264.
106. Pritchard June 16, 1849, 35.
107. Starr, June 24, 1849, 82–83.
108. Hale, June 30, 1849, 87.
109. Searls, July 19, 1849, 50–51.
110. Bruff, July 29, 1849, *GR* 57.
111. Frink, June 22, 1850, *CWW* 2:103–104.
112. Parsons, August 24, 1850, *CWW* 2:264–265.
113. Wellenkamp, June 21–22, 1850, 4.
114. Pritchard, June 17, 1849, 37.
115. Starr, June 27–28, 1849, 86–88.
116. Hale, July 1–3, 1849, 87–88.
117. Searls, July 19, 1849, 52.
118. Bruff, August 1, 1849, *GR* 60.
119. Jamison, June 10, 1850, 13.
120. Wellenkamp, June 23, 1850, 4.
121. Frink, June 23–24, 1850, *CWW* 2:105–106.
122. Frush, July 3–6, 1850, 40–41.
123. Edmundson, July 19, 1850, 525.
124. Littleton, July 29, 1850, 35–36.
125. Parsons, August 30, 1850, *CWW* 2:266.
126. Pritchard, June 19, 1849, 38.
127. Starr, June 29–30, 1849, 88–89.
128. Josselyn, July 1, 1849, 32.
129. Searls, July 19–20, 1849, 52–53.
130. Hester, July 4, 1849, *CWW* 1:239.

Notes—Part III

131. Bruff, August 2, 1849, *GR* 62.
132. Bruff, August 3, 1849, *GR* 63.
133. Bruff, August 3, 1849, *GR* 66–67.
134. Jamison, June 11, 1850, 13.
135. Frink, June 25, 1850, *CWW* 2:106.
136. Davis, July 28, 1850, *CWW* 2:186.
137. Littleton, July 30, 1850, 36–37.
138. Pritchard, June 20–21, 1849, 39.
139. Starr, June 30–July 1, 1849, 90–92.
140. Hale, July 6, 1849, 88.
141. Searls, July 22, 1849, 53–54.
142. Bruff, August 4, 1849, *GR* 70–71.
143. Wellenkamp, June 25–26, 1850, 4.
144. Frink, June 26–27, 1850, *CWW* 2:106–108.
145. Hill, July 4, 1850, 8.
146. Davis, July 29–30, 1850, *CWW* 2:186–187
147. Josselyn, July 3–7, 1849, 32–33.
148. Jamison, June 12–15, 1850, 13–14.
149. Littleton, August 1–4, 1850, 37–40.
150. Parsons, September 4–14, 1850, *CWW* 2:266–269.
151. Pritchard, June 22, 1849, 40.
152. Starr, July 3–6, 1849, 95–99.
153. Hale, July 6–7, 1849, 88–89.
154. Searls, July 23, 1849, 54.
155. Bruff, August 6, 1849, *GR* 73.
156. Pritchard, June 22, 1849, 41.
157. Pritchard, June 22, 1849, 41.
158. Starr, July 6–7, 1849, 100–101.
159. Wellenkamp, June 27, 1850, 4.
160. Frink, June 27, 1850, *CWW* 2:108.
161. Frush, July 12, 1850, 44.
162. Frink, June 28, 1850, *CWW* 2:109.
163. Frink, July 1, 1849, *CWW* 2:110.
164. Hale, July 8–9, 1849, 89.
165. Starr, July 7–8, 1849, 101–104.
166. Pritchard, June 24, 1849, 42.
167. Searls, July 25–26, 1849, 56.
168. Bruff, August 7, 1849, *GR* 74.
169. Bruff, August 7–8, 1849, *GR* 75–77.
170. Pritchard, June 25, 1849, 43–44.
171. Hale, July 12–13, 1849, 90–91.
172. Searls, July 27, 1849, 56.
173. Bruff, August 9, 1849, *GR* 81–83.
174. Bruff, August 10, 1849, *GR* 85–86.
175. Frink, July 3–4, 1850, *CWW* 2:110–111.
176. Hill, July 6–11, 1850, 8–9.
177. Frush, July 15, 1850, 46.
178. Davis, August 1–6, 1850, *CWW* 2:186–189.
179. Wellenkamp, June 28–29, 1850, 4.
180. Pritchard, June 25, 1849, 43–44.
181. Starr, July 10, 1849, 106–108.
182. Hale, July 12–13, 1849, 90–91.
183. Bruff, August 11, 1849, *GR* 86.
184. Bruff, August 13–15, 1849, *GR* 89–90.
185. Pritchard, June 27, 1849, 45.
186. Pritchard, June 28, 1849, 45.
187. Hale, July 16–17, 1849, 92.
188. Searls, August 5, 1849, 56–57.
189. Bruff, August 12, 1849, *GR* 87–88.
190. Frink, July 5, 1850, *CWW* 2:112.
191. Frink, July 6–8, 1850, *CWW* 2:113.
192. Hester, July 29, 1849, *CWW* 1:239.
193. Pritchard, June 29, 1849, 46.
194. Starr, July 13, 1849, 112–114.
195. Starr, July 14, 1849, 115–116.
196. Hale, July 19–20, 1849, 93.
197. Searls, August 5, 1849, 57–58.
198. Bruff, August 17, 1849, *GR* 92.
199. Hill, July 15, 1850, 9.
200. Frink, July 9, 1850, *CWW* 2:114.
201. Frush, July 22, 1850, 51.
202. Bruff, August 17, 1849, *GR* 94.
203. Bruff, August 18, 1849, *GR* 94–95.
204. Searls, August 5, 1849, 57–58.
205. Searls, August 12, 1849, 58–59.
206. Frink, July 8, 1850, *CWW* 2:115.
207. Frink, July 9, 1850, *CWW* 2:115–116.
208. Wellenkamp, July 4–9, 1850, 5–6.
209. Pritchard, June 30–July 1, 1849, 48.
210. Pritchard, July 2, 1849, 48–49.
211. Hale, July 22, 1849, 94.
212. Bruff, August 18, 1849, *GR* 97–99.
213. Bruff, August 20–21, 1849, *GR* 100–101.
214. Frink, July 10, 1850, *CWW* 2:117.
215. Pritchard, July 2, 1849, 49.
216. Pritchard, July 3, 1849, 49.
217. Hale, July 23, 1849, 94.
218. Bruff, August 24, 1849, *GR* 104.
219. Hill, July 18, 1850, 10.
220. Frink, July 12, 1850, *CWW* 2:117–118.
221. Frush, July 26, 1850, 55.
222. Josselyn, July 8–14, 1849, 34–35.
223. Jamison, June 15–18, 1850, 14.
224. Edmundson, July 28–August 1, 1850, 526.

225. Littleton, August 6, 1850, 42.
226. Littleton, August 8, 1850, 43.
227. Davis, August 9–16, 1850, *CWW* 2:187–188.
228. Parsons, September 18–19, 1850, *CWW* 2:270.
229. Jamison, June 19–20, 1850, 14–15.
230. Littleton, August 11, 1850, 44–45.
231. Edmundson, August 9, 1850, 526–527.
232. Davis, August 19–20, 1850, *CWW* 2:191.
233. Parsons, September 22–23, 1850, *CWW* 2:271.

Part III. From Fort Hall and Salt Lake to the Sierra Nevadas

1. Josselyn, July 16–20, 1849, 35–36.
2. Booth, July 28–August 4, 1850, 14–15.
3. Littleton, August 20–24, 1850, 46–47.
4. Davis, August 22–29, 1850, *CWW* 2:193–194
5. Jamison, June 26–29, 1850, 15–16.
6. Littleton, August 26–29, 1850, 48.
7. Pritchard, July 3–4, 1849, 51.
8. Hale, July 24, 1849, 94–95.
9. Bruff, August 25, 1849, *GR* 108.
10. Hill, July 19, 1850, 10.
11. Pritchard, July 5, 1849, 51.
12. Hale, July 25, 1849, 95–96.
13. Bruff, August 26, 1849, *GR* 111.
14. Hill, July 20, 1850, 10.
15. Frink, July 13, 1850, *CWW* 2:119.
16. Hale, July 26, 1849, 96.
17. Pritchard, July 6, 1849, 52.
18. Hale, July 27, 1849, 97.
19. Hale, July 28, 1849, 97–98.
20. Bruff, August 28, 1849, *GR* 116.
21. Frink, July 14–15, 1850, *CWW* 2:120.
22. Hill, July 22, 1850, 11.
23. Pritchard, July 8, 1849, 53.
24. Hale, July 29, 1849, 98.
25. Hester, August 3, 1849, 1:239.
26. Bruff, August 29, 1849, *GR* 119–120.
27. Wellenkamp, July 11, 1850, 6.
28. Frink, July 17, 1850, *CWW* 2:120–121.
29. Hill, July 24, 1850, 11.
30. Littleton, August 29, 1850, 49.
31. Pritchard, July 9–11, 1849, 54.
32. Hale, July 30–31, 1849, 99.
33. Hale, August 2–3, 1849, 100.
34. Hester, August 18, 1849, *CWW* 1:239–240.
35. Bruff, August 29–31, 1849, *GR* 120–122.
36. Wellenkamp, July 13–14, 1850, 6.
37. Frink, July 19, 1850, *CWW* 2:122.
38. Frink, July 20–21, 1850, *CWW* 2:122–123.
39. Hill, July 25–30, 1850, 11–12.
40. Littleton, August 30–31, 1850, 50.
41. Littleton, September 2, 1850, 51.
42. Booth, August 14–19, 1850, 17–18.
43. Davis, September 3–5, 1850, *CWW* 2:195.
44. Davis, September 7–8, 1850 *CWW* 2:196.
45. Davis, September 9, 1850, *CWW* 2:196.
46. Hale, August 5–7, 1849, 101–103.
47. Hester, August 20, 1849, *CWW* 1:240.
48. Pritchard, July 12–13, 1849, 56.
49. Hale, August 9, 1849, 104.
50. Searls, August 19, 1849, 59–60.
51. Bruff, September 3, 1849, *GR* 124.
52. Bruff, September 3–4, 1849, *GR* 125.
53. Starr, August 5, 1849, 125–130.
54. Jamison, July 1–3, 1850, 16.
55. Frink, July 22–23, 1850, *CWW* 2:123–124.
56. Booth, August 20–22, 1850, 18.
57. Littleton, September 4, 1850, 52.
58. Davis, September 15–17, 1850, *CWW* 2:198.
59. Bruff, September 5, 1849, *GR* 126.
60. Pritchard, July 14–15, 1849, 57–58.
61. Josselyn, August 4, 1849, 40.
62. Hale, August 10, 1849, 104–105.
63. Bruff, September 7, 1849, *GR* 127–128.
64. Hill, August 2, 1850, 13.
65. Littleton, September 6, 1850, 53.
66. Edmundson, September 3, 1850, 531.
67. Pritchard, July 18–19, 1849, 60–61.
68. Frink, July 25, 1850, *CWW* 2:124.
69. Hale, August 11–12, 1849, 105–106.
70. Frink, July 27, 1850, *CWW* 2:125–126.

Notes—Part III

71. Wellenkamp, July 20, 1850, 7.
72. Littleton, September 10, 1850, 55.
73. Starr, August 6, 1849, 134–135.
74. Hale, August 13, 1849, 106–107.
75. Frink, July 29–31, 1850, *CWW* 2:126.
76. Hill, August 6, 1850, 14.
77. Hester, August 25, 1849, *CWW* 1:240.
78. Pritchard, July 20, 1849, 62.
79. Littleton, September 15–16, 1850, 57.
80. Hale, August 14, 1849, 107–108.
81. Bruff, September 8, 1849, *GR* 129–130.
82. Frink, August 2, 1850, *CWW* 2:127.
83. Searls, August 19, 1849, 59–60.
84. Davis, September 17, 1850, 2:198.
85. Bruff, September 9, 1849, *GR* 131–132.
86. Starr, August 8–10, 1849, 135–138.
87. Frink, August 4–5, 1850, *CWW* 2:127–128.
88. Wellenkamp, July 21, 1850, 7.
89. Davis, September 19, 1850, 2:199.
90. Hale, August 15, 1849, 108–109.
91. Pritchard, July 22, 1849, 62–63.
92. Hale, August 16, 1849, 109–110.
93. Wellenkamp, July 22, 1850, 7.
94. Jamison, July 7, 1850, 17.
95. Hale, August 17, 1849, 110.
96. Bruff, September 12, 1849, *GR* 135–136.
97. Starr, August 15, 1849, 151–153.
98. Frink, August 6, 1850, *CWW* 2:128–129.
99. Hale, August 18, 1849, 111.
100. Bruff, September 14, 1849, *GR* 139.
101. Frink, August 7, 1850, *CWW* 2:129.
102. Davis, September 20–21, 1850, *CWW* 2:201.
103. Hale, August 20, 1849, 112–113.
104. Booth, August 26–31, 1850, 19–20.
105. Josselyn, August 12, 1849, 41.
106. Bruff, September 14, 1849, *GR* 139–140.
107. Josselyn, August 13, 1849, 42.
108. Hale, August 21, 1849, 113–114.
109. Bruff, September 18, 1849, *GR* 141–142.
110. Starr, August 16, 1849, 153–155.
111. Wellenkamp, July 23, 1850, 8.
112. Edmundson, September 8, 1850, 532.
113. Josselyn, August 13, 1849, 43.
114. Hale, August 22, 1849, 114.
115. Bruff, September 19, 1849, *GR* 145–146.
116. Josselyn, August 13–14, 1849, 43–44.
117. Bruff, September 20, 1849, *GR* 147–148.
118. Hale, August 23, 1849, 114–115.
119. Bruff, September 21, 1849, *GR* 151–152.
120. Josselyn, August 15–17, 1849, 44–45.
121. Hale, August 24, 1849, 116.
122. Bruff, September 21, 1849, *GR* 152.
123. Hale, August 25, 1849, 117.
124. Bruff, September 23, 1849, *GR* 156.
125. Hale, August 26, 1849, 118.
126. Josselyn, August 18–21, 1849, 45.
127. Hale, August 27–28, 1849, 119–120.
128. Bruff, September 24, 1849, *GR* 157–158.
129. Bruff, September 25, 1849, *GR* 158–159.
130. Bruff, September 25–26, 1849, *GR* 161–162.
131. Hale, August 29–30, 1849, 122–123.
132. Bruff, September 27, 1849, *GR* 164.
133. Hale, August 29–31, 1849, 122–123.
134. Bruff, September 29, 1849, *GR* 167.
135. Josselyn, August 22–24, 1849, 45–46.
136. Hale, September 2–4, 1849, 124–126.
137. Bruff, September 30–October 1, 1849, *GR* 169–171.
138. Pritchard, July 21–22, 1849, 63.
139. Pritchard, July 23–24, 1849, 64.
140. Starr, August 12–13, 1849, 141–143.
141. Wellenkamp, August 24–27, 1850, 8.
142. Frink, August 8, 1850, *CWW* 2:130.
143. Wellenkamp, July 28, 1850, 8.
144. Jamison, July 11–13, 1850, 22.

145. Frink, August 9, 1850, *CWW* 2: 131.
146. Wellenkamp, July 29, 1850, 8.
147. Edmundson, September 13, 1850, 532.
148. Littleton, September 18, 1850, 58.
149. Booth, September 5–6, 1850, 21.
150. Frink, August 10, 1850, *CWW* 2:131–132.
151. Starr, August 18–19, 1849, 162–164.
152. Wellenkamp, July 30–August 1, 1850, 8.
153. Frink, August 11, 1850, *CWW* 2:132–134.
154. Frink, August 12–13, 1850, *CWW* 2:135.
155. Davis, September 27–28, 1850, *CWW* 2:201.
156. Pritchard, August 25, 1849, 64–65.
157. Searls, August 26, 1849, 60–61.
158. Starr, August 22, 1849, 166–167.
159. Wellenkamp, August 2, 1850, 9.
160. Frink, August 14, 1850, *CWW* 2:135–136.
161. Littleton, September 19, 1850, 58.
162. Pritchard, July 25, 1849, 65.
163. Frink, August 15, 1850, *CWW* 2:137.
164. Davis, September 29, 1850, *CWW* 2:201.
165. Starr, August 26, 1849, 171–173.
166. Hester, September 4, 1849, *CWW* 1:240–241.
167. Littleton, September 20, 1850, 59–60.
168. Starr, August 23, 1849, 174–176.
169. Littleton, September 20, 1850, 59–60.
170. Davis, October 1, 1850, 2:202.
171. Littleton, September 23–24, 1850, 60–61.
172. Hester, September 7, 1849, *CWW* 1:241.
173. Hester, September 14, 1849, *CWW* 1:242.
174. Littleton, September 27, 1850, 62.
175. Littleton, September 28–29, 1850, 63.
176. Pritchard, July 26, 1849, 66.
177. Jamison, July 14, 1850, 22.
178. Wellenkamp, August 3, 1850, 9.
179. Searls, September 3, 1849, 61–62.
180. Pritchard, July 26–27, 1849, 66–67.
181. Frink, August 16, 1850, *CWW* 2:138–139.
182. Edmundson, September 18, 1850, 533.
183. Pritchard, July 27, 1849, 67.
184. Wellenkamp, August 3, 1850, 9.
185. Frink, August 16, 1850, *CWW* 2:139–140.
186. Pritchard, July 27, 1849, 68.
187. Wellenkamp August 4, 1850, 9.
188. Frink, August 17, 1850, *CWW* 2:140–141.
189. Pritchard, July 28, 1849, 68–69.
190. Searls, September 23, 1849, 62.
191. Frink, August 17, 1850, *CWW* 2:140–141.
192. Jamison, July 15–17, 1850, 22–23.
193. Wellenkamp, August 5–6, 1850, 9–10.
194. Edmundson, September 18, 1850, 533.
195. Pritchard, July 28, 1850, 69.
196. Frink, August 18, 1850, *CWW* 2:141–142.
197. Wellenkamp, August 7, 1850, 10.
198. Pritchard, July 30, 1849, 70.
199. Frink, August 19, 1850, *CWW* 2:142–143.
200. Wellenkamp, August 8–10, 1850.
201. Frink, August 20, 1850, *CWW* 2:143–144.
202. Pritchard, August 1–2, 1849, 72.
203. Wellenkamp, August 11–12, 1850, 10.
204. Frink, August 21, 1850, *CWW* 2:144–145.
205. Frink, August 24–26, 1850, *CWW* 2:146–147.
206. Jamison, July 18, 1850, 23.
207. Edmundson, September 26, 1850, 534.
208. Davis, October 9, 1850, *CWW* 2:202.
209. Pritchard, August 3, 1849, 73.
210. Pritchard, August 4, 1849, 74.
211. Searls, September 30, 1849, 62.
212. Frink, August 27–28, 1850, *CWW* 2:147–148.
213. Wellenkamp, August 13, 1850, 12.
214. Frink, August 28, 1850, *CWW* 2:149–150.

215. Edmundson, October 2, 1850, 534.
216. Davis, October 10–11, 1850, *CWW* 2:203.
217. Pritchard, August 5, 1849, 75.
218. Frink, August 30, 1850, *CWW* 2:152–153.
219. Jamison, July 19–20, 1850, 23.
220. Pritchard, August 7, 1849, 77.
221. Wellenkamp, August 14, 1850, 10.
222. Frink, August 31, 1850, *CWW* 2:153–154.
223. Edmundson, October 4, 1850, 535.
224. Pritchard, August 9, 1849, 79.
225. Frink, September 3, 1850, *CWW* 2:155–156.
226. Davis, October 12, 1850, *CWW* 2:204.
227. Searls, October 1, 1849, 63.
228. Jamison, July 21–25, 1850, 24.
229. Frink, September 3, 1850. *CWW* 2:156–157.

Epilogue

1. King, letter to his brother James from Sacramento, August 28, 1850.

Index

Alexander & Hall 28–30
American Falls 162, 198–201
American Fur Company 99, 101–102
Ancient Bluffs 84–85
Ash Hollow 74–75, 78–85

Bear River 161–165, 167–168, 170, 172–173, 187, 193, 195–197
Bear River Mountains 148, 165, 167
Bellevue, Nebraska 10
Big Meadow 246–252
Big Sandy River 148–155, 158
Black Rock Desert 233–234
Black Rock Spring 235–238
Black Hills 91, 105, 107, 109–115, 118
Black's Fork 154–156
Blue River 15, 17, 19, 23, 25, 27, 35–40, 44
Booth, Caleb 5, 48–51, 62, 88, 103, 110, 114, 153, 195–196, 210, 216, 230, 247
Bruff, Joseph Goldsborough 5, 7, 30–31, 33–34, 42–43, 56, 62–63, 71, 75, 79, 88–89, 91, 94–95, 97, 101–102, 104, 109, 113, 116–117, 121, 123, 126–128, 131, 134, 136–139, 142, 147, 151, 158, 164, 166–167, 170–171, 173, 175–178, 181, 183, 199–200, 203, 208–209, 215, 217, 224–225, 228–229, 232–234, 238–239, 241–243

Cache Cave 187–189
Carlin Canyon 217–219, 230
Carson, Kit 103, 122, 185, 263
Carson Canyon 266–268
Carson River 253–255, 260–264, 267

Castle Rock 84–85
Cheyenne Indians 41, 82
Chimney Rock 85–90
cholera 14, 21–22, 26, 32, 36, 39, 51–56, 63, 67–69, 78, 80, 88, 95, 97, 102, 104, 148, 161, 248
City of Rocks 193, 198, 204–206, 211
Columbia River 181–182
Council Bluffs (Kanesville), Iowa 9–11, 13, 48–50
Courthouse Rock 85–87
Crow Indians 93, 161, 201

Davis, Sarah 5, 31, 36, 39–40, 57, 66–67, 71, 76, 79, 93, 129, 133, 148, 153, 168, 188, 190, 196, 197, 211, 217, 225–226, 230, 253, 256, 269, 272
Deer Creek 115–120, 122
Devil's Gate 124, 130, 132–138
Digger Indians 203, 212, 215, 220, 226, 264
Donner Party 15, 246, 257
Dry Sandy River 147–148
Duncan's Ferry 33–34

Edmundson, William 5, 48–51, 90, 104, 117, 122, 128, 144, 153, 188, 190, 219, 233, 250, 260, 263, 267
Elkhorn River 51

Farris, Tom 12–13
Forks of the Platte 58, 70, 72, 74
Fort Bridger 146, 148–149, 151, 153–156, 158, 161–162, 186–187
Fort Hall 147, 153, 158, 161–162, 169, 174, 177–185, 198, 224

Index

Fort Kearney 33–34, 44, 47–48, 54–59, 63, 66–67, 69, 97–98, 106
Fort Laramie 48, 54, 56–57, 69, 74, 76, 79–80, 83, 93–105, 107–111, 139–140, 156
Fort Leavenworth 10, 27–28, 144
Forty Mile Desert 258
Fremont, John C. 158, 215, 270
Fremont's Peak 147, 152
Frenchmen (traders) 161, 165, 171
Frink, Margaret 5, 30, 32–34, 41–44, 57, 65–66, 71, 75, 79, 81, 85, 87, 102, 109, 113, 117, 122, 128, 132, 137, 139, 142, 148, 152, 160–161, 167, 173, 176, 179, 182, 185, 203, 209, 216, 221–222, 226, 228–229, 246–250, 252–253, 260–265, 268–269, 272–273

Goose Creek 204–211
Goose Lake 231, 233, 244
Grand Island 45–46, 54–57, 65
Grant, Captain 183–185
Great Boiling Spring 237–238
Great Plains 14–15, 21–22, 31, 59, 83
Great Salt Lake 98, 102, 146, 155, 160–162, 170, 176, 186, 189, 191, 193, 196, 204
Green River 146, 148–167

Hale, Israel 5, 32, 36–37, 40, 46, 55, 59, 60–61, 70, 74, 77–78, 81–82, 85–87, 94, 99, 101, 108, 112, 116, 120, 125, 130, 134, 139, 141, 150, 157–158, 162, 165, 170–172, 181, 183, 199, 201–202, 207, 211–212, 218, 221–222, 224, 227, 230–233, 235, 239–240, 242, 244
Ham's Fork 154–156
Harris, Black 10, 26
Hasting's Cut-off 217
Hester, Sallie 5, 30, 38, 63, 99, 119, 130, 134, 147, 177, 205, 208, 223, 255–257
High Rock Canyon 240–243
Hill, John Birney 66, 82, 114, 133, 153, 167, 176, 185, 199, 201, 203, 205, 209, 219, 223
Hudson Bay Company 169, 182–183, 185
Hudspeth (Emigrant's or Myers) Cut-off 177–180, 185, 193, 198, 202–203, 205, 215
Humboldt (St. Mary's) River 103, 172, 178, 202, 206–228, 230, 233, 247

Humboldt Sink 219, 229–231, 245, 250–255, 258–259

Ice Spring 138–140
Independence, Missouri 9–12, 15, 17–19, 23, 25–27, 30, 44
Independence Rock 124, 130–134, 138

Jamison, Samuel 5, 15, 19–20, 56, 65, 72, 82, 88, 93, 102, 107, 128, 131, 137, 148, 153–155, 187, 189, 195–197, 227, 247, 262, 265, 270–272
Josselyn, Amos 5, 15, 19, 20–21, 24–25, 38, 55, 59–60, 74, 84, 91, 112, 116, 119, 125, 135, 146, 153–154, 187, 193, 217–218, 230–231, 233, 235, 237, 239, 243

Kansas River 23–25, 56
King, John Nevin 6, 28–29, 47, 64, 97, 105, 274

Laramie Fork 98, 101–102, 105
Laramie Peak 91, 108, 114
Lassen, Peter 182
Lassen Cut-off 230–234, 238, 244–246
Lee Springs 147
Little Blue River 15, 36–41, 44
Little Sandy River 147–149
Littleton, Micajah 6, 17, 23–24, 67–68, 72–73, 76, 78–79, 82, 87, 93–94, 110, 112, 118, 133–134, 144, 149, 153–155, 188–190, 195–197, 210, 219, 222–223, 252, 255–257
Loup Fork 44, 51

Mineral Springs 127–128
Missouri River 10, 15, 23, 30–33, 35–36, 45, 48, 51, 57, 74, 94, 98, 143
Mormons 48, 56, 70, 116, 119, 121–122, 137, 139, 146, 154, 158, 187, 195, 217, 225, 267
mosquitoes 40, 63, 82–83, 95, 164, 182, 185, 198–200, 203, 223
Mud Lake 241–243

North (fork of) Platte River 70–71, 74, 76, 79–80, 82, 84, 87, 107–108, 115–116, 118, 122–123, 138

Omaha Indians 50
Oregon Battalion 120, 125, 166
Otoe Indians 50

Index

Pacific Springs 124, 135, 141–144, 146–149
Panack Indians 173, 181–182
Parsons, Lucena 6, 48–54, 57, 68, 72, 76, 82–83, 85, 88, 90, 93, 105, 110, 114, 118, 129, 133, 138–139, 144, 153, 155–156, 189, 191
Pawnee Indians 26, 38–39, 41–43, 50–51, 54, 57, 77, 81
Platte River 36–37, 41–42, 44–47, 51–55, 60, 63, 65–66, 69, 75–77, 85, 88, 90, 97–99, 104, 128, 133
Port Neuf River 180–181, 198–199
Pottowatamie Indians 24–26, 48
prairie dogs 61–62
Pritchard, James A. 6, 15, 23, 25, 39–40, 44–45, 54, 58–62, 64, 70, 74–75, 78, 81, 83, 85–86, 91, 94, 98–99, 107, 111, 115, 117, 119, 123, 125–126, 130, 133, 135–136, 138–140, 146, 149–151, 157, 159, 163, 165, 169–171, 174, 177, 180–183, 198–200, 202, 204, 206, 214, 221, 223, 226, 245, 251, 253, 258–263, 265, 267, 269–272

Rabbit Hole Spring 234–237
Raft River 201–205
Rattlesnake Mountains 136
Red Hills 107, 112
Red Lake 269, 272
Robidoux 91–93
Rocky Mountains 71, 93–94, 107, 133, 135, 139, 142–143

St. Joseph, Missouri 9–13, 25, 27, 29–35, 41, 44, 63, 103, 143
St. Louis, Missouri 10, 15, 28, 52, 70, 85
Salt Lake City 146, 148, 152–153, 161–162, 186–187, 190, 193, 195–196
Salt Valley 239–240
Savannah, Missouri 10, 32–33
Scotts Bluff 90–94, 98
Searls, Niles 3, 6–7, 14, 17–18, 20–27, 38, 40, 46–47, 56, 58, 62–63, 70–71, 75, 77, 79, 82, 84–85, 87, 91, 101, 109, 11, 120, 125–127, 130–131, 134, 136, 139, 141, 144, 146, 150, 158, 164–166, 172–173, 175, 178, 214, 225, 251, 259, 262, 267, 272

Shoshone Indians 159, 167, 174–176
Sierra Nevada Mountains 15, 212–213, 224–225, 231–232, 244–245, 252–254, 257, 261–262, 264–271
Sioux Indians 41, 56, 77, 79–82, 93
Smith, Elizabeth Dixon 14
Smith, Jedediah Strong 140
Smith, Peg Leg 171–172
Snake Indians 153, 156, 170, 173
Snake (Lewis) River 181–182, 199–201
Soda Springs 162,174–180
South Pass 124, 132, 135, 139–146
South (fork of) Platte River 60, 70–79
Starr, Franklin 6, 33, 35, 38–39, 41, 46, 55, 81, 83, 86, 90, 111, 115, 121, 133, 139, 146, 150, 157, 159–160, 163, 170, 174–175, 177, 181, 215, 222, 226, 228, 232, 245, 248, 251, 254
Steamboat Springs 174–176, 179
Stockton, Robert 10
Sublette (Greenwood) Cut-off 41, 146–147, 149–153, 160
Sweetwater Mountains 129, 137
Sweetwater River 42, 71, 123–139

Thomas' Fork 169–173
Thousand Springs (Hot Springs) Valley 204, 206, 208–210
Truckee River 253–257

Vermillion Creek 26, 38

Wakaruska River 23–24
Washington City Company 131,164, 167, 178, 218, 235, 242
Weber River 187–189, 193, 195–196
Wellenkamp, Henry 6, 27–28, 82, 88, 93, 122, 132–134, 137, 140, 142, 152, 160, 177, 179, 205, 209, 222, 226–227, 232, 246–247, 249, 252, 259, 261, 263–265, 271
Weston, Missouri 10, 27–29, 44, 47
Willow Springs 125–129
Wind River Mountains 135, 140, 141, 144, 148, 152
Wolf River 35–36
wolves 44, 61–62, 72, 82–83, 135, 139

www.ingramcontent.com/pod-product-compliance
Ingram Content Group UK Ltd.
Pitfield, Milton Keynes, MK11 3LW, UK
UKHW041926140426
5217IPUK00014B/340